ANALYZING AND FORECASTING FUTURES PRICES

WILEY FINANCE EDITIONS

ANALYZING AND FORECASTING FUTURES PRICES

A Guide for Hedgers, Speculators, and Traders

Anthony F. Herbst

Wiley Finance Editions
John Wiley & Sons, Inc.
New York • Chichester • Brisbane • Toronto • Singapore

Copyright © 1992 by John Wiley & Sons, Inc.

Library of Congress Cataloging in Publication Data

Herbst, Anthony F., 1941–
    Analyzing and forecasting futures prices: a guide for hedgers, speculators, and traders / Anthony F. Herbst.
       p.   cm. -- (Wiley finance editions)
    Includes bibliographical references and index.
    ISBN 0-471-53312-2
    1. Futures.   2. Business cycles.   3. Prices--Forecasting.
    4. Futures market.   I. Title.   II. Series.
    HG6024.A3H467   1992
    332.64'5--dc20   91-41062

Printed in the United States of America.

Printed and bound by the Hamilton Printing Company.

10 9 8 7 6 5 4 3 2 1

Preface

This book reveals, for the first time in one volume, techniques used by some of the most consistently successful commodity futures traders. The focus is on proven techniques for finding evidence of cycles in price series data and for gauging the significance and estimating the parameters of those cycles. Those cycles that are judged to be genuine are then used in combination to forecast the direction of commodity futures prices and, most importantly, turning points in the trend of price. This differs from the naive and ineffectual exercise of simply performing a fast Fourier transform of the data and then projecting the series into the future with the entire set of parameters.

It may be, as some contend, that market price evolution follows a chaotic process, in the mathematical sense of the word *chaos*. The path of a time series following such a process is sensitive to the conditions at the starting point. In a chaotic process, minor variations in the initial conditions produce greatly different results after sufficient time has elapsed. However, as long as one restricts forecasts to a reasonably short period into the future, the techniques presented in this book work well, even if the prices series is chaotic.

Although I have developed computer programs to facilitate and automate the techniques covered, most of them can be applied with a spreadsheet program on a personal computer, at least while learning how they work. Examples are provided, where appropriate, of spreadsheet applications. Those who may wish to obtain the specialized programs may contact either me or the Foundation for the Study of Cycles for information. Department of Economics & Finance, The University of Texas at El Paso, El Paso, Texas 79968-0543, FAX: (915) 833-4813.

I wish to thank my wife, Betty, and our children Mya and Geoff for their forbearance during the time the manuscript was in preparation, a process to which they are now accustomed. Although many persons assisted me in a variety of ways, special thanks are offered to E.T. Garrett for his guidance and thoughtful questions on some of the nuances of the analytical techniques covered in this book. Also, an acknowledgment is owed to Gertrude Shirk for initially sparking my interest in the subject of cycles long ago and encouraging my study of the techniques presented. Finally, I thank those who pioneered the use of cycle analysis for market forecasting, in particular Walt Bressert, Peter Eliades, Jake Bernstein, and Perry Kaufman for their work over the years which validates the efficacy of the analysis of cycles for calling market moves when carefully applied.

CONTENTS

List of Figures

ANALYZING AND FORECASTING FUTURES PRICES

1

Introduction

The theme of this book is analysis and forecasting of futures prices. Everyone who speculates in commodity[1] or financial futures has a notion of where prices are going. Otherwise there would be no rational purpose for trading. The aim of this book is to provide a solid foundation for forecasting the likely movement of futures prices or, for that matter, any other time series. Thus the techniques are also applicable to forecasting individual stock prices and interest rates even though the emphasis is on futures contracts.

I invite you to travel along on a journey of exploration in the following chapters. Along the way you will see how commodity and financial price series can be analyzed, how cycles in the series can create the patterns that technical analysts look for and attribute so much significance to, and how to make forecasts of prices. You will also see how to use your spreadsheet program to gain some insights into cycles in time series. And we will look into how the performance of a forecasting method can be measured in a formal, statistical sense.

For those who believe strongly in the dogma of the efficient markets hypothesis, the idea that prices can be forecast will be heresy. However, I urge those readers to bear with me through the chapters that follow. I believe many will be converted to accept that price trends, and even turning points, can be forecast despite the inability to predict any given day-to-day change.

---

[1]The word *commodity* will be used to refer to any item for delivery against an expiring futures contract or whose cash price is used for settlement of the contract at maturity. This term, therefore, will include financial securities as well as agricultrical products, metals, and other physical commodities.

The successes of some traders who have adopted the analytical methods discussed in this book as part of their repertoire stand as testimony to what the techniques can help a trader do. Some have had what can only be called spectacular success, and not just in one year or two, but over a long enough time span that accident or pure luck can be dismissed as a very unlikely explanation. This is not to assert that the forecasting methods can claim all the credit for such success. They *must* be combined with close attention to money management in order to realize profits successfully; the methods cannot merely be right about prices in the longer term but have trading capital wiped out in the short run. Besides, most successful traders use a combination of the techniques in their repertoire.

FUTURES MARKETS TODAY

The small margin requirements for commodity trading (generally around 10 percent of the contract value, give or take a few percentage points) provide exciting opportunities for leveraged profits (and losses) to speculators. Those who recognize that the stock market is not the only financial arena worthy of attention can find futures either an interesting alternative to a dull stock market or, more prudently, a useful adjunct to an overall portfolio. Futures need be no more risky than stocks or bonds; by putting up the same margin as on stock purchases, the risk per dollar of equity would on average be no more. But putting up more margin than required is neither necessary nor desirable.

Volatility and uncertainty in recent years, coupled with chronic inflation, have led many business managers to use futures markets to reduce risk exposures of their firms by hedging.[2] The main impediment to hedging by nonagricultural firms has been, and continues to be, a shortage of personnel who understand how futures markets may be used to reduce risk. At the same time, misconceptions and ignorance at the policy-making level of many enterprises prevent them from either hiring knowledgeable persons or training individuals already in the organization. If top management either does not understand futures markets or, worse yet, thinks it understands but has incorrect or outdated perceptions that stand in the way of policies allowing or requiring hedging, it is unlikely the organization will use them.

---

[2]We define a hedge as a means of reducing cash position risk by taking an appropriate position in the futures market. For example, a copper fabricator, who makes electrical wire for sale, may buy futures contracts in copper to provide protection against a price increase in raw copper that the firm will need to buy at a later date. A copper smelting firm, having a large inventory, may sell futures contracts to gain protection against a decline in the price of copper.

Seldom has the world financial scene undergone such a wave of innovation and growth as occurred in futures markets in the 1970s and 1980s. Traders are attracted by the potential for leveraged profits and the opportunity to match their analytical, economic, and money management skills in one of the few true financial auction markets. More and more business managers are learning to use futures markets for risk reduction by hedging. As more stock traders and hedgers turn to the futures markets, we can predict that these markets will grow in economic importance. Availability of additional futures contracts, in different underlying commodities, will contribute to industry growth through market segmentation; that is, more diversity will attract a larger number of potential participants to the markets. The larger and more active the futures markets, the better the opportunities for traders with superior skills to achieve consistent high returns on their capital.

Until recently, futures trading was overwhelmingly an American and British phenomenon, although markets existed elsewhere. Innovation of contracts in financial futures was once almost exclusive to the United States. But today, the British have made significant progress, and new futures contracts are being developed in Europe and Asia. As recognition of the advantages to be gained from these markets spreads, we might reasonably expect further worldwide growth.

Unfortunately, futures trading has attracted opponents.[3] Whatever their motivation, if the opponents of futures trading succeed in their lobbying efforts to curtail futures trading in the United States, other futures markets will become much more important. Killing the industry in the United States will cause it to flourish elsewhere. Futures trading is simply too important today as a business management tool in hedging cash positions. And for speculators, these markets have no acceptable alternative. Trading will continue, if not in the United States, then elsewhere.

The danger of ill-advised regulation is very real and persistent. The point will not be dwelt upon here, but some see the regulatory battle lines as being drawn between Chicago and New York. Before the advent of financial futures and stock index futures in Chicago, New York was the unchallenged financial center of the United States and the world.[4]

---

[3]Opposition is nothing new, except perhaps that today the enemies are better funded and politically more powerful. There were efforts in the mid-1800s to ban futures trading in the United States. The popular argument, which is *not* supported by the majority of research, is that futures trading increases the volatility of the underlying commodity, financial instrument, or index.

[4]"There were plenty of grand pronouncements 10 years ago when the New York Stock Exchange held a gala opening for its . . . New York Futures Exchange. 'Whatever Chicago can do, we can do better,' boasted then-Mayor Ed Koch as the new market burst upon the scene." Stanley W. Angrist and William Power, "Futures Aren't Bright at Big Board Unit," *Wall Street Journal*, July 13, 1990, pp. C1, C17.

WHAT FORECASTING
CAN AND CANNOT DO

How much can one expect from a good forecasting method? What is reasonable? First, one should *not* expect *any* forecasting theory or technique to predict the precise value at which a futures contract price will settle tomorrow, or the next day, or any given day, or what the exact high or low will be. A good forecasting method will on average have a small forecast error; that is, the difference between the forecast price and the actual market price will be small. The forecast should also be *unbiased*, which means that the errors should overshoot the actual price as often and by as much as they undershoot it.

Why should a trader bother to forecast prices if it cannot be done precisely? The answer is that (1) any time someone trades, it is on the basis of some forecast of the market, if only an intuitive, informal one; and (2) consistent profits can be made by using a forecasting method that can (a) indicate the direction of price changes in the future, and (b) provide early notice of likely turning points. The ability to signal turning points may be the most important characteristic of a superior forecasting method. In a trending market, profits can be made by simply extrapolating the trend. But such simple, naive methods will always be inadequate at market turning points—when it is most important to be correct!

A forecasting method that can provide an indication of market direction, a sense of whether or not the movement will be small or large, and a generally accurate warning well ahead of turning points will be profitable if combined with good money management. Why is good money management necessary? Without it a trader will do such things as trade with too little capital, overcommit too early in a new market trend, let losses accumulate rather than cutting them short, or take small profits instead of letting profits ride until action in the market closes out the trader's position. Money management is as important as market analysis and forecasting; that is the reason that a significant portion of Chapter 3 is devoted to it.

CYCLE-BASED FORECASTING
METHODS

There are many methods of forecasting. Some work reasonably well. Others are not worth the time and effort required to use them. It is not the purpose of this book to cover all forecasting methods. Only those that have been shown to work well with futures prices are covered. The approach to forecasting adopted in this book is not available elsewhere. Indeed, the author believes this is the first book to be published on the approach.[5] At the heart of the forecasting methods presented in this book is the conviction that there exist *cycles* in price series. If cycles exist in price time series then it should be possible to (1) detect them, (2) measure them, and (3) use knowledge of their characteristics to anticipate future prices, that is, to forecast them. Are there genuine cycles in price data? The evidence supports the belief that there are. Consider the following example.

A graph of the Dow Jones Industrial Average from the early 1900s to 1988 clearly shows evidence of a four-year cycle in stock prices (Figure 1.1). And the visual evidence is supported by statistical testing of the proposition that the cycle is not only genuine, but also that its timing qualifies it as a "political" cycle in stock prices. The four-year cycle in U.S. stock prices tends on average to reach a peak at an ideal time for the incumbent president, immediately following the November election.[6] In the more recent elections the cycle has not been manifest in the data, but economic cycles often fade from view only to appear again later, and with the same phase. This cycle may have faded as a result of fundamental economic causes that temporarily suspended its effects.

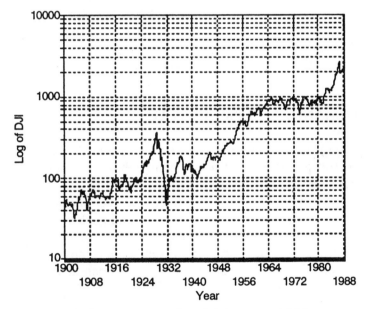

Figure 1-1   Dow Jones Industrial Average, 1900–present.

[5]Sometime in or about the 1960s forecasting based on a combination of trend, seasonal (an annual, 12-month cycle), and cyle methods faded in popularity. That may be viewed as a precursor to the methods covered in this book.

[6]See A.F. Herbst and C.W. Slinkman, "Does the Evidence Support the Existence of 'Political Economic' Cycles in the U.S. Stock Market?", *Financial Analysts Journal* Vol. 40, No. 2 (March 1984), pp. 38–44 for the details on this cycle. The same issue contains other articles on the subject of the presidential, or political economic, cycle in the United States.

What fundamental factors could cause a four-year cycle in the stock market with peaks just after presidential elections? Yale Hirsch[7] suggests that most administrations in Washington want to get the business of raising taxes and other politically unpopular matters out of the way quickly. Voters, it is thought, have short memories. If the second half of the president's term has "no new taxes", or other bad news, as well as a rising stock market, these are considered to be favorable to re-election.[8]

In support of this view, Hirsch mentions a simple strategy developed by David MacNeill of Boston: invest in stocks for the two years preceding an election; then sell all of them and switch to Treasury bills for the following two years. Such a strategy over 22 years made a total return of 1860.4 percent. That is $3\frac{1}{2}$ times the buy-and-hold return for the same period. Over the 38 presidential administrations since 1832 that he examined, Hirsch found a total market gain of 515 percent, with only 8 percent coming from the second two years of each president's term.[9] One does not have to be a rocket scientist to see that the difference is significant. It is so strongly different that there would be little point in testing the hypothesis that the returns are the same except as an academic exercise.

Can there be cycles other than a political economic stock market cycle? Indeed there can. In analyzing U.S. T-bond prices, for example, there is a persistent cycle of approximately one month of trading days. By itself, knowing of this cycle is not enough to make for profitable trading in T-bond futures, but in combination with other cycles it can be.

SUPPLY, DEMAND, AND PRICE CYCLES

In addition to cycles that correspond to activities by U.S. political parties at regular four-year intervals, we must recognize those of industrial consumers and producers who may purchase and sell commodities on a monthly, quarterly, or other schedule. Other cycles reflect scheduled meetings of the Board of Governors of the Federal Reserve and the central bank committees of other nations. There are the monthly, quarterly, or other regular inflows of premiums at insurance companies and pension funds, who must invest most of it as it is received. And beyond these scheduled human activities nature can induce very strong cycles.

[7]*Don't Sell Stocks on Monday (Stock Trader's Almanac)* (New York: Penquin Books, 1986).

[8]By the time you read this we may know whether President Bush erred in reversing his 1988 campaign words, "Read my lips. No new taxes." In the last week of June 1990 Bush agreed with the opposition liberal Democrats to consider tax increases. For Republican candidates running for election in November 1990 this was bad news. The Bush administration and its advisors apparently did not think so. From your perspective following that election, and possibly the presidential election of 1992, you can judge whether Bush was correct in going against the belief of presidents before him.

[9]Hirsch, *Don't Sell Stocks on Monday*, p. 82

The temperate zone seasons and tropical rainy-to-dry-to-rainy changes are predictable cycles. But on top of them and within them is a great deal of variation. Some summers are hotter and drier than others, some winters colder and snowier than others. Some growing seasons are too wet or too dry to allow planting at the ideal time, others have too much or too little rain at critical times after planting. These variations create expectations about the quantity that will eventually be harvested, with consequences for market prices.

The reactions of producers to price changes can take some time to manifest themselves in the market. Consider the thought processes of a farmer in the U.S. Gulf states. On such land either cotton or soybeans can be grown. Let us suppose that at planting time the price of cotton is historically low, the price of soybeans, high. If the farmer plants soybeans, there is the risk, on top of the normal risks faced by farmers, that many other farmers will plant soybeans also, and that abundant supplies at harvest will cause the price to be low. If the farmer plants cotton there is risk that the price will continue to be low at harvest. Clearly, once the crop is up it is too late to reverse the planting decision for this growing season. In temperate climates it is usually not feasible to plow up a crop and plant another in the same growing season that will be more profitable.

The production of many agricultural crops, and also of minerals that must be extracted from the earth by mining, is such that supply tends to be rather fixed until the next harvest has matured, or new mine shafts have been sunk and miners hired. Economists refer to this as *inelastic* supply. The demand curve responds to expectations based on the changing condition of the growing crop still in the fields. Reports of factors that would cause a reduced harvest will nudge prices higher both in the cash market and in futures contract prices. Expectations of a larger harvest will move prices lower. Nothing much can be done to produce more, or less, of a particular crop until the next planting season. That may be as distant as the next year, or in the case of crop commodities grown in both Northern and Southern temperate zones and traded in world commerce, half a year. For some agricultural products, such as live cattle, it is more than a year. For others, such as orange juice, cocoa, and coffee the production cycle is measured in years.

Changes in demand can of course alter prices. These changes can result from gradual shifts in consumer tastes and preferences or from conversion to substitute or complementary products. For example, a very poor soybean crop would tend to make corn prices higher for reasons beyond the fact that they have experienced similar weather conditions within the same growing regions. A poor soybean crop with the resulting high prices would mean that feedlot operators and others such as egg and chicken producers would try to keep their costs down by substituting other feed items, among them corn. The increased demand for corn would tend to move prices higher. Such substitutions occur in other commodities also. High copper prices tend to reward substitution of aluminum in some applications, like automobile radiators and some electric power transmission facilities. And, once the substitution has been successful it may not be reversed when prices adjust to their old levels.

From the foregoing discussion in this section you may have formed the impression that if you could anticipate such things as weather in critical growing regions you might be able to do well at forecasting prices of agricultural commodities. That is certainly a correct perception. But it is not necessary to become a meteorologist to forecast price cycles in agricultural commodities. Weather changes that induce price changes are often revealed in the price series of the commodities themselves. Thus it is not necessary to become a weather forecaster. Of course, if you are interested in long-term phenomena that are weather-driven, you may need to analyze weather data if there are a lot of those and few price data.

CONCLUSION

In a general sense, human mass behavior over the centuries has exhibited a tendency to move in cycles and trends that have sometimes had explosive culminations. History is filled with examples of speculation gone awry as the Great South Seas Bubble, the Dutch Tulip Mania, and so on.[10] The same psychological factors that motivate such remarkable episodes probably also fuel some of the shorter term cycles in financial and commodity markets. To ignore their manifestations in market cycles is to reject the opportunity for profits that might result from better forecasting and also possibly to incur losses that could have been avoided.

This book concentrates on the analysis and forecasting of futures prices, but our forecasts should be tempered by the observation that mass psychology can and often does influence market price behavior in ways that seem to defy logic. This is particularly true at market bottoms and tops, most especially at tops. Others may find a rich harvest in determining *how* human behavior determines some of the cycles we find in price series. For our purposes it is sufficient to understand that it does, and that it is intrinsic in the action of the market.

[10]Many of these are carefully detailed in a very entertaining book written in the 19th century: George Mackay, *Memoirs of Extraordinary Popular Delusions and the Madness of Crowds*. (London: Richard Bentley, 1841). This work was recently reprinted (1980) by Bonanza Books, New York. It is must reading for all investors and anyone who wants to try to understand how and why whole nations get into situations that only later, or from outside, seem clearly irrational.

In his computer simulation model of the U.S. economy, Massachusetts Institute of Technology Professor Jay Forrester found cycles corresponding to some well-known hypothetical economic cycles, such as the Kondratieff wave, considered to be some 50 to 60 years in length. The remarkable thing is that Professor Forrester did not make any attempt to program the cycles into the model; they resulted naturally from interactions among the variables and equations that define the model.

Again I invite you to join me on a journey through the territory of forecasting that is covered in the chapters that follow. You will see how commodity and financial price series can be analyzed, how cycles in the series can create the patterns that technical analysts look for and attribute so much significance to. Of perhaps greatest importance, you will see how to make your own forecasts of prices. To facilitate your understanding you will also examine a spreadsheet program to gain some insights into cycles in time series, in addition to inspecting the analysis that is done by specialized programs. And to look at forecasting objectively we will see how to measure the performance of a forecasting method in a formal statistical way.

2
Market Efficiency and Price Behavior

The behavior of securities and futures prices has long been a matter of controversy. Those who hold different opinions have been polarized into two main camps: those who believe the markets are highly efficient, and those who believe the markets are not so efficient, and that with proper analysis one can achieve larger returns than with a naive "buy and hold" strategy. The latter group is further divided into those who advocate technical analysis, those who believe fundamental analysis holds the key to superior profits, and those who combine the two approaches into an eclectic course of analysis and action.

Advocates of fundamental analysis and proponents of technical analysis often have feelings for one another that can be likened to those of those of two groups within a family who are not on speaking terms. Those using both approaches correspond to the family members who get along with both factions and, because they do, are held suspect by both. As in family feuds, the apparent hostility between the technical and fundamental factions often seems to surpass that between those who believe in market efficiency and those who do not.

RANDOM WALK

A price series that follows a random walk is one that is modeled by the equation

$$P_{t+1} = a + bP_t + \epsilon_t \qquad (2.1)$$

where P denotes price, the subscript $_t$ the time period, and ϵ (epsilon) a stochastic error term often assumed to be normally distributed with zero expected value. The a term represents "drift" in the random walk and b represents a coefficient of correspondence between today's price and tomorrow's. In a trendless market with the a term equal to zero, one would expect the b term to be 1.0. That is, tomorrow's price would differ from today's by a purely random amount, ϵ.

In more formal terms, if futures contract prices follow a random walk, then the best time series forecasting model will be a first order autoregressive model.[1] Equation (2.1) contains such a model. If this model accurately represents the price time series then none of the correlations or partial autocorrelations will be found to be statistically significant.

The implication of a random walk model for commodity traders is this: If commodity prices follow a random walk, then no method of forecasting can improve upon Equation (2.1), and therefore both technical and fundamental analyses are futile efforts to catch a will-o'-the-wisp.

MARKET EFFICIENCY

If a market is perfectly efficient the price of the commodity will follow a random walk. However, there may be different degrees of market efficiency. In a perfectly efficient market, price at all times reflects the consensus of value determined by buyers and sellers acting upon their assessments of all pertinent information. If this is the case, then any new information (i.e., unexpected news) will cause prices to change quickly until a new consensus of value is reached, too quickly for traders to profit from the news. Unanticipated events tend to occur randomly, and to be as often bullish as bearish. Thus, price changes are as likely to be positive as they are to be negative.

Surprises are what move prices significantly away from an equilibrium range in large, actively traded markets. Formal confirmation of expectations seldom causes prices to move in the direction that the uninitiated would expect. For example, the U.S. Department of Agriculture (USDA) crop reports have little influence on price *unless* they surprise traders with significant differences from what was expected before the announcement. If widespread drought and hot weather in the central United States have damaged the corn crop, that information will be contained in the market price of corn. Confirmation of the crop damage will not, therefore, elicit a large, predictable price change. However, if the USDA reports that the damage was much more

---

[1] In such a model the forecast value for a given period is a weighted sum of one or more previuos values. See, for instance, S. Makridakis and S. Wheelwright, eds., *The Handbook of Forecasting: A Manager's Guide* (New York: Wiley, 1982).

extensive than had been thought, the price will rise from the current level for cash corn and many futures contract delivery months.

Forms of Market Efficiency

To facilitate empirical testing of it, researchers have labeled three forms of market efficiency: weak, semistrong, and strong. Each form of market efficiency has its own implications for technical or fundamental analysis.

Weak-form market efficiency exists if price follows a random walk model. Weak-form efficiency implies that it is not possible to forecast tomorrow's price accurately using only the historical series of prices extending through today's price. If a market is weak-form efficient, traditional technical analysis of price charts and price series will be of no help in predicting future prices. Weak-form efficiency, however, does not in itself imply that fundamental analysis might not be worthwhile.

Semistrong-form market efficiency is defined by the proposition that no *publicly* available information will enable one to predict tomorrow's price.[2] If true, this means that fundamental analysis will be no more useful than technical analysis in the effort to trade futures profitably. If a market is semistrong-form efficient, price fully reflects not only its history but also all other information in the public domain . The effects of articles in the *Wall Street Journal*, or a television news story about drought in the Corn Belt, or civil war in a copper-exporting nation are already reflected in the price by the time the public gets the news.

The fact that a market may test out to be semistrong-form efficient does not preclude the possibility that the particular model tested was misspecified. The possibility remains that another model, perhaps using different variables, or the same variables in different ways, may prove useful in predicting future prices. For an analogy, if life as we define it on Earth is not discovered on Mars or on Venus, that does not rule out the possibility that life will be found on another planet, perhaps in another star system.

In contrast to tests for semistrong-form efficiency, the tests for weak-form efficiency are much less complex because they concentrate only on price, and perhaps a limited number of variables closely related to price, such as volume of trading activity and futures contract open interest. However, most of the testing on weak-form efficiency has used techniques that cannot recognize patterns unless they repeat over and over within the same data series without much variation.

---

[2]One must rule out such cases as new information released *after* the markets close on a given day. Such information may enable one to predict the direction of price movement the following day, but not in such a way as to profit from it; the market will open at the appropriate price the following day.

Strong-form market efficiency holds if even "insider" information cannot enable those who possess it to "beat the market", to earn returns consistently above a buy-and-hold strategy. That such information can indeed be useful is not seriously doubted. However, there is a question of the degree to which different types of inside information are useful in forecasting the direction prices are likely to take. For example, there would seem to be a strong a priori rationale to assume that a U.S. Weather Service forecast of an exceptionally hot summer in the central United States would elicit market reaction different in degree, if not direction, from the information of the poor Soviet Union wheat harvests in 1974 and 1979. Initially, such information is known only to a few "insiders". In the case of the Soviet crop failures, orders were placed in the futures market before the public became aware of the situation, and at prices far lower than they would have been otherwise.[3]

Where the potential exists for insiders to profit from special knowledge at the expense of the public, special measures are sometimes employed. For example, the USDA takes measures to prevent anyone being tipped off about its crop reports before the formal press release. To implement this security, anyone entering beyond a certain point within the USDA offices is not allowed to leave until after the report is released. And, to prevent anyone inside the building signaling to a confederate on the outside, the blinds on all windows in the office where the report is prepared are drawn.

Market efficiency implies that "beating the market", earning a return over and above that of a simple buy-and-hold strategy, will be at best a difficult undertaking. At worst, it will be impossible. Examination of some specific empirical studies may shed some light on the question of market efficiency.

EMPIRICAL STUDIES OF MARKET EFFICIENCY

Since the advent of the random-walk efficient-markets hypothesis, countless studies have tested the propositions that it implies. Of necessity, only a few studies are discussed here. The choices reflect this author's preferences and should not be interpreted to mean that these are necessarily better than those that were omitted. In recent years, published academic studies of market efficiency have tended to focus on such matters as weekend, expiration day, end-of-year and January effects in markets. Studies of trading rules and strategies are notably lacking in that literature, and for that reason some of the better early studies are included to fill what would otherwise be a significant

---

[3]Failure by U.S. government agencies to disclose this information to the public could be said to be tantamount to subsidizing grain sales to the Soviet Union by victimizing those holding short positions in the market at the time.

void. Where available, recent published studies are mentioned. Many of the studies cited are reprinted in the readings books published by the Chicago Board of Trade.

Empirical studies have generally followed one of two methodologies: tests of serial correlation and other related statistical relationships, or tests of various "filter" rules for buying and selling. Serial correlation tests are based on a calculation of the correlation of a price series with itself, lagged by one day, two days, or whatever. If there is a regular and persistent pattern in the data, one or more of these serial correlations will be statistically significant. Filter rules are based on a rigid system of buying after a price change of a specified amount or percentage, and selling after a price change of another amount in the opposite direction.

Serial Correlation Tests

Larson (1960) conducted serial correlation tests on corn futures and concluded that 81 percent of new information is incorporated into the price within one day. Then, apparently because of a tendency to overreaction, a contrary 8 percent move spread over four days follows. After that, over the next 45 days the remaining 27 percent of price adjustment occurs, bringing the price to a level appropriate to a new equilibrium. Larson's results are based on averages and data collected before 1960. Whether they hold today is a question that researchers may wish to address.

Larson's results suggest that the corn market is reasonably efficient and that a trader would have some difficulty profiting from publicly available information. However, if there is a contrary reaction to new information, followed by further movement of almost 30 percent to a new equilibrium, it would appear that there is hope for a skilled trader to profit from the corn market.

Brinegar (1970), pursuing the observation by Working (1967) that futures prices react to new information that is randomly as likely to be bullish as bearish, found positive serial correlation in wheat, corn, and rye prices over periods of 4 to 16 weeks. He concluded that there was a statistically significant tendency for trends to continue, though it was not especially strong.

Labys and Granger (1970) used spectral analysis to study monthly futures prices over the period January 1950 through July 1965. Of the commodities studied, they concluded that only wheat had a significant seasonal cycle. However, it should be noted that monthly data are not especially helpful in identifying cycles of less than a month that might be present. Because spectral analysis is a very important part of the forecasting techniques covered in this book, a great deal more is said about it later. You may judge for yourself whether or not their conclusion holds today, when there are many more futures contracts, and futures contracts on many things besides agricultural products.

Filter Studies

Filter studies are based on examination of the profit and loss performances resulting from different mechanical trading rules, rules that can be programmed easily on a computer without effort or sophistication. Because the rules are mechanical, it might be argued that they cannot be expected to do so well as a human trader, who is capable of incorporating the subtleties and nuances of the market into his or her decisions. Of course, the filter rule does not suffer from whatever bad decisions might be made as a result of human emotion either, thus providing some counter benefit.

If a mechanical trading system can yield positive returns over long periods of time this would suggest that the market in question is not entirely efficient. And if a mechanical system can "beat the market" there is hope for traders who are trying to do the same.

Houthakker (1961) examined wheat and corn futures using filters based on different stop orders ranging from 0 to 100 percent. His data covered the span of October 1, 1921, to October 1, 1939, and then February 1, 1947, to October 1, 1956. The war years were not included because of the suspension of trading.

Houthakker found that different contract months gave markedly different results with the stop[4] percentages he used. For instance, long positions in May wheat gave consistently good results (except for a 1 percent stop that yielded a small loss of 2¢ per bushel), while September wheat yielded consistent losses. However, for short positions these were reversed.

For corn futures he found that long positions in the December contract yielded consistently large profits, the May contract consistently moderate profits, and the September contract losses for all but a 2 percent gain when a zero stop percentage was used. For short positions the results were reversed, but the magnitudes were different. It is noteworthy that December corn gave better results with relatively small stop percentages, while for May corn large stop percentages performed better.

Smidt (1965), using daily price data for May soybeans for 10 consecutive May contracts expiring in 1952 through 1961, used a set of fairly complex filter rules. He examined the results of two systems that would have the trader be either long or short one futures contract once any position had been established. Each contract was assumed to be liquidated 10 days before its expiration.

Smidt's first rule requires the trader to buy (or sell) soybeans if an N-day moving average moves upward (or downward) by K cents. For example, if a five-day moving average were being used with a K of 3¢, and the five-day moving average went up by 3¢ or more a long position would be established;

---

[4]Orders to buy and sell were stop orders triggered by the price hitting the filter percentages.

if the five-day average were to fall by 3 or more cents a short position would be established. Smidt tested values for N of 1, 2, 3, 5, and 10 days.

His second trading rule is similar to the first. However, the value of K is not fixed, but rather is based on a proportion of the 10 most recent daily price *ranges*. Smidt used proportions ranging from 0.05 to 0.20. Results of Smidt's study show that losses are incurred in most years even under the most profitable moving average lengths and action prices or proportions. It is remarkable that if the large profits from the bull markets of 1954, 1956, and 1961 are eliminated, none of the filter rules produced significant profits, and most yielded losses.

Smidt also reversed his decision rules to test the proposition that a contrarian strategy might be more useful. He found that profits were both higher and more evenly spread over time than with the original rules, even if the most profitable year was not included. He concluded that profits could be obtained by selling strength and buying weakness in May soybeans. This suggests some inefficiency in this market and contract.

However, Working (1967) observed that Smidt's results could be retabulated to show that Smidt's contrarian rule worked well in only half the years examined, with an average gain of only 1.26¢ per bushel. In these years, prices were generally more volatile and at higher levels. In the other years gains and losses were approximately equal. Many more studies have been conducted on the question of market efficiency for common stock shares than for commodity prices, either cash or futures. Most have concluded that filter rules provide consistent profits only to one's broker when transactions cost are taken into account.[5]

Of filter rule studies on commodity prices, one of the more interesting is by Stevenson and Bear (1970). They examined the performances of three trading rules:

1. Buy and hold with a stop loss X percent under the entry price. Sell on last trading day of the contract.
2. After a move of X percent, establish a position in the direction of the market. Place a trailing stop X percent below entry price for a long position, X percent above for a short. The stop is moved if and as the price goes in the trader's direction.
3. When the price changes by X percent, go with the market; that is, go long if the market has risen X percent, short if it has fallen X percent. Hold for an X percent change from the entry price.

[5]See for instance Paul Cootner, "Stock Prices: Random vs. Systematic Changes," reprinted in P. Cootner, ed., *The Random Character of Stock Market Prices* (Cambridge, MA: M.I.T. Press, 1964), pp. 231–252; or Eugene Fama and Marshall Blume, "Filter Rules and Stock Market Trading," *Journal of Business* 39 (Supp. 1966): pp. 226–241.

Stevenson and Bear simulated the performance of the trading rules with filters of 1.5, 3, and 5 percent. Unlike many other studies, theirs included commission costs. They examined two markets, corn and soybeans, over the period 1957 to 1968 (12 years).

Of the trading rules, only the second performed well with both corn and soybeans. The 5 percent filter provided the best profitability, and profitability increased as the filter size was increased over the range they considered. Rules 1 and 3 worked well only with soybeans, and then only with a 5 percent filter. Of the rules, the third gave the poorest results.

Recent Evidence

Although most recent studies have concentrated on the stock market, the questions they raise about market efficiency have implications for the commodity markets also.

Recent studies, such as those by Holloway (1981), Hall and Tsay (1988) and Huberman and Kandel (1990), support the conclusion of Black (1973) that even when transactions costs are included, the Value Line ranking system shows excess returns, suggesting the market is not, after all, so efficient as most researchers had thought. The Value Line rankings appear to be able to predict systematic factors in the market.

The fact that several researchers reached similar conclusions over a span of almost two decades strengthens the view that the market is not so efficient as had once been thought. It also weakens the inferences drawn by those who note sponsorship of Black's study by Value Line. It is interesting that public knowledge of the studies apparently has not seriously diminished the usefulness of the Value Line rankings.

Joy and Jones (1986) claim that traditional studies of market efficiency often misstate transaction costs and conclude that technical analysis has not been adequately tested. They point out also that technical analysis encompasses much more than weak-form market efficiency analysis.

Lehmann (1990) points out that in an efficient market systematic changes in fundamental valuation over intervals such as a week should not occur. His evidence suggests the existence of overreaction in the prices of common stock. The winners and losers of one week show sizable reversals that indicate the presence of persistent arbitrage profits after adjustment for bid-ask spreads and transactions costs.

It should be mentioned that the evidence presented on market efficiency suggests that some markets appear to be more efficient than others, and that markets tend to become more efficient as traders gain experience with them. Ogden and Tucker (1987) found that U.S. futures contract options on currencies provide little opportunity for arbitrage profits. They found that fewer than 0.7 percent of their data offer profit opportunity after transaction costs are considered. Brenner, Subrahmanyam and Uno (1990) found that Japanese stock index futures showed fewer departures from their fair price as the markets for them matured and as transaction costs and restrictions on trading declined.

CONCLUSION

Evidence suggests that the question of market efficiency had been laid to rest prematurely by academic researchers. That the markets are less than perfectly efficient will surprise few brokers, speculators, or other practitioners, even if many academics are chagrined by the revelation.

If markets are *somewhat* inefficient, this should not lull anyone into the error of thinking that profits are easy to achieve. The markets are *relatively* efficient. Thousands of market participants strive with their wits, analytical techniques, and financial resources to make profits in the commodities markets. It would be hazardous to assume that a naive scheme for beating the market, such as one based on filter rules, can offer consistent profits over the long run. The adoption of such a rule by a large number of traders would assure a decline in its usefulness.

One may be able to earn large profits in the commodities markets, but only with difficulty. It should be remembered that in the commodities markets equal amounts are lost as are made by traders. In fact, when commissions are included, trading becomes a negative-sum game.

To profit in the commodities markets one must *anticipate* developments before they occur, and establish positions in harmony with the market. To do this, one may find contrary opinion useful along with technical analysis, fundamental analysis, and econometric techniques, and especially the forecasting techniques covered in this book.

3
Speculation, Risk Bearing, and Money Management

When one speaks of a person who buys and sells stocks and bonds, whether for the dividends and interest or for an anticipated price appreciation, the term *investor* is generally used. However, a person who buys or sells commodity futures contracts in expectation of profits from correctly forecasting the movement of prices is usually termed a *speculator*. Yet what is the difference between an individual who expects the price of a stock to rise, and accordingly purchases shares, and the individual who buys a futures contract because of a similar prognosis about the price? Let us set the record straight on this before going further. It can be important to your self-esteem and, as that affects trading, to how well you do financially to understand that by risking your capital in trading futures contracts you are performing a valuable service. You need not feel inferior to those who confine their trading to the stock market.

Using the term *investor* to connote socially desirable traits and the term *speculator* to convey disparagement reflects ignorance. The "investor"—that is, stock buyer or seller—is in no demonstrable sense morally, socially, or ethically superior to the "speculator" in commodity futures. Buying existing shares or bonds in the secondary market is an exchange of claims and, in itself, does not result in investment in the economic sense; that is, no new productive physical capital is created by the change in stock or bond certificate ownership. This is not to say that active secondary markets in equity and debt instruments are not vital to a modern industrial or postindustrial economy. Such markets provide the liquidity necessary to ensure that firms can raise capital; without active secondary markets it would not be possible to have efficient primary markets. However, it makes no sense to impute moral or ethical superiority to "investors" in stocks or bonds vis-à-vis "speculators" in futures. Speculators are necessary to provide liquidity, and their activities facilitate the process of price adjustments to levels reflecting supply-demand expectations.

Is there any distinction between buying and selling stocks or bonds and futures? Yes. Technically, the stock or bond purchaser takes title to the securities purchased. The commodity futures purchaser does not take title unless a long position is held to delivery. Thus, a long futures position is not an ownership, but rather a contract to purchase the commodity at a set price. The holder of a long futures position profits or loses as a result of price movements above or below the price at which the contract was purchased because the futures contract conveys both the right and the obligation of the holder to take delivery if held to maturity. The technicality of when and if title passes to the purchaser by itself provides an insubstantial rationale for distinguishing between an investor and a speculator. If there is a difference, it must be in other attributes. In futures trading, a speculator is any market participant who is not in the market for the purpose of risk reduction. Thus speculators are those who are not hedgers.[1]

Compared with stock trading, the similar normal volatility of commodity prices, but far greater leverage provided by futures trading, affords proportionately greater volatility in the speculator's account equity. The magnifying effect of leverage increases the price volatility present in commodities: a small price change produces a proportionately much greater change in the speculator's wealth.[2] This characteristic makes money management skills much more important than in stock and bond trading if the speculator is to make profits rather than have his or her capital wiped out.

IS SPECULATION NECESSARY?

If hedgers were in the futures markets such that a balance always existed between short and long hedgers, there would be little need for speculators. However, such is not the case. In most markets hedgers tend to be concentrated on one side of the market, either long or short. Because both a long and a short position must exist for every unit of open interest, it is speculators who take up the slack. Without speculators, hedging in most markets would at the very least be difficult, and at the worst impossible. If the amount of copper production hedged by smelters with short futures positions is not equal

---

[1] A third class of market participant, the arbitrager, can be distinguished. Arbitrage is the process of simultaneously buying in one market and selling in another in order to make a virtually risk-free profit from price anomalies.

[2] If the speculator has to put up margin equal to 10 percent of the value of a futures contract, then a 1 percent change in the unit price of the commodity will cause a 10 percent change in the speculator's wealth.

to the amount hedged by copper fabricators, then speculative positions are necessary for balance.

The benefits of hedging to reduce the risks faced by producers and con-sumers of basic commodities are well known. Not only do the hedging en-terprises themselves benefit but also, because they can pass them to their customers and shareholders, the advantages gained are widely shared. Hedgers gain protection from adverse price changes in return for relinquishing wind-fall gains from favorable price changes. Speculators provide hedgers with the opportunity to gain price protection; they expect to earn a suitable return for accepting the risk that hedgers want to get rid of. The transfer of risk from hedgers would not be possible without speculation.

Besides the balancing effect of speculation, speculative interest provides liquidity. Without speculators standing ready to take positions, a futures con-tract could not be bought of sold quickly and at a price at or near that of the last trade. The greater the speculative interest in a futures market, the greater the liquidity.

COMMODITY VS. STOCK SPECULATION

Those who have read the preceding portions of this chapter may have noted the word *speculation* applied to both commodities and stocks. This usage puts both on the same basis, removes any imputed moral or ethical superiority connoted by the word *investment*, and thus facilitates objective comparison. Such comparison is useful because most persons going into commodities have had experience in the stock market. So, speculators, walk tall and walk proud! By trading futures contracts you are performing a valuable service to society and the economy. Don't be bothered by those who use the term "speculator" in a pejorative sense; educate them if they will listen, ignore them if they will not.

Leverage in Commodities Trading

In stock purchases the margin requirement has been 50 percent for many years. The purchaser (or short seller) must put up at least half the cost of the stock bought (or sold short). The broker lends the balance to the customer. On this loan, an interest rate of some 1.5 to 2 percent over the prime, or broker loan rate, is charged. In commodities the situation is quite different.

In commodities purchases (and sales), margin requirements are set by the respective exchanges for the commodities they trade. Margin is generally from 5 to 10 percent of contract value. Unlike stocks, where the minimum margin requirement is specified as a percentage of value, in commodities trading margin is specified as a dollar amount. Thus the actual percentage of contract value varies with price fluctuations. When there are substantial price changes, margin requirements are altered so that the approximate 5 to 10 percent is restored. In particularly volatile markets the exchanges may raise margin requirements substantially, both to cool off the market and to provide additional safety to the exchange. Margin should be adequate to absorb losses; it is much more difficult to collect additional money from a losing trader than to debit his or her account.

Unlike the situation in stocks, commodities margin requirements are not a down payment but a good faith deposit. And, since ownership is not transferred unless a contract is held to delivery at maturity, there is no borrowed money to accrue interest to be paid to the broker.

With margin for most commodities at roughly 10 percent of contract value and for stocks at 50 percent, leverage is much greater in commodities. A 2 percent change in the price of the underlying commodity will produce a 20 percent change in the trader's equity (assuming initial margin to be the trader's equity). A 2 percent change in the price of a stock will cause only a 4 percent change in equity for the stock trader.

The far greater leverage in commodities than stocks, provided by the lower minimum margins, makes commodities trading seem much more risky. However, if the trader chose to use the same margin in commodities as in stocks there would be no inherent difference in risk. Some commodities positions would be more risky than some stocks, and vice versa. There is nothing to prevent the commodity trader from putting up more than the minimum requirement. However, there is no need to do so because the funds can be placed in an interest-earning money market fund and transferred as needed to the commodities account.

The Role of Margin

In stock trading, margin deposit is a down payment, or partial payment, on stock actually bought. The remaining cost is financed with a margin loan from the customer's brokerage firm. The stock bought this way is held by the broker until fully paid for. Thus the broker has both a lien on the shares bought and custody of them.

Margin in commodity trading is not a down payment but a performance deposit or buffer. Margin in commodity trading provides funds to absorb losses that may be incurred by the trader. Without this money the broker would have to make good on the losses and then try to get repaid by the trader afterward. This would be both a nuisance and a difficulty; some traders would delay payment, others might try to refuse paying altogether. When commodities margin falls below approximately 75 percent of the initial requirement the trader receives a margin call, requiring that additional funds be deposited or that some open positions be liquidated.

Because margin in commodities is not a down payment or partial payment there is no corresponding margin loan on which interest accrues.

Trading Costs

Several costs are associated with trading futures: commissions, information, and opportunity. For traders not temperamentally conditioned for futures trading we may add the physical and emotional costs incurred from the stresses imposed on the trader.

In futures trading commissions are small compared with the value of the contract bought or sold. Unlike stock and bond commissions, futures commissions are "round-turn". Commission is paid only once, on exit from a long or short position. Also, the commission is a flat fee per contract for commodities: it is not figured as a percentage of contract value.[3]

Information costs include all those costs the trader incurs to obtain information necessary to trade profitably. Among these costs are the subscription fees to chart services, newsletters, and telecommunications hot lines. For those who use computers to analyze data, the cost of the computer equipment and supplies must be included.

Opportunity costs are the alternative profits a trader gives up as a result of the decision to trade commodities. For example, if the trader can earn a return of 9 percent per annum on bonds, but sells the bonds to obtain margin for commodity trading, then the opportunity cost is the foregone interest income.

WHO SHOULD (AND SHOULD NOT) TRADE?

Whether or not to trade commodity futures, or financial futures, is a question that only the potential trader can answer.[4] Of course, if he or she cannot meet the minimum financial requirements the only possible answer is negative. But how should the person who meets the financial requirements reply?

Some assert that futures trading should be undertaken only by those who are well established professionally and financially—by those who can afford the risks involved using what might be considered discretionary funds. Those

---

[3]There is conderable variation from broker to broker on commissions. A discount broker may charge only a small fraction of what a "full service" broker charges, for example.

[4]In some countries the question may be answered in law. In Germany, for example, futures contracts are not enforceable in court because of section 762 BGB (*Burgerliches Gesetzbuch*), which states that *"Durch Spiel oder Wette wird eine Verbindlichkeit nicht begrundet"* [Games and bets do not create liabilities]. Nor do they generally in the United States, but the nature of futures contracts is recognized to be different and socially beneficial.

proffering such a view seldom can provide a satisfactory response to the question of why such a financially well-off individual should wish to trade futures. If one is financially secure then why venture into an unfamiliar and presumably risky new area?

An alternative view is that persons who are willing to face relatively high risk for commensurately high reward should consider trading futures. In this view individuals can use futures as a part of their overall wealth-building strategy. This alternative view stands up under the illumination provided by modern portfolio theory and other money management principles, unlike the view that futures trading should be only for the financially secure.

If futures trading can be considered within an overall financial program, then what remains is for the individual to decide whether or not to do so. The nonfinancial aspects of futures trading may well be decisive for many people. To trade futures successfully a person must be willing to invest the time required to analyze the markets, to plot strategy, to establish and follow tactics based on sound principles of money management. These tasks require not only time but also a large measure of self-discipline. Because of the leverage that futures markets provide, traders cannot neglect following market developments unless plans for action are formulated in advance and instructions are provided to a reliable broker (that is, the customer representative at the brokerage holding the account).

Once strategy and tactics have been worked out, the futures trader must have the discipline to stay the course. It is often difficult to adhere to a trading plan in the face of market action and the commentary and analysis of others.[5] Work out strategy and tactics carefully, then have faith in your program until facts, not opinions, demonstrate the need for revision. But do keep in mind that it is very difficult to determine the line between "courage of one's convictions" and "bullheaded stubbornness".

Finally, the potential futures trader must look inward into his or her own psychological depths to determine whether futures trading should be undertaken. If losses will weigh so heavily as to ruin one's disposition, influence job performance and relations with family and co-workers, and even adversely affect physical and mental health, then one should avoid futures trading. In some cases a person cannot tell in advance how he or she will handle the adversities that even the most successful traders face from time to time. Thus, it may become evident only after trading for some time that a person is ill-suited to it and should quit.

[5]It is important to avoid discussing the market with one's broker representative unless he or she has demonstrated *trading* expertise and a style congruent with yours. Beware especially of brokers who are never at a loss for words, even in regard to futures they know little about. Their unsolicited opinions can have an unsettling effect, even on experienced traders, consciously or subconsciously. If necessary, change brokers.

CHOOSING THE GAME

Having made the decision to trade commodities, the investor/speculator/trader has a number of alternatives from which to choose. A sound and workable rationale for analysis and forecasting futures prices can benefit all these choices. Some persons may prefer to concentrate on grains, others on meats, and still others on currency or financial futures. Some may adopt an eclectic approach to trading, selecting on the basis of fundamental or technical analysis what appear to be especially promising trades. Besides choosing which commodities to trade, one must answer other questions regarding the approach to and style of trading.

Straight Long or Short Positions

The simplest approach to futures trading, although not necessarily the best, is to establish either a long or short position; that is, to buy in anticipation of a price increase, or sell in anticipation of a decline. The appropriate position to establish is a matter for the trader to determine from fundamental and/or technical analysis, or from some hunch about the likely direction of price.

For hedgers the question of whether to be long or short is answered by the cash position held. The hedger with an inventory of wheat in storage is long cash wheat and thus should be short wheat futures: that is, have a short hedge. The copper fabricator who will need to buy copper bars in the coming months is short cash copper, and thus should be long copper futures.

Hedgers are in futures for a different reason from speculators. Hedgers—it they are truly hedging—are seeking to reduce their risk and willing to forgo possible cash position profits in order to pass on potential cash position losses.

Traders who hope to profit from price movements through straight long or short positions have relatively uncomplicated strategies: "Buy low, sell high" or, for short positions, "Sell high, buy low." While simple in concept, the profitable execution is far from easy. And, the risk incurred is large in the sense of swings in the trader's equity being relatively wide. In technical terms the variance tends to be great relative to the expected return: that is, the coefficient of variation tends to be large. Equivalently, the risk-to-reward ratio is large, to use trade jargon.

Spreads and Straddles

At one time there was a distinction made between the terms *spread* and *straddle*. Today they are used synonymously, with spread being encountered more often among traders. Those who trade spreads or straddles are referred to as "spreaders," never as "straddlers," though the term would seem equally appropriate.

In trading spreads, the speculator anticipates making a profit from correctly predicting the *relative* price movements between two futures contracts. The contracts may be for different delivery months of the same commodity, in which case one has an *intracommodity* spread, or for different commodities, whether in the same delivery month or not. In the latter case one has an *intercommodity* spread.

In agricultural commodities there may be differences between contracts in different crop years of the same commodity that are as great as, or greater than, the differences between two different commodities in the same crop years. For example, the old and the new crop May and November soybeans may be more different in terms of the fundamentals driving their prices than May corn and May beans, both old crop contracts.

When shortages develop in carryover, old crop inventories, the old crop futures prices can move above those of the new crop contracts. There is no limit on how far the nearby, old crop contract prices can go above the deferred contracts, except that the price rise will be moderated by the price elasticity of demand for the commodity and the availability of substitutes.

In normal circumstances *carrying charge* markets prevail in physical commodities. That is, the difference in price between an October and a March contract for a commodity will reflect what it costs to store the commodity for five months. If the price differential is greater than carrying charges traders could earn arbitrage profits by taking delivery of the October contract at its expiration, storing it till March, then making delivery against the expiring March contract. In the contrary case of the price differential being less than carrying charges, arbitragers would sell the October and buy the March. For this to produce a profit, however, time must remain before the October expires because there is no way to put a short position into storage. Only those who use the commodity in question can be assured of a profit, provided the deliverable grades are acceptable for their purposes. These arbitragers will deliver cash inventory against the expiring October contract if necessary. They will take delivery of the March at expiration. What they have done by this is to exchange the higher actual inventory carrying charges for the lower implied charges of the futures markets.

Those who use the physical commodity, and thus have an inventory of it, may be able to make arbitrage profits when the implied carrying charges in the futures markets are too low. However, speculators cannot hope to have the same chance to profit. They must instead put on the spread with sufficient time remaining before the nearby contract expires for it to work to their advantage. If their analysis is correct, the relative prices will move apart to reflect full carrying charges. But, since short positions cannot be stored, they cannot carry a position between contract expirations. In principle they could, of course, purchase cash commodity to deliver against the expiring nearby contract, then carry the open long position to expiration, or as long as necessary to make the anticipated profit. In practice, persons outside the trade will be well advised to avoid such complication to their lives.

Interest Rate Spreads. For many commodities a major component of carrying costs is the cost of the money tied up in inventory, that is, interest. Thus, if interest rates are expected to decrease, carrying charges should consequently decrease; if rates rise, so too will carrying charges. In the case of commodities like precious metals, interest costs loom large in the picture of total carrying costs. For example, if gold is at $350 an ounce, a contract for 100 ounces is worth $35,000. If at the same time interest is at 10 percent per annum, by having funds tied up in cash gold inventory the trader forgoes $3500 in earnings. If the inventory is financed with borrowed funds, the cost is a cash outflow of $3500, a forceful reminder of the cost of money!

Continuing the previous gold example, if interest rates were to rise to 12 percent the interest cost would rise $700 to $4200. If rates were to fall to 8 percent, the interest cost would decrease $700 to $2800. One assumes, of course, that there is no change in the price of gold. Rising interest rates not only increase carrying costs, but also tend to accompany expectations of increased inflation. This rise favors an increase in the price of gold, which is magnified in the deferred months by the interest effect. If the relationship between the price of a nearby (P_N) and a distant (P_D) contract (with a maturity one year beyond it) is given by

$$P_D = P_N(1 + i) \tag{3-1}$$

where iP_n is the cost of carry, then the change in P_D is expressed in differential form as

$$dP_D = dP_N + i\,dP_N + P_N\,di \tag{3-2}$$

The first term on the right-hand side is the change in the price of the nearby contract. The second term is the effect of the interest on the change in nearby price, and the last term reflects the effect of a change in interest rate. Together, the second and third terms reflect the interaction of price change in gold and interest rate change.

What makes carrying charge interest rate spreads worthwhile is that the margin requirement is low (around $500 per spread) and the potential for loss or gain is comparatively well defined, at least considering the extremes of interest rate range experienced in the past decade. For a $500 margin deposit the spreader stands to make well over 100 percent if he or she is right. If not, losses will not mount so quickly that the trader has no chance to act defensively and exit the position.

It must be mentioned that interest rate spreads like those in precious metals do not work the same way in other commodities. In fact, with other commodity futures, a *bull spread* means one is long the nearby contract, short the deferred; a *bear spread* means short the nearby, long the deferred. The reason for these appellations is that in a bull market prices of nearby futures tend to rise faster than those of the more distant contracts. Conversely, in a bear market, nearby prices tend to fall faster. With precious metals, however, one finds just the opposite tendencies. There are no crop year effects in the case of the metals to cause a squeeze in the near months. And interest rate effects outweigh those from other carrying charges because the precious metals have great value density. One hundred ounces of gold, worth perhaps $35,000, occupies only a few cubic centimeters. A hundred ounces of gold thus occupies a very small space in a vault, and the storage charge and insurance do not amount to much. Contrast this with a contract for 5000 bushels of corn, for example, worth perhaps $15,000 and occupying space approximately equivalent to a railroad car. Or compare a contract for gold with one for live cattle; 40,000 pounds of cattle on the hoof not only occupy space but also must be fed, watered, and otherwise looked after, including veterinary care if necessary. Obviously the carrying charges are vastly different.

Intracommodity Spreads. Interest rate spreads in the metals are intracommodity spreads. Other intracommodity spreads are based on perceived price anomalies between different contract months of the same commodity. For example, a trader may feel that market sentiment about old crop corn usage and remaining stocks may be overdone, vis-à-vis expectations concerning the prospects for a bumper crop in the coming year. He or she may decide in February to sell a May contract and buy a December if the trader believes that old crop supplies will prove more abundant relative to new crop than the market reflects. Another trader, believing that old crop carryover will be less than expected relative to the new crop, may buy the May and sell the December.

Intracommodity spreads based on a long position in a nearby, old crop contract and a short position in a new crop contract have a well defined cap on the loss that may be incurred. That loss is equal to the change in carrying costs plus commissions and opportunity cost on the margin deposit. The trader, if necessary, can generally take delivery of the nearby contract, store the commodity, then deliver against the deferred.[6]

Intracommodity spreads in which the trader is short the old crop and long the new have the potential for disaster. The reason for this is that a severe run-

---

[6]This condition is not true in a few commodities, such as lumber, which cannot be taken in delivery and then later retendered for delivery. A trader must learn always to check on the details of delivery with his or her broker before putting on a spread.

down in old crop inventory can cause a sharp run-up in price, and just how far the price can go relative to the as yet unharvested new crop is indeterminable in advance. The price spread will be braked by availability of substitutes and by slackened demand as the price of the old crop rises. But the spread trader should be aware that severe losses can be incurred in such a spread.

Intercommodity Spreads.   An intercommodity spread is based on a long position in one commodity with a simultaneous short position in another. Not all such combinations can be considered as spreads. There must be a reasonable linkage in the prices of the two commodities, and the linkage must be direct for a spread to be a recognized spread. *On recognized spreads* the margin requirement is usually the larger of the two individual margins rather than their sum. And the commission is somewhere between the commission on one and the commission on both commodities if they were traded separately.

Recognized intercommodity spreads include corn versus wheat, soybeans versus end products (oil and meal)[7] gold versus silver, T-bills versus T-bonds, and lumber versus plywood. The common thread running through such spreads is that each set of long and short positions is in futures that are affected by the same factors of supply and demand. Some spreads, such as T-bonds or Government National Mortgage Association (GNMA) securities versus lumber, are not recognized as spreads. However, if the trader can make a plausible case as to how and why two such different commodities react similarly to the same factors, many brokers will try to make some accommodation.

The common influence on both futures makes for a spread. The two should normally move together in response to certain major factors, such as weather or interest rates. The normal price relationship provides the trader with a sense of which way prices are likely to move when the normal relationships become distorted. The risk in intercommodity spread trading is that the price relationship might become still more abnormal before it comes back. Spread profits can be made on either movement from normal or back to it; so too can losses.

Risk Considerations

It is often said that spread trading is less risky than trading straight positions. This is generally true. In trading different crop years of pork bellies, for example, the risk can be greater in a spread than in trading within one crop year; and this may be reflected in the margin being larger, not smaller, for

---

[7]This spread is called the "crush" or "reverse crush" spread, depending on whether the trader is long beans and short end product or the opposite.

such a spread. Generally, however, a spread presents less risk than a straight long or short position.

The reason that spreads tend to be less risky is that both contracts tend to move in the same direction, so that convergence or divergence will seldom be abrupt. At least in intracommodity spreads this is the case. In intercommodity spreads there may be occasions when there is a sharp movement in one future and not the other because of a fundamental influence that affects only one of the two commodities. Spread margin requirements reflect this; they are higher for intercommodity spreads.

If one confines trading to intracommodity bull spreads the risk will be less than in straight long or short positions. The trader must be careful, however, to ascertain that retendering is permitted in case taking delivery is a consideration. In Chicago Mercantile Exchange lumber, for example, delivery is permitted only at mill site and retendering by traders not permitted. This policy can lead to price anomalies that would otherwise be arbitraged away. The reason that spreads tend to be lower risk than straight long or short trades is that, by combining long and short positions in highly correlated commodities, one creates a portfolio with negatively correlated assets. More will be said about this later in this chapter. Portfolio theory has an important bearing on money management and risk-return considerations.

Entering and Lifting the Spread

Spreads are usually entered by a spread order, which implies both sides will be put on simultaneously, or as near as conditions on the floor permit. There are spread brokers who specialize in these affairs, and they are good at it; nevertheless, traders will find it advisable to use limit orders in spreading to avoid regrets. Limit orders put the burden on the spread broker to fill within the limit specified. Otherwise, the fill might be at a less favorable price differential than the trader anticipated.

Intracommodity spreads present fewer problems in entering and exiting simultaneously than intercommodity spreads. The fact that in intracommodity spreads both sides are put on in the same trading pit makes them less troublesome than spreads where commodities at different parts of the trading floor, or on different exchanges, are involved. Yet for most recognized spreads, such as Chicago Wheat/Kansas City wheat, even the geographical distance involved does not seriously impair broker performance.

In some intercommodity spreads it may be necessary or advisable to "leg in" one side at a time, rather than simultaneously. One should not attempt such a move without the aid of a broker experienced in such matters. It should seldom be necessary to leg in to a spread. If your broker recommends it, you should ask for reasons why it is preferable to a spread order in the particular circumstances. By legging into a spread the trader has a larger risk exposure than desirable until the other leg is put in. If there should be trouble in getting the other leg in, perhaps because it is in a distant contract with low volume currently, the in-leg could move to create a larger than anticipated loss.

When lifting a spread both sides are generally done at once. However, a spread may be lifted one leg at a time. Why would anyone want to? One good reason is that the trader has come to believe strongly that the market is going to move decisively one way and wants to have a pure play on it. This may coincide with the imminent expiration of the nearby contract if it is an intracommodity spread.

Spreading for the Wrong Reasons

Spreads can be less risky than pure long or short plays. However, they can, and are, sometimes used by traders for other reasons.

A trader whose position endures an adverse price move, perhaps one that precipitates a margin call, may put on a spread. The spread margin is less than that of the original open long or short position. Thus, the margin call is put off.

Besides forestalling a margin call, converting a losing pure long or short into one side of a spread can buy time for the trader to think. The spread prevents the situation from further rapid deterioration; it may still deteriorate, but more slowly than before. Unfortunately, converting to a spread does not often improve a losing situation. While it may buy time for the trader to assess the situation more calmly than before, the conclusion is likely to be the same: Get out of the position.

If the trader was bullish he or she probably was long a nearby contract, for it is these that usually have the greatest liquidity and potential for price movement. The fact that the trader was wrong implies that the market may continue to fall. By converting to a spread the trade creates a bull spread: long the nearby, short the deferred (except in the precious metals).

A trader who had a bull spread in a falling market will continue to lose money. The losses will tend to mount more slowly than they did with the original long position. Nevertheless, the losses will grow inexorably. A bull spread in a bear market is a losing situation. No less so is the bear spread in a bull market.

Only if the market turns, vindicating the trader's original prognosis about price direction, will a spread improve matters. But just as losses accrue more slowly in the spread, so too do profits. If the situation were to improve it would do so more slowly than if the trader had kept the original position in the first place. And, although the margin on a spread is less, the commission is greater than a pure long or short trade.

Trying to convert a losing trade into a profitable one is not the only flawed rationale for spreading. Traders have tried spreading gold versus silver on the basis of an historical gold/silver price ratio to which some writers impute an almost mystical significance. A trader must not assume that an intercommodity spread will pan out as hoped because the price spread is wider (or narrower) than the historical norm. There may very well exist fundamental reasons to account for the price disparity; it might persist and even go far against the trader's position. In 1984, for example, July corn went to a substantial premium over July wheat, and the premium continued to grow for some time. Normally, wheat is at a large premium to corn, but dry weather during the prior growing season had harmed the corn crop, while winter wheat in the field and the approaching harvest were considered to be faring well.

MONEY MANAGEMENT—PLAYING TO WIN!

The importance of proper attention to money management cannot be overemphasized. Please, before trading futures contracts on a scale that could mean the difference between prosperity (if all goes well) and poverty (if all does not go as planned), make it a point to learn and never lose sight of the fundamental principles of money management. Those professionals who have consistently made superior profits know the importance of sound money management and rank it no less important than methods for forecasting market prices of futures contracts. If it is of such great importance to them, can it be any less important for you?

According to one authority, "The money management approach is a group of tools and techniques for managing the rewards and costs of trading."[8] These tools, or techniques, are useful within a conceptual framework that treats commodity trading as a business enterprise. And, the enterprise will only succeed over the long term by their application.

In general terms, money management is concerned with minimizing risk for a given expected return (or equivalently, maximizing return for a given level of risk). It is also concerned with avoidance of catastrophic loss (i.e., financial ruin). Money management must relate to the individual trader's circumstances and temperament. The trader of modest means should not expect to trade in the same manner as one with great financial resources.

Money management encompasses concepts, techniques, models, and behavioral traits that assist the commodity trader who is in the market to win to earn profits on money and time invested. Therefore, one who trades commodities for entertainment might not need money management. But one who plays to win, who expects to profit from commodities trading, can hardly expect to do so without sound money management.

Unsound money management in stock market trading may go undetected for a long time, as equity gradually declines. But, in commodity trading

[8]Fred S. Gehm, *Commodity Market Money Management* (New York: Wiley, 1983), p. 4.

unsound money management will quickly be revealed, because the markets are both ruthless and swift in meting out profits or losses.

UTILITY AND RISK AVERSION

Risks and trading results cannot be meaningfully measured solely in dollar terms. The trader's attitude and feelings—his or her *utility*—must play a role. Each individual feels and reacts differently toward the same situation. Some prefer to keep their funds in the safe harbor of U.S. T-bonds rather than to brave the vicissitudes associated with a potentially far more profitable trade in commodity futures.

Long ago economists developed the basic concepts of risk and utility to augment the growth of economic theory in what is termed micro-economics.[9] Utility is a measure of personal satisfaction. If something provides a feeling of greater pleasure than something else, it has greater utility.

Recently psychologists have added to the theory of utility by analyzing the choices of test subjects who were posed questions aimed at determining their attitudes toward risk and reward. In particular, they discovered that people generally view a cost of a given amount as acceptable, while a loss of the same amount is not; that is, losses have greater negative utility and thus are more "aversive" than costs. Two researchers who have made important contributions in the area suggest that:

> The framing of an expenditure as an uncompensated loss or as the price of insurance can probably influence the experience of that outcome. In such cases, the evaluation of outcomes in the context of decisions not only anticipates experience but also molds it.[10]

This idea has a bearing on the futures trader, who can view the small losses resulting from protective stop orders either as losses or as costs of trading. Viewing them as losses will be more stressful for most traders than the alternative. Yet the dollars are no different in either case. Therefore, traders would do well to condition themselves to view the ordinary diminishments in equity that are part and parcel of the trading as costs and to avoid referring to

---

[9]Perhaps the earliest existing published work on risk is that of D. Bernoulli, "Exposition of a New Theory on the Measurement of Risks," *Papers of the Imperial Academy of Science in Petersburg*, Vol. 2 (1730), 175–192. A translation by L. Sommer appeared in the January 1954 issue of *Econometrica*. Two classic articles on risk and utility are those by M. Friedman and L. J. Savage, "The Expected Utility Hypothesis and the Measurability of Utility," *Journal of Political Economy*, Vol. 60 (1952): 463–475; and by J. Tobin, "Liquidity Preference as Behavior Towards Risk," *The Review of Economic Studies*, Vol. 67 (February 1958): 65–86.

[10]D. Kahneman and A. Tversky, "Choices, Values, and Frames," 1983 American Psychological Association Award Address, p.10.

them as losses. Otherwise the stress created may adversely affect the trader's performance.

A risk-averse person experiences diminishing marginal utility for increasing amounts of wealth. Each extra dollar adds less utility than the last. This person would reject a "fair bet" (one with zero expected value from equal probabilities of gaining or losing the amount of the bet) because the expected utility is negative.

A risk-neutral person experiences the same utility from each dollar of wealth. Fair bets would be acceptable to such a person.

Finally, a risk seeker, or risk lover, would receive greater utility from each additional dollar, suggesting greed. The utility of a potentially large gain in a gamble is so much larger than the utility of the amount bet for such persons that they will take the bet even though the expected monetary value is zero or even negative. One should not expect to find many persons with this utility function since their tendency to prefer the riskier of two propositions when it offers the greater possible dollar gain is self-destructive.

Most persons will have a utility function like that shown in Figure 3-1. Eventually he or she has a risk-averse function for large dollar amounts. For small amounts the function may indicate risk seeking, phasing into risk neutrality, then risk aversion.

In the range of wealth gains and losses regularly experienced, the trader will have a reliable sense of the utilities associated with them. However, for gains or losses outside the range of experience, the trader will be less sure of the associated utilities, confusing his or her instincts and rendering decision-making less reliable. For this reason traders should attempt to ascer-

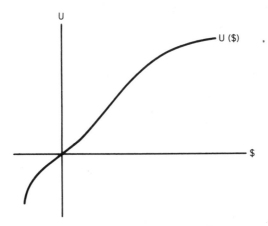

Figure 3-1   Utility of money function for typical person. (Source: *The Handbook of Capital Investing*, Anthony F. Herbst, copyright 1990, Harper & Row. Reprinted with permission of HarperCollins Publishers.)

tain their own utility profiles, especially before scaling up the size of trades significantly.

CALCULATING PERSONAL UTILITY*

This section presents a method for estimating an individual's utility function. The method could also be used to try to determine a composite utility curve for a group. The treatment here parallels the presentation contained in Teweles, Harlow, and Stone.[11]

The first step is to determine the largest dollar gains and the largest dollar losses your investment decisions have regularly made. This may be impossible for many readers. Thus, persons who have not made such decisions will have to imagine what the amounts would be, and try to be perfectly honest about it. This is not a test; there are no right or wrong answers. It is not necessary to do any calculations in reaching your answers, although you may if you prefer.

Let us begin by developing the utility function for a speculator who tells us that he (individually) has regularly made decisions that have resulted in gains of as much as $5000 and losses of as much as $2000. We shall not concern ourselves here with whether these are gains and losses over several months, or with other details of the timing of the amounts. The procedure would not be materially different anyway. Having established the largest regular gains and losses, we write them down as shown in Table 3-1, Column (4). The value $5000 is associated with utility of 1.0 and the loss of $2000 with utility 0.0. Other values could have been used for the utilities, such as +1.0 and −1.0, but the scaling is unimportant. By assigning zero utility to the worst outcome the calculations are a little easier.

Having established utilities of 1.0 for a gain of $5000 with a probability 1.0, and 0.0 for loss of $2000 with probability 1.0, we now need to find intermediate values. We ask our speculator if he would accept an investment offering a gain of $5000 with probability 0.9 and loss of $2000 with probability 0.1; in other words, there are nine chances in 10 of gaining $5000 and one chance in 10 of losing $2000. He answers yes, certainly he would accept such investment. Now we ask if he would pay us $3000 for the opportunity to make such an investment. Yes, he would. $3200? No, not this much. How about $3100? Maybe. At $3100 he is not sure. For $100 more he will not take the investment, for $100 less he will. Thus in Table 3-1 we write $3100 in the second row, Column (4).

---

* This section is adapted from A.F. Herbst, *The Handbook of Capital Investing*, (New York: Harper & Row, 1990) 247-253.

[11]R.J. Teweles, C.V. Harlow, and H.L. Stone, *The Commodity Futures Game* (New York: McGraw-Hill, 1977).

Table 3-1 Computation of a speculator's utility for monetary gains

Probability of			
(1) Best Result	(2) Worst Result	(3) Computed Utility	(4) Dollar Cash Equivalent
1.0	0.0	1.0	$ 5,000
0.9	0.1	0.9	3,100
0.8	0.2	0.8	2,300
0.7	0.3	0.7	1,500
0.6	0.4	0.6	900
0.5	0.5	0.5	500
0.4	0.6	0.4	− 300
0.3	0.7	0.3	−1,000
0.2	0.8	0.2	−1,300
0.1	0.9	0.1	−1,800
0.0	1.0	0.0	−2,000

We repeat the process for gain of $5000 with probability 0.8 and loss of $2000 with probability 0.2. Our speculator will pay up to $2300 but no more for an investment offering these prospects. For each missing value we repeat the process until Column (4) is completed. Then we can plot the results obtained, as shown in Figure 3-2, and fit an approximate curve to the points.

In constructing his or her utility curve for monetary gains and losses, the reader can perform a self-interview or work with someone who will perform the function of interviewer. Further insight into the process is found in Teweles, Harlow and Stone.

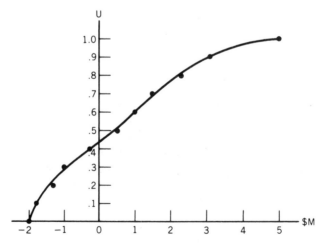

Figure 3-2 Speculator's plotted utility function. (Source: *The Handbook of Capital Investing*, A.F. Herbst, copyright 1990, Harper & Row. Reprined with permission of HarperCollins Publishers.)

The curve obtained and plotted in Figure 3-2 is reasonably satisfactory, except that we do not have enough data points between $-$1000$ and $+$1000$ to be confident in the shape of the curve in that range. We can obtain more information by continuing the interview process. Let us begin by constructing Table 3-2 with best result now $1000 and worst result $-$1000$. The associated utilities are, respectively, 0.6 and 0.3.

Values between $1000 gain and $1000 loss are obtained as before. The decision maker is asked if he would accept an investment project offering $1000 gain with 0.9 probability and $1000 loss with 0.1 probability. Yes. Would he pay $1000? No. $950? No. $900? Maybe. $850? Yes. We write $900 in Column (6) of Table 3-2. The process is repeated until Column (6) is filled and then the results are plotted. Figure 3-3 contains the graph for the section of utility curve between $-$1000$ and $+$1, 000$. The scale is enlarged from that used in Figure 3-2. After combining the information contained in Table 3-2 with that of Table 3-1 and plotting the results, we obtain Figure 3-4. The additional detail for utility between $-$1000$ and $+$1000$ enables a more refined approximation. The tentative judgment that our investor is a risk seeker for monetary gains seems to be vindicated by the additional information over the range of about $0 to $1000. Because of the rather wide spread between utility values for dollar amounts in the ranges $-$1000$ to $-$2000$ and $1000 to $5000, we might want to repeat the procedure for obtaining detail over these ranges if our speculator's patience has not been exhausted. We shall not do this here, however, since the procedure has been illustrated.

The results obtained from our speculator do not deviate very widely from the fitted curve. In fact, they are very close to it, thus indicating a high degree of consistency in evaluating alternatives over the range of values regularly experienced by the decision maker. We should not have been surprised if

Table 3-2 Computation of refined utility function for a speculator

Best outcome		Worst outcome			
(1)	(2)	(3)	(4)	(5) Computed	(6) Dollar Cash
Utility	Probability	Utility	Probability	Utility	Equivalent
0.6	1.0	0.3	0.0	0.60	$ 1,000
0.6	0.9	0.3	0.1	0.57	900
0.6	0.8	0.3	0.2	0.54	650
0.6	0.7	0.3	0.3	0.51	550
0.6	0.6	0.3	0.4	0.48	400
0.6	0.5	0.3	0.5	0.45	100
0.6	0.4	0.3	0.6	0.42	− 100
0.6	0.3	0.3	0.7	0.39	− 400
0.6	0.2	0.3	0.8	0.36	− 550
0.6	0.1	0.3	0.9	0.33	− 700
0.6	0.0	0.3	1.0	0.30	−1,000

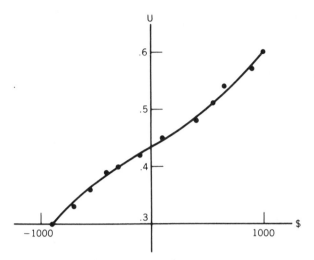

Figure 3-3   Plot of refined utility for a specula-
tor. (Source:*The Handbook of Capital Investing*,
A. F. Herbst, copyright 1990, Harper & Row.
Reprinted with permission of HarperCollins Publishers.)

the points were much more scattered about the fitted curve. What happens
if we now attempt to obtain utility values for dollar gains and losses beyond the range of the decision maker's regular experience? If we attempt to
do this, we will most likely find that the decision maker becomes increasingly

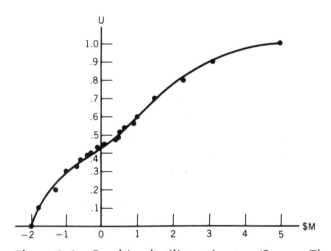

Figure 3-4   Combined utility estimates. (Source:*The
Handbook of Capital Investing*, A. F. Herbst, copyright 1990, Harper & Row. Reprinted with permission of HarperCollins Publishers.)

inconsistent as the monetary values become further and further removed from the domain of his or her experience.

To compute the utility of larger monetary gains, the formula used is

$$U(Gain) \times Pr(Gain) + U(Loss) \times Pr(Loss)$$
$$= U(Cash\ Equivalent) \qquad (3\text{-}3)$$

where

$$
\begin{aligned}
U(Gain) &= U(G) = \textit{utility of gain} \\
Pr(Gain) &= p \quad\;\; = \textit{probability of gain} \\
U(Loss) &= U(L) = \textit{utility of loss} \\
Pr(Loss) &= (1\text{-}p) = \textit{probability of loss} \\
and\ U(CashEquivalent) &= U(C) = \textit{utility of cash equivalent}
\end{aligned}
$$

is equivalent to

$$U(G)p + U(L)(1 - p) = U(C) \qquad (3\text{-}4)$$

By rearranging the terms, we obtain formulas for computing the utilities of gains and losses outside the range of the decision maker's experience:

$$U(G) = \frac{U(C) - U(L)(1 - p)}{p} \text{ and } U(L) = \frac{U(C) - U(G)p}{1 - p} \qquad (3\text{-}5)$$

In calculating the utilities of gains and losses to commodity traders for extended amounts, it may be advisable to compute them several times for different hypothetical amounts. The reason behind repeating the procedure is to find out how consistent the decision maker is in making decisions outside the range of his or her experience. The reader is referred to the excellent discussion by Teweles, Harlow and Stone for a detailed treatment. The main reason for concern about the decision maker's consistency for larger gains and losses than he or she has regularly experienced is this: If judgments do become increasingly inconsistent for larger gains and losses, then the decision maker should either exercise greater caution (something the person will probably do anyway) in evaluating such prospects, or else avoid them entirely if possible. Otherwise it is likely that decisions will be made for which the perceived a priori and a posteriori utilities are different and the decision maker will regret making such decisions even before the results are in.

PYRAMIDING

To make large amounts of money, the trader may wish to have multiple contracts. Strategies for adding to the number of contracts carried are called *pyramiding* strategies.

At Time	Action	Pictorial	Total Contracts
t = n	Add one	X	10
t = m	Add two	X X	9
t = 1	Add three	X X X	7
t = 0	Buy four	X X X X	4

Figure 3-5   Pyramid with a broad base.

In pyramiding, the trader adds to his or her positions as the price moves favorably by using the growth in equity to provide margin funds. A pyramid can have a broad base with a narrow top or a narrow base with a broad top.

By starting out with several contracts, and adding progressively fewer as equity grows, a broad-based pyramid is created. Figure 3-5 illustrates the process. The broad base and narrow top suggest stability and, in fact, this type of pyramid is far more stable than its narrow-base opposite. Figure 3-6 depicts a pyramid with a narrow base and wide top. This type of pyramid is unstable, as its physical analog suggests.

In the wide-base pyramid, as additional contracts are added, there is more equity created toward the bottom of the structure than toward the top. Thus, a reversal in the market is less likely to wipe out the equity unless it is prolonged. With the narrow-base pyramid, however, the additional contracts are added with equity generated more by contracts added recently than by those at the bottom. Not only that, but also the greater number of contracts rests on an equity cushion that is supported by a small set of contracts. For a given reversal in the price of the futures contract, it is thus more likely that the narrow-base pyramid will collapse under the cascading effect of margin calls.

If one wishes to pyramid gains then one should do it with a broad-based pyramid. There are many variations on the basic theme. The sequence 4, 3, 2, 1 is but one of many. It could just as well have been 5, 3, 1; or 4, 2; or 4, 3, 1. The strategy for adding additional contracts also is variable.

Additional contracts may be bought or sold as the commodity price moves favorably by a given amount, say 10¢ per bushel in the case of corn. Or, the

At Time	Action	Pictorial	Total Contracts
t = n	Add four	X X X X	10
t = m	Add three	X X X	6
t = 1	Add two	X X	3
t = 0	Add one	X	1

Figure 3-6   Pyramid with a narrow base.

trader may add contracts when the increase in equity is some percentage of the required margin (100 percent, 150 percent, and so on). With this latter strategy additional contracts can be added more quickly as the equity growth accelerates with the addition of contracts. (Warning! The decline in equity upon a price reversal is also greater.)

Judicious pyramiding can lead to great wealth. One can easily take a price chart and show how a successful pyramid can be constructed. However, it is difficult to do so without benefit of hind-sight. As the pyramid grows, even small price changes induce great equity changes, and few trends continue long without volatility increasing. And, for a pyramid to be successfully executed requires that a trend develop after the trader enters the market. Often, there will be no prolonged trend to allow a pyramid to work.

USING STOP ORDERS

The phrase "Damned if you do; damned if you don't" has never been applied more aptly than to the use of stop orders in futures trading. The skilled placement of stop orders can do much to preserve profits and reduce losses, yet the placement of such orders is one of the most difficult aspects of futures trading to master. Those who have used stop orders invariably can recall occasions when it seemed the market changed course just long enough to stop out their position, then reversed course and moved in the erstwhile trader's favor. Reversals happen often enough to give credibility to the notion in the minds of some traders, "I'm not paranoid, they're out to get me!" But to trade without using stops is to play the game under a handicap. For this reason, stops are used by many traders despite their uneasiness about them.

Traders frequently use stop orders to enter a position upon the triggering of a technical signal based on chart analysis. At the same time, they often place a stop-loss order to try to limit their losses if the trade does not turn out as expected. Unfortunately, certain chart signals tend to be rather obvious. Other speculators will tend to place their stop orders at the same levels, and floor traders are well aware of this. The floor traders, or "locals" as they are known, will "fish for stops" and, finding them, move the market temporarily to their profit. Price charts contain ample cases of price spikes that may be explained on the basis of stops being cascaded like a set of dominoes placed on end. Given this situation, what can the trader do?

In using stops, there are some guidelines that may help. They are far from perfect but likely to be better than the naive use of a stop order. First, avoid placing stops at obvious chart points. Second, try to use "stop-close only" orders for stop-loss protection if your broker will accept them and execute them reliably even though they may have to be renewed daily. Some exchanges will not accept "stop-close only" orders as such; then you must rely on your broker's representative to place the appropriate order at the right time. These orders will often prevent the trader from being stopped out only to see the market reverse and close away from the stop. In cases where the floor traders run the stops, they generally unload positions acquired in the process before the close rather than carry them overnight or over a weekend.

Third, consider using "mental" stop, if one has the time to follow the market and self-discipline to act. Unfortunately, most people cannot monitor the market continuously, and most brokers cannot be expected to do it for traders unless the latter's accounts are large enough to warrant the effort. Even those who can follow the market action may find it difficult to act appropriately while under the stress of a market gone against them unless they have worked out a plan of action in advance and strictly follow a policy with regard to enacting the plan.

Fourth, place formal stops only after a large, sharp price move or "spike" that would have hit a resting stop has occurred. This strategy will work except in cases where the move continues rather than reversing, thus depriving the trader of the advantage afforded by a stop. It also will not work in cases where a second price spike follows the one the trader waited to see before placing his or her stop.

Limit Moves and Lock-In

Occasionally a futures market moves so strongly that few or even no trades occur within the allowed price range. This sometimes goes on for several days of limit moves. Those who are adversely affected cannot get out until a price is reached at which trading resumes. Stop orders provide little protection against such situations, and losses can be devastating. In many cases, however, they could have been avoided.

For most agricultural commodities locked-limit moves tend to occur more frequently to the upside because they can be induced by weather events that threaten supplies. For example, severe freezes in Florida can propel orange juice futures to sharply higher prices in a series of limit moves that lasts for several days. Similarly, a dry, hot spell in the Corn Belt can cause grain and soybean prices to go limit up once the drought is acknowledged by crop damage reports. Or, a report that the Soviet Union will be purchasing much greater amounts of grain than expected can induce a sharp upward move in limit steps.

Although there tends to be more limit up moves than limit down, they occur with some regularity as markets top out after a prolonged rise. Traders need to be especially wary of the possibility of a sharp decline upon release of a crop report after a bull market has prevailed for some time. If the report reverses the bullish sentiment with news of less severe crop damage than expected, or larger carryover stocks, for example, the bull market may collapse sharply, perhaps in a series of limit declines.

To reduce the possibility of being caught in a locked-limit situation traders can do several things. First, they should not be short orange juice futures during the freeze season; that should be left to hedgers and gamblers (those who undertake unnecessarily risky trades). Second, positions should be reduced or offset after a favorable trend has existed for a long time. That is, if long in an aging bull market or short in an old bear market, positions should be reduced or offset. Third, traders must beware the effects of a major crop report. For instances, in 1983 the prices of grains and soybeans were shocked one way, then the other, within a span of less than two weeks by conflicting USDA crop reports.

CUTTING LOSSES, LETTING PROFITS RUN

One of the mistakes speculators make most frequently is to take small profits and to get out of losing trades only after incurring large losses. There are brokers who encourage this behavior—taking small profits, if not large losses. Brokers live by commissions, and traders who take small profits and small losses generate more commissions than those who let profits or losses run. They rationalize their advice to clients on the basis that a small profit is better than no profit at all. This advice is true, and probably well-meant, even if self-serving. However, speculators cannot hope to make large profits by taking small ones. Unfortunately, having ignored a broker's advice to sell and secure a small profit, a speculator who ends up with a loss will be vulnerable to similar advice in the future. Having been wrong once when the broker was right, one has a natural reluctance to risk a recurrence: this can lead to trading errors.

The hard-and-fast rule that all commodity futures speculators should adopt is to let profits run, cut losses short. That is, hold onto winning positions, perhaps with a stop order to exit on a market reversal. And, get out of losing trades quickly, taking small losses rather than letting them grow to large losses. This may be accomplished with stops.

A technique that deserves attention is that of using trailing stops. With this the trader puts a stop-loss order under his or her entry price. If this is touched the position is liquidated with a small loss. If the trade is successful, the stop is ratcheted behind the market price. The position is liquidated when the market moves against the position, thus preserving most of the profit. In principle the technique is simple; in practice it is most difficult to apply successfully. Stops placed too close will take the speculator out with small losses in almost every case. Stops placed too far away lead in many cases to larger losses than necessary on trades that are bad to begin with, and on good trades they give up too much profit in taking the trader out. To be successful in using this technique, speculators cannot place stops naively and expect them to work well. They should plan to spend a good deal of time analyzing past market action and volatility as a guide to effective use of stops.

PORTFOLIO THEORY AND DIVERSIFICATION

So far, attention has been focused on individual futures trades. However, few speculators trade only one commodity, and there are good reasons why one should trade several.

The expression "Don't put all your eggs in one basket" was an early pre-cursor of modern portfolio theory.[12] The basic idea of risk reduction through diversification rests on the principle that two or more risky investments in combination are less risky than they are individually. Assume the specula-tor has two independent trades (that is, the results are uncorrelated, they do not depend on one another), each with a probability of success of 0.60 (and probability of failure of $1.0 - 0.60 = 0.40$). There is only a 0.16 ($= 0.40 \times 0.40$) probability of both failing; the trade-off is that there is only a 0.36 ($= 0.60 \times 0.60$) probability of both succeeding.

If we measure risk by the variance or standard deviation, as is the norm in the literature of finance and economics, then the combination of futures positions can be portrayed as in Figure 3-7. The hatched region depicts the set of feasible (that is, achievable) combinations of positions.[13] Note that the same return can be achieved with different levels of risk, and for the same level of risk different returns are available.

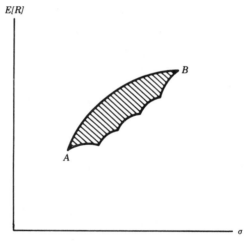

Figure 3-7 Portfolio risk and return

[12]The trite counterpart, "Put all your eggs in one basket and watch the basket very care-fully," will be seen to lack any risk-reducing benefits.

[13]Because futures contracts are not infinitely, or even finely divisible, the feasible set is not dense. The graphic portrayal is thus not wholly accurate since it suggests a dense feasible set and smooth transition from one portfolio to another.

In Figure 3-7 the set of points along AB is termed the efficient set. This set dominates all other feasible points. A point along AB is preferred to all points below it because, for the same risk, points on AB offer higher returns. A point along AB is also preferred to all points to its right because, for the same return, points on AB incur less risk. Therefore, the only portfolios of interest are those along AB.

Given that points in the efficient set AB are the only ones of interest, how can we say which of them the individual speculator will choose? The answer lies in the person's utility function, specifically in the set of curves in the expected return $E[R], \sigma$ space on which the trader is indifferent. These give the risk-return trade-offs for the individual trader. Figure 3-8 shows the interaction of the efficient set with the trader's risk-return indifference set. The chosen portfolio is at point P. Another person, having a different set of risk-return indifference curves, would select a different portfolio.

The essential ingredients of portfolio diversification are these: expected return $E[R_i]$ on the ith investment, variance or standard deviation on the ith asset, and the covariance between the ith and jth assets.

Expected returns are additive. That is, the return on a portfolio (p) composed of assets i and j in proportion a and b is given by

$$E[R_p] = aE[R_i] + bE[R_j] \tag{3-6}$$

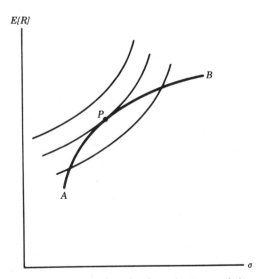

Figure 3-8   Individual trader's portfolio.

The variance, which we are using to measure risk, is given by[14]

$$\text{Var}(ai + bj) = a^2\text{Var}(i) + b^2\text{Var}(j) + 2ab\text{Cov}(i, j) \qquad (3\text{-}7)$$

Assume that a speculator has identified two possible trades, the characteristics of which are given in Table 3-3. The expected net return on a portfolio of one unit of trade A and one of trade B is $175. The variance of return is given by the calculation[15]

$$\begin{aligned} \text{Var}(A + B) &= (0.67)^2(81) + (0.33)^2(144) + (2)(0.67)(0.33)(-100) \\ &= 7.82 \end{aligned}$$

The relative riskiness of an investment is given by the ratio of risk to expected return. The ratio of variance to expected return is 0.81 for trade A, 1.92 for trade B, and 0.40 for the portfolio of one unit of A and one of B. The risk has been substantially reduced.

In the example just discussed, covariance between A and B is negative and this makes the risk reduction stronger than if the trades were positively correlated. Nevertheless, as long as the trades are not perfectly positively correlated, there will be a diminishment in risk.

What if the covariance were 64 not -100? The correlation coefficient would be $+0.59$, and the portfolio variance would be 80.34. The ratio of risk to expected return would be 0.46, which is still less than either trade A or B by itself. This calculation illustrates the principle that as long as the assets selected are not perfectly positively correlated, the portfolio will be relatively less risky than the individual assets.

Table 3-3   Hypothetical Commodity Trade Data

	Trade A	Trade B
Cost	$1000	$ 500
Expected return	100	75
Variance of return	81	144
Covariance		-100
Correlation coefficient		-0.93

[14]More generally, the variance of a linear combination of variables, with weights $a, b, c,$ ..., is

$$\text{Var}(ax + by + cz + \ldots) = a^2\text{Var}(x) + b^2\text{Var}(y) + c^2\text{Var}(z) + \ldots + 2ab\text{Cov}$$

$(x, y) + 2ac\ \text{Cov}(x, z) + 2bc\ \text{Cov}(y, z) + \ldots$

[15] Note that the weights for A and B are given by $1000/(1000 + 500)$ and $500/(1000 + 500)$, respectively.

Although trade B alone offers the higher return, it is also the more risky. Risk and return invariably go hand in hand—the higher the expected return, the greater the risk. Otherwise, everyone would want to buy the asset, driving up its price and reducing the potential return.

The principle of risk reduction through portfolio diversification plays an important role in money management. Traders who recognize and incorporate into their trading the concept that the same return at less risk is better will improve their performance. The principles are simple; nevertheless, speculators will find their successful application far from a trivial challenge.

In practicing portfolio diversification, one finds that obtaining the requisite statistical measures can be an elusive goal. In commodity futures, there is some question as to the continuity and stability of statistical parameters from one contract month to another; for example, whether the variance of May wheat is the same as that of September wheat, and whether it is the same for May wheat in one year as it is for another year. Similar problems of parameter constancy exist in other investments, but they are perhaps more troublesome in futures trading. Nonetheless, the concepts of portfolio diversification, even if not meticulously applied, provide a useful framework for action.

RISK OF RUIN

A futures trader will likely either succeed by growing wealthy or fail by losing the funds committed to speculation. Few will continue for long neither prospering nor losing, with equity locked in a sideways pattern over time. One thing is certain: if the odds are against the speculator, if he or she has no advantage, then eventually trading capital will be gone. We define *ruin* as the condition of having lost all one's trading capital.

If a given speculator assumes he or she has a certain probability advantage, yet continues to find himself or herself being ruined, then the speculator should try to reassess the assumed advantage realistically. The examples we consider are simple, yet they serve to illustrate the principles involved.

Like many useful risk-related concepts, risk of ruin has its origins in gambling. The probability of eventual loss of all trading capital (that is, ruin) is given by the equation

$$R = \left(\frac{1 - A}{1 + A}\right)^C \tag{3-8}$$

where R is the probability of eventual loss of all trading capital, A is the trader's advantage, and C the number of investment units the trader starts with and continues to risk in each trade.[16] Given that p is the probability of

[16]William Feller, *An Introduction to Probability Theory and Its Applications* (New York: Wiley, 1957).

a favorable outcome, the trader's advantage is $A = p - (1 - p)$ or $2p - 1$. Thus, if the odds of a favorable outcome are 55 out of 100, p is 0.55 and A is 0.10. C is found by dividing the trader's initial capital by the amount risked on each trade.[17]

To illustrate, let us assume a speculator is considering a futures trade that offers a 0.60 chance of earning 100 percent and a 0.40 chance of losing the entire margin deposit. The speculator has \$16,000 trading capital, and the required margin is \$4,000. The risk of ruin is given as

$$R = \left(\frac{1 - 0.2}{1 + 0.2}\right)^4 = 0.198 \tag{3-9}$$

or about one chance in five of eventual ruin. In other words, even with the relatively large assumed advantage, there is a genuine threat of eventual loss of all trading capital.

A somewhat different formulation of risk of ruin is necessary to answer the question of what the probability of ruin is before the trader can successfully accumulate W additional units of wealth:

$$R = \frac{[(1 + A)/(1 - A)]^W - 1}{[(1 + A)/(1 - A)^{C+W} - 1} \tag{3-10}$$

where A and C are as formerly defined.[18]

Continuing the previous example, what is the probability that the speculator will be ruined before the initial \$16,000 grows to \$36,000? It is

$$R = \frac{[(1.2)/(0.8)]^5 - 1}{[(1.2)(0.8)]^{5+4} - 1} = 0.176 \tag{3-11}$$

or a little more than one chance in six. That this is a lower probability than the risk of *eventual* ruin merely shows that even if the trader has an early run of successes, if he or she continues to trade *on the same scale*, ruin can still occur. However, after initial success, the trader might decide to scale back the relative amount risked on each trade (that is, increase C).

By increasing the advantage (perhaps by careful study of fundamentals, or technical analysis) the trader's chances for avoiding ruin increase. However, the effect of scaling back the amount risked on each trade can have a similar effect. If the advantage were to increase to 0.25 the risk of eventual ruin drops to 0.130. But traders can exercise much better control over C than over the odds of success on each trade. And, by reducing the amount risked to

---

[17]This formulation assumes a double-or-nothing situation in which the trader makes or loses 100 percent on each trade.
[18]Ibid.

half as much as before, the risk of ruin drops to 0.039 (C is 8), a remarkable reduction from the former 0.198.

The implications are clear. Speculators should strive for as large an advantage as possible in the odds of success on a trade. They should also risk only a small amount of their trading capital on each trade. It is left as an exercise for the reader to determine the risk of ruin if the trader's advantage is negative, and whether or not a large C value is advantageous in such a case.[19]

---

[19] For the nonmathematical a reminder: a probability cannot exceed the value of certainty, which is 1.00.

4

Fundamental and Technical Analysis

Analysis of investments, including commodity futures, can be labeled as fundamental or technical. Although the end results they seek to accomplish may be the same, the means for obtaining them are different, and the underlying philosophical foundations are separate.

If markets were perfectly efficient, the practice of either fundamental or technical analysis as a predictive tool would be in vain. No one could hope to earn consistently higher returns than could be had by a naive "buy-and-hold" strategy. However, if everyone were to abandon these analytical methods, it is debatable whether or not the markets would continue to be efficient.

The variety of high-priced commodity newsletters published by independent commodity advisors and those newsletters sent to clients by the major brokerage firms attest to investors' demands for news and analysis. Brokerage firm letters generally concentrate on fundamental analysis. Technical analysis coverage typically ranges from next to none to almost equal to the fundamental. In contrast, the independently published newsletters are overwhelmingly oriented to technical analysis. It would seem that the investing and speculating public prefers to spend its money for technical analysis and information rather than for fundamental.

Some commodity traders use fundamental analysis to try to determine the direction of the market trend and technical analysis for timing their entry to and exit from market positions. In other words, some traders use fundamental analysis to gauge the long-term market factors, and technical analysis to deal with the shorter-term influences.

Now, let us examine fundamental and technical analysis. Discussion will be based on the assumption that the commodity markets are less than perfectly efficient.

FUNDAMENTAL ANALYSIS

The foundation for fundamental analysis is supply of and demand for the commodity in question. Fundamental analysis involves modeling the supply-demand relationships in a market. Supply and demand are far more difficult to analyze and model than generally realized. To provide useful results, the analyst cannot deal only with static equilibrium conditions for a commodity (itself not an easy task) but must incorporate dynamic influences also. The analyst must identify the relationships within the system being modeled. In a formal model, these relationships become equations in an interlinked system of equations.

Variables within the model will be either endogenous or exogenous. The former have values determined within the model, whereas the latter are determined by factors external to and possibly independent of the model. An example of an exogenous variable would be average rainfall in a particular corn growing state over some time span, while an endogenous variable might be the amount of acreage planted.

Since fundamental analysis is concerned with supply-demand modeling, it is useful to examine each of these separately. However, remember that in a dynamic model supply and demand may have to be treated as interrelated rather than independent. For example, next season's crop production may be a function of this year's demand and the consequent farm production plans and intentions.

Demand

Demand for a commodity may be seasonal or cyclical. For instance, there are seasonal influences on the consumption of beef due to changes in consumer life styles from season to season as evidenced by summer-time backyard barbecues. Seasonal variation is, of course, a type of cyclical change. For cycles of approximately one year we use the term seasonal, reserving the term cycle for all other periodicities.

Demand for a commodity is influenced by prices and availability of substitutes. Consumers may drink less coffee as the price rises, substituting tea or soft drinks. If the price of beef gets too high, consumers will substitute pork, poultry, or fish.

Some commodities may be consumed in lesser quantities as consumer incomes rise or their prices fall. These goods are referred to as inferior goods, or Giffen[1] goods. These commodities behave contrary to the usual price-

---

[1]There is a technical difference. Inferior goods have a negative substitution effect while Giffen goods (named after the economist who first described them) have a negative income effect. In the case of Giffen goods, as income rises consumers desire less of them. For inferior goods consumers spend less on them when the prices of substitutes become relatively less.

quantity model in which quantity demanded is a decreasing function of unit price. If consumers really prefer other goods to potatoes, they may not consume more potatoes at a lower price but instead use the money no longer needed for potatoes to buy their preferred consumption. If consumers would like to consume more beef, but have been substituting poultry because of its lower price, then as their incomes rise, they may cut back on poultry and expand purchases of beef.

Social and political factors may influence demand for some commodities. For example, consumption of sugar may be limited by health and weight concerns of consumers. Consumption of commodities like palladium may be affected by the warmth or coolness of the current relationship between the Soviet Union (the major producer) and other nations.

The interconnections, or cross-elasticities, in demand between the commodity in question and substitutes have a bearing on specifications for a demand model. As an example, demand for corn is not solely determined by the price of corn. It is strongly influenced by the prices of substitutes like grain sorghum or milo, and by those of soybean meal, oats, and so on. Similarly, the price of platinum may be constrained by the substitutability of palladium in some applications, such as petroleum cracking.

Supply

Estimation of supply is no less complicated than for demand. For many agricultural commodities supply may be fixed for all practical purposes from harvest to harvest. This situation can create an inelastic supply; that is, quantity cannot increase in response to higher prices until the next planting season.

For many commodities, supply is heavily influenced by weather conditions and crop diseases. For others, it may be affected by the foreign exchange needs of less-developed nations that depend on export earnings. For some commodities, supply may be managed by a dominant producer (as in the case of palladium) or consortium (the Organization of Petroleum Exporting Countries is the outstanding contemporary example).

Cross-elasticities influence supply as well as demand. For example, if the price of cotton as an alternative crop on the same land is low while that of soybeans is high, significant acreage may be diverted from growing cotton to growing soybeans.

In the case of such futures as U.S. Treasury bills and bonds, supply is a function of the financing and refunding requirements of the Treasury. For certain others, like silver, supply is determined in large measure by production of other products (copper, lead, zinc, and so on) for which it is a by-product. Copper ore is not mined and processed to produce silver, yet silver is a valuable residual from copper refining.

Price Determination

The objective of fundamental analysis is to determine the commodity price that will prevail for a given set of circumstances. Consider Figure 4-1; the demand curve is representative of an agricultural commodity. In this case demand is relatively inelastic because supply is fixed between harvests. The supply curve is not perfectly inelastic because higher prices can elicit additional supply from sources outside normal channels, such as inventories of consumers who become suppliers as they substitute other commodities for their own use. A perfectly inelastic demand curve would be vertical.

A shift in demand from DD to D*D* causes price to increase a relatively large amount from P_0 to P_1. Quantity supplied, however, increases a comparatively small amount, from Q_0 to Q_1. Knowledge of the nature of the supply and demand curves and the forces causing a demand shift may thus help the fundamental analyst to predict the relative magnitude of price change.

Figure 4-2 depicts a shift in supply, such as might be the effect of a severe drought on corn. The price response in Figure 4-2 is fairly small but, in contrast to the situation shown in Figure 4-1, the change in quantity demanded is large. This is what one would expect for a commodity for which consumers can readily use substitutes.

In Figure 4-3 both supply and demand are relatively inelastic. A shift upward (or to the left) in supply results in a large price increase accompanied by a relatively small decrease in quantity consumed. Commodities for which good substitutes are not available and for which consumer have strong pref-

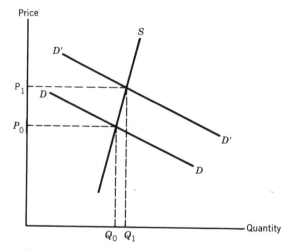

Figure 4-1   Supply-demand interaction.

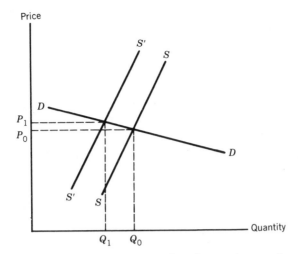

Figure 4-2   Shift in supply, elastic demand.

erences can be expected to behave as illustrated in Figure 4-3. Commodities like cocoa, coffee, and cotton might be expected to conform to this model in varying degrees.

Market Equilibrium

At any given time, price will move to ration supplies. However, even though a market will adjust to a new equilibrium in a particular time frame, the decisions of producers and consumers will impinge upon the supply-demand balance in subsequent time frames. Under certain conditions, their decisions

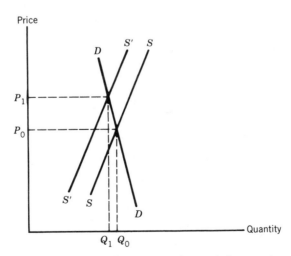

Figure 4-3   Inelastic supply and demand.

will lead to a new price equilibrium; under other conditions, price may oscillate explosively.

Consider the supply-demand conditions portrayed in Figure 4-4. If the market were to have a price of P_0 at a given time, suppliers would be willing to provide quantity Q_0, but consumers would only want Q_1 units at that price. Suppliers will only be able to sell Q_1 units. In the next production decision, suppliers will plan to produce Q_1 units, for which they will ask a price of P_1 per unit. However, at a price of P_1, consumers will want Q_2 units. They will decide to buy Q_2 units but, because only Q_1 are available the price will be bid up. Producers will be able to sell the production of Q_1 easily and realize they could have sold more, and at a higher price. In the next round of production, they will produce Q_2 units. The process repeats, with production gradually converging toward equilibrium with demand. The process may take some time with agricultural markets or others requiring substantial lead times for production plans to reach fruition. Any disturbance to supply or demand may either shorten or lengthen the time for an equilibrium to be reached.

A market may have explosive divergence from equilibrium, until the market eventually collapses. This is portrayed by the cobweb model shown in Figure 4-5. Starting at P_0 only Q_1 units will be sold, not the Q_0 units suppliers would like to sell. Producers will have unsold inventory unless they drop the price. For the next production cycle, producers will plan to supply only Q_1 units, and at the lower price, P_1. However, at this price Q_2 units will be demanded, and this will lead producers to plan for stepped-up production in the next production cycle. In this system, the divergence from equilibrium becomes greater and greater until eventually the system must collapse to a level of price and quantity from which the evolution may again begin.

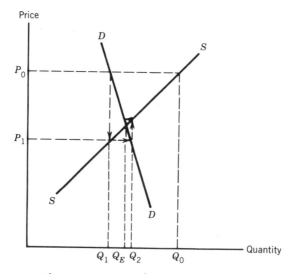

Figure 4-4 Market convergence.

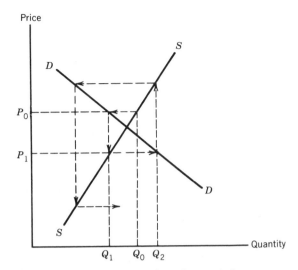

Figure 4-5 Cobweb model.

It should be noted that the cobweb model portrayed has a supply function that is relatively less elastic than the demand function. This is precisely the stuff of which many agricultural markets are made: A long production cycle on the supply side couples with demand that is conditioned by availability of substitutes. In the real world, cobweb models are constrained by the availability of resources for production, so that the explosive divergence is contained.

Practical Considerations

The foregoing discussion of fundamental analysis has attempted to convey what it is about while avoiding specific models for individual commodities. For those who would develop models of their own using fundamental analysis, it will be useful to keep several thoughts in mind.

A supply-demand model, to be useful in commodity trading, must be able to forecast. That is, the model must be able to use available historical data to yield likely values for future time periods. Identification of leading variables and relationships incorporating them is fundamental to model development.

Likewise, one must recognize that models based on contemporaneous observations on all possible variables will be of little if any value to the commodities trader. The difficulty of identifying and including significant variables and relationships, while excluding the myriad that do not contribute to better forecasts, must not be ignored. Nor should the necessity of revalidating and re-estimating shifts in relationships be overlooked.

In principle, fundamental analysis has strong rational appeal. In practice, it may more often than not fail to perform as well as reason would lead one to expect. It fails either from model misspecification or absence of useful leading variables.

Case Study: The Sugar Market

To illustrate what is involved in construction of a model for fundamen- tal analysis let us consider sugar, which is traded in New York (in two different contracts—domestic, and world or No. 11) and overseas, most notably in London and Paris. Table 4-1 summarizes factors affecting the supply of and the demand for sugar. It is clear that a number of influences cannot be easily dealt with quantitatively, such as the social and political-economic or those involving crop diseases and weather. It is also clear that to try to include all the listed influences would be expensive in terms of time and resources and would still yield a model that is far from perfect.

In practice, one would not attempt to include all supply and demand in- fluences in a model. The marginal value of each additional variable declines just as the cost of incorporating it increases; eventually the cost of adding another factor is no longer justified. Thus, a crucial consideration in con- structing a model for fundamental analysis is to identify those variables that contribute most in explanatory power and put them into the formal model while excluding the others. This is not to say that the omitted variables are of no importance (they may be used to refine the results of the formal model, for example). Certain variables may have to be excluded from the formal model because they are mathematically awkward to deal with or because in- sufficient history exists for their parameters to be estimated. Nevertheless, the effect of some influences may be inferred in light of their likely impact

Table 4-1 Factors in the supply/demand model for sugar

Supply	Demand
Climate factors	End product categories
Northern temperate	Soft-drinks and beverages
Southern temperate	Confectionary
Tropical and sub-tropical	Commercial baking
Crop factors	Individual/household use
Cane	Chemical and miscellaneous
Beets	Alternative products
Crop diseases and weather	Substitutes (corn sweetener and
Alternate crops/land uses	synthetics)
Inventory factors	Social
Carryover stocks in supplier hands	Tastes, health and lifestyle factors
Political-economic factors	Inventory factors
Cartel pricing, production	Carryover stocks in hands of consumers
Government subsidies to producers	Political-economic factors
Political factors affecting production	Government subsidies to consumers
	Political factors affecting demand

on the market, assuming the market is in equilibrium at the current price. For example, a hurricane which crosses Cuba and destroys much of the cane cannot be included in a model of sugar prices except stochastically. However, once landfall of the hurricane is imminent, or past, one can surmise the effect on equilibrium price.

The German firm of F.O. Licht & Company is the world's authoritative source of data on sugar. Anyone who wishes to construct a model for the price of sugar would have to utilize their data or else try to duplicate the expensive process of gathering and processing information into usable form. The main types of information that seem to be used in fundamental analysis are such things as planting intentions, crop conditions during the growing season, carryover stocks, and rate of disappearance (that is, usage). The measure and influence of the more subtle factors are up to the model builder to determine.

A good model for fundamental analysis provides statistically reliable price forecasts (at least the direction of likely price movement) while using variables parsimoniously. That is, a good model should be as simple as possible while still yielding useful forecasts.

TECHNICAL ANALYSIS

At the core of technical analysis is the premise that the market price at any time is revealed by the pattern of prior price movements. As a result, those who employ technical analysis use price patterns to predict the direction of future price movement. Although price data are at the center of technical analysis, some practitioners also employ other related data such as trading volumes and open interest as well as modified price series. (One unit of open interest equals one long and one short contract position.)

In its traditional form, technical analysis relies solely on price patterns for what they may portend about the likely future direction of price movement. Two different methods for graphically recording prices are commonly used: the bar chart and the point and figure, or reversal chart.

In recording prices on a bar chart, one draws a vertical line representing the price range in a given time span (day or week typically). Then a short horizontal tick is drawn out from the settlement price to the right. Sometimes the opening price is recorded with a dot or a short, horizontal tick to the left of the appropriate price.

Figure 4-6 illustrates the construction of a bar chart. This is the type of chart published by the Commodity Research Bureau, Inc. and several other popular services. These charts are straightforward: The price activity of each time period is plotted immediately to the right of that of the prior period.

Some chart services plot volume and open interest at the bottom of certain bar charts. The additional information these provide is used by some technical analysts to confirm or augment the price data.

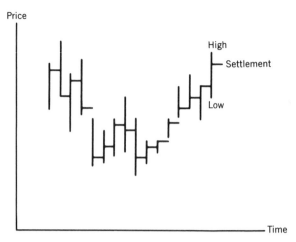

Figure 4-6   Commodity bar chart.

TRADITIONAL TECHNICAL PATTERNS

Head-and-Shoulders

It is probably safe to say that the head-and-shoulders (H&S) patterns for tops and bottoms are the best known of all technical formations. Figure 4-7 depicts these formations in several variations. The "neckline" is a vital part of H&S patterns. It is penetration of the neckline that provides signals for trade initiation.

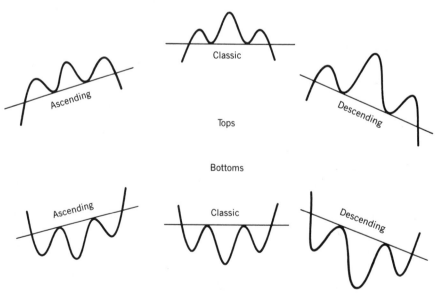

Figure 4-7   Head-and-shoulders patterns.

Figure 4-8 shows an H&S top in May 1991 Chicago Wheat that follows an H&S bottom. The sharp price rise on March 1 represents the type of breakout often seen when traders who have short positions place protective stop buy orders over a falling trend line. A price rise triggers these buy orders, which have a snowballing effect. As the price reaches higher levels, new stop orders are touched, and these put further upward pressure on price as they are executed. In essence, when stop buy orders are hit this way, supply temporarily increases anomalously in response to lower price levels. The reverse to this scenario applies for an H&S top.

Double Tops and Bottoms

Sometimes instead of a head-and-shoulders formation reaching full development, one finds two lobes extending to the same or nearly the same level. Figure 4-9 illustrates a double bottom in the 1989 Deutsche mark.

Unfortunately for those who sold December 1991 cotton in *anticipation* of an H&S top, rather than on its *confirmation*, the price rose steadily from March 1991, as Figure 4-10 shows. The double H&S "top that wasn't" in 1991 cotton illustrates a basic difficulty with technical analysis: One does not know whether a particular chart pattern applies until afterward. All too

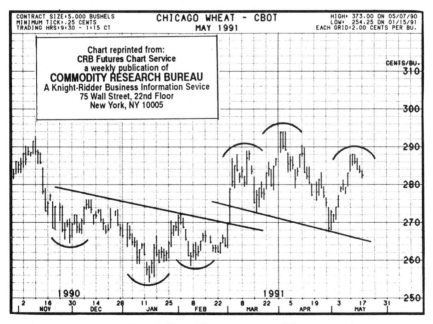

Figure 4-8 Head and shoulders, tops and bottoms alternating.

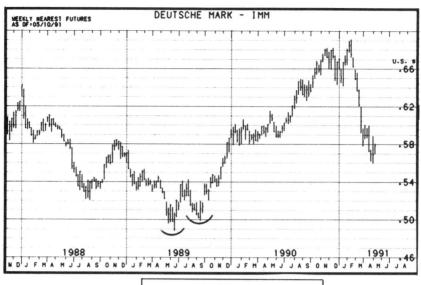

Figure 4-9   Double bottom.

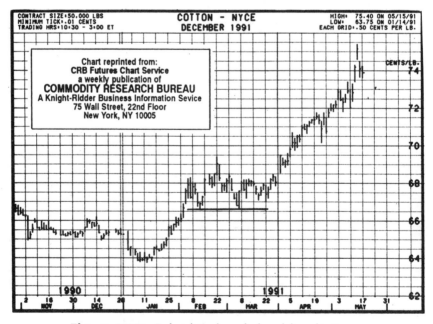

Figure 4-10   False head-and-shoulders bottom.

often, what appeared to be a budding H&S or double top (or bottom) evolves into something else. For the trader, this implies that one should enter the market by using stop orders at prices that confirm the pattern. This strategy, however, is no panacea, since there may be a cluster of such orders that causes erratic market action and poor order fills when the crucial level is attained. One thus has a dilemma: whether to anticipate confirmation of a technical pattern and risk being wrong or to wait for confirmation and hope to get a good order fill when other technical analysts have the same idea. Decisions such as these separate successful technical analysts-traders from the failures. Likewise, such decisions favor those with trading experience in the markets and some appreciation of market fundamentals.

Trends and Channels

Successful commodity traders follow trends. Perhaps one can find surer roads to ruin than fighting a trend, but bucking the market trend will remain close to the top of any list of losing strategies. Certainly one can play the "trends within a trend"—the short-term trends that go counter to the long-term market trend—*if* one recognizes the direction of the major trend and enters and exits accordingly. But those plays are different from blindly going counter to the major trend—and staying with a losing trade.

Figures 4-11, 4-12, and 4-13 contain typical trend channels (indicated by the author) in Paris MATIF June 1991 Notional Bond, spot French franc, and the Chicago IMM September 1991 Swiss franc. Such formations are so ubiquitous that one can scarcely pick up a set of commodity charts published in any given week and not find a least one example.

Figure 4-14 illustrates a more complex trend channel for the prices of the nearest-to-expiration Coffee, Sugar, and Cocoa Exchange (CSCE) No. 11 sugar contract. Within the broad channel of the dominant uptrend is a variety of price movements. Nevertheless, most of the prices are contained within the dominant channel (the center of the three bands). It is the mark of a skilled trader to capture profits from the sub-trends within the main channel, rather than simply rely on the main trend.

Paul H. Cootner,[2] while postulating that prices move in a random walk around their intrinsic value, stated that prices would be contained within "reflecting barriers." He based this idea on the behavior he felt likely from professional investors, who would buy or sell as price reached these barriers, thus tending to keep price within them. Though Cootner wrote of stocks, it is likely that the same principles apply to commodities.

---

[2]P. H. Cootner, "Stock Prices: Random versus Systematic Changes,"*Industrial Management Review* 3 (Spring 1962):24–45.

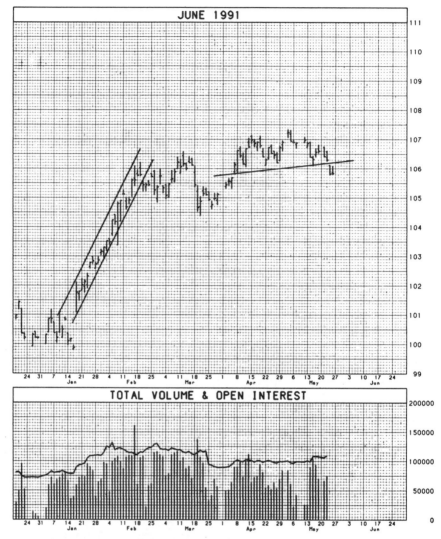

Figure 4-11   Trend channel with head-and-shoulders top.

Triangles and Wedges

Figure 4-15, which contains the chart for the June 1991 U.S. dollar index (IMM, Chicago), shows a triangle consolidation in a rising price trend. Figure 4-16 illustrates a triangle that follows a complex H&S bottom in the June 1991 Winnepeg canola contract. At the right in that figure is a down "flag" from which the price breaks sharply to lower levels (flags and pennants will be discussed shortly). According to some writers[3] price tends to continue in

[3] Although there are more sophisticated works, a good non-technical treatment is provided by Ted Warren, *How to Make the Stock Market Make Money for You* (Los Angeles: Sherbourne, 1966). Two chapters specifically on futures markets are included.

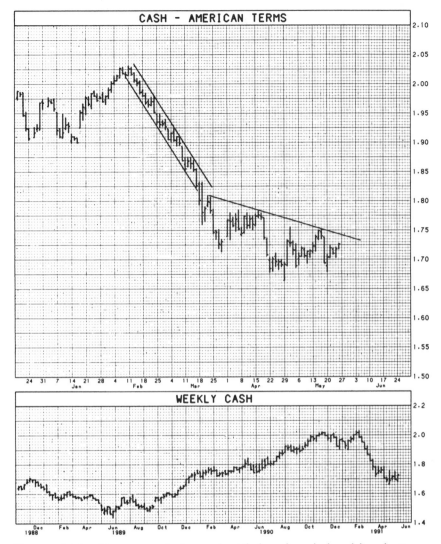

Figure 4-12 Downtrend channel with head-and-shoulders bottom.

the same direction upon leaving the triangle or wedge as it was moving on entry, and such movement is most reliable when the breakout occurs about two-thirds into the triangle.

Although triangles and wedges are common technical patterns,[4] one seldom finds such a pattern with the apex at the left. That is, the price volatility tends to dampen as one moves further into the triangle from left to right, rather than to become explosive. If markets followed a truly random walk, one would expect a priori to find as many triangles with their apexes to the left as to

---

[4]Perhaps the operative word should be "were." Triangles and wedges have been far less common in charts during the early 1990s than they were a decade before.

Figure 4-13   Narrow downtrend channel.

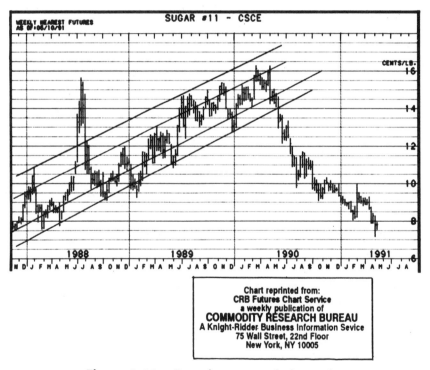

Figure 4-14   Complex uptrend channel.

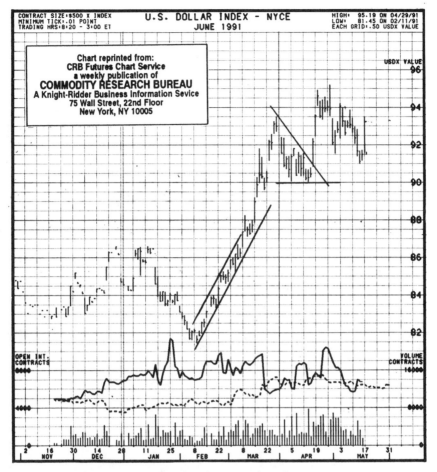

Figure 4-15 Island reversal with pennant.

the right. An interpretation that may explain the damped oscillatory pattern that is actually found in almost all occurrences of triangles is that the market tends to converge to a new equilibrium. In doing this, price volatility lessens until there is new information considered significant by the market.

Island Reversals

Figures 4-17 and 4-18 contain examples of island reversals for Chicago May oats and May corn, respectively. The "island" for the corn contract is noteworthy for having taken a month to evolve.

Island reversals result from powerful news that causes a market to reverse direction abruptly, often from a consolidation range wherein prices move in a narrow range. Because these patterns result from significant news devel-

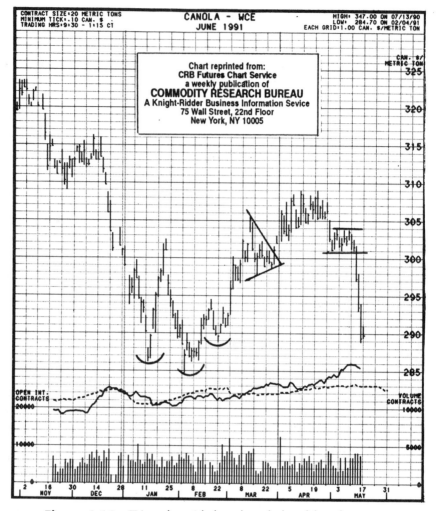

Figure 4-16 Triangle with head-and-shoulders bottom.

opments, the price often continues in the direction of the breakout for quite some time beyond the breakout from the "island."

Other Patterns

Certain other patterns occur with sufficient frequency to warrant identification and labeling, and some traders attach significance to them. Figure 4-19 illustrates some of them. A *pennant* (Fig. 4-19 *a* and *b*) is a large price move that, when plotted, serves as the staff, with a triangle or wedge following the large move. A *flag* (Fig.4-19 *c* and *d*) is similar, but without the triangle shape on the staff. A *key reversal* (Fig.4-19 *e* and *f*) is a price move to a new

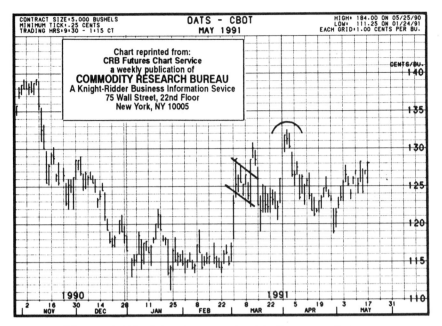

Figure 4-17 Island reversal with flag, oats futures.

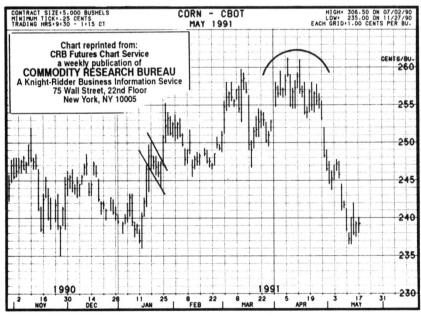

Figure 4-18 Island reversal with flag, corn futures.

71

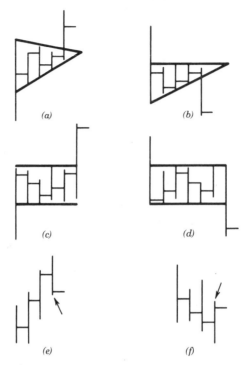

Figure 4-19 Some additional technical patterns.

high, followed on the same day by a settlement below that of the prior day or a price move to a new low followed by a settlement at a price above that of the prior day. Figure 4-16 contains a flag.

Figure 4-20, containing a chart for July 1991 soybeans, is especially rich in technical patterns. In May–June 1990 one finds a double bottom. Then in the first week of July 1990 there is a two-day island top. A sharp downtrend follows to culminate in an island reversal taking three weeks to form. Then a head-and-shoulders top develops. A key reversal can be seen at the beginning of August 1990, and another the last week of May 1991. Careful examination of the chart will reveal still more patterns.

Other technical analysis patterns have been named. The reader interested in gaining depth in traditional technical analysis is advised to consult some of the excellent works devoted solely to the topic.

Point-and-Figure Charting

An alternative to the bar chart is the point-and-figure or reversal chart. This method of recording prices requires that the price move some specified dis-

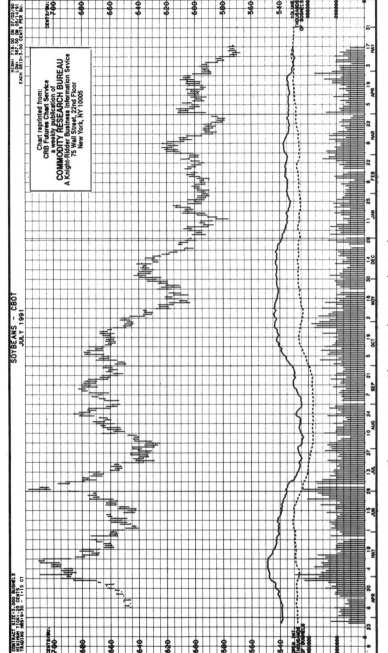

Figure 4-20 Chart rich in technical patterns.

73

tance to be placed on the chart, and thus provides for some filtering of the raw data. With this charting method, there is no time axis, for reference dates may be recorded in the plot area itself.

Figure 4-21 contains a point-and-figure price chart for the Japanese yen along with the corresponding bar charts for both daily and weekly price ranges.[5] The smoothing effect that the point-and-figure chart has on the data is apparent. So, too, is the smoothing effect of recording the weekly rather than the daily price data.

This point-and-figure chart is based on a reversal of four points, with each point set at 0.002. Each vertical distance between lines is worth 0.002, and only reversals in the direction of price of *greater* than 4 × 0.002, or 0.008 are recorded.

What rules determine whether one adds Xs or Os, or switches from one to the other? Assume we have a column of Xs because the price has been rising for some time. We record one or more Xs in the same column only if the high for the day is *at least* one box (that is, 0.002) above the previously plotted price. The high must reach or exceed the scale price for the box in the column to receive an X. We record as many Xs as are required.

We continue with our column of Xs until we cannot add another X and the low price for the day is at least three boxes under the box containing the highest X. Then we move one column to the right and fill in the appropriate number of Os. For an O to be recorded, the price must have gotten *at least* as low as the scale price.

The process works in reverse order if we are currently in a column of Os. We add one or more Os to the bottom of the column only if the low of the day is at least one box under the lowest O in the column. We switch to Xs only if the low of the day is not low enough to warrant another O in the column and the high of the day is *at least* three boxes above the scale price of the lowest O.

In addition to the patterns that are held to be useful with bar charts, several additional formations have been defined and are used in point-and-figure charting.

Far fewer firms offer point-and-figure charts than bar charts. One that provides such charts for a comprehensive set of commodity futures is the Chart Craft Commodity Service.[6] Traders can avail themselves of special offers advertised in *Barron's* or *Futures* magazine to order a sample issue or trial subscription to a variety of chart services at a minimal cost, and then choose the best for an annual subscription.

[5]From the Dunn & Hargitt Commodity Service, Lafayette, IN.
[6]Chart Craft Commodity Service, Larchmont, N.Y.

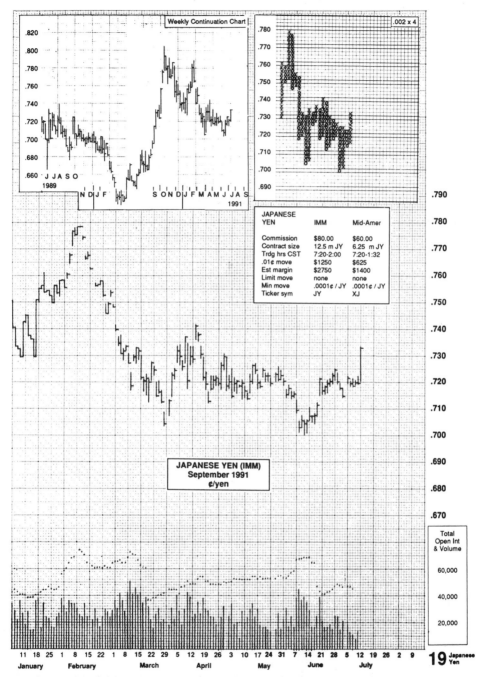

Figure 4-21 Point-and-figure chart with bar chart. (Source: Dunn & Hargitt, 22 North Second Street, P. O. Box 1100, Lafayette, IN 47902, (317)423-2624)

CYCLES AND TECHNICAL PATTERNS[7]

Both traditional technical analysis and cycle analysis have strong followings. However, the two approaches are generally treated independently and seldom is cycle analysis mentioned in the same breath as a "double top" or "H&S" bottom, except coincidentally, and without regard to cause and effect. Yet, if it were not for cyclical effects, the traditional technical patterns would be much less common than they are.

It can be shown that double tops and H&S tops (and bottoms of both types) can be repetitively generated by the interactions of just two cycles of different periodicity. Trend channels also can be generated by just two cycles. The repetitive generation of uniform patterns in the markets is, of course, unlikely over long spans because of random influences that may cause parameter shifts; there are also cyclical influences external to any simple model containing only a few cycles. Here we shall consider only two cycles at a time. Even so, the results are unambiguous.

Representative patterns appear over time when the period of the longer of two cycles is an odd or an even multiple of the shorter cycle. A number of multiples were examined in preparing this section. However, because of space constraints only the odd multiples of 3 and 7 and the even multiple of 6 are shown.

When the period of the longer cycle is exactly three times the shorter cycle, a pattern of repeating H&S tops and bottoms results, with a smooth transition from one into the other. This is illustrated in Figure 4-22.

When the longer cycle contains an *even* multiple of the shorter, the pattern that the interaction traces is one of H&S tops (bottoms) alternating with

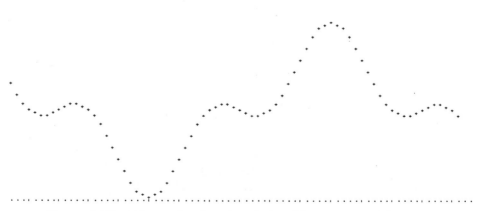

Figure 4-22 Alternating head-and-shoulders tops and bottoms.

[7]A. Herbst and B. Herbst, "Bringing Cycles and Technicals Together," *Futures* 13, No.3 (March 1984): 104,106. Reprinted from *Futures* magazine, 219 Parkade, Cedar Falls, Iowa 50613.

Figure 4-23 Long cycle is six times the shorter.

double bottoms (tops). This combination also yields the type of trend channel between tops and bottoms that is often found in actual commodity price movements. This interaction is illustrated for multiples of six cycles in Figure 4-23.

If the multiplicity of the longer cycle is a large odd multiple of the shorter, the H&S tops and bottoms alternate. Also, there is clearly indicated trend channel, and breaks of the trend coincide with the transition from head to right shoulder as seen in Figure 4-24.

We have seen only a few representative samples from a great many different combinations of two cycles (a literally infinite number if we allow for non-integer multiples or very long period for the longer of the two cycles). However, examination of these and other combinations allows some generalizations to be drawn.

- When the longer cycle is an even multiple of the shorter cycle, H&S tops (bottoms) alternate with the double bottoms (tops).

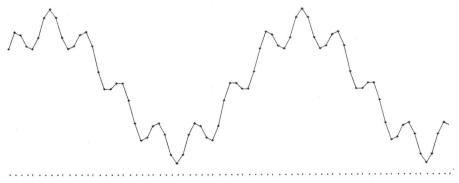

Figure 4-24 Long cycle is seven times the shorter.

- When the longer cycle is an odd multiple of the shorter cycle, H&S tops alternate with H&S bottoms.
- When two cycles are combined, with one having a much longer period than the other, trend channels arise.

It should be apparent that cycle analysis and traditional technical analysis of price charts should not be viewed as competing methods, but rather as complementary tools for putting price action into perspective. The technical analyst who combines the two approaches will have a trading advantage over those who do not. The chart analyst who understands how cycles influence chart patterns should be better able to anticipate the evolution of a pattern from a given point into the future. And, cycle analysts who refer to the charts should be less surprised if prices do not react as the cycles alone would suggest when important chart points are crossed and chartists react. Market action evoked by violation (or confirmation) of important chart support or resistance levels may cause phase shifts in otherwise consistent cycles. Market participants are not, and should not be considered to be, passive with respect to market action, including that influenced by cycles that may be present.

For those who would like to examine combinations of two cycles on their own, the following equation will be useful:

$$y = A_1\sin(\omega_1 t + p_1) + A_2\sin(\omega_2 t + p_2) \qquad (4\text{-}1)$$

where y = the value of the combined cycles at time t
A_i = the amplitude, or relative strengths of the component cycles ($i = 1,2$)
$\sin$ = the trigonometric sine function
ω_i = the number of cycle repetitions in 360° (2π radians)
p_i = phase-shift parameters (Assume these are zero if both cycles are to start together.)

For cycle one to contain seven replications of cycle two, $\omega_1/\omega_2 = 7$. In the figures used in this example, the ratio of A_1 to A_2 was taken to be in the same proportion. In other words, if cycle one was assumed to be seven times as long as cycle two, it was also assumed to be seven times as strong. Those who would rather not work with trigonometric functions can nevertheless examine the combination of two or more cycles. They can do this by drawing the individual cycles carefully on a sheet of graph paper, then measuring the combined values and plotting these as a single cycle on the same page.

Previous work indicates that the traditional technical patterns of triangles, wedges, pennants, and so on require at least three cycles in combination to become evident. Additional insights may be gained by reading the excellent work by Bernstein on commodity cycles.[8]

[8]Jacob Bernstein, *The Handbook of Commodity Cycles: A Window on Time* (New York: Wiley, 1982). Bernstein has authored several more recent works, but this remains a favorite with many traders.

CONCLUSION

This chapter has examined basic precepts of fundamental and technical analysis. Fundamental analysis, while appealing to reason, nevertheless suffers from the inherent difficulty associated with building a model useful for forecasting as opposed to an ex post or contemporaneous explanation. Technical analysis assumes that the pattern of price behavior over time reveals all that is important about supply and demand and further that this knowledge gives one an advantage in predicting the likely direction of future price movement.

While fundamental analysis suffers from the problems of model building, technical analysis suffers from problems related to pattern validation. One does not know with certainty whether one has a particular pattern until after the fact. The trader who would use technical analysis to enter or exit the market may therefore be wise to enter with stops at prices validating the pattern, even though these may frequently result in less-than-desirable order fills, and occasionally may respond to false price moves.

It was shown that some traditional technical patterns can be constructed by the interaction of cycles in price series. In particular H&S and double tops and bottoms, plus trend channels, can be produced by the interaction of price cycles. Price cycles in agricultural commodities may have fundamental causes, such as seasonal or weather-induced effects; in the case of financial futures, cycles can stem from the fiscal and monetary activities of the federal government or action of the Federal Reserve. Thus, there may be linkage from fundamental to technical analysis.

Occasionally one hears the proposition that fundamental analysis should be used to pick the market to trade, and technical analysis should be used for the timing of entry and exit. This notion would seem to deserve more attention from traders.

Ultimately, what determines the merit of a particular mode of analysis is how well it works. A study by Taylor suggests that different futures contracts have different "personalities" and that technical patterns, therefore, have more or less reliability depending on the particular commodity.[9] He found that some patterns not only occur with high frequency, but also are reliable (H&S tops and bottoms in pork bellies, for example, are 85 and 87 percent reliable). Whether his conclusions remain valid two decades later remains to be seen.

That technical analysis, in principle, works may help to explain why thousands of traders are willing to spend hundreds of dollars on each annual subscription from among many weekly charting services, and why many keep charts of their own. What Taylor's study did not address are the means by which technical analysis can be implemented. One can, for example, become an expert on the rules of poker or bridge, or on riding a bicycle or flying an

[9]R. J. Taylor, "Technical Personalities of Major Commodities," *Commodities* (August 1972).

airplane by reading and study. However, there is no substitute for hands-on experience. And, as in other things, different persons have different talents and aptitudes. Some may be able to adapt to trading futures profitably while others less suited by ability or temperament fail.

Analysis and forecasting techniques based on cycles present in future prices can help in predicting price movements. The aim of the following chapters is to provide a working knowledge of the more useful techniques.

5

Time Series Analysis and Forecasting

Participants in futures markets engage in forecasting prices or, at least, the directions of price movements. Some may produce forecasts informally, or with little or no conscious analytical effort. Others may resort to complex mathematical modeling based on supply-demand fundamentals. Still others may rely on analysis of price data, alone or in combination with a few closely related variables, to form opinions as to the likely course of coming price movements. It is to this last group that this chapter will likely be of greatest interest.

There would seem to be a paradox for an author to discuss market efficiency and the obstacles it puts in the way of traders in one chapter, and then discuss the application of methods for overcoming those difficulties in other chapters. Let us address this basic issue. First, while much evidence tends to support the efficient markets hypothesis (EMH), there exists a growing body of published research indicating the existence of imperfections. Second, the establishment of a speculative position in a futures market implies that the speculator has forecast that the market price will move favorably to his or her position. Otherwise what would be the point of being in the market, other than to satisfy some masochistic impulse? Third, technical analysis based on chart configurations remains popular, and chart formations can be explained in terms of interactions of cyclical influences. Thus an understanding of time series analysis may help the chartist anticipate how a given chart pattern is likely to evolve, and whether the expected pattern is likely to be realized. Fourth, the hedger may wish to incorporate forecasts into a hedging program, for timing purposes.

Forecasting financial markets and futures markets is a task neither easy to do well nor susceptible to naive, mechanistic approaches. Nevertheless, a forecasting approach that consistently provides better odds than tossing a coin for pointing to the correct direction of price movement merits examination. The techniques discussed in this chapter have proven their worth in business forecasting. Classical applications of these methods are found in forecasting airline passenger numbers, demand for telephone services, and traffic volume across urban bridges.

FORECASTING METHODS

Many forecasting methods have been developed over the years. It is not the purpose of this work to evaluate or even enumerate all of them. Instead we will focus on those methods this author has found to be especially useful, with brief mention of some of the popular methods that are less efficacious.

The methods discussed in this chapter are based on time series analysis. This is the analysis of historical data within the series one wishes to forecast. The simplest of such methods is that of trend projection, a technique of undeniable value in a trending market, though always wrong at the crucial turning points. In this chapter we shall focus on spectral analysis and the popular and much misused Box-Jenkins methodology. The purposes of the two approaches and the underlying philosophies are somewhat different even though both are based on the notion that past data are prologue for the future.

Spectral (or spectrum) analysis has typically been used to study long time series in which the cyclical components do not vary greatly over time. Box-Jenkins modeling has been developed for the shorter time series generally found in economic data. Spectral analysis does not directly provide a forecasting model. However, it can detect cycles within a time series, even those not apparent to the eye. This can be useful in determining the likelihood of a potential chart formation evolving into a confirmed action signal. Spectral analysis can also be useful in sequence with other applications, including Box-Jenkins, and for examining the residuals (that is, forecast errors) after fitting a Box-Jenkins model. Also, with knowledge of prominent cycles within a time series one may combine the cycles into a synthetic time series that extrapolates into the future their combined effects. This works well with cycles that are relatively invariant over time, and even some that are not. Fortunately many economic series are amenable to this approach. Box-Jenkins methodology can provide a forecasting model directly, without resort to other procedures.

Note that spectral analysis assumes that any cycles present in the data persist over time, that cycles do not fade away. Box-Jenkins analysis, in contrast, does not make this assumption and can handle cycles that are induced by shocks to the system, producing the time series under analysis. Such induced cycles are assumed to die out in the absence of new shocks to the system, and thus the series is assumed to revert to "white noise." A white noise series has no cycles that stand out as more significant or dominant than others.

Both spectral analysis and Box-Jenkins methodology depend on computers for their practical application. The amount of calculation required for practical applications is so great that neither method is practicable without a computer. However, this poses a less formidable obstacle than might at first appear. Not only are computer programs implementing these models available on large computers,[1] but programs that perform the necessary calculations on microcomputers are also available at modest cost.[2]

SPECTRAL ANALYSIS

Spectral analysis is a method for finding evidence of cycles that exist in time series data, if any do. It is based on Fourier analysis, named after a French mathematician. The formal mathematics of spectral analysis is the topic of Chapter 7. Rather, in this chapter we shall consider an illustration of what one can expect to get from application of spectral analysis.

Examination of Figure 5-1 suggests that cycles may be present in this price (that is, index) series. Let us consider this possibility further. These data were selected not because they contain the strongest cycles one might expect to find in futures data, but because these cycles are generally rather faint and thus present a challenge to those who would discover them. The data employed will be restricted to the last 156 settlement prices so that actual market data may be used and no exchange-determined settlement prices will be included from the period of light trading early in the life of the contract. The data analyzed ended July 9, 1990.

---

[1]For those near a large university it may be possible to purchase computer time directly (usually under the restriction that sale of such time would not be in competition with commercial services in the area) or to obtain access by enrolling in a course, either for credit or as an auditor, or non-credit student. For the business firm or affluent individual the fine Biomedical P-Series programs (BMDP) developed at the University Of California at Los Angeles are available for a variety of computers, and the programs one gets include many other statistical applications in addition to spectral analysis and Box-Jenkins modeling. Similar program packages are available from SAS Institute,Inc. in Cary, North Carolina. As an alternative to applying the forecasting methods directly oneself, it may be more efficient and cost-effective to hire a consultant for a specific project.

[2]Versions of the popular mainframe computer programs that can perform various statistical analyses are available for personal computers, and there are specialized programs designed to perform the work of fitting a Box-Jenkins model. One of the most powerful and flexible programs for personal computers is *RATS* (Regression And Time Series) by VAR Econometrics, 134 Prospect Ave. South, Minneapolis, MN 55419,(612) 822-9690. However, it does require some knowledge of both computer and econometrics (statistics adapted to economics). This author has developed computer programs for use on personal computers that perform spectral analysis and other methods illustrated in this book.

Appendix 5-1, at the end of this chapter, contains a periodogram presentation of the results of a spectral analysis on the T-bond settlement prices. The column labeled "Harmonic" represents the frequency of a cycle in terms of the number of cycles that will fit into the number of data points analyzed. Thus, with 156 data points, a harmonic of 1.0 corresponds to a cycle of period 156, a harmonic of 2.0 to 78, and so on. One should never bother with harmonics corresponding to cycles less than two days (if using daily data). And one should never attach much significance to cycles longer than about one-fifth of the number of data points analyzed, nor use cycles longer than one-third the data series length except for the purpose of removing "trend" or reintroducing it.

In Appendix 5-1 the column labeled "Amplitude" contains measures of the relative strength indicated for a cycle of each period. The "Slope" term is a measure of the degree to which a given amplitude stands out from surrounding amplitudes, a large value indicating a sharply defined cycle. And the "Phase"[3] column contains numbers indicating at which point after the beginning of the data each cycle first reaches its peak amplitude. This is useful for compar-

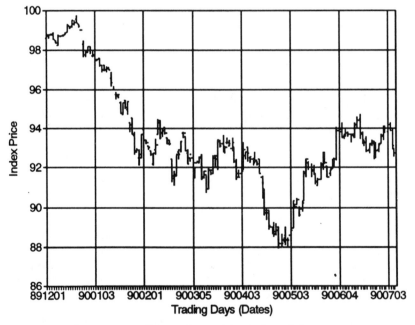

Figure 5-1   December 1990 T-bond futures.

---

[3]Phase has a different meaning when used with cross-spectral (or bivariate spectral) analysis, which examines relationships between two time series in terms of cyclical components. We shall not get into cross-spectral analysis in this work.

ing results with a graph of the original price data and required for the purpose of synthesizing a data series for forecasting. Note that because cycles of fractional length may be estimated the total number of cycle values contained in the Appendix 5-1 is greater than the 156 data points used.

The indications of cycles in the data shown in the column for amplitude in Appendix 5-1 are plotted in Figures 5-2 and 5-3. Figure 5-2 contains the spectrum of the lower frequency cycles. Figure 5-3 displays the spectrum of the higher frequency cycles. These graphs suggest that cycles appear to be present in the T-bond settlement prices.

It is almost always true that longer period cycles have the greatest amplitudes. However, the shorter period (that is, higher frequency) cycles tend to be more numerous and can be tested for statistical significance. And, the combined effects of shorter period cycles can be greater than for any given long cycle as well as changing the direction of the time series more quickly. The fundamental reasons for the existence of cycles of any given length can change; and an analysis on data performed several years later on a futures price series may not uncover the same cycles in all cases, though some will often be fairly persistent over long intervals of time.

Appendix 5-2 contains the results of examining the 37.14 day cycle indicated in Figure 5-2 to be present in the T-bond settlement prices. It is also

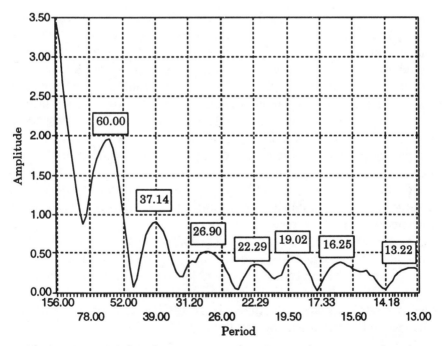

Figure 5-2   Higher frequency cycles, December 1990 T-bonds.

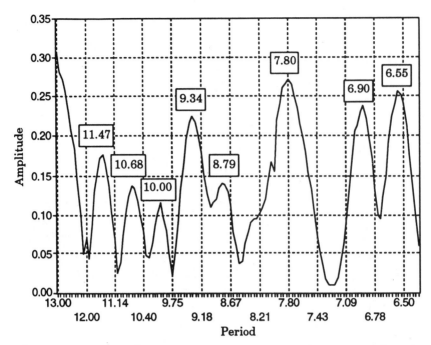

Figure 5-3   Lower frequency spectrum, December 1990 T-bonds.

the longest indicated cycle in our data series of 156 points to which we can attach any real significance.(Recall that cycles longer than about one-fifth of the number of data points analyzed, in this case 156, should not normally be considered very significant.) The array analysis presented examines each third of the data separately, then each half, then overall, and shows the phase, and so on for each. It also provides some estimates of improved measures of the cycle length, phase, and strength. The technique used to create the data in Appendix 5-2 is discussed in depth in Chapter 8.

The phases presented indicate the data point from the base, or beginning of the data, at which a cycle first reaches its peak. The term thus has the meaning normally used in describing a cycle with a single sine or cosine wave rather than the combination of a sine and a cosine wave with different coefficients for which the phase is implicit.[4]

The most useful measure from the array analysis is the Bartels test statistic of probability, printed toward the bottom of Appendix 5-2. The Bartels test provides a direct measure of the likelihood that a given cycle is genuine. The closer to zero the Bartels statistic is, the less likely it is that the cycle could be due to random influences. Appendix B to Chapter 8 fully describes the Bartels test and illustrates its application.

[4]For a discussion of why this is so see Chapter 7, Equations 1–4.

A great deal more will be said in Chapters 7 and 8 about both spectral analysis and array analysis. The purpose of this chapter is to provide an introduction and a sense of what the methods provide. Later chapters that are devoted to the methods provide detail.

THE BOX-JENKINS METHODOLOGY

The methodology developed by Box and Jenkins is based on the analysis of time series over the time domain.[5] That is, it does not use frequencies as spectral analysis does, but instead works with days, weeks, months, and so on. Persons outside the physical sciences and engineering are generally more comfortable with these measures than frequency.

There are three separate steps to Box-Jenkins methodology: (1) identification, (2) estimation, and (3) validation or diagnostic checking. While mathematically demanding and rigorous in its theoretical development, the method nevertheless involves a great amount of artistry and judgment. Sometimes different models will yield quite similar results, and choosing the best from several will be based on ease of use. A simpler model will be preferred in most cases.

Box-Jenkins models are referred to as ARMA (autoregressive moving average) or ARIMA (autoregressive, integrated moving average) forecasting models. Besides these designations there are the simpler AR (autoregressive) and MA (moving average) models that are special cases of the ARMA or ARIMA classes. The following discussion focuses on the ARIMA model because it is the more general.

The basic ARIMA model can be written

$$\phi(B)(1 - B)^d Z_t = \theta(B)\epsilon_t \tag{5-1}$$

where Z_t is the value of the time series observation at time t, ϵ_t is a series of random shocks which are assumed to be independently, normally distributed with zero mean and variance σ^2.

$\phi(B)$ is a polynomial of order p in the backshift operator B, which is defined as

$$\phi(B) = 1 - \phi_1 B - \ldots - \phi_p B^p \tag{5-2}$$

$\theta(B)$ is defined similarly to be a polynomial of order q in B:

$$\theta(B) = 1 - \theta_1 B - \ldots - \theta_q B^q \tag{5-3}$$

---

[5]See G. E. P. Box and G. M. Jenkins, *Time Series Analysis, Forecasting and Control*, rev'd ed'n. Oakland, California: Holden-Day, 1976.

Finally, $(1 - B)^d$ denotes the differencing operator. Differencing is frequently necessary to achieve stationarity. What this all means is that if a time series is not stationary one must take steps to make it stationary. A nonstationary time series is one for which the parameters are functions of time, and thus one for which its mean, variance, and so on, change over time. If a time series is not stationary, its mean, variance, and autocovariances of the stochastic process we wish to model do not exist, thus invalidating estimation techniques that rely on them. Fortunately, for purposes of analysis, most time series can be made stationary by replacing the original data points with their differences; that is, the differences between successive observations. Usually first or (rarely) second differences are sufficient to obtain stationarity. Overdifferencing must be avoided because it introduces artifacts into the autoregression structure.

In the case of a series that is stationary for $d = 0$ the model is termed ARMA if it contains both ϕ and θ terms. Otherwise, if $d > 0$ it is termed an integrated model (ARIMA).

For Box-Jenkins models a useful shorthand notation is often used: ARIMA (p, d, q). For various values of these parameters the model labels shown in Table 5-1 are obtained. For example, if we assume $d = 0$ and $p = 2$, the left-hand side of Equation (1) becomes

$$(1 - \phi_1 B - \phi_2 B^2)Z_t = Z_t - \phi_1 Z_{t-1} - \phi_2 Z_{t-2} \tag{5-4}$$

It is clear that there exist a virtually unlimited number of ARIMA models. The situation is not hopeless, however, because there are two tools to help us narrow the ranges of p, d, and q. The first tool is the autocorrelation function of Z_t, which is the correlation of Z_t with Z_{t-k} for lags of $k = 0, 1, 2, 3$, and so on. The second tool is the partial autocorrelation function, which is the correlation between Z_t and Z_{t-k} after removal of the effects of Z_{t-1} through Z_{t-k+1}. The partial autocorrelation thus provides a measure of the strength of the relationship between data points at times t and $t - k$ when the influences of intervening time periods have been removed.

Each category of ARIMA (p, d, q) has a unique pair of autocorrelation and partial autocorrelation patterns. Figure 5-4 illustrates the patterns characteristic of simple MA(1) and AR(1) models. Note that either the autocorrelation

Table 5-1 Box-Jenkins models in terms of their parameters

	p	d	q
ARIMA models	> 0	> 0	> 0
ARMA models	> 0	$= 0$	> 0
AR models	> 0	≥ 0	$= 0$
MA models	$= 0$	≥ 0	> 0

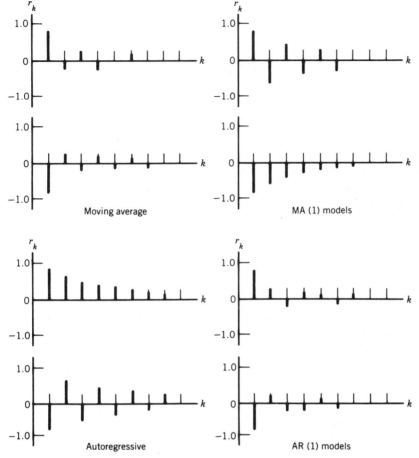

Figure 5-4 Characteristics autocorrelation and partical autocorrelation patterns for first-order Box-Jenkins model.

or partial autocorrelation function "cuts off" or truncates at lag $k = 1$ in the first-order models. Second-order MA(2) and AR(2) models have similar patterns but truncate after two lags. Thus, for a pure MA(q) or AR(p) model the order of the model is indicated by the lag at which truncation occurs.

That is the good news. Now what about mixed models? Unfortunately the situation tends to be much less straightforward. We may find that there is no truncation in either the autocorrelation or partial autocorrelation series; or, that spikes occur irregularly at various values of k. Such models can present significant challenges, even to experts in the application of Box-Jenkins modeling.

After tentative identification of an appropriate model the next step is estimation of model parameters. Procedures for this are mathematically complex and not applied without a computer. The reader interested in such details as the computational procedures is referred to the books that are devoted to Box-Jenkins modeling.[6]

A Case Study: Spot Gold

For this example daily gold prices covering a span of over 1300 days were analyzed. The control card setup for using the Statistical Analysis System (SAS) program package on an IBM mainframe computer is shown in Figure 5-5. It is included because it can be used with only minor modification by those who may wish to apply the method to other market data. Missing data values, due to holidays (but not weekdays), are filled in using values forecast from the observations preceding each missing value. This step is important

```
 1.  /BJAUSAS JOB B138-AFH,'AFH'
 2.  /*LINES 5
 3.  /*TIME 1
 4.  //EXEC SAS, OPTIONS = 'LS = 70'
 5.  //CASHAU DD DSN = B138.AFH.CASHAU,DISP = SHR
 6.  TITLE DAILY CASH GOLD PRICE;
 7.  DATA GOLD;
 8.  INFILE CASHAU;
 9.  INPUT @6 DAY YYMMDD8,
10.      @16 PRICE 4.1
11.      @23 INT 4.0
12.      @ VOL     ;
13.  T = _N_;
14.  KEEP DAY T PRICE INT VOL;
15.  LABEL PRICE = CASH GOLD PRICE;
16.  LABEL INT  = OPEN INTEREST–FUTURES
17.  LABEL VOL  = DAILY VOLUME–FUTURES
18.  FORMAT DAY MMDDYY8.;
19.  ;
20.  PROC ARIMA DATA = GOLD OUT = GOLD;
21.      IDENTIFY VAR = PRICE(1) CENTER NLAG = 10;
22.      ESTIMATE Q = 1 PLOT;
23.      FORECAST LEAD = 1 NOPRINT ID = T;
24.  DATA GOLD;
25.      SET GOLD;
26.      IF PRICE = 0 THEN PRICE = FORECAST;
27.      LNPRICE = 0 = LOG(PRICE);
28.  PROC ARIMA DATA = GOLD OUT = GOLD;
29.      IDENTIFY VAR = LNPRICE(1) CENTER NLAG = 20;
30.      ESTIMATE P = (1)(5) NOCONSTANT ML GRID PRINTALL PLOT;
31.      FORECAST LEAD = 1 ID = T PRINTALL;
```

Figure 5-5   IBM and SAS control cards for running a Box-Jenkins analysis.

[6]A very nice introduction is provided in J.P. Cleary and H. Levenbach, *The Professional Forecaster* (Belmont, CA: Lifetime Learning Publications, A Division of Wadsworth, Inc, 1982).

because without it a shift occurs every time a day is omitted. Note that first differences of the data have been taken to achieve stationarity.

Figure 5-6 exhibits the correlations and partial correlations for cash gold. The inverse correlations, which the SAS program provides, are also shown but are not widely used for model identification. The autocorrelations and partial autocorrelations suggest that a first-order moving average model may be appropriate.

```
                        DAILY CASH GOLD PRICE
                                      18:48 TUESDAY, JUNE 5, 1984
                          ARIMA PROCEDURE
          NAME OF VARIABLE              = PRICE
          PERIODS OF DIFFERENCEING = 1.
          MEAN OF WORKING SERIES = 0
          STANDARD DEVIATION      = 52.1479
          NUMBER OF OBSERVATIONS = 1304
                          AUTOCORRELATIONS
LAG   COVARIANCE   CORRELATION  -1 9 8 7 6 5 4 3 2 1 0 1 2 3 4 5 6 7 8 9 1
  0     2719.41      1.00000                        |******************
  1    -1360.8      -0.50040           **********   |
  2      71.9889     0.02647                        .|*
  3     -23.8429    -0.00877                        .|.
  4       0.937199   0.00034                        .|.
  5     -12.5282    -0.00461                        .|.
  6     -29.4635    -0.01083                        .|.
  7      28.2386     0.01038                        .|.
  8     -24.6285    -0.00906                        .|.
  9      49.6341     0.01825                        .|.
 10      -0.572223  -0.00021                        .|.
                      INVERSE AUTOCORRELATIONS
          LAG        CORRELATION  -1 9 8 7 6 5 4 3 2 1 0 1 2 3 4 5 6 7 8 9 1
           1          0.78071                        |****************
           2          0.60167                        .|*************
           3          0.46823                        .|*********
           4          0.36253                        .|*******
           5          0.27570                        .|******
           6          0.19912                        .|****
           7          0.12922                        .|***
           8          0.07322                        .|*
           9          0.02995                        .|*
          10          0.01825                        .|.
                       PARTIAL AUTOCORRELATIONS
          LAG        CORRELATION  -1 9 8 7 6 5 4 3 2 1 0 1 2 3 4 5 6 7 8 9 1
           1         -0.50040            *********  .|
           2         -0.29873              ******   .|
           3         -0.20661                ****   .|
           4         -0.14967                 ***   .|
           5         -0.11789                  **   .|
           6         -0.11130                  **   .|
           7         -0.08578                  **   .|
           8         -0.08017                  **   .|
           9         -0.04468                   *   .|
          10         -0.02023                       .|.
```

Figure 5-6   Identification phase of Box-Jenkins analysis of cash gold.

DAILY CASH GOLD PRICE

18:48 TUESDAY, JUNE 5, 1984

AUTOCORRELATION CHECK FOR WHITE NOISE

TO LAG	CHI SQUARE	DF	PROB	AUTOCORRELATIONS					
6	328.48	6	0.000	-0.500	0.026	-0.009	0.000	-0.005	-0.011

ARIMA LEAST SQUARES ESTIMATION

PARAMETER	ESTIMATE	STD ERROR	T RATIO	LAG
MU	$-.00639256$	0.251048	-0.03	0
MA 1,1	0.778685	0.017346 1	44.89	1

CONSTANT ESTIMATE   = $-.00639256$
VARIANCE ESTIMATE   =   1672.87
STD ERROR ESTIMATE   =   40.9007
NUMBER OF RESIDUALS =   1304

	MU	MA 1,1
MU	1.000	-0.001
MA 1,1	-0.001	1.000

AUTOCORRELATION CHECK OF RESIDUALS

TO LAG	CHI SQUARE	DF	PROB	AUTOCORRELATIONS					
6	1.43	4	0.839	-0.014	0.017	-0.005	0.010	-0.016	-0.014
12	6.34	10	0.736	0.010	0.013	0.036	0.023	0.012	0.038
18	23.94	16	0.091	0.014	0.014	0.101	-0.029	-0.027	-0.036
24	75.12	22	0.000	-0.012	-0.023	-0.024	0.191	-0.019	-0.023
30	77.35	28	0.000	-0.027	-0.025	-0.002	-0.012	0.011	0.006
36	85.23	34	0.000	-0.007	-0.007	-0.025	-0.034	0.051	-0.037
42	92.31	40	0.000	-0.031	-0.057	-0.021	0.005	0.005	0.024

Figure 5-7   Fitted Box-Jenkins model for cash gold price.

Figure 5-7 contains a moving average model for cash gold, centered about the mean of the time series. The t-ratio of 44.89 for the MA1, 1 term indicates that this term is statistically highly significant, and the autocorrelations and partial autocorrelations of the residuals are shown in Figure 5-8. The model is adequate, as indicated by the disappearance of the lagged correlations.

The real significance of this model vis-à-vis the efficient market hypothesis is that the cash gold market is shown to be less than fully efficient over the time for which the data used in fitting this model was generated. Whether or not the inefficiency remains and is such that it could be profitably exploited today remains to be answered. Nevertheless, results such as these provide both hope and justification to those who seek ways to forecast the direction of market price movements and thus to gain an advantage over those who do not make forecasts.

The Box-Jenkins methodolgy will not be developed further in this book for several reasons. First, the method has in this author's experience shown itself to be overly sensitive to errors in data. This means that just two or three bad data points out of many can lead to misspecification of the model and incorrect forecasts. Second, for forecasting futures prices other methods, such as projection of combinations of cycles shown by spectral analysis to be present, have in my experience performed better, especially for long-term

DAILY CASH GOLD PRICE

18:48 TUESDAY, JUNE 5, 1984

ARIMA PROCEDURE

NAME OF VARIABLE   = PRICE
PERIODS OF DIFFERENCING = 1.
MEAN OF WORKING SERIES = 0
STANDARD DEVIATION   = 52.1479
NUMBER OF OBSERVATIONS = 1304

AUTOCORRELATIONS

LAG	COVARIANCE	CORRELATION	−1 9 8 7 6 5 4 3 2 1 0 1 2 3 4 5 6 7 8 9 1
0	1672.87	1.00000	|******************
1	−23.3907	−0.01398	. | .
2	29.204	0.01746	. | .
3	−8.9757	−0.00537	. | .
4	−16.9529	−0.01013	. | .
5	−27.2767	−0.00461	. | .
6	−23.2225	−0.01388	. | .
7	17.1973	0.01028	. | .
8	22.4613	0.01343	. | .
9	60.7038	0.03629	. |*
10	39.0475	0.02334	. | .

INVERSE AUTOCORRELATIONS

LAG	CORRELATION	−1 9 8 7 6 5 4 3 2 1 0 1 2 3 4 5 6 7 8 9 1
1	0.01684	. | .
2	0.01630	. | .
3	0.00354	. | .
4	0.00835	. | .
5	0.01553	. | .
6	0.01388	. | .
7	−0.00970	. | .
8	−0.01416	. | .
9	−0.03647	*| .
10	−0.02343	. | .

PARTIAL AUTOCORRELATIONS

LAG	CORRELATION	−1 9 8 7 6 5 4 3 2 1 0 1 2 3 4 5 6 7 8 9 1
1	−0.01398	. | .
2	0.01727	. | .
3	−0.00489	. | .
4	−0.01587	. | .
5	−0.01642	. | .
6	−0.01401	. | .
7	0.01036	. | .
8	0.01394	. | .
9	0.03588	. |*
10	0.02350	. | .

Figure 5-8 Analysis of residuals after model fitting.

forecasts. And spectral analysis is very robust even with data sets having sharp discontinuities. Third, proper use of Box-Jenkins methods requires a level of experience and judgment that demands a significant investment of time to obtain. Without this the method can provide ill-specified models and poor forecasts. And fourth, the method is poorly suited to many data sets, especially when many data points are available and whatever cycles are present are not exact or near-exact sine waves throughout the data set.

Appendix 5-1   Spectral (Periodogram) Analysis of DEC90
T-Bond Futures Settlement Prices

Harmonic	Period	Amplitude	Slope	Phase
1.000	156.0000	3.420310	0.087700	20.24431
1.200	130.0000	2.684316	0.082594	29.35201
1.400	111.4286	1.920192	0.068930	31.58632
1.600	97.5000	1.265493	0.051918	26.83438
1.800	86.6667	0.867703	0.040048	18.84650
2.000	78.0000	1.271546	0.065208	11.28458
2.200	70.9091	1.700098	0.095903	14.14139
2.400	65.0000	1.897088	0.116744	16.07597
2.600	60.0000	1.962849	0.130857	18.51130
2.800	55.7143	1.620713	0.116359	21.97686
3.000	52.0000	0.937520	0.072117	23.39855
3.200	48.7500	0.330143	0.027089	26.96608
3.400	45.8824	0.178215	0.015537	3.69236
3.600	43.3333	0.591123	0.054565	7.64047
3.800	41.0526	0.829534	0.080826	10.52674
4.000	39.0000	0.901590	0.092471	12.35113
4.200	37.1429	0.781183	0.084127	15.62674
4.400	35.4545	0.526970	0.059453	18.30378
4.600	33.9130	0.264836	0.031237	22.35361
4.800	32.5000	0.211254	0.026001	29.51511
5.000	31.2000	0.372163	0.047713	1.84649
5.200	30.0000	0.392677	0.052357	3.86171
5.400	28.8889	0.506036	0.070067	6.09211
5.600	27.8571	0.523273	0.075137	7.61032
5.800	26.8966	0.486643	0.070885	8.87061
6.000	26.0000	0.402591	0.061937	9.46571
6.200	25.1613	0.217194	0.034528	10.99761
6.400	24.3750	0.049608	0.008141	9.76554
6.600	23.6364	0.149667	0.025328	3.59580
6.800	22.9412	0.291971	0.050908	4.91841
7.000	22.2857	0.362801	0.065118	6.38099
7.200	21.6667	0.343136	0.063348	8.41003
7.400	21.0811	0.245565	0.046594	10.91784
7.600	20.5263	0.172301	0.033577	15.25535
7.800	20.0000	0.214571	0.042914	17.71962
8.000	19.5000	0.398322	0.081707	1.69732
8.200	19.0244	0.444642	0.093489	3.67329
8.400	18.5714	0.405345	0.087305	5.36069
8.600	18.1395	0.282534	0.062302	6.85102
8.800	17.7273	0.098724	0.022276	8.55201
9.000	17.3333	0.101148	0.023342	17.20612
9.200	16.9565	0.261108	0.061595	1.58755
9.400	16.5957	0.355557	0.085698	2.87625
9.600	16.2500	0.386592	0.095161	3.85766
9.800	15.9184	0.345281	0.086763	4.57044
10.000	15.6000	0.302202	0.077488	4.87563
10.200	15.2941	0.271894	0.071111	5.29242
10.400	15.0000	0.275514	0.073470	5.20643
10.600	14.7170	0.197818	0.053766	6.46978
10.800	14.4444	0.102928	0.028503	7.622675
11.000	14.1818	0.040821	0.011514	12.27448

(continued)

Appendix 5-1 *(continued)*

Harmonic	Period	Amplitude	Slope	Phase
11.200	13.9286	0.150148	0.043119	0.97766
11.400	13.6842	0.246415	0.072029	2.05885
11.600	13.4483	0.303638	0.090313	2.97983
11.800	13.2203	0.314258	0.095083	3.71743
12.000	13.0000	0.307009	0.094464	3.72802
12.200	12.7869	0.271921	0.085063	4.71618
12.400	12.5806	0.229474	0.072961	5.19330
12.600	12.3810	0.183216	0.059193	5.80374
12.800	12.1875	0.100201	0.032887	6.42139
13.000	12.0000	0.069971	0.023324	6.05076
13.200	11.8182	0.088308	0.029889	2.21892
13.400	11.6418	0.155213	0.053330	3.19439
13.600	11.4706	0.177089	0.061754	4.04770
13.800	11.3043	0.137063	0.048499	5.03360
14.000	11.1429	0.067046	0.024068	6.25144
14.200	10.9859	0.038276	0.013936	10.92176
14.400	10.8333	0.106233	0.039224	1.72921
14.600	10.6849	0.136698	0.051174	2.70187
14.800	10.5405	0.118072	0.044807	3.46564
15.000	10.4000	0.077484	0.029802	3.98800
15.200	10.2632	0.044613	0.011733	2.75136
15.400	10.1299	0.085689	0.033836	2.39953
15.600	10.0000	0.115461	0.046184	2.98596
15.800	9.8734	0.080353	0.032553	4.05022
16.000	9.7500	0.022687	0.009307	6.04001
16.200	9.6296	0.083403	0.034644	9.40670
16.400	9.5122	0.156598	0.065852	0.84682
16.600	9.3976	0.206584	0.087930	1.65986
16.800	9.2857	0.211067	0.090921	2.32905
17.000	9.1765	0.179414	0.078206	2.94670
17.200	9.0698	0.138894	0.061256	3.09504
17.400	8.9655	0.115578	0.051566	2.90155
17.600	8.8636	0.134585	0.060736	2.94347
17.800	8.7640	0.138693	0.063301	3.42547
18.000	8.6667	0.112129	0.051752	4.14364
18.200	8.5714	0.057151	0.026671	5.08608
18.400	8.4783	0.040621	0.019165	7.45822
18.600	8.3871	0.077329	0.036880	0.49249
18.800	8.2979	0.095108	0.045847	1.13020
19.000	8.2105	0.102706	0.050034	1.21087
19.200	8.1250	0.121048	0.059593	1.20302
19.400	8.0412	0.166762	0.082954	1.28786
19.600	7.9592	0.220598	0.110865	1.62165
19.800	7.8788	0.260398	0.132202	2.03452
20.000	7.8000	0.271224	0.139089	2.44912
20.200	7.7228	0.252202	0.130628	2.90097
20.400	7.6471	0.215923	0.112944	3.27006
20.600	7.5728	0.180188	0.195176	3.67840
20.800	7.5000	0.133044	0.070957	4.06926
21.000	7.4286	0.072533	0.039056	4.55331
21.200	7.3858	0.031897	0.017339	5.01577

(continued)

Appendix 5-1 *(continued)*

Harmonic	Period	Amplitude	Slope	Phase
21.400	7.2897	0.010264	0.005632	6.46510
21.600	7.2222	0.010633	0.005889	6.71176
21.800	7.1560	0.035628	0.019915	6.89887
22.000	7.0909	0.090906	0.051280	0.12703
22.200	7.0270	0.163996	0.093352	0.82052
22.400	6.9643	0.213027	0.122354	1.43242
22.600	6.9027	0.237862	0.137838	2.10587
22.800	6.8421	0.200619	0.117285	2.79402
23.000	6.7826	0.132903	0.078379	3.72216
23.200	6.7241	0.094201	0.056037	5.32469
23.400	6.6667	0.149054	0.089432	0.09032
23.600	6.6102	0.225118	0.136225	0.96465
23.800	6.5546	0.256739	0.156677	1.60996
24.000	6.5000	0.240757	0.148158	2.19106
24.200	6.4463	0.176255	0.109368	2.73084
24.400	6.3934	0.103066	0.064483	3.06977
24.600	6.3415	0.043617	0.027512	2.59168
24.800	6.2903	0.056090	0.035668	1.90623
25.000	6.2400	0.076643	0.049130	2.06342
25.200	6.1905	0.057343	0.037052	2.33497
25.400	6.1417	0.039803	0.025923	2.14980
25.600	6.0938	0.053198	0.034920	1.49175
25.800	6.0465	0.074798	0.049482	1.42980
26.000	6.0000	0.046904	0.031270	1.23590
26.200	5.9542	0.102657	0.068964	1.56900
26.400	5.9091	0.125727	0.085107	1.70161
26.600	5.8647	0.131027	0.089367	1.94882
26.800	5.8209	0.122409	0.084117	2.16513
27.000	5.7778	0.096416	0.066750	2.48657
27.200	5.7353	0.060510	0.042202	2.26035
27.400	5.6934	0.072473	0.050917	1.75275
27.600	5.6522	0.117103	0.082873	1.89818
27.800	5.6115	0.147126	0.104875	2.25565
28.000	5.5714	0.146466	0.105155	2.81090
28.200	5.5319	0.114711	0.082945	3.44257
28.400	5.4930	0.083944	0.061129	4.37276
28.600	5.4545	0.093050	0.068237	5.40169
28.800	5.4167	0.124964	0.092281	0.74746
29.000	5.3793	0.145593	0.108262	1.30213
29.200	5.3425	0.132792	0.099424	1.76210
29.400	5.3061	0.108276	0.081623	2.06359
29.600	5.2703	0.077505	0.058824	2.23429
29.800	5.2349	0.051345	0.039233	2.01887
30.000	5.2000	0.049464	0.038049	1.82468
30.200	5.1656	0.055271	0.042799	1.66774
30.400	5.1316	0.066224	0.051621	1.67158
30.600	5.0980	0.078216	0.061370	1.77638
30.800	5.0649	0.078257	0.061803	1.86798
31.000	5.0323	0.078971	0.062772	1.99708
31.200	5.0000	0.078310	0.062648	1.88962
31.400	4.9682	0.048717	0.039223	2.11115

(continued)

Appendix 5-1 *(continued)*

Harmonic	Period	Amplitude	Slope	Phase
31.600	4.9367	0.031767	0.025740	1.86566
31.800	4.9057	0.048204	0.039305	1.26172
32.000	4.8750	0.068465	0.056177	1.43491
32.200	4.8447	0.084487	0.069756	1.51567
32.400	4.8148	0.092703	0.077015	1.60402
32.600	4.7853	0.092358	0.077202	1.81407
32.800	4.7561	0.077346	0.065050	1.98505
33.000	4.7273	0.069622	0.058911	1.82511
33.200	4.6988	0.060444	0.051455	1.73844
33.400	4.6707	0.087286	0.074753	1.79416
33.600	4.6429	0.093482	0.080539	2.10778
33.800	4.6154	0.084339	0.073094	2.53031
34.000	4.5882	0.044163	0.038501	3.00779
34.200	4.5614	0.035956	0.031531	0.08698
34.400	4.5349	0.083156	0.073348	0.86910
34.600	4.5087	0.116430	0.103295	1.38352
34.800	4.4828	0.129775	0.115799	1.79062
35.000	4.4571	0.105856	0.094999	2.15034
35.200	4.4318	0.062005	0.055964	2.54896
35.400	4.4068	0.017377	0.015773	2.55191
35.600	4.3820	0.034440	0.031437	1.47844
35.800	4.3575	0.057160	0.052470	1.80270
36.000	4.3333	0.059897	0.055289	2.12012
36.200	4.3094	0.046734	0.043378	2.39293
36.400	4.2857	0.017760	0.016576	3.08122
36.600	4.2623	0.012578	0.011804	0.74831
36.800	4.2391	0.022098	0.020851	0.96674
37.000	4.2162	0.027350	0.025948	1.03741
37.200	4.1935	0.038723	0.036935	0.96008
37.400	4.1711	0.052865	0.050696	1.15684
37.600	4.1489	0.074192	0.071529	1.31711
37.800	4.1270	0.064315	0.062336	1.56175
38.000	4.1052	0.050930	0.049624	1.59832
38.200	4.0838	0.020565	0.020144	1.29766
38.400	4.0625	0.049615	0.048852	0.99518
38.600	4.0415	0.086376	0.085490	1.15655
38.800	4.0206	0.100292	0.099778	1.45006
39.000	4.0000	0.084890	0.084890	1.06010
39.200	3.9796	0.075041	0.075426	1.74630
39.400	3.9594	0.042452	0.042887	1.76860
39.600	3.9394	0.040153	0.040770	1.38215
39.800	3.9196	0.059700	0.060924	1.38655
40.000	3.9000	0.076549	0.078511	1.47047
40.200	3.8806	0.075427	0.077748	1.64254
40.400	3.8614	0.074017	0.076675	1.75822
40.600	3.8424	0.053049	0.055225	1.90337
40.800	3.8235	0.048251	0.050478	2.04018
41.000	3.8049	0.014839	0.015600	2.15454
41.200	3.7864	0.030237	0.031943	1.16993
41.400	3.7681	0.051436	0.054602	1.22723
41.600	3.7500	0.066615	0.071056	1.49610

(continued)

Appendix 5-1 *(continued)*

Harmonic	Period	Amplitude	Slope	Phase
41.800	3.7321	0.071545	0.076681	1.80991
42.000	3.7143	0.039836	0.042901	2.24361
42.200	3.6967	0.013247	0.014334	3.02540
42.400	3.6792	0.050318	0.054704	0.51334
42.600	3.6620	0.074049	0.080885	0.87592
42.800	3.6449	0.092676	0.101706	1.25637
43.000	3.6279	0.071602	0.078946	1.53066
43.200	3.6111	0.059404	0.065801	1.58099
43.400	3.5945	0.041770	0.046483	1.37224
43.600	3.5780	0.066637	0.074494	1.30874
43.800	3.5616	0.083634	0.093927	1.51204
44.000	3.5455	0.081283	0.091704	1.79281
44.200	3.5294	0.048931	0.055455	2.06324
44.400	3.5135	0.021442	0.024410	2.47058
44.600	3.4978	0.032148	0.036765	0.74540
44.800	3.4821	0.051557	0.059224	1.07137
45.000	3.4667	0.064812	0.074784	1.30266
45.200	3.4513	0.059834	0.069346	1.62980
45.400	3.4361	0.030395	0.035383	1.63277
45.600	3.4211	0.028140	0.032903	1.11448
45.800	3.4061	0.046339	0.054419	1.08897
46.000	3.3913	0.060411	0.071254	1.20887
46.200	3.3766	0.079234	0.093861	1.35550
46.400	3.3621	0.083778	0.099675	1.49737
46.600	3.3476	0.075759	0.090522	1.64973
46.800	3.3333	0.066914	0.080297	1.81033
47.000	3.3191	0.044149	0.053205	2.05674
47.200	3.3051	0.019623	0.023749	1.89061
47.400	3.2911	0.013737	0.016696	1.26159
47.600	3.2773	0.043147	0.052661	1.16142
47.800	3.2636	0.053923	0.066090	1.42048
48.000	3.2500	0.052295	0.064364	1.62645
48.200	3.2365	0.047566	0.058787	1.76560
48.400	3.2231	0.018638	0.023130	1.88289
48.600	3.2099	0.020151	0.025112	1.37149
48.800	3.1967	0.034916	0.043689	1.39665
49.000	3.1837	0.032623	0.040988	1.50806
49.200	3.1707	0.037196	0.046924	1.65038
49.400	3.1579	0.023942	0.030326	1.78248
49.600	3.1452	0.010843	0.013790	1.62922
49.800	3.1325	0.011871	0.015159	1.18537
50.000	3.1200	0.026579	0.034076	0.86978
50.200	3.1076	0.036861	0.047446	0.97207
50.400	3.0952	0.049736	0.064274	1.06394
50.600	3.0830	0.059630	0.077367	1.23429
50.800	3.0709	0.062950	0.081996	1.41530
51.000	3.0588	0.048150	0.062966	1.62935
51.200	3.0469	0.033872	0.044467	1.71707
51.400	3.0350	0.014150	0.018649	0.80174
51.600	3.0233	0.005590	0.007396	1.22910
51.800	3.0116	0.015532	0.020630	0.89180

(continued)

Appendix 5-1 *(continued)*

Harmonic	Period	Amplitude	Slope	Phase
52.000	3.0000	0.055340	0.073787	1.88781
52.200	2.9885	0.051834	0.069378	0.78278
52.400	2.9771	0.072705	0.097686	0.92487
52.600	2.9658	0.083157	0.112155	1.05948
52.800	2.9545	0.091151	0.123404	1.18584
53.000	2.9434	0.065150	0.088537	1.32628
53.200	2.9323	0.059935	0.081758	1.39283
53.400	2.9213	0.061890	0.084741	1.39256
53.600	2.9104	0.060155	0.082675	1.53315
53.800	2.8996	0.055894	0.077105	1.73958
54.000	2.8889	0.037132	0.051414	2.08210
54.200	2.8782	0.019010	0.026419	2.86490
54.400	2.8676	0.049406	0.068915	0.54608
54.600	2.8571	0.057861	0.081005	0.88359
54.800	2.8467	0.084854	0.119230	1.14652
55.000	2.8364	0.058308	0.082229	1.26258
55.200	2.8261	0.033681	0.047671	1.32119
55.400	2.8159	0.048557	0.068976	1.05317
55.600	2.8058	0.068005	0.096951	1.03985
55.800	2.7957	0.084563	0.120990	1.29541
56.000	2.7857	0.086547	0.124273	1.52560
56.200	2.7758	0.068907	0.099297	1.70877
56.400	2.7660	0.029350	0.042444	1.89938
56.600	2.7562	0.007474	0.010847	0.63892
56.800	2.7465	0.030715	0.044734	0.85399
57.000	2.7368	0.036251	0.052982	1.18109
57.200	2.7273	0.034287	0.050288	1.41808
57.400	2.7178	0.018116	0.026663	0.95393
57.600	2.7083	0.019259	0.028445	0.84219
57.800	2.6990	0.049191	0.072904	1.00315
58.000	2.6897	0.068940	0.102526	1.10168
58.200	2.6804	0.055722	0.083154	1.29259
58.400	2.6712	0.050474	0.075582	1.32391
58.600	2.6621	0.042862	0.064402	1.34566
58.800	2.6531	0.033968	0.051213	1.32616
59.000	2.6441	0.025490	0.038562	1.42262
59.200	2.6351	0.022808	0.034621	1.38924
59.400	2.6263	0.021272	0.032399	0.85589
59.600	2.6174	0.030990	0.047359	0.83994
59.800	2.6087	0.043450	0.066623	0.99119
60.000	2.6000	0.057834	0.088975	1.11945
60.200	2.5914	0.050449	0.077873	1.25135
60.400	2.5828	0.040568	0.062828	1.27170
60.600	2.5743	0.043454	0.067521	1.26477
60.800	2.5658	0.047257	0.073673	1.23350
61.000	2.5574	0.039296	0.061463	1.28299
61.200	2.5490	0.036249	0.056883	1.38642
61.400	2.5407	0.036851	0.058016	1.22827
61.600	2.5325	0.036961	0.058380	1.22631
61.800	2.5243	0.051172	0.081087	1.30607
62.000	2.5161	0.047531	0.075563	1.35193

(continued)

Appendix 5-1 *(continued)*

Harmonic	Period	Amplitude	Slope	Phase
62.200	2.5080	0.034037	0.054285	1.55822
62.400	2.5000	0.012209	0.019534	1.60376
62.600	2.4920	0.010704	0.017181	0.83764
62.800	2.4841	0.034439	0.055456	0.98942
63.000	2.4762	0.049199	0.079475	1.06078
63.200	2.4684	0.045206	0.073256	1.25439
63.400	2.4606	0.044478	0.072305	1.23837
63.600	2.4528	0.031131	0.050767	1.21450
63.800	2.4451	0.030559	0.049991	1.25729
64.000	2.4375	0.030945	0.050781	1.32033
64.200	2.4299	0.042607	0.070138	1.35494
64.400	2.4224	0.034324	0.056678	1.39238
64.600	2.4149	0.020410	0.033807	1.51435
64.800	2.4074	0.017280	0.028712	1.26827
65.000	2.4000	0.013527	0.022544	0.94468
65.200	2.3926	0.029870	0.049937	0.95982
65.400	2.3853	0.046322	0.077679	1.04388
65.600	2.3780	0.043936	0.073902	1.18690
65.800	2.3708	0.044678	0.075380	1.32331
66.000	2.3636	0.037748	0.063882	1.33158
66.200	2.3565	0.022977	0.039003	1.21342
66.400	2.3494	0.028078	0.047805	0.92547
66.600	2.3423	0.036892	0.063001	1.11430
66.800	2.3353	0.059206	0.101409	1.19306
67.000	2.3284	0.050766	0.087214	1.25999
67.200	2.3214	0.040117	0.069125	1.44260
67.400	2.3145	0.025133	0.043435	1.46962
67.600	2.3077	0.009171	0.015896	1.53884
67.800	2.3009	0.015682	0.027263	1.24613
68.000	2.2941	0.021328	0.037188	1.11610
68.200	2.2874	0.034181	0.059773	1.11362
68.400	2.2807	0.038931	0.068279	1.10997
68.600	2.2741	0.034468	0.060629	1.17306
68.800	2.2674	0.036338	0.064103	1.25372
69.000	2.2609	0.024757	0.043802	1.32139
69.200	2.2543	0.028739	0.050994	1.27245
69.400	2.2478	0.036824	0.065528	1.17644
69.600	2.2414	0.040731	0.072690	1.25589
69.800	2.2350	0.048454	0.086721	1.35210
70.000	2.2286	0.039807	0.071448	1.45484
70.200	2.2222	0.031098	0.055976	1.65535
70.400	2.2159	0.010553	0.019050	1.80123
70.600	2.2096	0.006859	0.012417	0.10508
70.800	2.2034	0.010264	0.018633	0.81671
71.000	2.1972	0.022117	0.040264	0.79194
71.200	2.1910	0.023324	0.042582	0.84447
71.400	2.1849	0.039698	0.072677	0.88794
71.600	2.1788	0.039812	0.073090	0.97245
71.800	2.1727	0.045304	0.083406	1.09789
72.000	2.1667	0.038786	0.071604	1.15896
72.200	2.1607	0.041857	0.077488	1.21017

(continued)

Appendix 5-1 *(continued)*

Harmonic	Period	Amplitude	Slope	Phase
72.400	2.1547	0.043118	0.080045	1.15889
72.600	2.1488	0.038660	0.071967	1.24740
72.800	2.1429	0.044076	0.082275	1.35138
73.000	2.1370	0.032060	0.060009	1.36877
73.200	2.1311	0.016967	0.031845	1.49257
73.400	2.1253	0.017084	0.032153	0.93504
73.600	2.1196	0.028831	0.054410	0.93501
73.800	2.1138	0.047193	0.089304	1.12133
74.000	2.1081	0.047018	0.089213	1.25340
74.200	2.1024	0.045579	0.086717	1.39353
74.400	2.0968	0.032542	0.062080	1.47121
74.600	2.0912	0.017657	0.033774	1.69057
74.800	2.0856	0.003913	0.007505	1.69033
75.000	2.0800	0.014881	0.028617	0.77135
75.200	2.0745	0.023618	0.045541	0.83551
75.400	2.0690	0.040873	0.079022	0.90311
75.600	2.0635	0.046504	0.090147	1.00357
75.800	2.0580	0.053897	0.104753	1.13006
76.000	2.0526	0.055666	0.108478	1.20058
76.200	2.0472	0.048228	0.094231	1.30083
76.400	2.0419	0.041078	0.080472	1.31327
76.600	2.0366	0.037729	0.074104	1.39544
76.800	2.0312	0.038926	0.076654	1.43764
77.000	2.0260	0.027858	0.055002	1.60152
77.200	2.0207	0.017538	0.034716	1.65053
77.400	2.0155	0.001629	0.003233	1.01023
77.600	2.0103	0.013723	0.027305	0.86710
77.800	2.0051	0.025028	0.049927	1.08199
78.000	2.0000	0.031601	0.063202	0.99997

Appendix 5-2   Illustration of Test of Significance for T-Bond Cycle of 37.14
                   Days.

* *
"Array" analysis program.—Series IV—Encoded Serial No.
©Copyright 1985–1991 by Anthony F. Herbst.
All rights reserved.
* *

Input file header lines are:
   "CT DEC 90—December CBOT T-Bond futures"
   "Data from 880623 thru 900713"
   521, 880623, −54

Enter number of data points to skip at beginning of file: 365
Enter period to examine, with decimal point: 37.14

37.140000 Item array

Number of points from input file = 156, base = 880623
Number of lines 4, points in array 152

Thirds

Section	Con A	Con B	Amplitude	Phase
1	−0.45994	1.14784	1.23656	12.04906
2	0.34667	2.27618	2.30243	8.90291
3.	−0.49305	−0.70914	0.86370	24.77507

Improved period 38.577653
Prediction for middle third 19.684665

Halves

Section	Con A	Con B	Amplitude	Phase
1	−0.45994	1.14784	1.123656	12.04906
2	−0.07319	0.78352	0.78693	10.34687

Probable period 36.288905

All lines

Section	Con A	Con B	Amplitude	Phase
1	−0.26656	0.96568	1.00180	11.38833

Individual Lines

Chi-square test on distribution of phases around their mean:
   0 0 0 3 0 0 1   Chi square = 13.500000, with 6 d.f.

Bartels' test = 0.192292
* *
Average amplitude   =   1.413231 (+ or −) 0.763840
Least squares period =   35.368709 (+ or −) 5.375950
Least squares phase   =   12.461993 (+ or −) 5.276788
Using 3 points
* *
Chi-square test on distribution of amplitudes around their mean:
   0 0 0 3 0 0 1   Chi square = 13.500000, with 6 d.f.

6

Visual and Manual Methods for Finding Cycles

This chapter is shorter than others in this book for several reasons. First, the general availability of powerful, low-cost, desktop computers renders the visual and manual methods for cycle study that once prevailed unnecessary for most purposes. Second, visual identification is suggestive, not definitive. What looks to be a cycle in plotted data may indeed reveal the presence of a cycle, but visual clues alone do not prove the existence of the cycle. Third, the presence of multiple cycles in data tends to distort the visual clues associated with any one cycle. Fourth, accurate visual identification even under ideal conditions requires a greater level of skill and experience than most persons have or can take the time to develop. And fifth, accurate manual identification of cycles requires more time and patience than most persons either can afford to devote to it or care to spend on such activity.

Why should we bother with visual or manual identification of cycles at all? One reason is that visual identification, however tentative it might be, provides us with a sense of what we might expect to find from computer analysis of the same data. Another is that with some data sets there may be one or two dominant cycles that manifest their presence strongly enough for visual identification to be useful. And once a cycle has been identified we may mark its expected highs and lows on a ruler and project on a price chart when we might expect it to reach its next peak or trough.

A definitive 1970s work on the subject of cycle analysis puts visual/manual methods for finding cycles into three activity classifications: (1) counting intervals between beats (high to high, low to low); (2) using rulers such as marked strips of paper to measure high to high and low to low; (3) using time charts, like those developed by Chapin Hoskins for instance, to measure "clearspan" and thus identify cycles.[1] We shall not get into the formalities of these methods since the work cited in footnote 1 covers them in great detail. Instead, we shall examine some futures price charts for cycles and then fit cycles of the suspected length to the data and see what we have.

Consider Figure 6-1, which depicts 90-day perpetual[2] futures contract settlement prices for U.S. T-bond futures. Careful measurement suggests possible cycles of about 62 days and 75 days, which are indicated by arrowheads in Figure 6-2. This is a rather "busy" time series, and a smoothing might offer some advantage in identifying possible cycles. However, smoothing can also introduce distortions even when performed by experts, and we shall not perform any such operations here.

A 62-day cycle that we have postulated has an average amplitude (that is, strength) like the pure 62-day synthetic cycle overlaid on the data in Figure

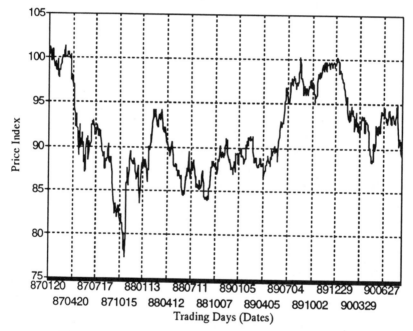

Figure 6-1   T-bond, 90-day perpetual contract.

[1]*Cycle Analysis: A Case Study* (Pittsburgh, PA: Foundation for the Study of Cycles, 1971–75). This is an anthology of articles that appeared in the Foundation's monthly publication, *Cycles*. It is available from the Foundation for the Study of Cycles, 2600 Michelson Drive, Suite 1570, Irvine, CA 92715.

[2]The concept of perpetual futures contracts appears to have been originated, or at least popularized, by Robert Pelletier of Commodity Systems, Inc., Boca Raton, FL. The concept is straightforward. For a 90-day perpetual contract price we take the prices of the two contracts that expire at dates bracketing a date 90 days from the present. Then we interpolate the price each day, centered at 90 days from the current day each time. These contracts have the advantage that the basis change tends to be minimized in contrast to what it would be for an actual, traded contract.

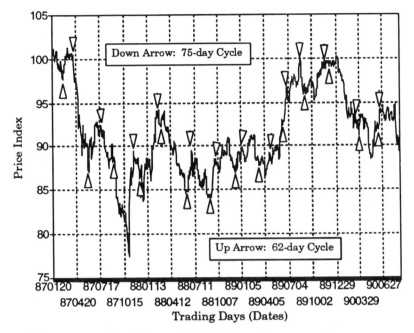

Figure 6-2 Possible cycles in T-bond perpetual contract.

6-3. It can account for about 2.4 points, or \$2,400 on a nominal \$100,000 T-bond contract. But before you mortgage the house, and so on, stop and look at the price graph and cycle plot in Figure 6-3 again. The optimal fit of a 62-day cycle is based on the entire span of data analyzed, and matches the peaks at the far left very well. But over to the center and right of the graph we should not be very confident in making money using only our knowledge of a possible 62-day cycle.[3] Other factors are at work that distort or offset this one possible cycle.

All right, so the 62-day cycle is no panacea for tracking the market. But what about a 75-day cycle? The news is not much better on it.[4] It is much stronger (4.5 amplitude) than the 62-day, and somewhat more statistically significant (a greater chance it is genuine).[5] A 75-day cycle is graphed as an overlay on the data in Figure 6-4.

---

[3]Independent analysis by computer suggests that we have a likely cycle of 60.7 days, rather than the 62 indicated by visual analysis. Not bad, you say, we missed by only 1.3 days. That is true, but the 60.7 day cycle turns out to be neither the strongest nor the most statistically significant cycle present in the data.

[4]Independent computer analysis suggests that a cycle of approximately 78.4 days may be present.

[5]Statistically, the Bartels test indicates a probability of 7 chances in 10 that the apparent presence of a 62-day cycle is due to chance influences in the data. The probability is 4 chances in 10 for the 75-day cycle.

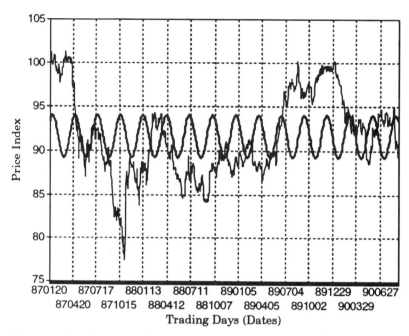

Figure 6-3 Overlaid 62-day cycle on perpetual T-bond prices.

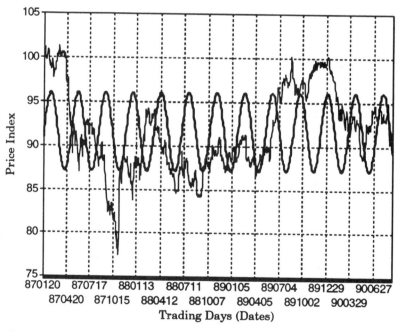

Figure 6-4 Overlaid 75-day cycle on perpetual T-bond prices.

Perhaps a person who is fortunate enough to have the 20/20 vision of youth, but mature enough to have the patience and experience to do so, can find signs of other cycles visually. Perhaps he or she might look for them after I mention those the computer says are present, and significant by the Bartels test at less than 1 chance in 7 of being due to random factors. Here are two for the settlement data shown in Figure 6-1: 56.0 (1 chance in 8 it is false) and 86.4 days (8 chances in 100 it is false). It should be noted that these cycle periods are based on analysis of a particular data set, containing close to a thousand 90-day perpetual contract values. Analysis of an actual futures contract or a shorter or longer data series may provide periodicities that vary somewhat.

TREND REMOVAL

There is one application for which visual estimation of a cycle can be most valuable. That is in trend removal prior to further analysis.[6] Figure 6-5 contains a pure sinusoidal cycle of 950 days overlaid on the settlement prices of the 90 day perpetual T-bond contract of Figure 6-1. It approximates the data rather well. In fact, it accounts for a large amount of the variability in the

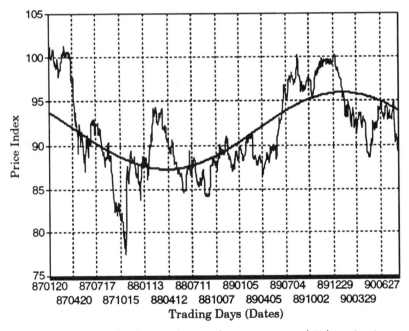

Figure 6-5 Overlaid 950-day cycle on perpetual T-bond prices.

[6]A *linear* (that is, straight line) trend is commonly removed from data to detrend it. Unfortunately, data seldom contain linear trends, although one may often approximate a segment of a very long trend *cycle* with a straight line.

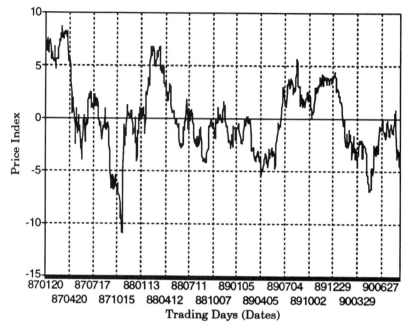

Figure 6-6   Residuals after fitting 950-day cycle on perpetual T-bonds prices.

data, and the standard deviation of the residuals (that is, differences between data and sine wave) is small.

Figure 6-6 contains the residuals after fitting a 950-day cycle to the data. The sine wave was fitted with a procedure that assures it is the best-fitting 950-day cycle for this data set.[7] The maximum deviation of the data from the 950-day sine wave is less than 12 index points. That is still a large amount, but now we have a series that lends itself better to analysis aimed at finding important cycles.

In general, how can we visually gauge, and then measure an appropriate long cycle that might represent the trend? First, we need to decide which data point is on the low of the cycle in question. Then we need to decide where the cycle peaks. The number of trading days between low and high (or high and low) is half the period of the cycle.

CONCLUSION

Visual fitting of cycles can assist in determining which approximate cycle lengths may warrant further investigation. However, in the case of "busy"

---

[7]Borland's Quattro Pro spreadsheet program was used to fit the cycle and also to produce all the graphs for this chapter. The template for performing this analysis is listed in Appendix A of this text.

data, such as that for U.S. Treasury Bonds used in this chapter, visual identification may be a frustrating exercise.

Perhaps the most useful application today of visual cycle identification and manual fitting (albeit computer assisted) is for removal of trend in a data set. There is some subjectivity in the process as described in this chapter. However, even an approximately correct identification of the trend can assist in better identification of cycles present in the data. Thus, one should not worry unduly whether the true long term or trend cycle is 933 days or 950 days or 961 days. With a sinusoidal wave it will not make an important difference in the residual series obtained by removing the trend cycle.

7

Finding Cycles in Data with a Computer: Spectral Analysis

This chapter covers the use of Fourier transform-based spectral analysis for detecting cycles in data. And, because of its widespread use for engineering and communications applications the strengths and weaknesses of the fast Fourier transform (FFT) are also discussed as they pertain to economic time series.[1] The emphasis is on computer determination of spectral analysis. The amount of calculation required to perform spectral analysis rules out practical application to manual methods. But today the low cost of powerful personal computers and software written for them puts spectral analysis and other powerful techniques within reach of almost everyone.

What is spectral analysis? Do you remember looking at the pattern of colors produced when a sunbeam passes through a prism? Or a rainbow? Or magazine photos that show the breakdown of light from a distant star? All of those show the spectrum, or array, of component wavelengths of light. Sunlight appears white to the human eye. But in reality it is made up of various colors of light mixed together. The different colors correspond to light of different *frequencies*. Red light, for example, has a lower frequency than blue light. Equivalently, red light may be said to have a longer wavelength, or wave period, than blue light. Period is the reciprocal of frequency.

Spectral analysis considers time series data, that is, historical data for which each successive value is associated with a later, and usually consecutive, pe-

---

[1]Treatment of maximum entropy spectral analysis (MESA) is deferred to a later chapter where it is covered with linear prediction.

riod of time. The technique breaks down the time series data into a spectrum of various frequencies. If the original data contain cycles that are genuine, then if we combine the pure cycles we should obtain a near approximation to the time series itself. It would be rare to obtain a perfect fit to the original time series because of noise (random influences) present in the data. Only if there were no random influences, if the data were deterministic rather than probabilistic could we obtain a perfect fit. What is in question is not whether spectral analysis can help us find a key to replicating a data series perfectly. It cannot. The truth is, no forecasting method can provide a perfect forecast of data containing random influences; randomness guarantees that the forecast will almost always be different from the data series. The relevant question is how well can spectral analysis help us to approximate the data and thus provide reasonably accurate forecasts. And how well does spectral analysis perform in comparison with other forecasting methods? The answer is, very well indeed for those time series containing cycles that are reasonably consistent and persistent.

The search for cycles in data can be enhanced substantially with a computer and appropriate software. In order to use those computer programs one does *not* have to be a mathematician. However, one should have a basic, intuitive understanding of what the programs do and, more importantly, what they cannot do as well as the problems that arise in using them and in interpreting their results.

Spectral analysis can often identify cycles present in data. The cycles can then be combined into a synthetic time series and used for forecasting. Identification of cycles may also offer clues to those who are interested in economic causality, and not solely in forecasting.[2] For example, a cycle of about 21 days would correspond to one month of market, or trading days. Such a cycle might then be linked to actions in the market by one or more participants.

Spectral analysis is a probabilistic Fourier analysis. It takes a time series (that is, a signal) that is assumed to be generated by a stochastic process and decomposes it into its "natural" frequency components. Because frequency is the independent variable, the impact of each cycle can be determined at any frequency component within the time series. Since period, or cycle length, equals the reciprocal of frequency, the results of spectral analysis can be related to cycles in the time domain, with measures in hours, days, or other units of time.

---

[2]In recent years spectral analysis has tended to become lost in the shadow of Box-Jenkins ARIMA (Autoregressive Integrated Moving Average) methodology for business and economic time series modeling and forecasting. However, Box-Jenkins methodology will not be covered in detail in this book. In the author's experience it is difficult to apply intelligently without a great deal of training and hands-on experience. Perhaps more important, the method can be very sensitive to what may seem to be relatively minor errors in the data. Spectral analysis, in contrast, is robust with respect to even strong discontinuities in the imput data.

To measure how important a cycle is in determining the overall time series, one examines the *power spectrum* produced by the spectral analysis. High power at a frequency indicates the presence of a cycle at that frequency. This is understandable by analogy with a radio tuning dial; one turns the dial until the desired station comes in, passing through other station broadcasts (strong power) with static ("noise") between. It is useful to consider spectral analysis as a procedure that provides a map of the stations found at various frequencies from a set of time series data.

THE MATH BEHIND SPECTRAL ANALYSIS[3]

A stationary[4] time series may be considered to be composed of the sum of periodic (that is, cyclical) series plus its mean in the finite Fourier transform

$$y_t = \bar{y} + \sum_{j=1}^{M} \alpha_j \cos(\omega_j t - \theta_j) \tag{7-1}$$

where $0 \le \omega_j \le 2\pi$, $\omega_j = 2\pi j/M$ the *angular frequency*, θ is the phase angle, and $M = 1 + N/2$ if N is even, otherwise $M = 1 + (N+1)/2$, with N here denoting the number of observations in the time series. This equation is equivalent to an alternate form in which the phase angle, a shift parameter determining when the cycle first reaches maximum amplitude after $t=0$, is not explicitly stated, as in

$$y_t = \bar{y} + \sum_{j=1}^{M} A_j \cos(\omega_j t) + \sum_{j=1}^{M} B_j \sin(\omega_j t) \tag{7-2}$$

The A and B coefficients in Equation (7-2) are found from the relationship

$$A = \frac{2}{M} \sum_{t=1}^{M} y_t \sin(\omega_j t) \tag{7-3}$$

and

$$B = \frac{2}{M} \sum_{t=1}^{M} y_t \cos(\omega_j t) \tag{7-4}$$

---

[3]This section may be skimmed or skipped by those not interested in the mathematics of spectral analysis, without seriously detracting from the balance of the chapter.

[4]A time series without a trend in the mean or variance is said to be stationary.

The *intensity* at a particular frequency is given by

$$I_j = \frac{M}{2}(A_j^2 + B_j^2) \tag{7-5}$$

and may be viewed as the squared *amplitude* associated with that frequency, weighted by $M/2$. Plotted as a group, the intensities yield the *periodogram*. The *power spectrum* at a given frequency is given by

$$p(\omega_j) = \lim_{N \to \infty} E[I_j], \qquad 0 \le \omega_j \le 2\pi \tag{7-6}$$

where E is the expected value operator and N is the number of observations.

An important fact is that the autocorrelation function is directly related to the Fourier transform. Because of this, the Fourier transformation of the sample autocorrelation function yields the estimated relative average power at any frequency. Also, the spectral density can be expressed as a function of the angular frequency

$$p(\omega_j) = \frac{1}{\pi}[1 + 2 \sum_{K=1}^{M-1} r(K) \cos(\omega_j K)], \qquad j = 1, 2, \dots, M \tag{7-7}$$

where $r(K)$ denotes the sample autocorrelation function, K the index for the number of lags over which the autocorrelation is calculated, and M the maximum lag in time periods.

Equation (7-7) can also be written in terms of *frequency* by substituting $2\pi f_j$ for ω_j and dividing the power at each frequency f by $1/M$ to obtain

$$p(f_j) = 2[1 + 2 \sum_{K=1}^{M-1} r(K) \cos(2\pi f_j K)], \qquad j = 1, 2, \dots, M \tag{7-8}$$

and $0 \le f_j \le \frac{1}{2}$. Unfortunately, Equations (7-7) and (7-8) do not provide a consistent estimator of the population[5] spectral density and must be modified to obtain improved estimation. A trade-off is involved.

Less bias may only be achieved at the expense of greater variance in spectral analysis. In practice one can choose several different values for the truncation point, $L(L \le M - 1)$, in Equations 7-9 and 7-10, and compute the spectral estimates for each of those values. Initially one uses a small value of L (on the order of a few percent of M) and then gradually increases it in what

---

[5]Remember, for economic data, we almost always must work from a sample. A consistent estimator should provide us with estimates that do not vary much with different amounts of data from the same time series.

is called "window closing." One should note that spectral density obtained with a small L yields estimates with low fidelity and thus a high order of bias.

With this method each $p(\omega_j)$ is estimated as a weighted average of neighboring intensities. The sample spectrum one obtains by substituting the sample autocovariances is a highly unstable estimate of the true power spectrum. The problem is reduced if the sample spectrum is obtained from smoothed spectral estimates through the use of lag windows.

Many lag windows have been proposed, but there has been a discernible tendency toward preference for the one proposed by Parzen. Consequently, it is often by default the window in computer programs.

If we denote the lag window by $\lambda(K)$, then Equation (7-8) becomes

$$p(f_j) = 2[1 + 2 \sum_{K=1}^{L-1} \lambda(K) r(K) \cos(\frac{\pi_j K}{2L})], \qquad j = 1, 2, \ldots, 2L$$

$$(7\text{-}9)$$

with the Parzen window defined in equation (10).

$$\lambda(K) = \begin{pmatrix} 1 - \frac{6K^2}{L^2}(1 - \frac{K}{L}), & 0 \le K \le \frac{L}{2} \\ 2(1 - \frac{K}{L})^3, & \frac{L}{2} \le K \le L \end{pmatrix} \qquad (7\text{-}10)$$

In many computer implementations, Equation (7-9) is not used. The reason is that the computational burden is heavy and increases rapidly with series length and the number of lags used. These make programs using (7-9) relatively costly to run for long time series. To overcome this problem a derivation of an equivalent form in Equation (7-11) is generally used.

$$p(f_j) = 2[1 + 2 \sum_{K=1}^{L-1} r(K) e^{-2\pi i f(K)}] \qquad (7\text{-}11)$$

Equation (7-11) takes advantage of the series expansion relationship between the trigonometric functions and e, the base of natural logarithms. The term i in the exponent is defined as $i^2 = -1$, and thus the equation uses complex numbers. Why bother with this? The reason is that this alternative formulation provides an avenue for greatly reducing the amount of computation when the data have a number of points that are an integral power of two (for example, 64, 128, 256, 512, 1024, and so on.)[6]

---

[6]Variations exist that can be even faster for some data series, such as when the number of data points is an integral power of four. Other variations can handle data series whose length is equal to the product of certain integers.

THE FAST FOURIER TRANSFORM (FFT)

While Equation (7-11) itself does not offer any advantage over (7-9), by using an equivalent but much more quickly calculated form called the *fast Fourier transform* (FFT), one saves remarkably on computational time. Newland[7] points out that direct evaluation of Equation (7-11) would require N^2 multiplications, whereas the FFT reduces the number of operations to $N\log_2(N)$. If $N = 2^{10}$, $N^2 = 2^{20}$, but we have $N \log_2(N) = 5 \times 2^{11}$. Thus, for even a moderately long time series the FFT requires less than 1 percent of the number of operations. The longer the series being analyzed, the greater the saving in computation.

The FFT is based on the complex series expansion expressed in Equation (7-11). If we recognize that frequency (omega) is defined by $\omega = \exp(2\pi i/N)$, where N (a positive integer) is the period, and i is defined as in Equation (7-11), and exp denotes raising e to that power within the parentheses, then

$$\omega = e^{2\pi i/N} = \cos(2\pi/N) + i \sin(2\pi/N) \tag{7-12}$$

and the Fourier series expansion of y_t is given by

$$y_t = \sum_{j=-\infty}^{\infty} f_j \omega^{jt} \tag{7-13}$$

where the f_j are the Fourier coefficients of y_t. As is usually the case with market data, we assume that the y series has values corresponding to observations at integer points along the time scale (for example, at intervals of a full day, not at points within a day). When this is the case, the Fourier transform provides a great deal of redundant information; in fact, the only non-redundant information is for values of y_t where $0 \le t \le N - 1$.

Market data normally are already "discretized" at N equidistant points in one period, or wave, of the cycle. Because $\exp[2\pi i(-1) (t/T)] = \exp[2\pi i(N - 1)(t/T)]$, where T/n is the cycle period, and n/T its frequency, for $n = 0, 1, 2, \ldots N - 1$, we may avoid redundant calculation by restricting our attention to terms of the form $\exp[2\pi i(n/T)]$. There are several complications, all of which are covered in great detail in several sources.[8]

---

[7]D. E. Newland. *An Introduction to Random Vibrations and Spectral Analysis* (London: Longman Group Ltd., 1975). Third impression, 1980, p.150

[8]References this author has found particularly useful include *Turbo Pascal Toolbox: Numerical Methods* (Scotts Valley, CA: Borland International, 1987), Ch. 10; W.H. Press, et al., *Numerical Recipes* (Cambridge, England: Cambridge University Press, 1986); and H. Flanders, *Scientific Pascal* (Reston, VA: Reston Publishing Co., Inc., 1984). These all include computer program listings in addition to explanations that run the gamut from summary of the mathematical theory to excruciatingly detailed treatment.

FALLING THROUGH THE GAPS

It is a characteristic of spectral analysis that periods corresponding to higher frequencies are much more closely clustered (that is, have a finer "mesh") than those corresponding to low frequency. For example, if one is analyzing weekly data a frequency of $f = 0.01$ cycles per week corresponds to a cycle of period 100 weeks, and $f = 0.02$ corresponds to a cyclical period of 50 weeks. Likewise, $f = 0.45$ corresponds to 2.22 weeks and $f = 0.46$ corresponds to 2.17 weeks, and the periods are much closer together. What this means is that high frequency, short period cycles are potentially more likely to be precisely identified while long cycles are likely to "fall through" the wider mesh associated with low frequencies.

The most commonly used FFT requires that the data to be analyzed have a number of observations that are equal to an integer power of two (16, 32, 64, 128, 256, 512, 1024, 2048, and so on). This is often not the case in economic data, even though in engineering applications like vibration analysis or communications it can usually be easily fulfilled. Another problem is that the FFT takes discrete steps as it goes through the frequency domain from 0 to 2π (steps of $0/N, 1/N, 2/N, \ldots 2$). For example, with 1024 data values one obtains spectral estimates at frequencies and periods as in Table 7-1.

Suppose, contrary to assumption of the FFT, that there is a cycle of period 183.25, a frequency of 5.588? Where will it be detected? The answer is that it will show up in the spectral power estimate for the frequencies surrounding it, at frequencies of 5 and 6. This is not a happy outcome, because its power will be mixed with power at other periods surrounding it, and thus a precise measure of the 183.25 period cycle will not be obtained. What can be done to avoid this? The first way is to avoid the FFT and programs that are built upon it; leave them to engineers and scientists who have data sets with thousands of data points. Use instead programs that allow non-integer steps through the frequency range of interest.

If you are determined to use FFT-based spectral analysis, a way in which the problem of wide mesh at the low frequency, long periodicity end of the spectrum may be somewhat alleviated (at the expense of introducing other problems) is to "pad" the data by appending a series of zeros to the end. However, when such padding is done, the data at the end of the series should be "tapered" to reduce problems introduced by the padding. Padding and tapering are subjective, somewhat controversial, and require experience in

Table 7-1 Frequency and Period Correspondence: FFT on 1024 Points

Frequency	0	1	2	3	4	5	6	...	511	512
Period	∞	1024	512	341.33	256	204.80	170.67		2.0039	2

their use. Adequate treatment of them would require more space than can be devoted to them here. Many texts devoted to spectral analysis cover them in detail and interested readers who prefer using FFT-based spectral analysis are referred to them.

LIFE WITHOUT FFT

Is there life without the FFT? Indeed, there is! With most economic time series and today's computers, one can perform spectral analysis without using the FFT. Yes, the calculations do take longer. If you have very long time series you want to analyze, you may well wish to use the FFT. But for most market forecasters, data series are typically under 1000 values, and almost always less than 2000 or 3000. Considering that 10 years of daily commodity data is less than 2500 values, few traders will use longer series. Nor is there really a need to.

The strength or amplitude of a cycle is generally proportional to its length. A long cycle is usually very strong, a short cycle comparatively weak. According to E. T. Garrett,[9] an authority on cycle analysis of economic time series,

> All spectra of economic time series show that in a general way large amplitudes go with long periods. Where a spectrum is derived from a time series of a given length no spectral analysis technique can bring out those lines which are long compared to the length of the series. The information content is just not there.
> . . .

But before you despair, consider this: Assume you have a cycle of 1000 days in the price series of a commodity, and that the cycle has an amplitude of $2.00 in a price series that averages $7.00 over the past 10 years. If the cycle follows the typical sinusoidal, or sine, wave, how much effect will it have on price over the next 20 days (almost a month of trading days)? Very little! The average daily price change attributable to the cycle is only $0.002, so over 20 days its effect will amount to 4¢ *on average*. But with a sine wave the amount depends upon where one starts. If the sine wave is at its crest (top) or trough (bottom), in 20 days the amount of change will be only 1.6 cents. So what is the practical impact of this?

Short-periodicity cycles *individually* usually do not have much amplitude. But *collectively* their amplitudes add up to significant price movement, and their combined influence can move the market *quickly* up or down. Consequently, rather than fretting about long-period cycles we would be better off searching for reliable shorter-period cycles that, when combined, can provide

[9]Correspondence of E.T Garrett with the author, May 11, 1990.

us with useful and reasonably accurate forecasts of what the market is likely to do in the near future.[10] Profits in futures trading are typically made by being right in the short run, not the long run. A trader who is wrong about price movements in the next day, week, or month might not have enough capital left to trade even though his or her long-run analysis of the market is right on target. A good short-run forecast provides a game plan, not a road map. It provides the *probable* direction of the market price; but because of random factors, and possibly cycles that have not been included in the forecast synthesis, there can be no guarantee. Anyone who trades from a forecast with the assumption that it is correct and the market wrong will soon see that the market is *always* right. What a good forecast does is indicate what the market is *likely* to do, not guarantee what it will do. A good forecast will tip the odds of a winning trade in the trader's favor, but the trader nevertheless must have adequate capital, money management skills, and trading ability.

APPLICATION OF SPECTRAL ANALYSIS

Now let us see what spectral analysis can and cannot do to help us anticipate the direction market prices are likely to follow. In order to see more clearly what happens with spectral analysis we shall first create a synthetic or artificial time series that contains only three things: (1) a trend, with a growth term that contains some randomness, (2) a seasonal cycle of 12 time periods, and (3) a long-term cycle of 120 time periods. The seasonal cycle has an amplitude, or distance from bottom to top of 30, and a phase of 5, meaning it reaches its first peak in the fifth period. The long-term cycle has an amplitude of 120 and a phase of 10. Figure 7-1 displays graphically the three components and their combination for 551 time periods. To facilitate discussion let us call them months.

Now let us examine a spectral analysis on the 551 artificial monthly values. Figure 7-2 contains a plot of the power spectrum of an analysis on the untransformed, undetrended data. The *x* axis (horizontal axis) contains periods, rather than frequency; those who prefer to think in frequency terms may simply take the reciprocals of the indicated periods. A full plot of all periods would run from 551 down to 2. However, because in this example there is virtually zero power at the high frequency, short-period end of the axis, those values are not plotted in order to make the others stand out more clearly.

Note that at a period of 551, the entire span of data in our sample, we have an indicated amplitude of about 200. Then there is an amplitude of

---

[10]For high frequency cycles the problem with gaps in the FFT frequency spectrum is of less concern than for low frequencies.

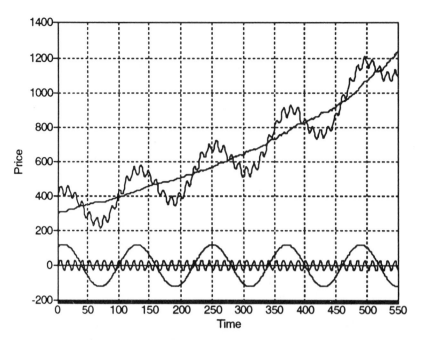

Figure 7-1 Synthetic combination of trend, seasonal, and cyclical time series.

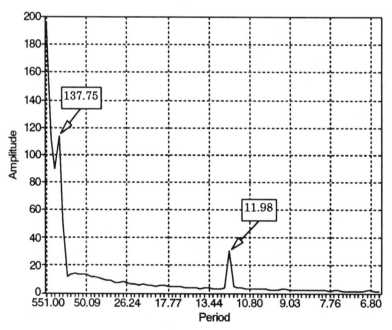

Figure 7-2 Spectrum of synthetic time series (trend, seasonal, cyclical).

about 112 at 137.75 months, and an amplitude of about 30 at 11.98 months. What happened? Why were the 12-month and 120-month cycles not identified precisely? There are at least two reasons. First, this spectral analysis was performed by going through the data in harmonic frequency steps of 1, 2, 3, 4, 5, . . . , 275. The corresponding periods are 551, 275.5, 183.67, 137.75, 110.2, . . . , 2.0036. Thus the 120 day cycle should show up in either or both of the surrounding periods: 137.75 or 110.2. We could, of course, redo the spectral analysis using much smaller steps, and refine our estimate of the periods and amplitudes of the cycles. But the second reason why the cycles were not correctly identified demonstrates why we would not normally be able to do so.

The second reason why the spectral analysis missed the two cycles we know to be present is that the data contain a trend. The presence of a trend distorts spectral analysis results and must be dealt with. How bad is the distortion? See for yourself! Figure 7-3 contains a pure straight-line trend, with values of 1, 2, 3, and so on. However, Fourier analysis of the straight line indicates that it also contains a combination of cycles. The Fourier analysis approximates the straight line with sinusoidal waves. Clearly the data that were analyzed, the first 100 data points, are approximated very well by just eleven such sinusoidals—let us not call them cycles, because a straight line

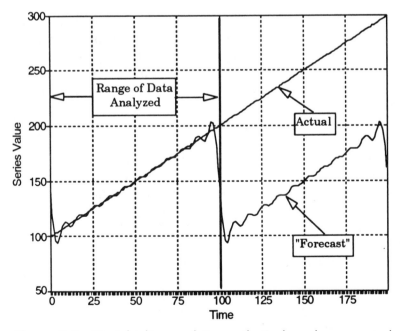

Figure 7-3 Straight line and its synthetic based on spectral analysis.

obviously does not contain cycles except in the sense that the line can be closely approximated by a Fourier transform of the data.

Now look in Figure 7-3 at what happens when the synthesis or combination of the eleven sinusoidals that fitted so well is projected into the future. It looks as though the "market," or whatever it is that has a pure straight-line trend, is due for an immediate doomsday crash. Not so! Fourier analysis, of which this type[11] of spectral analysis is a refined variant, is based on the assumption that the data sample is just one set out of an *infinite number* of *identical* sets. And it does its job very well under that assumption. But economic data sets are not infinite nor even long enough to give credibility to the fiction that they come close enough for the method to be useful. Note that the "forecast" in the second half of the graph reproduces exactly the synthetic series fitted to the first 100 data points. What we see in this graph is not very encouraging about the applicability of spectral analysis results for useful forecasting. Can anything be done about it? Fortunately the answer is "Yes."

Removal of a linear trend, as we have done by first differencing, is a form of *filtering*. To be more precise, it is a form of *high pass* filtering, in which high-frequency cycles are allowed to pass through the filter, while low-frequency cycles are not. Because of the problems with identifying low-frequency, long-period cycles mentioned above, our interest is mainly in these filters and not in *low pass* or in *notch* filters, the latter allowing only a certain range of frequencies to pass. The subject of filtering is taken up in Chapter 9, where we examine its application for smoothing data and removing cycles from data.

In Figure 7-4 are the results of a spectral analysis on the combination of trend, seasonal, and cycle after removing the trend by taking first differences. First differencing is based on creating a new time series from the original by defining the differenced values as the original values minus their predecessors: $D_1 = P_2 - P_1$, $D_2 = P_3 - P_2$, and so on. The differenced series has one fewer observation than the original series. To see what happens to a pure linear trend when the data are differenced, try it with the series 1, 2, 3, 4, 5, and so on.[12]

The spectral peaks in Figure 7-4 stand out clearly. If the harmonic steps through the frequencies had been smaller than one, the periods of the seasonal and cycle would have been more precisely identified. Nevertheless, the spectrum is unambiguous—there is definitely something cyclical going on with periods about 110 and about 12. Because the linear trend was removed by differencing the data, it could not distort the spectral analysis. Now what happens when we attempt to fit the waves revealed by differencing the data to the original, untransformed data?

---

[11]Maximum entropy spectral analysis, or MESA, is based on a different mathematical foundation. It is covered in a later chapter.

[12]Trend removal may also be performed by removal of very long cycles that are judged to be present.

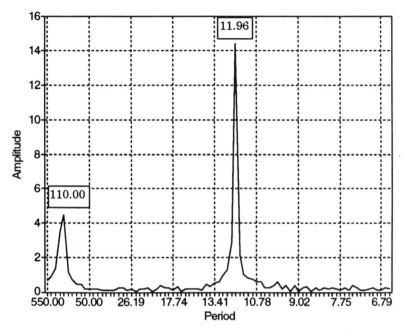

Figure 7-4   Spectrum of first differences of trend, seasonal, and cyclical time series.

To fit the results of the spectral analysis on the differenced data to the original series we do the following: First, generate a series containing cycles of the differenced data. This is a synthetic differences series. Next, add the first number in the differences series to the first number in the original data. This yields the second number in the synthetic counterpart of the original, untransformed data. Then, for the third and subsequent values, add the number in the synthetic differences series to the preceding number in the synthetic untransformed series. This is very easy to do in a spreadsheet program.

Figure 7-5 displays both the original data containing trend, seasonal, and cycle, and the synthetic produced by the process described in the preceding paragraph. For the first hundred or so points the fit is very good. But then the two series begin to drift apart. What happened? The differencing process removed the *linear* (straight line) portion of the trend. Unfortunately, differencing also removed most of the longer cyclical effects and slightly affected shorter period cycles. The linear trend was put back in constructing the synthetic counterpart to the original data. But any effect of the trend on the cycles was lost. Again, E.T. Garrett offers advice[13] on what limits what we can or cannot do about trend:

[13]Op.cit.

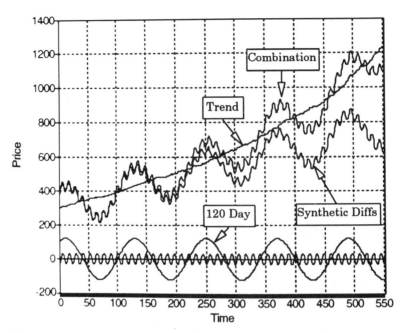

Figure 7-5   Combination and spectral synthetic of trend with seasonal and cycle.

The bias toward short cycles and against long cycles . . . works against the projection of the synthetic by depriving it of long cycle input. Within the constraints of [available] methodology nothing can be done about this. On a broader basis longer cycles from related series . . . could be brought in . . . but the ad hoc nature of this process [undermines credibility of the entire methodology].

As a practical matter, how important is it that the synthetic series drifts away from the original? The answer is, "Not very." Remember, for trading performance we want to be right in the short run. The effect of trend over short time intervals will be insignificant, but the effect of shorter-period cycles will be comparatively strong, especially when there are many shorter-term cycles combined. In making a forecast from the data that were analyzed, one would begin with a projection from the last actual value. Thus the gap between the actual series and the synthetic would not exist initially. And, because of the short seasonal cycle, the forecast would be accurate for a reasonably short-term forecast.

There is a lot more to say about spectral analysis, fitting cycles to data, and especially about determining whether or not a cycle that seems to be present is genuine. These matters are covered in Chapters 8, 9, and 10.

SUMMARY

This chapter discussed Fourier transform-based spectral analysis and some of the mathematics behind it. Also covered was the fast Fourier transform and the advantages and disadvantages it offers.

The undesirable influence of a trend in data was examined. It was shown with an example that a strong trend in the data casts a distorting spell over the power spectrum. It was also shown that the effect of trend on the spectrum can be removed by the simple technique of taking first differences of the time series data prior to the analysis.

It was emphasized that in making projections for market forecasting cycles of long period (low frequency) are less important than shorter cycles. Consequently, it is not crucial to identify cycles that are long relative to the amount of available data. That is very fortunate because, even if we wanted to, we could not. Nevertheless, it is important to remove the effects of trend (linear trend, low-frequency cycle or cycles) before doing spectral analysis, by applying an appropriate high pass filter such as first differencing.

8

Judging Whether a Cycle Is Genuine: Array Analysis

The previous chapter showed one way of finding cycles in data, using spectral analysis. Now we shall see how to determine whether the indication of a cycle given by a spectral peak corresponds to a genuine cycle in the data. Spectral analysis itself does not provide us with measures of the statistical validity of a cycle indicated to be present. Therefore, we turn to an older, almost forgotten, methodology to measure the genuineness of a given cycle, *array analysis*.

Array analysis was popular in the early 20th century but fell into general disuse after World War II. The method is described in some detail in a book by Whittaker and Robinson,[1] which may still be available in paperback reprint from Dover Publications in the United States.

DEFINITION OF GENUINENESS

What do we mean by a cycle being genuine? The definition that we shall use is this: A cycle is genuine if it is both *consistent* and *persistent*. Consistent means that the cycle is of reasonably constant amplitude [2] and phase through-

---

[1]Sir Edmund Whittaker and G. Robinson, *The Calculus of Observations: A Treatise on Numerical Mathematics* (London: Blackie & Son, Ltd., 1924).

[2]There is a qualification to this. If a cycle is *amplitude-modulated* by another, longer cycle its amplitude will not be constant. The methods discussed in this chapter are not designed to deal with such cycles. In fact, we do not have good methods for dealing with such cycles.

out the data. Persistent means that the cycle is always in the data; it does not fade out from a section of the data only to come back in a subsequent section.

ARRAY ANALYSIS

The goal of array analysis is to fill an array with the time series one is interested in. Assume that we are interested in a cycle of length 12 in monthly data (a seasonal cycle). We would fill the first row with the first 12 observations in our time series, the second row with observations 13 through 24, the third row with observations 25 through 36, and so on. If we do this with a time series that contains a genuine 12-month cycle we shall find that the sums across the rows have less variance between them than the sums of the columns do. The reason for this is that the rows contain one complete cycle, and thus the amplitude at various points along the cycle is averaged out. In contrast, the columns each contain the amplitude at a particular point of the cycle, and thus column sums have a greater variance. This concept will be illustrated with an example.

EXAMPLE: A PURE CYCLE

To illustrate what is involved in array analysis we shall use a pure 5-period cosine wave. Table 8-1 contains the worksheet values for the parameters and first 15 values of the series. Table 8-2 contains the cell formulas. Those who wish to duplicate the process can enter them and copy down the column for as many values as are desired.

Figure 8-1 contains a graph of the cycle values for a 5-period cosine wave. This cycle reaches its peak at time $t = 0, 5, 10$, and so on. Its minimums are at $t = 2.5, 7.5, 10.5$, and so forth. The values for time used to generate this smooth cycle ranged from 0 to 5.0 in increments of 0.10. However, when we test for a cycle of period 5 in the units of data in a time series we sample the cycle at discrete intervals. Figure 8-2 contains a graph of the sample values, indicated by the boxes (□) in the plot. (The lines that connect them are solely to guide the eye.) It would be better to have data that are more nearly continuous than at whole units of time, but that is simply not possible with most data.

Now that we have a synthetic time series, albeit one with only the 5-period cycle, we can apply array analysis. By using a pure cycle like this we can see what results from the array technique when a strong, pure cycle is present.

Table 8-3 contains the spreadsheet section holding the array. It contains 110 values, arranged in 22 rows of 5 items each. The array is constructed by placing data items 1 to 5 in the first row, items 6 to 10 in the second row, and

Table 8-1 Pure 5-period cycle

	A	B	C
4	Ampl. =		10
5	Period =		5
6	Omega =		1.2566
7	Phase =		0
8	Plus		25
9			
10			
11	1	0	35.0000
12	2	1	28.0902
13	3	2	16.9098
14	4	3	16.9098
15	5	4	28.0902
16	6	5	35.0000
17	7	6	28.0902
18	8	7	16.9098
19	9	8	16.9098
20	10	9	28.0902
21	11	10	35.0000
22	12	11	28.0902
23	13	12	16.9098
24	14	13	16.9098
25	15	14	28.0902
26	16	15	35.0000
27	17	16	28.0902
28	18	17	16.9098
29	19	18	16.9098
30	20	19	28.0902
31	21	20	35.0000
32	22	21	28.0902
33	23	22	16.9098
34	24	23	16.9098
35	25	24	28.0902
36	26	25	35.0000
37	27	26	28.0902
38	28	27	16.9098
39	29	28	16.9098
40	30	29	28.0902
41	31	30	35.0000
42	32	31	28.0902
43	33	32	16.9098
44	34	33	16.9098
45	35	34	28.0902

so on. Table 8-4 contains the computer instructions that create the worksheet cells.

Note that in the array in Table 8-3 each column contains a number that is constant down the column. The number is constant because in each row we are at the same point on the cycle. If the cycle were not exactly five periods long we would see some variation within the columns. Note also that the row sums are a constant 125, and thus the row averages a constant 25.

Table 8.2   Computer formulas for calculating the
5-period cycle

B4:	'Ampl. =
C4:	10
B5:	'Period =
C5:	5
B6:	(F4) 'Omega =
C6:	(F4) (2*@PI)/C5
B7:	'Phase =
C7:	0
B8:	'Plus
C8:	25
A11:	1
B11:	0
C11:	(F4) = $C$4*(@COS($C$6*B11+$C$7))+$C$8
A12:	2
B12:	1
C12:	(F4) +$C$4*(@COS($C$6*B12+$C$7))+$C$8
A13:	3
B13:	2
C13:	(F4) +$C$4*(@COS($C$6*B13+$C$7))+$C$8
A14:	4
B14:	3
C14:	(F4) +$C$4*(@COS($C$6*B14+$C$7))+$C$8
A15:	5
B15:	4
C15:	(F4) +$C$4*(@COS($C$6*B15+$C$7))+$C$8
A16:	6
B16:	5
C16:	(F4) +$C$4*(@COS($C$6*B16+$C$7))+$C$8
A17:	7
B17:	6
C17:	(F4) +$C$4*(@COS($C$6*B17+$C$7))+$C$8
A18:	8
B18:	7
C18:	(F4) +$C$4*(@COS($C$6*B18+$C$7))+$C$8
A19:	9
B19:	8
C19:	(F4) +$C$4*(@COS($C$6*B19+$C$7))+$C$8
A20:	10
B20:	9
C20:	(F4) +$C$4*(@COS($C$6*B20+$C$7))+$C$8
A21:	11
B21:	10
C21:	(F4) +$C$4*(@COS($C$6*B21+$C$7))+$C$8
A22:	12
B22:	11
C22:	(F4) +$C$4*(@COS($C$6*B22+$C$7))+$C$8

Table 8-3 Array for analysis of 5-period cycle

	E	F	G	H	I	J	K	L	M
5									
6				Correlation Ratio					
7				Eta =	1.000				
8							All Lines:		
9	Y =	26950	17359.27	6290.732	6290.732	17359.27	F =	1.44E+16	
10	Avgs =	35.000	28.090	16.910	16.910	28.090			
11	Base Per.			Period after base					
12	Number	1	2	3	4	5	RowSum	RowAvg	
13	1	35.000	28.090	16.910	16.910	28.090	125.000	25.000	1
14	6	35.000	28.090	16.910	16.910	28.090	125.000	25.000	2
15	11	35.000	28.090	16.910	16.910	28.090	125.000	25.000	3
16	16	35.000	28.090	16.910	16.910	28.090	125.000	25.000	4
17	21	35.000	28.090	16.910	16.910	28.090	125.000	25.000	5
18	26	35.000	28.090	16.910	16.910	28.090	125.000	25.000	6
19	31	35.000	28.090	16.910	16.910	28.090	125.000	25.000	7
20	36	35.000	28.090	16.910	16.910	28.090	125.000	25.000	8
21	41	35.000	28.090	16.910	16.910	28.090	125.000	25.000	9
22	46	35.000	28.090	16.910	16.910	28.090	125.000	25.000	10
23	51	35.000	28.090	16.910	16.910	28.090	125.000	25.000	11
24	56	35.000	28.090	16.910	16.910	28.090	125.000	25.000	12
25	61	35.000	28.090	16.910	16.910	28.090	125.000	25.000	13
26	66	35.000	28.090	16.910	16.910	28.090	125.000	25.000	14
27	71	35.000	28.090	16.910	16.910	28.090	125.000	25.000	15
28	76	35.000	28.090	16.910	16.910	28.090	125.000	25.000	16
29	81	35.000	28.090	16.910	16.910	28.090	125.000	25.000	17
30	86	35.000	28.090	16.910	16.910	28.090	125.000	25.000	18
31	91	35.000	28.090	16.910	16.910	28.090	125.000	25.000	19
32	96	35.000	28.090	16.910	16.910	28.090	125.000	25.000	20
33	101	35.000	28.090	16.910	16.910	28.090	125.000	25.000	21
34	106	35.000	28.090	16.910	16.910	28.090	125.000	25.000	22
35									

133

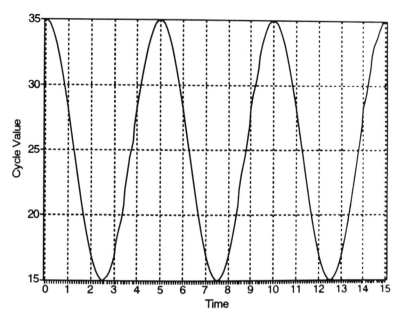

Figure 8-1 Pure cosine wave, sampling interval 1.00.

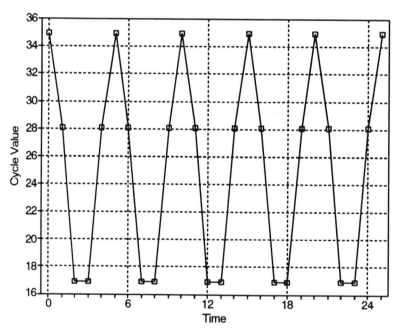

Figure 8-2 Pure cosine wave, sampling interval 1.00.

We can judge the statistical significance of the cycle in a number of ways. In this case it is easy to do so with the *correlation ratio*, and somewhat less easy to do with an analysis of variance using the *F statistic* with 4 and 105 degrees of freedom. The correlation ratio is defined as the standard deviation of the column averages divided by the standard deviation of the entire set of observations. According to Whittaker and Robinson,

> ... in the course of one horizontal row ... the part of the phenomenon which is of period *p* will pass through all the phases of one complete period, so that this periodic part is in the same phase at all terms which are above or below each other in the same vertical column.... The part of the phenomenon which is of period *p* therefore appears with *m*-fold amplitude in the row of column sums ... and therefore appears with its own proper amplitude in the row of means.

> ... Any accidental disturbance on the other hand, or any periodic disturbance of period different from *p*, will be enfeebled by the process of forming means, since positive and negative deviations will tend to annul each other; and therefore, when a periodicity of period *p* exists, the standard deviation of the M's has a value much larger than when a periodicity of this period does not exist in the phenomenon.[3]

In the present case we have a perfect value of correlation ratio η (eta) = 1.00. If there were no 5-period cycle present in the data, the value would have been close to zero. Calculation of the F statistic is more complicated. Any of the many books on standard statistics that cover analysis of variance can be consulted for the details. Later we shall apply another statistical measure, the Bartels test, which provides a direct measure of the probability of the genuineness of a cycle.

Figure 8-3 contains a bar graph of the column averages for each third of the array of Table 8-3, plus the overall array (all lines). Note that because we have a perfect, 5-period cycle, each bar is of identical height. Furthermore, the height of the bars in each column helps reveal the amplitude of the cycle and the base value upon which it is superimposed. The amplitude of the cycle is 10 and the base value 25.

Now that you have seen how an array analysis is conducted on a cycle of whole number period (integer) length, we will consider how a cycle of non-integer period can be analyzed. For this purpose we should have a cycle that is realistic, yet not so long that the array has so many columns as to be unmanageable in a worksheet. For this purpose Wolfer's data[4] on the number of sunspots will be useful, because their occurrence has a strong cycle of 11.4 years. Figure 8-4 contains a graph of the data with a synthetic pure cycle of 11.4 years. It is clear that the fit is very close, especially in the more recent years. In the early years it is possible that the data are not so reliable because the instruments available then were more primitive.

---

[3] Whittaker and Robinson, op. cit., p. 346.

[4] As an illustration of spectral analysis, a listing of these data is provided in the *SAS/ETS User's Guide*, 5th ed. (Cary, NC: SAS Institute, Inc., 1984).

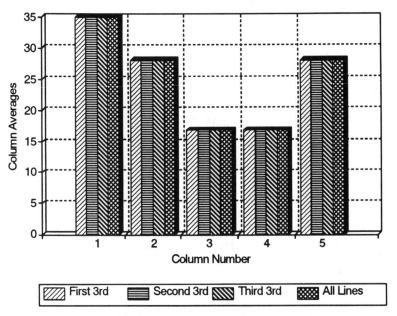

Figure 8-3 Column averages of sections of array.

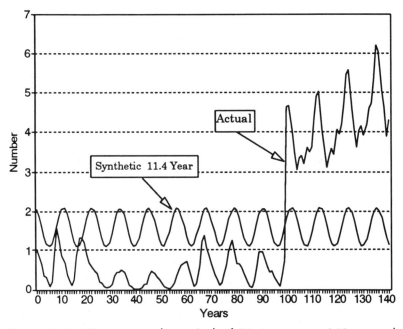

Figure 8-4 Fitting a cycle period of 11.4 years to 142 annual sunspots numbers.

Table 8-4 Worksheet of computer formulas for analysis of 5-period array

H6:	(F4)	[F5] "Correlation Ratio
H7:	(F4)	[F5] "Eta =
I7:	(F3)	[F5] @STD(F10..J10)/@STD(F13..J34)
K7:	[F5]	'All Lines:
K8:	(F4)	[F5] 'F =
L8:	(S2)	[F5] +L9/L10
E9:	[F5]	"Y =
F9:	[F5]	(@SUM(F13..F34)^2)/@COUNT (F13..F34)
G9:	[F5]	(@SUM(G13..G34)^2)/@COUNT (G13..G34)
H9:	[F5]	(@SUM(H13..H34)^2)/@COUNT (H13..H34)
I9:	[F5]	(@SUM(I13..I34)^2)/@COUNT (I13..I34)
J9:	[F5]	(@SUM(J13..J34)^2)/@COUNT (J13..J34)
L9:	(H)	[F5] (((@SUM(F9..J9)-(@SUM(F13..J34)^2)/110))/(5-1)
L10:	(H)	[F5] (@SUMPRODUCT(C11..C120,C11..C120)-@SUM(F9..J9))/(110-5)
E10:	(F4)	[F5] "Avgs =
F10:	(F3)	[F5] @AVG(F13..F34)
G10:	(F3)	[F5] @AVG(G13..G34)
H10:	(F3)	[F5] @AVG(H13..H34)
I10:	(F3)	[F5] @AVG(I13..I34)
J10:	(F3)	[F5] @AVG(J13..J34)
L10:	(H)	[F5] @AVG(L13..L33)
E11:	(F4)	[F5] "Base Per.
H11:	[F5]	'Period after base
E12:	(F4)	[F5] "Number
K12:	(F0)	[F5] "RowSum
L12:	(F4)	[F5] "RowAvg
E13:	(F0)	[F5] 1
F13:	(F3)	U [F5] @VLOOKUP(1,$SERIES,2)
G13:	(F3)	U [F5] @VLOOKUP(2,$SERIES,2)
H13:	(F3)	U [F5] @VLOOKUP(3,$SERIES,2)
I13:	(F3)	U [F5] @VLOOKUP(4,$SERIES,2)
J13:	(F3)	U [F5] @VLOOKUP(5,$SERIES,2)
K13:	(F3)	[F5] @SUM(F13..J13)
L13:	(F3)	[F5] @AVG(F13..J13)
M13:	[F5]	1
E14:	(F0)	[F5] +E13+$C$5
F14:	(F3)	U [F5] @VLOOKUP($E13+$C$5+F$12-1,$SERIES,2)
G14:	(F3)	U [F5] @VLOOKUP($E13+$C$5+G$12-1,$SERIES,2)
H14:	(F3)	U [F5] @VLOOKUP($E13+$C$5+H$12-1,$SERIES,2)
I14:	(F3)	U [F5] @VLOOKUP($E13+$C$5+I$12-1,$SERIES,2)
J14:	(F3)	U [F5] @VLOOKUP($E13+$C$5+J$12-1,$SERIES,2)
K13:	(F3)	[F5] @SUM(F13..J13)
L13:	(F3)	[F5] @AVG(F13..J13)
M13:	[F5]	1
E14:	(F0)	[F5] +E13+$C$5
F14:	(F3)	U [F5] @VLOOKUP($E13+$C$5+F$12-1,$SERIES,2)
G14:	(F3)	U [F5] @VLOOKUP($E13+$C$5+G$12-1,$SERIES,2)
H14:	(F3)	U [F5] @VLOOKUP($E13+$C$5+H$12-1,$SERIES,2)
I14:	(F3)	U [F5] @VLOOKUP($E13+$C$5+I$12-1,$SERIES,2)
J14:	(F3)	U [F5] @VLOOKUP($E13+$C$5+J$12-1,$SERIES,2)
K14:	(F3)	[F5] @SUM(F14..J14)
L14:	(F3)	[F5] @AVG(F14..J14)
M14:	[F5]	2

Whether we do the array analysis manually or in a spreadsheet program, we obviously cannot have 11.4 columns. We can have either 11 or 12. Which will it be? And having determined the number of columns, how shall we proceed to fill the array? There are three ways to do this.

The first way to fill the array is to follow Whitakker and Robinson's prescription:

> When the trial period is not a whole number of days, we modify the arrangement slightly so as to secure that terms in the same phase are still in the same vertical column: thus if the trial period were $31\frac{1}{2}$ days, we should write the values corresponding to days 1 to 31 in the first horizontal row, and the values corresponding to days 32 to 62 in the second horizontal row, then we should omit altogether the value corresponding to day 63 in order to bring the value corresponding to day 64 to the beginning of the third row, and so on.[5]

This method is easy to use once it is understood, and yields good results provided one has enough data. With a long enough time series the omitted values have such little influence that the analysis is not diminished in their absence. The key to applying this approach is to remember to throw out the data values corresponding to integer multiples of the cycle in question. For example, with an 11.4 year cycle we should fill the first row with observations 1 to 11, the second row with observations 12 to 22, and so forth, remembering to discard the 57th observation.

The second way to fill the array is one recommended by The Foundation for the Study of Cycles.[6] Discussion concerns the array for a cycle of $8\frac{2}{3}$ periods in length.

> If the period being investigated is not a whole number, then the number of columns is equal to the next whole number larger than the period. Thus, for our period of $8\frac{2}{3}$, a nine column array is used. The first base number is 6, 1 before 7, 7 being the position of the first value. The decimal form of the period (8.67) is added successively to the first base number (6) to give 14.67, 23.34, 32.01, etc. These numbers are then rounded to whole numbers to give the base column numbers of 6, 15, 23, 32, 41, 49, 58, and 67. These numbers are then entered into the base column of the array.

> It takes nine entries on the body of the table to get from 6 to 15, but only 8 to get from 15 to 23. When the table is first filled in, the last place in the second line is left blank. The last column in any other line which requires only eight values is also left empty. On an array with a fraction $\frac{2}{3}$, that would be every third line.

[5]Whitakker and Robinson, op.cit., p. 354.

[6]"Cycle Analysis—A Case Study, Part 3: Detailed Analysis for a Single Cycle," *Cycles* (May 1971): p. 125. This is further dicussed in "Cycles Analysis—A Case Study, Part 18: More on the Use of the Array," *Cycles* (December 1972): pp. 303–320, based on Edward R. Dewey's earlier work.

The error that accumulates because our data readings are at whole number intervals, but our period is fractional, is, in effect, jerked back into place every third line. . . .

After the table is filled in, the spaces left blank in the ninth column are filled in with the next following datum, and parentheses differentiate these entries.

Whenever the assumed cycle on which the array is constructed is different from the true cycle, the positions of the cycle highs and lows in the array will drift. If the correct period is longer, the highs and lows will drift to the right. If the correct period is shorter, they will drift to the left. By comparing sets composed of the top, the middle, and the bottom third of the array rows we can obtain a sense of such drift and of whether the cycle is consistent over the data under analysis.

A third method of building an array uses a computer to do the calculations. In this approach we "stretch" the data to fit the next higher integer. For example, if we are interested in examining Wolfer's annual sunspot data for a cycle of 11.4 years, and we have 142 observations, we map the original data into 144 observations[7] in a 12 by 12 array. Figure 8-5 illustrates the result by plotting the original data series with the 'stretched' or adjusted data series.[8] The following discussion is based on a computerized array analysis of this adjusted data series. Figure 8-6 contains analysis of the Wolfer data.

First, we analyze the data by looking separately at each set of rows in the first third, middle third, and last third of the array. Then, we look at each half separately. Finally, we take the entire set of rows. The parameters to fit the cycle in question, in the present case 11.4 periods, are estimated for each third, each half, the overall array, and for each row by itself. (The reason for this will soon be evident.)

The A and B coefficients from the array analysis are the parameters in the equation for a cycle of the form $A \sin(\omega t) + B \cos(\omega t)$, where $\omega = 2\pi/\text{Period}$ and t is the index of a data point. The amplitude and phase can be found from this information, and then the cycle equation can be written in the alternative

---

[7]The mapping process actually produces some extra adjusted data points which are discarded because their inclusion would mean the array would have missing values in the last row. For instance, the integer part of $(12/11.4) \times 142 = 149$. Since we need 144, five are discarded.

[8]The process involved is as follows: First, find $11.4/12 = 0.95$. If the original data series $e(1)$, $e(2)$, and so on, are 1.02, 0.83, 0.67, and so on, we perform the following calculations to obtain the interpolated data series data(1), data(2), and so on. Let data(1) = $e(1)$ = 1.02. Then data (2) = $1.02 + 0.95 \times (0.83 - 1.02) = 0.8395$. And data (3) = $0.83 + 0.90 \times (0.67 - 0.83)$. The remianing values to fill the 12×12 array are generated by continuing the process. Note that the multiplier 0.95, 0.90, and so on can be obtained from $0.95 - i \times (1.00 - 0.95)$, where i is the value of the data subscript less 1 (that is, $t - 1$), and 0.95 the aforementioned ratio of 11.4 to 12. If the multiplier should become less than or equal to zero we again set it equal to the ratio, 0.95, and continue.

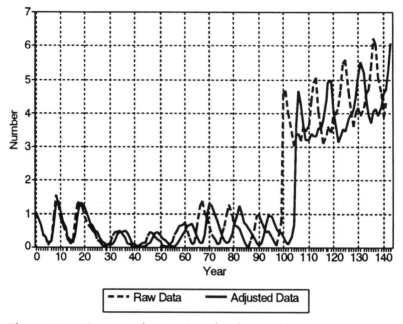

Figure 8-5   Sunspot data, original values and array remapped.

form $R\cos(\omega t - \phi)$, where R is the amplitude, and ϕ (phi) is the phase. The phase is the number of periods from the base before the cycle reaches its first peak.

If a genuine cycle is present in the data, and is consistent throughout, then the A and B coefficients should be relatively constant over all sections. Examination of the coefficients is indicative, but not definitive. That is, visually based judgments about the constancy of the coefficients may suggest something, but they do not prove anything. For the latter we need to employ formal methods based on statistics.

The F test for the array divided into thirds tests the hypothesis that the sections contain the same cycle. The calculated F statistic of 0.16728 is less than the tabulated value for 11 and 24 degrees of freedom and implies that we cannot reject the hypothesis. The F test for the halves similarly tests the hypothesis that the two contain the same cycle. This time we again see that the tabulated F value for 11 and 12 degrees of freedom is greater than the computed value of 0.15749, and again we cannot reject the hypothesis. The final F test is for the hypothesis that we examined early in this chapter, at that time for a pure 5-period cycle. It tests the hypothesis that the column sums are equal (that there is no cycle, since without a cycle of period corresponding to the number of columns in the array the column sums would tend to be equal). The computed F value again is less than the value tabulated for 11 and 132 degrees of freedom, so we cannot reject the hypothesis. It appears that an 11.4 year cycle is statistically significant in these data.

```
***********************************************************************
      "Array" analysis program.  -- Series  IV -- Encoded Serial No.
           (C) Copyright 1985-1990 by Anthony F. Herbst.
                      All rights reserved.
***********************************************************************


Input file header lines are:
"Wolfer Sunspot Data"
"Annual Observations"
   142, 0, 1


Enter period toexamine, with decimal point:  11.4
11.400000 Item array

Number of points from input file = 142, base = 0
Number of lines 12, points in array 144
                          Thirds
Section      Con A          Con B       Amplitude          Phase
   1        0.12730       -0.17904       0.21968         10.19637
   2        0.34149       -0.03243       0.34302          0.35320
   3        0.77667       -0.69950       1.04524         10.59477


Improved period 11.275805


Phase prediction for middle third 10.395571


F-ratio = 0.16728 with 11 and 24 d.f.


                          Halves
Section      Con A          Con B       Amplitude          Phase
   1        0.17147       -0.10477       0.20094         10.92987
   2        0.65883       -0.50255       0.82862         10.74270


Probable period 11.368805


F-ratio = 0.15749 with 1 and 12 d.f.


                         All lines
Section      Con A          Con B       Amplitude          Phase
   1        0.41515       -0.30366       0.51435         10.77920


                      Individual Lines

Chi-square test on distribution of phases around their mean:
   0   1   0   6   4   1   0    Chi square = 19.500000, with 6 d.f.


Bartels' test = 0.002825


F-ratio = 0.70128 with 11 and 132 d.f.
```

Figure 8-6 Computer array analysis.   **141**

```
========================================================================
Average amplitude     =       0.592138 (+ or -)   0.455617
Least squares period =       11.463922 (+ or -)   0.078932
Least squares phase  =       10.135782 (+ or -)   0.269595
Using 12 points
========================================================================
```

```
Chi-square test on distribution of phases around their mean:
   0    0    1    6    4    1    0     Chi square = 19.500000, with 6 d.f.
```

Figure 8-6   (*continued*)

In Figure 8-6 the first chi-square test is on the timing, or phase of the cycle. It is based on the following: The period contained in the array is arbitrarily sectioned into seven parts. If the cycle we suspect to be present is consistent over time, then we should find that the peak occurs at the same point from the start in each row of the array. In such a case the middle section (fourth of seven) would contain all occurrences of the peak in the cycle. To the extent that the cycle peak varies, we shall find values on either side of the middle section. The chi-square statistic tests the hypothesis that the observed frequency distribution over the seven sections is the same as a uniform distribution over the sections (that is, one-seventh of the observations are in each of the seven sections). With seven frequency bins, we have $N - 1 = 6$ degrees of freedom for the chi-square. A calculated value of 19.5 for 6 degrees of freedom exceeds the tabulated value of 18.5 at a confidence level of .995, so we can reject the hypothesis at the .995 level. This result may be interpreted as meaning that the calculated result should be obtained by chance only 5 times in 1000; that is, if a cycle of the suspected length is not contained in the data.

The second chi-square statistic in Figure 8-6 tests the strength, or amplitude of the cycle. If the cycle is genuine its amplitude should be the same in each row of the array. In all other respects this chi-square follows that described in the previous paragraph. Again in this case we strongly reject the hypothesis that the distribution of amplitude frequencies is no different from a uniform distribution.

The *Bartels* test[9] is another statistical measure that experience has shown to be both dependable and easier to interpret than F test and chi-square statistics. It also has the advantage that it does not require the use of supplemen-

---

[9]This test is named after Julius Bartels, who developed it in the 1930s while employed as a geophysicist with the Carnegie Institution of Washington, D.C. The detailed mathematics behind the development are contained in the article "Random Fluctuations, Persistence, and Quasi-Persistence in Geophysical and Cosmical Periodicities," in what is now the *Journal of Geophysical Research*, then titled *Terrestrial Magnetism and Atmospheric Electricity* 40, No. 1 (March 1935): pp. 1–28.

Bartels Test Applied to the Harmonic Coefficients of an
11.4 Year Cycle in Wolfer's Data

Section					
1	0.36145	-0.31595	0.23047	0.48007	10.62168
2	-0.25396	-0.45923	0.27539	0.52477	8.15847
3	0.22384	-0.02468	0.05071	0.22520	0.32579
4	0.17786	0.08368	0.03864	0.19656	1.32287
5	0.14634	0.13501	0.03964	0.19911	1.87693
6	0.37329	-0.04744	0.14160	0.37629	0.29566
7	0.45462	-0.19018	0.24285	0.49280	11.20614
8	0.39169	-0.02712	0.15416	0.39263	0.39958
9	1.43311	-1.18406	3.45580	1.85898	10.67214
10	0.46561	-0.55107	0.52047	0.72144	10.34784
11	0.50586	-0.64884	0.67689	0.82273	10.27648
12	0.70212	-0.41402	0.66439	0.81510	10.95832

Column	Sum	4.98183	-3.67890	6.49100	7.10567	76.46190
	Avg.	0.41515	-0.30366	0.54092	0.59214	6.37183

Average Amplitude = $\qquad$ 0.51435 $\quad = (0.41515^2 + (-0.300366^2))$

Average Vector $\quad =$ $\qquad$ 0.73547 $\quad = \sqrt{(6.49100/12)}$

"Expectancy" of

Average Vector $\quad =$ $\qquad$ 0.21231 $\quad = 0.73547/\sqrt{(12)}$

$\qquad$ and $\qquad =$ $\qquad$ 0.21231 $\quad = \sqrt{(6.4910)/12}$

Bartels' Test Probability = $\quad$ 0.00283 $\quad = 1/127.1$

$$= 1/\exp[(0.51435/0.21231)^2]$$
$$= 1/\exp[(4.98183^2 + 3.64390^2)/6.49100]$$

Figure 8-7 Application of the Bartels test.

tary tables to look up probabilities. The Bartels test is based on the A and B coefficients of the cycle that are fitted to the data. If we fit the cycle to each row separately, and then to the row containing the average of the columns, we obtain $N + 1$ sets of A, B terms. If we have a perfect cycle, the As and Bs will be constant. On the other hand, if we have no cycle they will follow a random walk about an A, B plane. The mechanics of applying the test are illustrated in Figure 8-7 in which the test statistic for an 11.4-year cycle in the sunspot data is calculated.

The Bartels test provides a direct measure of the probability that the evident presence of a cycle is due to chance. Thus, a value of 0.0 indicates a true periodicity, a value of 1.0 that no cycle of the suspect length is present in the data.[10]

Computerized array analysis can provide some additional calculations that offer alternative measures. For example, the phase prediction for the middle third of the array is based on the phases for the first and last thirds. If there were a uniform phase shift, or drift, the Section 2 phase would agree closely with the phase prediction. The "improved period" and "probable period" measures are based on adjusting the period entered in response to the program prompt in light of the calculated values.

Other measures that are not indispensable can nevertheless assist in our determination of whether or not a cycle is genuine. Among these is the standard technique of least squares. The least-squares period and phase are found by fitting a least-squares regression equation to the parameters for each row (that is, each line) in the array. If we throw out the extreme high and low values we usually obtain a more representative picture of the true relationships. The (+ or −) tolerances are determined from the standard errors of the regression estimates. These indicate the likely range of values into which the true period and phase fall. If the cycle is genuine, the least-squares period and phase should be in close agreement with those for the overall array (all lines).

In forecasting work it is suggested, based on experience with various measures, that the "all lines" parameters or "Section 3" parameters be used. The Section 3 parameters, having been fitted from the last third of the rows in the array, would normally be considered to provide a better projection into the future because the data on which they are based are nearer to it than the others. One could, of course, use the parameters for the last row in the array, but that is a dangerous alternative because the random effects that can strongly influence any one row are usually minimized when a number of rows are averaged together. If one wishes to fit a synthetic time series to the original data, rather than forecast, the "'all lines" parameters or least squares parameters should normally be used.

CONCLUSION

Array analysis provides a means for validating indications of cycles that are obtained from spectral analysis or by other means. The method offers some advantages over spectral analysis. For example,

> ... the actual properties of a cycle—its waveform, amplitude, regularity, etc.— can be as important as the per cent of the variance that it explains. Array analysis

---

[10]More precisely, a test value of 0.001 means that there is one chance in 1000 that we could obtain such results by chance alone. We thus should keep in mind that if we examine a thousand possible cycles in random data, we should on average obtain one indication of a cycle with a test value of 0.001 even though none truly exists.

can verify the existence of cycles that do not explain a major portion of the variance of a series and it reveals the properties of existing cycles.

... array analysis ... is valid not only for periodicities but also for disturbed fluctuations. The waveform need not be sinusoidal but may be of almost any form, e.g., triangular, square, sawtoothed, etc.; the amplitude may vary; and even the phase position may vary, provided the variation is not so great that a repetitive pattern is no longer important.[11]

Thus, array analysis provides a robust means of determining the properties of cycles that may exist in data, and in gauging the genuineness of cycles.

[11]James E. Vaux, Jr., "Array Analysis." Unpublished paper, about 1968. James Vaux developed most of the computer programs used by the Foundation for the Study of Cycles in the 1960s and 1970s, when it was located in Pittsburgh, PA. His efforts in that capacity, and in providing scientific documentation for the techniques used, merit recognition. The Foundation has since relocated to Irvine, CA.

9

Moving Averages, Filtering, and Turning Points

Moving averages are popular for determining turning points, that is, when a market trend changes direction. The basic concept behind application of moving averages is that, when a price series crosses the correct moving average of itself, the price series will continue in the direction of the crossing. More complex applications use two or more moving averages to ascertain turning points. With two moving averages, when the one with the shorter period crosses the one with the longer period, there will probably be a change in trend.

Moving averages are also useful for filtering (that is, removing) the effects of cycles of known period in data. When used for filtering, moving averages must be applied with caution to avoid introducing unnecessary distortions into the filtered series. There are two basic types of moving average, simple and exponential. The simple moving average has been popularly thought to require much more computation than the exponential, but it need not if care is taken in specifying the algorithm used for the calculation.[1]

The simple moving average can completely remove a cycle of given length in a data series, and substantially diminish cycles in the range of approximately ±20 percent the length of the moving average. The closer the length of the moving average is to that of a cycle in the data, the more the diminution of the effects of the cycle on the data. The exponential moving average does not fully remove the effects of a cycle from the data, but does reduce it significantly. The choice between the simple and exponential moving averages is largely a matter of personal preference. However, one might prefer to use

---

[1]For an efficient program (in C language) see J.S. Glazier, "Moving Average Myths," *Stocks & Commodities*, 4 (November 1990): pp. 70–72.

an exponential moving average for calling turning points in a price series and a simple moving average for removing the effects of a cycle of given length.

SIMPLE MOVING AVERAGE

Almost everyone has used a simple moving average at one time or another. The method provides a useful and easily understood way of smoothing time series data. What it does is filter out randoms and short-period (that is, high frequency) cycles contained in the raw data.

A simple n-period moving average is computed by adding the first n data points together and dividing by n to find their average. In mathematical terms, this is denoted by

$$X_{t+n-1} = \frac{1}{n} \sum_{i=t}^{t+n-1} x_i \qquad (9\text{-}1)$$

In calculating a simple moving average of n periods one will end up with $n - 1$ fewer data points in the adjusted series than in the raw data. Note that each moving average value in the equation is assumed to correspond to the last raw data value used in its calculation. In other words, it is "uncentered." To center an odd period (3, 5, 7, 9, and so on) moving average one simply shifts the moving average values so that the moving average value corresponds to the middle value used in its calculation. That is, moving average value t corresponds to raw data value $[t + (n - 1)/2]$. Thus, for a 5-day moving average, the first moving average value corresponds to the third raw data value. Centering an even period moving average value presents some problems because the moving averages fall "between" raw data observations. An easy way of handling this is to use the average of each consecutive set of two moving averages,[2] but this sacrifices an additional point in the moving average series.

Consider Figure 9-1. The raw data are simply a pure sinusoidal wave combined with a linear trend. Notice what happens when a simple moving average (SMA) of appropriate length is applied to the raw data. The sinusoidal wave is entirely removed, and only the trend remains. Whenever the length of a simple moving average corresponds to that of a cycle in the data the cycle will be removed. When the length of the moving average is an even multiple of the cycle, it will also be removed. Thus, a 20-day moving average would remove the effects of a 5-day cycle in the data. So would moving averages of

---

[2]A superior, albeit complicated, procedure for centering a 12-month moving avearge is discussed in J.I. Griffin, *Statistics* (New York: Holt, Rinehart, and Winston, 1962), pp. 339–362. Newer references on statistics typically do not contain such information on moving averages, emphasizing instead statistical inference.

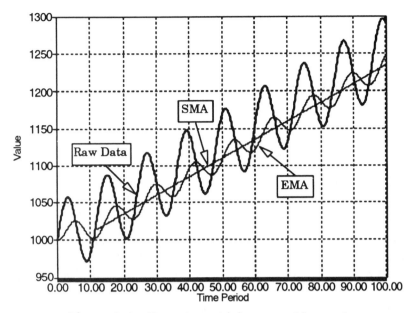

Figure 9-1 Pure sinusoidal wave with trend.

10, 30, 40, and so on days. But moving averages of an odd multiple would not eliminate the cycle. The reason for this is that one full manifestation of the cycle remains in the moving average.

The moving average values in Figure 9-1 are not centered. Thus the SMA lags (is slower) than its raw data series by one-fourth cycle, or 90°, because we have a sinusoidal wave as the only cyclical component in the raw data.

It is widely believed that the SMA requires a great deal of computation effort and thus tends to be slow even on fast computers. This is not necessarily true. If one calculates each term in the moving average series as defined in Equation 9-1, a considerable amount of unnecessary extra computation is performed, a wasted effort. To compute an n-period SMA efficiently, calculate only the first n terms using Equation 9-1. Then calculate the remaining terms according to the equation

$$\sum_t = \left[\sum_{t-1} + x_t - x_{t-n} \right]; \qquad X_t = \frac{\sum_t}{n} \tag{9-2}$$

Thus, it is only necessary to keep the running sum of n terms, modify it by removing the oldest, add the current raw observation, and finally divide by n.[3] It is waste of computer time to re-create the entire sum for each term

---

[3]In a spreadsheet program the procedure is somewhat different but equivalent. The moving average for the current cell is found by adding to the previous moving average value the result of $(x_{t-1} - x_{t-m})/n$. For example, if we are calculating a 7-period simple moving average in column C, the formula in cell C21 would read + C20 + (C21 − C14)/7. Of course, the *first* SMA value must still be calculated the old fashioned way.

in the moving average. With this attention to efficiency, the SMA compares well with the exponential moving average.

EXPONENTIAL MOVING AVERAGE

With an exponential moving average (EMA) the effects of a particular raw data point never completely disappear from the moving average. The EMA thus can be said to have an infinite memory. An n-period EMA is calculated according to

$$X_t = \alpha x_t + (1 - \alpha)X_{t-1} \tag{9-3}$$

where α is defined by $\alpha = 2/n$.[4] The EMA is thus very easy to calculate by simply adding α times the raw data value, x_{t-1}, to the quantity $(1 - \alpha)$ times the previous EMA value, X_t. (To start the process, use the first raw data value as if it were the first EMA value.)

Figure 9-1 also contains an EMA of the same period as the simple moving average plotted in it. Note that the EMA greatly diminishes but does not completely eliminate the influence of the sinusoidal wave contained in the raw data. Note also that the EMA and the SMA are equal at points where the sinusoidal wave incorporated in the raw data plotted in Figure 9-1 crosses the horizontal axis. (A large constant was added to the sinusoidal values to make all plotted values positive. Sine and cosine waves are symmetrical with half the values positive, half negative.)

MOVING AVERAGES AND MARKET TURNS

Why bother to calculate moving averages? One reason is to smooth raw market data and eliminate the random noise that tends to obscure the true, fundamental movements of the market. The smoothed data can often be analyzed more easily, although one must beware of distortions that naive or careless application of moving averages can induce.[5] Such distortions are

---

[4] See J. Ehlers, "Moving Averages," *Stocks and Commodities*, Vol. 3 (June, 1988), pp. 37-40 for details on the derivation of alpha and reference to an alternative derivation that defines alpha as $1/(n - 1)$.

[5] A very powerful alternative to a moving average is a method recommended by Tukey. It is a three-point moving *median*. For each set of three values take the middle value. This simple procedure is very easy to perform in a spreadsheet program with the formula: @SUM(C4..C6)−@MIN(C4..C6)−MAX(C4..C6). This finds the middle value from the data contained in column C, cell C4 through C6. The data are smoothed without introducing distortions or retaining the effects of outliers in the raw data that might be due to errors in recording market activity.

not normally a problem when only one moving average is taken of a raw data series. However, when a moving average is taken of a moving average, distortion can become significant.

A second reason for calculating moving averages is to remove the manifestations of cycles in a particular frequency range. The resulting data obtained from application of moving average calculation often can reveal the presence of cycles that were formerly hidden. Again the caveat applies: Be careful of distortions that the process of taking moving averages may introduce.

A complete treatment of moving averages for data filtering requires far more space than can be allocated here. Since the theme in this work is to analyze and forecast market prices, the reader is directed to other references for additional applications of moving averages for data filtering.[6]

The third reason for taking moving averages is to use them for calling or confirming turning points in market trends and sub-trends. This is the reason many stock and commodity traders work with moving averages. And, to some extent, they work.

Consider Figure 9-2, which contains a pure cosine wave with a linear trend and both simple and exponential moving averages. Figure 9-3 contains

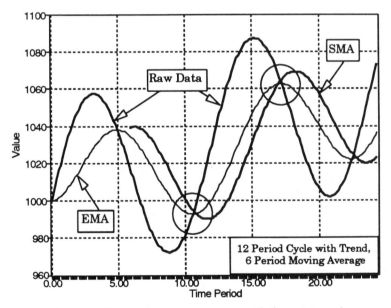

Figure 9-2 Pure cosine wave with linear trend.

[6]An excellent and detailed treatment of moving averages is by H. Brooks, *Investing with a Computer: A Time Series Approach* (New York: Petrocelli Books, Inc., 1984).

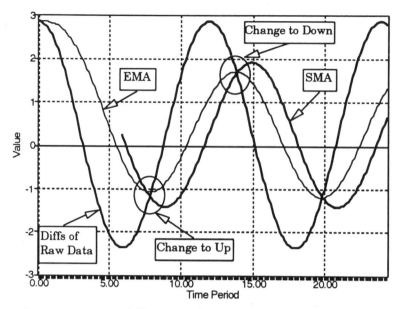

Figure 9-3   First difference of pure cosine wave with trend.

first differences of the same data series. The differencing process completely eliminates the linear trend, and can be characterized as a high-pass filter because it reduces the effects of long (low frequency) cycles present in a data series. Note that the "change to up" contained in the circled area at lower left is signaled when the actual, or raw market data series, penetrates the moving averages to the upside from below. Similarly, the "change to down" indicated in the circled area at upper right-center is indicated when the raw market data penetrates the moving averages to the downside from above. But note also that the signaling is delayed and thus might better be called a confirmation than an early indicator of change in direction. For an early indication, a trader might do better to see what is happening to the *rate of change* in the market data, reserving the penetration of moving average for confirmation of the change. A rate of change series can be obtained by taking first differences of the first differenced series. Thus one might enter a small trading position on the basis of rate of change and enlarge the position if the moving average confirms the change.

But what does one do in a real market situation? A simple example might not relate well to what traders actually do. Analysis of daily closing prices for the Dow Jones 30 Industrials over the 1980s using the techniques covered in previous chapters reveals several statistically significant cycles. We shall use two moving averages together to compare effectiveness.

Using moving averages of half their respective lengths offers maximum sensitivity in calling turning points. This suggests moving average lengths of

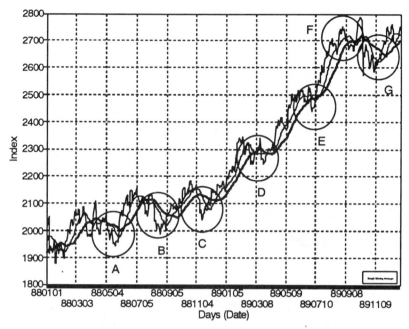

Figure 9-4 Dow Jones Industrial Average daily closes with 35-day and 17-day simple moving averages, 1988–1989.

35 days and 17 days. Figure 9-4 contains a graph of market data with simple moving averages of these lengths. The heavier line is the 35-day. Figure 9-5 contains a graph of market data with exponential moving averages of the same lengths.

The tactic to use with these moving averages is this: When the 17-day moving average crosses the 35-day moving average from below, go long the market. Hold the long position until the 17-day moving average crosses the 35-day to the downside. Then go short and stay short until there is again a crossing to the upside.

How well does this strategy work? You be the judge. Draw vertical lines from the crossing points to the market price. Then measure the distance (that is, the price change) from crossing point to crossing point. In the strongly trending stage of the market the technique would have performed nicely for long positions, but not so well for short selling. And, in the more or less sideways section of market price movement the results are far from conclusive.

Does it make any real difference whether one uses a simple or exponential moving average for confirming turning points? The answer to this question is evident in the figures. The simple moving average provides sharper signals, and more of them. As a consequence, more trades would be made, some unprofitable. Use whichever you prefer. With an efficient calculation algorithm

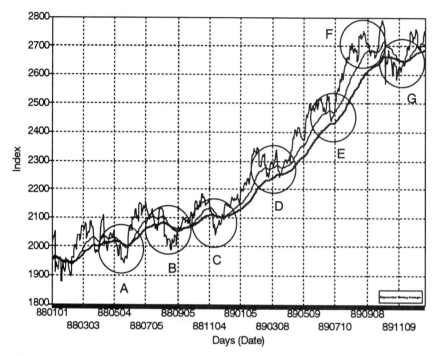

Figure 9-5 Dow Jones Industrial Average daily closes with 35-day and 17-day exponential moving averages, 1988–89.

like Equation 9-2, the time required to calculate the simple moving average is insignificantly different from that to calculate the exponential.

Although one can use moving averages to attempt to call, or to confirm, market turning points, if there are one or more cycles in the market there are better tools for the purpose. These are discussed in subsequent chapters.

10

Forecasting with Cycle Combinations

Many successful futures markets traders rely on cycles in market behavior to guide them. Knowledge of cycles in market prices allows a trader to anticipate market action rather than just confirm it. The trader who uses cycles already knows the probable direction or market price and thus can prepare for the action before it occurs or establish a position in advance of the market moving.

This chapter illustrates the procedures involved in identifying cycles in market data, judging their statistical significance or probability of genuineness, and then combining cycles to obtain the direction that they indicate the market will take. The technique disclosed here is used by some of the most consistently successful futures traders. It is not available in standard texts on forecasting.

Many persons who have a passing acquaintance with Fourier transform series from their college days are under the impression that, although the Fourier transform can fully *describe* a data series, it cannot be used for forecasting. They repeat the idea that any time series can be described by its transform over the entire frequency range of 0 to 2π, but that an extrapolation of the corresponding cycles will merely repeat the data set for which they are the transform. This argument would be convincing if there were no frequencies for which a genuine cyclical influence is at work.

Our task is to try to determine which, if any, frequencies (that is, periods) stand out above the others and thus correspond to probable cycles in the data. Are there significant cycles embedded in the market data, with all the apparent "noise"? The answer is yes, there often are. And when there are, we can profit from knowledge of them.

Market price series often contain cycles that are present over long spans of time. But sometimes a cycle may be found in one span of data and not in another. What is one to make of this? Can cycles that are not consistently present still be useful? They can be, with some limitations. If one views market price series as output from a chaotic system,[1] then such ephemeral cycles may arise from the particular pattern that the market established over a recent span of time. For short-range forecasting these can be very useful if they track the market well. But their usefulness quickly vanishes as forecasts are carried further into the future. For reliable longer-term projections one must try to use cycles that are genuinely present over the long haul and not just a symptom of recent events.

In determining which cycles to use in forecasting one must make some choices that result in tradeoffs. For a short-range forecast should we use a relatively short data series, or a long series that will average out aberrations that tend to distort cycles in any given short span of time? If we use a short data series we can estimate the parameters of short cycles that are manifested in that data. But longer term cycles cannot be estimated. Remember the rule of thumb expressed in Chapter 5: To have any reliability in identification of a cycle we need a data series that spans at least five replications of the cycle in question. Is that a serious problem?

If we want a short-term forecast we can usually obtain one that works very well without including longer-term cycles. Short-period cycles are by their nature responsive over short periods of time. Long-period cycles usually do not rise or fall much in any given time interval. For example, a cycle with period 30 days and amplitude 3.0 will change by an average of $3/30 = 0.100$ per day. A much stronger long cycle, say one with period 350 days and amplitude 30, will change by an average of $30/350 = 0.086$ per day. Thus the longer cycle contributes less to the price movement of each day even though it is ten times as strong as the shorter cycle. In market price data cycle amplitude is usually proportional to cycle length or period.

SUCCESSIVE REMOVAL VS. ONE-PASS ANALYSIS

There are two main ways to estimate the cycles present in market data. The first is easier, but not so useful as the second. It is to perform a spectral

---

[1] In this context "chaotic system" is meant in the modern sense of one that may be modelled mathematically, but that is sensitive to initial conditions and minor random influences. The literature on chaos and the related fractal geometry is so extensive and readily available that we shall not venture off on that tangent here.

analysis of the time series of interest and then associate the peaks in spectral power (that is, amplitude) with particular cycles. To determine if the indicated cycles are significant, one can perform an array analysis for each cycle, and it may be accepted as significant if the Bartels' test value is below the selected cutoff.

A variant of the first method is to perform an array analysis on each cycle in a selected range of cycles, selecting for further consideration only those cycles that meet a specified Bartels test value. This technique has the ability to find cycles that are statistically significant even when they are not very strong.

Nevertheless, the second method is better for most forecasting applications. It is based on repeated spectral analyses. In each spectral analysis the cycle with the highest amplitude is identified. Then that cycle is removed from the data series. The resultant residual series is then subjected to spectral analysis again, and the process repeated. Longer-term cycles, which can be as long as the data series or as short as one-third the data series, are also removed in the process if they happen to have the highest amplitude even though their statistical significance cannot be determined from the data sample. These should be considered as trend or sub-trend cycles whose removal helps to sharpen the resolution with which the shorter cycles may be identified.

In performing the process of successive cycle identification and removal it is useful to calculate the Bartels test probability for each cycle as it is identified. In the synthesis of identified cycles that culminates the process, it is thus possible to combine only those cycles that are found to be significant.[2] One would have more confidence in a forecast based on a projection of such cycles than in one which included cycles with low probability of being genuine.[3]

EXAMPLE: SOYBEAN PRICES

To illustrate the process for identifying and forecasting with cycles we shall use daily closing (that is, settlement) prices for soybeans from January 1988 through December 1990. To avoid the problem of contract expiration, 90-day perpetual contracts[4] are used.

---

[2] As a practical matter the Bartels test is only calculated for cycles whose period is one-third or less the span of the data series being analyzed.

[3] The Bartels test takes into account the persistence and consistency of a cycle, which taken together indicate genuineness.

[4] A 90-day perpetual contract is based on a weighted average of two actual contracts that expire on either side of the 90-day ahead time. The concept appears to have originated with Robert Pelletier of Commodity Systems, Inc., Boca Raton, FL. Perpetual contract data are available from that and other firms. They can, of course, also be generated from raw commodity futures data.

Step 1: Spectral Analysis

First we shall perform a spectral analysis of the data to see if there are any encouraging signs of cycles. If there are not, then we should not waste our time by trying to use a technique not suited to the data.

Figure 10-1 contains a plot of spectral amplitude versus frequency in cycles per day. Because of the crowding of points it is useful to look at sections of the graph separately.

Figure 10-2 contains a plot of the low-frequency cycles. Note that the horizontal axis is now scaled in days in order to see more readily the periods that correspond to the peaks in amplitude.

Figure 10-3 contains a plot of the spectral amplitudes for cycles in the range of 19.9 days to 273 days. There are indications of several likely cycles in the data.

Finally, Figure 10-4 shows a plot of high-frequency cycles ranging from 8.88 to 21.3 days in length. This is a rather congested spectrum, although it may contain some significant cycles.

Note that the scale for the vertical axis is different for each of the graphs. Thus, the strength of cycles indicated at the higher frequencies (shorter periodicities) is generally less than at the lower frequencies (longer periodicities). Indications of cycles do not depend on the absolute strength of the spectral amplitude, but rather on the strength relative to cycles at surrounding frequencies.

Step 2: Successive Removal

Since it appears that several likely cycles exist in daily soybean settlement prices we shall proceed with the analysis. In order to obtain better resolution of the medium- to short-period (high- to medium-frequency) cycles we shall successively remove the cycles with the greatest amplitude in each pass. In the first pass the cycle we shall remove is one with a period spanning the entire data set of 750 days. It has an amplitude of 122.48. This is essentially a trend in the data. Because this cycle covers the entire data series we cannot use the Bartels test to judge its significance.

After removing the effects of a 750-day trend cycle, we find that the residual data series contains a cycle of 375 days, with an amplitude of 52.54. This may be viewed as a sub-trend in the data. Again, we cannot apply the Bartels test to judge its statistical significance, its probability of being genuine, because it is longer than one-third the length of the data series. We remove this cycle and then repeat the analysis.

Next we find a cycle of 187.5 days in the residual data series, with an amplitude of 30.68. This cycle has a Bartels test value of 0.1577, which

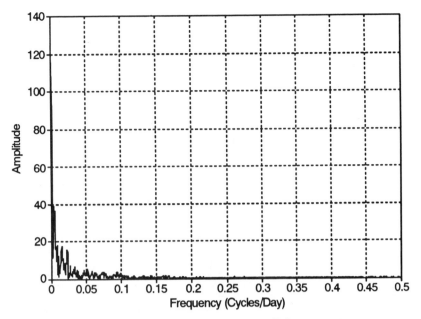

Figure 10-1 Spectral analysis—all frequencies.

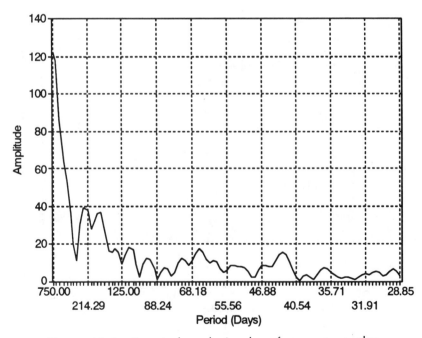

Figure 10-2 Spectral analysis—low-frequency cycles.

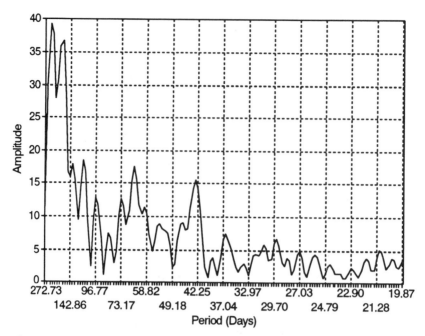

Figure 10-3 Spectral analysis—medium- to low-frequency cycles.

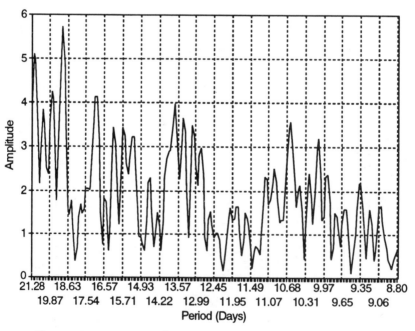

Figure 10-4 Spectral analysis—high-frequency cycles.

Table 10-1 Cycle parameters from 750 daily soybean settlement prices, January 1988–December 1990

"CY CC3 99T—Soybeans, 3 month perpetual contract"
"Parameters for synthesis/subtraction"

Amplitude	Phase	Period	Bartels Test
122.483052	178.822708	750.000000	−1.000000
52.541626	189.780969	375.000000	−1.000000
30.682811	120.050386	187.500000	0.157703
30.428261	115.500486	250.000000	−1.000000
17.000969	4.635193	115.384615	0.075965
13.649818	127.680608	150.000000	0.027419
13.384457	42.844705	65.217391	0.076073
13.282656	27.332664	42.857143	0.004142
11.994386	33.353413	71.428571	0.071890
10.589628	8.401895	51.724138	0.045409
9.989256	17.453357	45.454545	0.025094
8.290020	24.931511	78.947368	0.069486
7.619789	52.855589	60.000000	0.021516
7.678047	98.656230	107.142857	0.070666
7.472053	2.177531	36.585366	0.005153
6.875940	10.611440	93.750000	0.006660
5.475519	26.668370	29.411765	0.029295
5.025075	9.202602	48.387097	0.025360
4.803311	54.264396	55.555556	0.006354
4.650816	13.608189	18.987342	0.019849
4.393101	8.530754	17.045455	0.011343

means that it could have arisen by chance, or random influences in the data, about 16 times in 100.[5] We remove this cycle and then repeat the analysis on the residual data series.

Table 10-1 contains the parameters obtained by repetitive removal of cycles in the time series of 750 daily soybean settlement prices. The first column contains the cycle amplitude, the second column contains the phase, or point from the beginning of the data at which the cycle first reaches a peak, the third column the cycle period in days, and the last column contains the Bartels test associated with the cycle. For those cycles too long to have a Bartels test calculated for them a value of −1.00 is printed.

Figure 10-5 contains a plot of the original time series of soybean prices with two other series. The first is intertwined with the data series, and is a synthesis of all those cycles listed in Table 10-1. The second is represented by a lighter line, and is composed of a synthesis of only those cycles with Bartels test values less than 0.17, cycles that are likely to be genuine. The 0.17 is somewhat subjective.

[5] We must be careful about this. If we examine 1000 cycles, then a cycle that could arise by chance one time in a thousand is likely to do so. But such a cycle is not genuine.

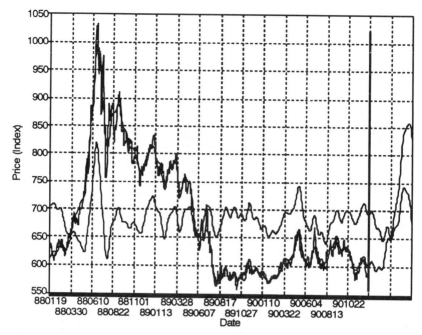

Figure 10-5 Time series of soybean prices, syntheses of cycles, and projections (time series Jan. 1988–Dec. 1990).

To the right of the dark vertical line at December 30, 1990, in the figure are projections, or forecasts, based on extending the synthesis of cycles into the future. The accuracy of the forecast may be verified by comparing these projections to the actual price behavior in soybean futures prices in 1991 for the first 100 trading days, or roughly five calendar months.

Are there any ways to judge how well a projection of cycles combined into a synthesized price series is likely to perform, other than to wait and see how the market behaves? Yes, there are. One way is to reserve some of the recent data—not use it to estimate the cycle parameters—and observe how well the cycle synthesis fits the unused data. Unfortunately, this method wastes some of the most valuable data, because recent data contain the essence of what drives the market today.

A second way to judge the ability of a cycle synthesis to track the market is to do a *backcast*. In this technique we reserve a holdout at the *beginning* of the data series. If the cycles used in the synthesis are genuine (or at least most of them are), then the combination of cycles should fit the early holdout sample that was not used in estimating the cycle parameters. This method has the advantage of not wasting the most recent market data, yet provides a fair test of how well a projection is likely to perform. In this case we judge effectiveness by forecasting back in time, thus the term backcasting.

USING A BACKCAST

Table 10-2 contains the parameters estimated for the last 300 points in the time series depicted in Figure 10-5 for daily soybean settlement prices. Comparison with Table 10-1 indicates that many of the cycles in both tables are close in period to one another. The 300-point series analyzed for Table 10-2 provides parameter estimates that are not so definitive as those contained in the 750-point analysis, but nevertheless some estimates are reasonably close between the two tables. The backcast holdout is thus 450 points, more than would normally be used, and more than necessary in order to indicate how well the forecasting technique of cycle synthesis can work. Figure 10-6 is a graph of the actual price data; a synthesis of all cycles, which is intertwined with the price data; and a synthesis of those cycles having Bartels test values under 0.10. To the right of the right-hand light vertical line we again have a forecast into the future. To the left of the left-hand light vertical line we have the backcast. In the "noisy" relatively sideways section at the middle of the graph the goodness of fit of the backcast to the data is a bit hard to discern. But matching up the major peaks and troughs in the data series to the synthesized series in the backcast suggests that the forecast should be useful in anticipating the price movement of the market.

Table 10-2 Cycle parameters from 300 daily soybean settlement prices, October 1989–December 1992

"CY CC3 99T—Soybeans, 3 month perpetual contract"
"Parameters for synthesis/subtraction"

Amplitude	Phase	Period	Bartels Test
22.641351	190.438168	300.000000	−1.000000
11.307057	28.994700	100.000000	−1.000000
11.269860	17.449172	38.709677	0.025644
7.091416	34.985267	48.000000	0.022703
5.615338	116.860587	150.000000	−1.000000
4.074962	12.695778	30.769231	0.090101
3.718371	40.643702	41.379310	0.071091
3.245899	17.327428	19.047619	0.043347
3.179139	34.432270	35.294118	0.024729
2.973311	8.254013	24.000000	0.025393
2.815408	18.097265	26.666667	0.014875
2.549981	16.341714	17.391304	0.012020
2.209506	50.833411	63.157895	0.068714
2.009190	8.713003	21.052632	0.045311
1.738498	6.327923	7.594937	0.016954
1.631857	14.330963	16.000000	0.115967
1.728848	11.443901	13.333333	0.053808
1.617297	6.124824	10.810811	0.044909
1.709589	4.589913	9.917355	0.037601
1.569642	4.050402	9.523810	0.037280
1.541303	2.243531	9.022556	0.033021

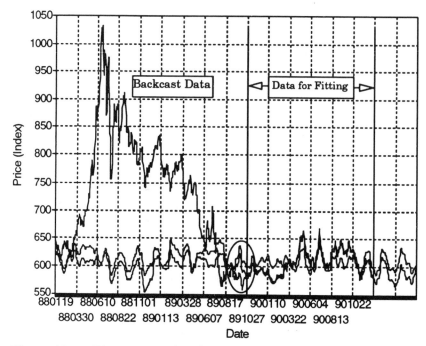

Figure 10-6 Time series of soybean prices, with forecast and back-cast syntheses and syntheses of cycles having Bartels' test values < 0.10 (time series Jan. 1988-Feb.1991).

Figure 10-7 contains a plot of a portion of the actual data series and of the two backcast series, enlarged to reveal detail. It is clear that the synthesized series are a good fit to the data in the backcast region, which was not used to estimate the cycle parameters. What is the basis of such a statement, when the synthesized series have different shapes from the price data? It is that the synthetic series call the *turning points* quite reliably and accurately in that region.

In Figure 10-8 boxes are labeled to focus attention on comparison between the data series and the synthesized backcast series. In the first two days of the backcast the synthetic series (that is, forecasts) indicate the market will head lower, and it does, with the exception of the second day before the end of the backcast period. In box A we see the forecasts calling a turn from up to down, and the market turns downward in that time frame. In box B we see the forecasts calling for a turn, and again the market turns on cue. In box C the forecasts show the market heading sharply lower, and it does. Box D has the forecasts turning from up to down, and the market turns as forecast. Similarly, box E indicates a turn that is realized. Box F suggests a dip in the market, and again this is realized in the price behavior. The forecast in box G

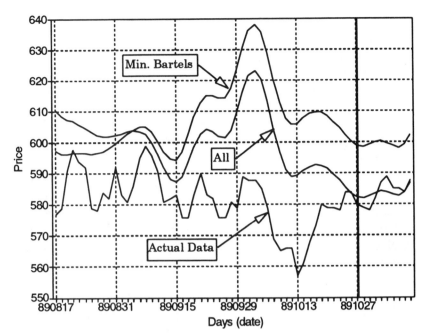

Figure 10-7 Enlarged graph of a portion of the soybean backcast, from Figure 10-6. (Points to the right of the dark vertical line are forecast.)

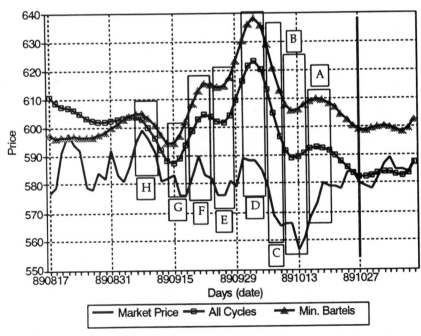

Figure 10-8 Annotated enlarged graph of a portion of the soybean backcast, from Figure 10-6. (Points to the right of the dark vertical line are forecast.)

shows a turn a day before the market switches from down to up. But this box is about six weeks away from the data used to estimate the cycle parameters for the forecast, so we might forgive it for not being so precise as it might be. Similarly, box H indicates a turn from up to down, and the market turns on cue.

It is very important to recognize that *a forecast that successfully calls turning points in market direction is a very useful forecast*. Never mind that it does not precisely indicate the market price. Any trader who can estimate turning points, and the relative magnitude of market movement, has a tremendous advantage over other traders who do not have such information. In comparison, those who use moving average penetrations to call market turns will be like the fellow who showed up for a date "a day late and a dollar short".

GOODNESS OF FIT

The goodness of fit between a forecast projection and the holdout data can be judged statistically by computing appropriate test values. Any standard text on statistics can be used to see how the chi-square test can be computed and used for this purpose. A test that is arguably better, but not so commonly covered, at least in elementary statistics tests, is the K-S (Kolmogorov-Smirnov). Both are easy to apply, especially with a spreadsheet program. Even with such formal tests, one must nevertheless decide upon a probability value for classifying whether the fit of forecast to actual data is precise enough. Often a judgment based on visual examination of forecast to holdout will be entirely satisfactory.

11

"PDQ" or "Q and D"?: Maximum Entropy Spectral Analysis and Linear Prediction

Maximum entropy spectral analysis (MESA) provides a useful alternative to Fourier analysis and the popular fast Fourier transform (FFT). MESA is a relatively new mathematical procedure. It was first proposed by John Parker Burg, who coined the acronym "MESA," in the 1960s.[1] According to Burg, the term *maximum entropy* " . . . corresponds to maximum information transformation rate . . . " in the channel capacity of a communication system.

In recent years MESA has received a great deal of attention from futures traders and publications aimed at them. As with many innovations before it, MESA has attracted both praise and scorn. To its dedicated followers, it has an almost magical ability to find cycles in data. To its detractors it is overrated and quirky. Which is it, pretty darned quick (PDQ) or quick and dirty (Q & D)? The answer is (1) neither and (2) both! For some time series the method is both fast and accurate. With other series it does not work well at all. And, to support those who call it quirky, there are time series for which it works well over some spans of the data but not others.

Unlike the FFT procedure, MESA does not assume that the data series used in an analysis repeats itself periodically. Thus it avoids "end effect" problems by making no assumptions about data outside the sample. Therefore it is useful even with small data samples, in contrast to the FFT.

---

[1] John Parker Burg, "Maximum Entropy Spectral Analysis," *Proceedings of the 37th Meeting of the Society of Exploration Geophysics,* 1967. Burg refers to the technique as *MESA* in his paper, "A New Technique for Time Series Data," presented at the NATO Advanced Study Institute on Signal Processing with Emphasis on Underwater Acoustics, Aug. 12-23, 1968.

THEORY AND MATH BEHIND MESA[2]

In mathematical terms, MESA can be expressed by the following equation,[3] which relates an unknown input u_n to an output signal s_n.

$$S_n = -\sum_{k=1}^{p} a_k s_{n-k} + G \sum_{\lambda=0}^{q} b_i u_{n-\lambda}, \qquad b_0 = 1 \tag{11-1}$$

where k, p, λ, and q are parameters such that $1 \leq k \leq p$, and $0 \leq \lambda \leq q$, and G is the gain of the model. In Equation 11-1, the output of the model, s_n, is a predictable, linear combination of historical model inputs and outputs. Consequently, the term *linear prediction* is applied to the model. Equation 11-1 may be transformed from the complex frequency plane to the z-plane by applying a z transform—defined as

$$z \equiv e^{2\pi i(f\Delta)} \tag{11-2}$$

where e is the usual base of natural logarithms and $f\Delta$ is the sampling frequency (frequency times sampling interval)—to both the input and output signals to obtain

$$S(z) = \sum_{n=-\infty}^{\infty} s_n z^n, \qquad U(z) = \sum_{n=-\infty}^{\infty} s_n z^n \tag{11-3}$$

The transformation yields the transfer function H(z) in Equation 11-4,

$$H(z) = \frac{S(z)}{U(z)} = G \frac{1 + \sum_{\lambda=1}^{q} b_i z^\lambda}{1 + \sum_{k=1}^{p} a_k z^k} \tag{11-4}$$

The numerator in 11-4 is the general "all-zero" model that corresponds to what is termed a pure moving average model in statistical forecasting literature. The denominator corresponds to the general "all-pole" model, a pure autoregressive model, which has been the most used, and useful, model.[4]

---

[2]This section may be skipped by those who are uncomfortable with mathematics without seriously detracting from the material that follows it.

[3]This section follows the article "Linear Prediction" by John Makhoul, *Proceedings of the IEEE*, 63 (April 1975), pp. 561–580; correction in *Proceedings of the IEEE*, 64 (Feb. 1976), p. 285.

[4]The mixed or autoregressive moving average model is referred to as the "pole-zero" model. The all-zero model is non-linear and thus less tractable than the all-pole model.

Readers who are familiar with the terminology of the Box-Jenkins methodology (Chapter 5) may recognize that the all-pole model is an AR (autoregressive) model. Unlike the usual Box-Jenkins method, here the forecast is fitted automatically by the procedure of MESA with linear prediction (hereafter MESALP), except that the forecaster may specify the number of poles to use, and whether the data are to be transformed before performing the forecast.

The all-pole model reduces to

$$s_n = -\sum_{k=1}^{p} a_k s_{n-k} + G u_n \tag{11-5}$$

where again G is the gain. And the associated all-pole transfer function model is

$$H(z) = \frac{G}{1 + \sum_{k=1}^{p} a_k z^k} \tag{11-6}$$

The *poles* of $H(z)$ are the roots of the denominator polynomial, and p is the order, or number of poles.

How does one compute the coefficients[5] in Equation 11-6? First the autocorrelation Φ_j for various lags is calculated

$$\Phi_j = < c_i c_{i+j} > \qquad j = \dots, -4, -3, -2, -1, 0, 1, 2, 3, 4, \dots \tag{11-7}$$

where the $<>$ indicate averaging over the sampled data from the function c_k: c_0 through c_N. If we have N data points, we can estimate the autocorrelation at N different lags of j, or

$$\Phi_j = \Phi_{-j} \approx \frac{1}{N-j} \sum_{i=0}^{N-1-j} c_i c_{i+j} \qquad j = 0, 1, 2, 3, \dots, N \tag{11-8}$$

According to the Wiener-Khinchin theorem, the Fourier transform of the autocorrelation is equal to the power spectrum of the data. And, in terms of the z transform, the Fourier transform is a Laurent series in z. The coefficients in Equation 11-6 must satisfy the relationship of Equation 11-9, where we now denote gain G by a_0. The *power*, $P(f)$, associated with a given frequency, f, is approximately

---

[5]This section is drawn from W. H. Press et. al, *Numerical Recipes* (Cambridge, England: Cambridge University Press, 1986).

$$\frac{a_0}{\left|1 + \sum_{k=1}^{M} a_k z^k\right|^2} \approx \sum_{j=-M}^{M} \Phi_j z^j \tag{11-9}$$

The series expansion on the left should agree term by term with the expression on the right in Equation 11-9. M, the *number of poles,* or *order,* must be less than N, but usually is chosen to be much smaller. As Press and coworkers point out, the left-hand side of Equation 11-9 "defines a sort of *extrapolation* of the autocorrelation function to lags larger than M, in fact even to lags larger than N . . . *larger than the run of data can actually measure.*" And they note "that this particular extrapolation can be shown to have . . . maximum *entropy* in a definable information-theoretic sense."

Solution of Equation 11-9 is facilitated by recognition of the fact that the relationship between the autocorrelations and the coefficients is linear and satisfies Equation 11-10 containing a symmetric Toeplitz matrix, with constant diagonal elements.

$$\begin{bmatrix} \Phi_0 & \Phi_1 & \Phi_2 & \cdots & \Phi_M \\ \Phi_1 & \Phi_0 & \Phi_1 & \cdots & \Phi_{M-1} \\ \Phi_2 & \Phi_1 & \Phi_0 & \cdots & \Phi_{M-2} \\ \cdots & & & & \cdots \\ \Phi_M & \Phi_{M-1} & \Phi_{M-2} & \cdots & \Phi_0 \end{bmatrix} \times \begin{bmatrix} 1 \\ a_1 \\ a_2 \\ \cdots \\ a_M \end{bmatrix} = \begin{bmatrix} a_0 \\ 0 \\ 0 \\ \cdots \\ 0 \end{bmatrix} \tag{11-10}$$

There are both direct and indirect methods for solving Equation 11-6. They require a great deal of computation, and there are important considerations regarding stability of $H(z)$, some of which arise from the inherent limitations upon accuracy of digital computers. Detailed consideration of these matters is beyond the scope of this work.[6]

USING MESA TO DETECT CYCLES

MESA can provide a useful alternative to Fourier transform-based spectral analysis (hereafter FBSA) for finding evidence of the presence of cycles in time series data. However, the frequency (or corresponding period) of cycles indicated to be present by the two basic methods will usually be somewhat different.

Spectral analysis based on the Fourier transform, as discussed in Chapter 7, requires smoothing, or filtering of either (1) the raw time series data or (2) the power spectrum. MESA does not require such smoothing. Also, FBSA

[6]The interested reader is referred to Makhoul, op. cit., or to Press et. al., ibid.

assumes that the data analyzed repeat indefinitely, that the data are a set identical to the set preceding and to the set following them. MESA makes no such assumption.

To illustrate what one may expect to find when a data set contains several strong cycles, a synthetic, or artificial time series will be analyzed here. Results from applying the method to market data can be compared to these idealized results. The synthetic data analyzed are for 1,100 points of a combination of 18 cycles for U.S. Treasury Bond futures. The cycles used in creating the synthesis were extracted from daily 3-month perpetual[7] T-bond futures.

Figure 11-1 contains a line graph of a MESA on the full 1,100 data points of the synthetic time series. The analysis used 500 poles and a grid, or mesh, of 20 points between the poles. The y-axis is on a logarithmic scale. Those spikes in the spectral power above 100 indicate the presence of strong and probably genuine cycles. The graph is annotated to show the precise periods corresponding to each spectral power peak. The frequency (that is, $f \Delta t$) for each may be easily calculated by taking the reciprocal of the period. For example, $1/327.9 = 0.00305$ cycles per day since daily observations were used in the analysis.

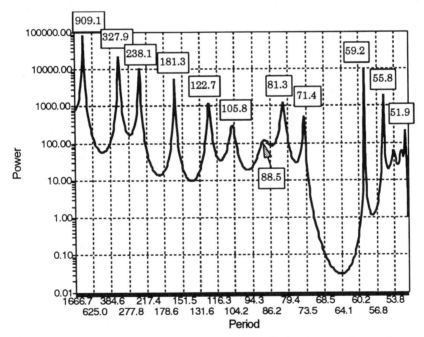

Figure 11-1 Maximum entropy spectral analysis of synthetic T-bonds (500 poles, grid 20).

[7]For a definition of perpetual contracts please refer to footnote 2 in Chapter 6.

Table 11-1   Parameters for synthesis/subtraction — 3-month
perpetual contract CBOT T-bonds

	Amplitude	Phase	Period	Bartels	MESA Period Nearest (500p,20g)
1.	5.060729	789.064881	891.000000	−1.000000	909.1
2.	0.506262	129.534163	405.000000	−1.000000	— —
3.	3.255525	10.855763	342.692308	−1.000000	327.9
4.	2.240240	31.685811	234.473684	0.078095	238.1
5.	0.693330	163.173354	171.346154	0.094282	161.3
6.	2.131873	133.524498	165.000000	0.038798	161.3
7.	0.830491	52.210811	165.000000	0.077700	161.3
8.	0.334789	129.867226	139.218750	0.019908	122.7
9.	0.810461	33.120792	103.604651	0.012043	105.8
10.	1.124230	69.145349	85.673077	0.028105	88.5
11.	1.247952	48.152887	82.500000	0.005050	81.3
12.	0.402158	58.360164	82.500000	0.001838	81.3
13.	0.773941	73.679298	74.250000	0.028169	71.4
14.	0.338710	36.946685	73.032787	0.021922	71.4
15.	0.564343	49.172378	59.400000	0.019009	59.2
16.	0.713650	6.272236	55.687500	0.023010	55.6
17.	0.213251	44.007623	55.687500	0.034352	55.6
18.	0.410745	15.074146	51.802326	0.007800	51.9

Table 11-1 displays the amplitudes, phases, and periods for each of the 18 component cycles contained in the synthetic data. Also, the Bartels test value is shown for each cycle. A Bartels test value of −1.0 is displayed for cycles for which the amount of data was insufficient to support the required calculations (cycles greater in length than one-third the number of days of raw data analyzed to obtain the cycles).

The last column in Table 11-1 contains the period of the MESA cycle corresponding most closely to the period of each cycle in the synthetic data. It is noteworthy that for cycles of period 165.0, 82.5, and 65.6875, where these cycles are present with a multiplicity of two, the MESA spectrum identified one cycle only. However, ordinary, one-pass FBSA would do no better. The reason is that the methods associate only *one* power or amplitude with each frequency (and thus each period). The parameters for the cycles in the synthetic series were obtained by successive elimination of the highest amplitude (greatest power) cycle in each pass through the raw market data.[8] Thus, the same period of cycle but with different phase and amplitude could be found.

Note that a given time series can usually be approximated by more than one combination of cycles! The question of the existence of a genuine cycle — caused by some economic, political, or other influence — is different from the

---

[8]That analysis was performed automatically with the program PowRcast^{tm}, developed by this author.

question of what combination of cycles provides a close approximation to a time series. The combination that provides a close approximation may, but is not required to, represent a combination of cycles that are genuine in the Bartels test sense of being both persistent and consistent over time. Given that the data analyzed here are synthesized by combining pure sinusoidal waves, it should be no surprise that MESA and FBSA often yield somewhat different cycle indications.

Figure 11-2 displays the power spectrum obtained by applying the MESA technique to the last 200 data points of the 1100 in the synthetic time series. Because of the much shorter data series, only 100 poles were used, with a fine grid of 50 divisions between poles. Although a large amount of power was indicated for cycles longer than 625 days, no spectral peaks were evident and thus that portion of the spectrum is not plotted. Comparison with Figure 11-1 reveals that the spectral peaks correspond to periods somewhat different from those obtained with the longer data series.

It is noteworthy that MESA, in contrast to FBSA, usually marks indications of cycles with unambiguous sharp spikes at the associated frequency or period. FBSA often shows gradually rising and declining power, and is characterized by the side lobes associated with "leakage" from power at strong cycles.

MESA is subject to a number of influences, some of which are beyond the user's control. The length of time series available for analysis, the fineness

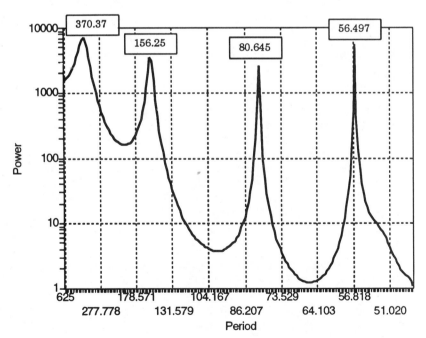

Figure 11-2 Maximum entropy spectral analysis of synthetic T-bonds (100 poles, grid 50).

of sampling interval, the number of poles, and the grid selected all influence the MESA power spectrum. Does that mean that MESA is difficult, or tricky to use in forecasting by extrapolation into the future? The answer, fortunately, is "No." The next section discusses using MESA with *linear prediction* (MESALP) for forecasting.

FORECASTING WITH LINEAR PREDICTION

The mathematics behind linear prediction are complex, and the method should not be confused with simple linear (straight line) extrapolation. Fortunately, one does not have to be a rocket scientist/mathematician to *use* MESALP with market data for forecasting. MESALP lends itself well to computer solution with suitable data sets. But one must nevertheless be cautious in interpreting and using any computer-generated forecasts because round-off errors that accumulate over lengthy strings of computations can sometimes invalidate the final results.

Computer programs exist[9] that implement MESALP, and it is not necessary to understand the underlying mathematics to use them. Of course, those do-it-yourself persons who wish to develop their own implementation can do so with investment of sufficient time and effort; the work by Press et al. should be consulted before undertaking such a project.

The left side of Equation 11-9 can be used to extrapolate, or forecast, into the future. Because the relationship between the autocorrelations and the coefficients is linear, a forecast based on it is referred to as *linear prediction*. Note that this should not be confused with linear (straight line) extrapolation of the data that one might perform with a least-squares projection. It is much more complex than that.[10]

---

[9]Several microcomputer programs that use the technique exist. The program used to illustrate the MESALP method here is this author's Autocast™. It should not be confused with another program, sold under the name of the mathematical procedure, MESA. Those who wish to develop their own adaptation should consult Press et al., *Numerical Recipes.*

[10]Press et al., *Numerical Recipes,* provide a complete description of the procedure for forecasting with MESA. It involves solving for the *linear prediction coefficients, d_j,* in the linear filter equation

$$y_n = \sum_{j=1}^{N} d_j y_{n-j} + x_N$$

where y_N is the *next* value, which is predicted from the *previous N* values. There is also a stability condition that must be satisfied. For stability of the predictor, the equation

$$z^N - \sum_{j=1}^{N} d_j z^{N-j} = 0$$

must have all N roots inside the unit circle ($|z| \leq 1$).

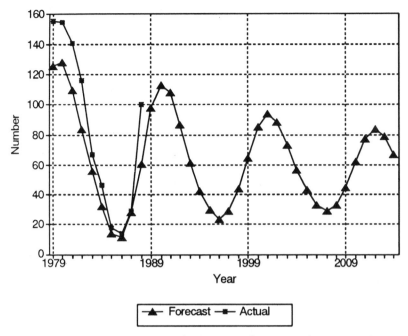

Figure 11-3 Sunspot annual averages, forecast (data 1847–1988, 23 poles, holdout 10).

Figure 11-3 illustrates the graphic output from analysis of annual sunspot data (see Chapter 8), which are characterized by the presence of strong and rather consistent cycles. The forecast data and the holdout data overlap for a purpose: The degree to which actual, historical holdout data correspond to forecast data indicates how good a fit there is. If the fit is good, with the turning points (tops and bottoms) well-matched, then one may be reasonably confident in the forecasts obtained from the data set used. Once a good fit has been achieved, the forecast can be redone with a holdout sample size of zero. Figure 11-4 illustrates the result from redoing the sunspot forecast with zero holdout.

In general, MESALP works best for forecasting when a relatively short data series, usually 100 to 200 data points, is used. It may be used with data transformed by taking logarithms, first differencing, or both. The method can often be used to obtain better results with short data series than FFT can provide. With long series, Fourier-based spectral analysis methods can provide better fits to data.

In using MESALP the number of poles must be specified. Computer implementations may initially select a number that will normally provide good results. The user then may adjust the number of poles until a satisfactory fit is obtained or the method is found unsuited to the data. If the number of poles specified is too large, a computer program may take too many iterations in searching for a solution or may project a forecast that is "explosive"—one

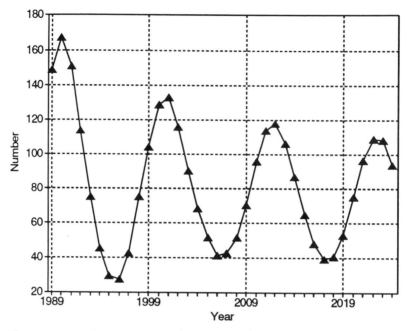

Figure 11-4   Sunspot annual averages, forecast (data 1847–1988, 23 poles, no holdout).

that jumps from larger to smaller values in each consecutive period. When that happens, fewer poles must be used. The fewer the number of poles it takes to achieve a satisfactory fit, the better. As the number of poles increase, computation time increases significantly.

MESA and Longer Cycles

Can MESA capture the presence of longer cycles even when a short data series is available for analysis? The answer is a qualified "Yes." If the data have cycles whose phases (timing of highs and lows) are constant, MESALP can find and use them. But over a long data set there are normally some shifts in phase. As a consequence, some cycles may not be identified and used.

Consider Figure 11-5, which contains plots of actual and forecast series for U.S. T-bond futures. The forecast series in this figure is a synthetic composite, or combination, of cycles found to be present in the data.[11] The vertical

---

[11]The analysis and forecast shown in the figure were carried out with PowRcast[TM], a program developed by this author to automate the lengthy analysis one would carry out with the set of CAP III[TM] programs. The program employs a proprietary algorithm designed to provide a close fit to the historical data.

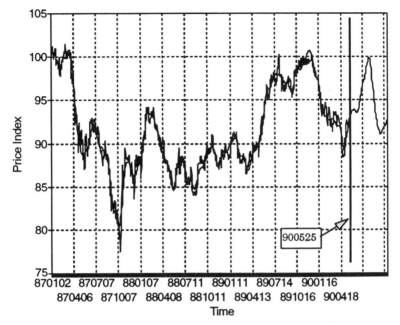

Figure 11-5 Three-month perpetual T-bond futures with forecast (data from January 2, 1987, to May 25, 1990). The forecast line is the one that extends to the right of the heavy vertical line.

line denotes the end of the historical data. Points to its right are the forecast. To the left, the historical and synthetic series closely intertwine, indicating a very good fit of synthetic to historical data.

Now refer to Figure 11-6. It contains the MESALP forecast obtained from the synthetic data series of T-bond futures (Jan. 2, 1987–May 25, 1990). There are no phase shifts in the pure sine wave cycles contained in the synthesis. The synthetic series is obtained by addition of the pure sine waves. Note how well the MESALP forecast fits the holdout sample (May 14–25, 1990). Such a close fit was not possible from the historical data. This illustrates how the MESALP method can provide a very close fit and useful forecast when the historical data contain cycles that are consistent in both length (period or frequency) and phase (timing).

Figure 11-7 repeats the analysis shown in Figure 11-6, but with a holdout sample of zero length. Comparison of the plotted series to that for the forecast in Figure 11-5 indicates a near-perfect fit. This suggests another use of MESALP.

For those who make predictions from a synthesis of cycles found to be present in historical data, MESALP may be used to *extend* the synthetic series because the fit is so precise. Thus, if one needs to extend a linear

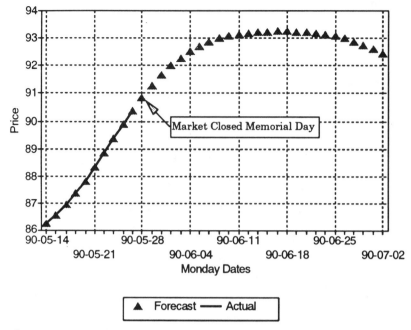

Figure 11-6 T-bond synthetic time series, actual and forecast (200 data points, 21 poles).

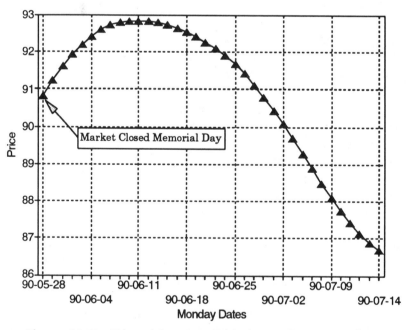

Figure 11-7 T-bond forecast (200 data points, 21 poles).

combination of pure sine waves MESALP can provide the numbers very quickly when there is no time to re-estimate the parameters of the component cycles.

Case Study: T-bond Futures Forecast

Now let us look at a forecast of U.S. T-bond futures made with MESALP. Figure 11-8 contains a forecast using 33 poles and a holdout sample of 5 points. Figure 11-9 contains a forecast with 44 poles and also a holdout of 5 points. It is apparent that there is little difference between the two forecasts. However, the forecast using 44 poles does take longer to run. In keeping with the principle that the fewer poles it takes to do the job, the better, we will use 33 poles and a holdout of zero to make our final forecast, contained in Figure 11-10. By the time you read this the forecast will have long been proven either accurate or inaccurate. You can judge whether or not the method merits your further attention. In fairness to both yourself and the method, however, you might see how well it works with other data series in your current time frame before deciding.

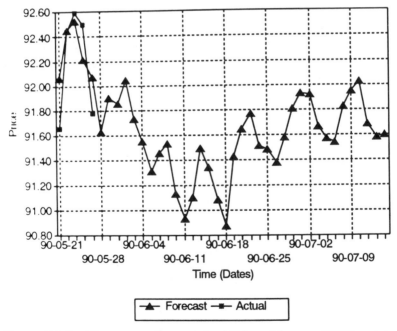

Figure 11-8 Three-month perpetual T-bond forecast (176 points history, 33 poles).

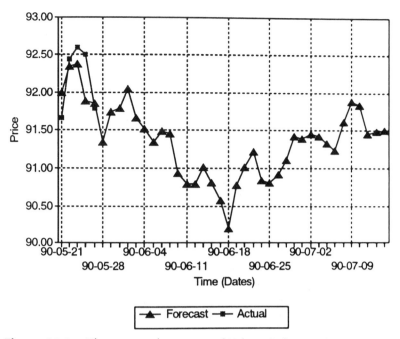

Figure 11-9 Three-month perpetual T-bonds forecast (176 points history, 44 poles).

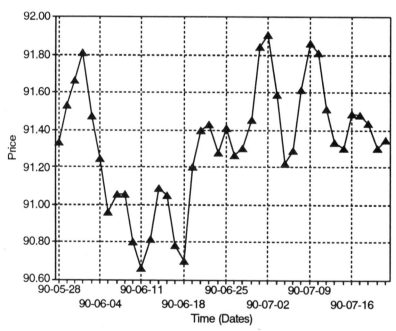

Figure 11-10 Three-month perpetual T-bond forecast with no holdout (176 points history, 33 poles).

CAVEATS

Like the allegorical "little girl who had a little curl," when MESALP is good it is very, very good, and when it is not it is impossible. Use of a holdout sample and experimentation with the number of poles and with first difference and/or logarithm transformations will reveal whether the technique is suitable for a given data set. Note that the method may work well for a data series for a while, and then not provide useful results for a time before again working well. There are no hard-and-fast rules about MESALP. Each user should try to develop an intuitive feeling about its application by using it on a variety of data. Finally, although it is often very useful, faster, and more convenient when it is suitable, MESALP should not be considered a substitute for techniques that are more robust with large data sets containing a lot of spurious "noise," or which may contain more than one cycle of the same period with different phases.

12

Comprehensive Case Study

Previous chapters covered the essential theory and application of the tools that will be used in this chapter to illustrate step-by-step what a complete analysis and forecast entails. You will be spared the details described in prior chapters without losing the essentials of the procedures involved. With an understanding of this chapter, and appropriate computer software,[1] you will be able to perform the analysis and interpret the results along with some of the world's most successful traders.

The focus for this comprehensive case study is the U.S. Treasury Bond contract traded on the Chicago Board of Trade (CBOT). The particular data employed are for a 90-day perpetual contract. The rationale for such contracts is to reduce the effects of expiration on traded futures contracts without seriously compromising the quality of analysis in regard to forecasting.[2] Perpetual contract data are available from several data sources, such as Commodity Systems, Inc. (CSI, Boca Raton, FL) and National Computer Network (Chicago). For those who wish to calculate them the procedure is described in a brochure available from CSI.

The CBOT T-bond futures are the most actively traded contracts in the world. They provide great liquidity and are volatile enough to offer opportunities for large profits to successful traders. T-bond futures are amenable

---

[1]Professional-quality programs by this author that automate the techniques illustrated are available. For those who prefer to develop their own, some of the software tools used to illustrate this chapter can be constructed from books such as W. H. Press et al., *Numerical Recipes* (Cambridge England: Cambridge University Press, 1986), which is available for both Pascal and C language compilers. Others can be constructed from publications available from the Foundation for the Study of Cycles, Irvin, CA, and books on spectral analysis and the calculus of observations.

[2]Footnote 2 in Chapter 6 (p. 106) explains how perpetual contracts are constructed.

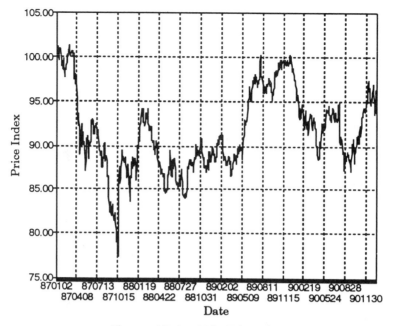

Figure 12-1 U.S. T-bonds.

to the procedures covered in previous chapters, even though somewhat challenging. Other futures may be even better suited, but offer less liquidity or present other problems.

Figure 12-1 contains a plot of T-bond futures settlement prices from January 2, 1987, through January 18, 1991. Holidays have been filled in with a weighted average of the two days before and the two days after. The day before and the day after receive twice the weight in the average as the days two before and two after. This provides a smooth transition into the holiday and out of it. Experience shows that simply putting the price of the last trading day in for the holiday works almost as well.

ORDINARY SPECTRAL ANALYSIS

The first step in determining whether or not forecasting based on cycles in the data is likely to be worth the effort is to run spectral analysis to see whether cycles seem to be present. We do this first with ordinary spectral analysis (*not* fast Fourier transform-based spectral analysis).

Figure 12-2 shows the spectrum for both long- and short-frequency cycles, plotted against time in days on the horizontal axis. Normally spectra are plotted with frequency on the horizontal axis, but it may be easier for some readers to appreciate the lengths of likely cycles in terms of trading days. It appears from the large amplitude at about 350 days, and the rising trend in amplitudes, that the raw data used in this analysis may contain a trend.

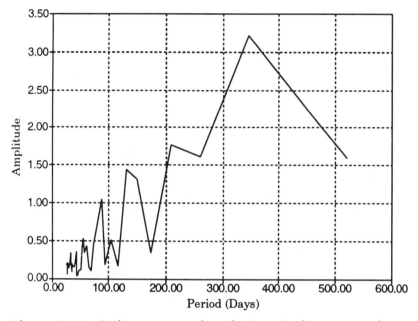

Figure 12-2   Ordinary spectral analysis, periods 2 to 520 days.

This might distort the signals of higher frequency cycles, so we need to be careful.

By examining Figure 12-2, it appears that cycles of about 350, 210, 140 to 160, 100, and 80 may be present. A clearer indication is found by simply replotting the data for cycles of less than about 170 days. Figure 12-3 contains

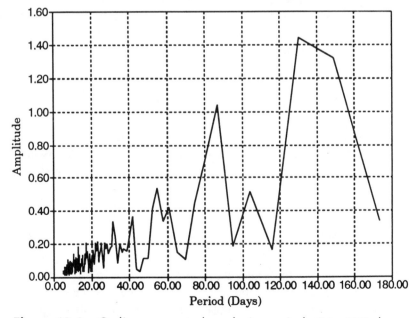

Figure 12-3   Ordinary spectral analysis, periods 2 to 175 days.

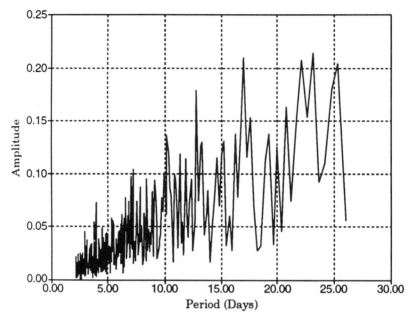

Figure 12-4   Ordinary spectral analysis, periods 2 to 27 days.

this graph. It suggests the presence of cycles of about 60, 55, 42, and 31 days in addition to those indicated in Figure 12-2. The spectrum for cycles of period less than 27 days is very "busy." Figure 12-4 contains a graph of this portion of the spectrum.

Ordinary spectral analysis is very useful but, as was shown in Chapter 11, maximum entropy spectral analysis as developed by Burg can provide a sharper picture of the spectrum. Therefore, let us next apply maximum entropy spectral analysis to the data.

MAXIMUM ENTROPY SPECTRAL ANALYSIS

The plots presented below of the spectrum from application of maximum entropy spectral analysis are for sections of the spectrum. This is necessary in order to reveal details that would be obscured if the entire spectrum were put into one graph.

On the Raw Data

To see how well the ordinary and maximum entropy spectral analysis agree, we first perform the maximum entropy method on the raw data (that is, without taking logarithms or differencing). Figure 12-5 contains a plot of the spectrum for cycles of period 200 to 500 days. It is rather uninteresting and

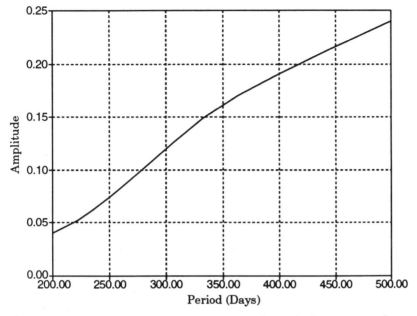

Figure 12-5 Maximum entropy spectral analysis on raw data, cycles 200 to 500 days.

reveals what we suspected from the ordinary spectral analysis: the presence of a trend. We shall deal with that later.

Things become more interesting in Figure 12-6, which contains a plot of the spectrum for cycles 200 days and less in length. Indications are present for cycles of about 140, 85, 70, and 40 days. Figure 12-7 focuses more closely on cycles of 25 days and less. Indications exist for cycles of about 22.5, 20, 17, 15, 13, and 10 to 11 days. Cycles may exist for shorter periods also, but although their cumulative effects can be significant, individually they seldom influence price movements as much as the longer cycles.

On the First Differences

Because a trend appears to be contained in the raw data, we next examine the first differences of the data. Remember that these are simply the settlement price on each day less the settlement price on the previous day. First differencing has a very powerful effect in eliminating a linear trend and reducing very long-period (very low-frequency) cycles. This is evident in the graphs of the spectrum for the differenced series.

Figure 12-8 displays a plot of the spectrum for the first differenced series for cycles of 200 days or less. Note how the upward trend in the spectrum has been eliminated. The indications of cycles of about 140, 85, 70, and 40 days remain, but now we may have more confidence in them.

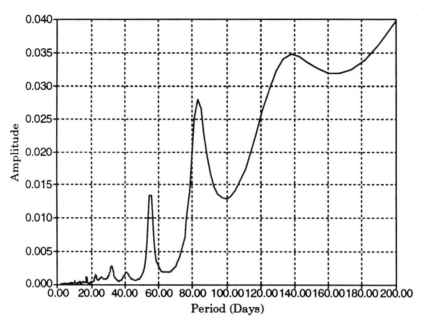

Figure 12-6 Maximum entropy spectrum analysis on raw data, cycles 200 days and less.

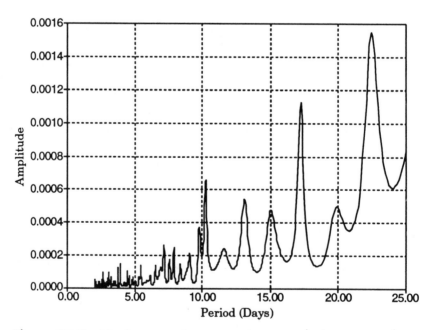

Figure 12-7 Maximum entropy spectrum analysis on raw data, periods 25 days or less.

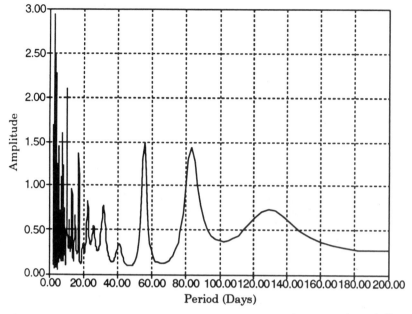

Figure 12-8 Maximum entropy spectrum analysis on first differences, periods 200 days or less.

Figure 12-9 is a similar plot of cycles of period 25 days or less. The cycle indicated to be present in Figure 12-7 at about 22.5 days now appears much weaker, as does the one for 20 days. However, some of the shorter-period (higher-frequency) cycles now appear relatively stronger than before.

MAXIMUM ENTROPY WITH LINEAR PREDICTION

The spectra of both ordinary and maximum entropy spectral analysis, the latter performed on both raw data and first differences, suggest that the price index of T-bonds may be forecast using techniques based on cycles. Thus, we shall first apply maximum entropy spectral analysis with linear prediction (MESALP), and see how well it works with this data series.

To see how well a MESALP will do, we first compare a forecast to a holdout sample of the most recent data. In the process of doing this we try several different values for the number of poles used in the MESALP process. This is largely subjective in the sense that the optimal number of poles used is a matter of judging when the best fit has been obtained.

When the holdout sample is very large we get a general sense of whether or not the method will provide a reasonably good fit to the holdout data, but we must realize that the further into the future we carry any forecast, the less reliable the forecast becomes. Thus, in Figure 12-10 we see that the forecast

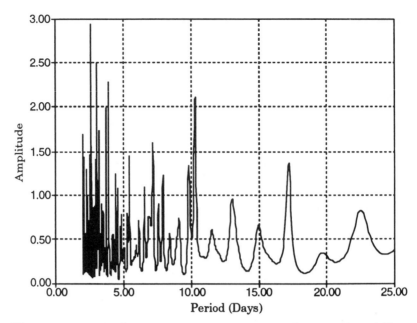

Figure 12-9 Maximum entropy spectrum analysis on first differences, periods 25 days or less.

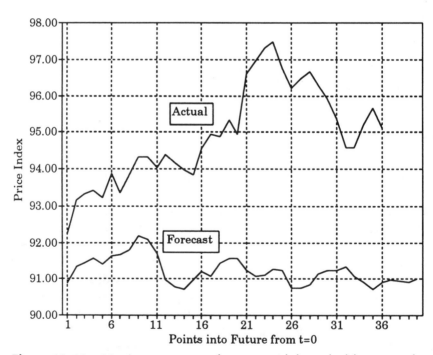

Figure 12-10 Maximum entropy forecast with large holdout sample.

accounts for many of the peaks and troughs along the 36 points in the holdout sample but does not show the proper amplitude for the peak at point 24, nor does it account for the apparent trend in the data.

Having established that the fit is reasonably good for the smaller peaks and troughs we next try a smaller holdout sample, five data points. The results of this are shown in Figure 12-11. The forecast at first glance does not appear to do well, but closer examination reveals it captures the direction of change in the first four points rather well. And, for the fifth point it does indicate a sharp downturn, albeit one day early. This suggests that this method should probably be more effective for position trading, where longer-term positions are established, than for day trading.

Now let us look at the results of using the method during a time in which no forecast method could be expected to perform well. The United Nations military action during early 1991 in the Persian Gulf,[3] affected all financial markets. Thus, a forecast that was made beforehand could not fairly be expected to perform well. Nevertheless, as Figure 12-12 shows, with the exception of January 18, 1991, the performance is not bad. It is actually quite good from day 6 to day 13 in the forecast. The actual market prices in the days shown in the graph were all affected by the prelude to war or the actual event of war. In a period without such a strong unexpected or random influence

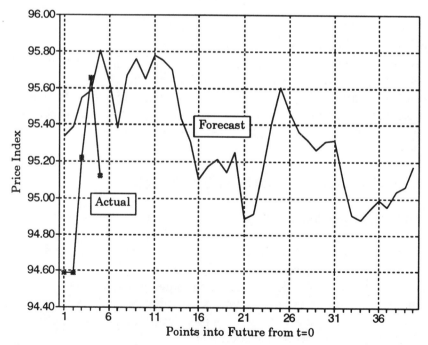

Figure 12-11 Maximum entropy forecast with small holdout sample.

[3]In Arab nations this body of water is known as the Arabian Gulf.

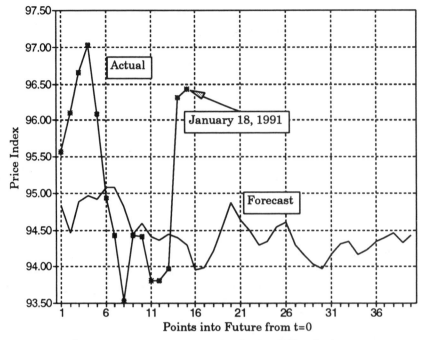

Figure 12-12   Forecast results in difficult times.

on the market we could expect better results. Regardless of how much faith we have in a forecasting method, in times of great uncertainty we should not fool ourselves into thinking that we can forecast the *short-run* direction of any market by forecasting. In fact, even in normal times random influences will practically guarantee that the forecast for any given period will be off the mark somewhat, even though on the average the forecast performs well.

FORECASTING WITH SYNTHESIS OF CYCLES

The ordinary and maximum entropy spectral analyses tentatively identified the presence of a number of cycles in the T-bond data. Now we will use these cycles to develop a forecast. The procedure used is to successively remove the strongest (that is, highest amplitude or power) cycle at each stage, and repeat the analysis. You will be spared the mountain of detail here, but just so you understand what is involved, here is what has been done to prepare the forecast. We shall use some 700 data points, reserving some at the beginning for backcast goodness-of-fit determination.

In Step One we remove a trend cycle, one that has a period the length of the data series being analyzed. It has an amplitude of 4.75 or, in terms of T-bond pricing, 4-24 ($4\frac{24}{32}$), and a phase of 383.798. Because the cycle is long relative to the data it is not possible to calculate the Bartels test value. Thus, we record a minus one for the Bartels test.

Next, after removing the 500-day trend cycle, we repeat the spectral analysis, and find that a 250-day cycle has the highest amplitude at this stage, 2.188 (2-6 or $2\frac{6}{32}$). Its phase is 143.82, and again we cannot calculate the Bartels test value. We remove this cycle and repeat the spectral analysis on the residual time series.

Now we find that a cycle of 125 days has the greatest amplitude, 1.66 (1-21 or $1\frac{21}{32}$). It has a phase of 61.69 and a Bartels test value of 0.05321, that is, the probability that this cycle could be due to chance is just over one in twenty. (The Bartels test is calculated in the array analysis covered in detail in Chapter 8. Appendix B provides detail on the test.) We remove this cycle and once again repeat the spectral analysis on the residual series.

Over and over again the analysis is repeated, each time removing the cycle with the greatest amplitude in the spectral analysis of the residual series at each stage. Eventually we get to a point at which the greatest amplitude suggests that we can stop the analysis without losing much valuable information.

Table 12-1 contains the parameters obtained from the analysis described above: amplitude, phase, period, and Bartels test value. These are used to create synthetic series that can be compared to the actual settlement prices of the T-bond futures.

Table 12-1 Forecasting 3-month perpetual contract CBOT T-bond futures with cycle synthesis

"CT CC3 99—3-Month Perpetual Contract CBT T-Bond Futures"
"Parameters for synthesis/subtraction"

Amplitude	Phase	Period	Bartels
4.751430	383.798493	500.000000	−1.000000
2.188391	143.819570	250.000000	−1.000000
1.663444	61.691806	125.000000	0.053210
1.669180	515.952526	700.000000	−1.000000
1.431332	240.114481	388.888889	−1.000000
1.154226	35.606604	92.105263	0.017231
1.017112	132.415658	194.444444	0.094762
0.735023	122.366652	145.833333	0.033476
0.521849	57.905936	63.636364	0.036163
0.427555	45.650894	50.000000	0.010527
0.331105	51.492233	72.916667	0.014809
0.308012	12.359890	30.973451	0.042069
0.290780	30.022631	81.395349	0.040487
0.283411	31.565880	36.842105	0.024018
0.282746	528.295174	700.000000	−1.000000
0.278596	9.864434	21.875000	0.015552
0.268973	2.505790	17.241379	0.003483
0.261323	40.231995	42.682927	0.019399
0.243413	8.547809	112.903226	0.061162
0.234957	21.535271	25.925926	0.006748
0.235607	7.165324	32.407407	0.003723

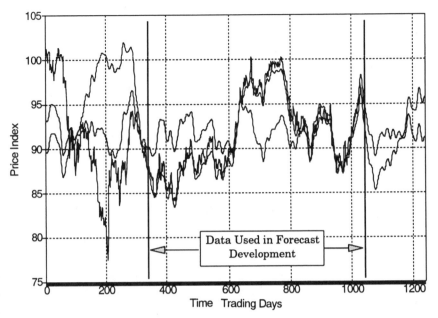

Figure 12-13   Forecast using cycle synthesis.

In Figure 12-13 three series are plotted: The darkest line is the actual T-bond settlement prices: the next darkest is the synthesis of all cycles, even those for which the Bartels test is large or could not be calculated; and the light line represents those cycles for which the Bartels test is less than or equal to a specified level. In the present case the light line is for cycles whose Bartels test values are 0.10 or less. The two vertical lines represent the boundaries of the data actually used in determining the cycle parameters. To the left of the vertical line at about point 350 are backcast points; the actual data in that region were not used in fitting the cycles. It is clear that combination of cycles with Bartels test values of 0.10 or less fits the actual data very well in the backcast region. This implies that the fit in the forecast region should also be good.

Points to the right of the vertical line at about 1050 are forecasts into the future—points not corresponding to data used to develop the forecast. Keeping in mind that the forecast period includes the outbreak of war in the Persian Gulf, you the reader may judge with perfect hindsight how well the forecast fits the period from mid-January 1991 to approximately the beginning of 1992.

CONCLUSION

This chapter has shown how forecasts of T-bond futures prices can be prepared using maximum entropy spectral analysis with linear prediction and using a combination, or synthesis, of cycles determined to be present in the data.

The procedures employed in this chapter require a considerable investment in time and effort. However, traders who successfully employ them will attest to their effectiveness. And for those who can justify the cost, computer software that automates the process of implementing the procedures illustrated are available.

Traders should realize that, no matter what technique of forecasting is used, there will be random influences that will prevent the forecast for any particular day from being perfectly on target. What one can hope to find in a technique that is close to perfection is a forecast that calls the turning points accurately and that tracks trends with a reasonable degree of precision.

13

Using Cycles for Spread Trading and Hedging

Many traders prefer to use spreads or straddles rather than to take outright long or short positions in futures. Motivations vary but often relate to the lower risk and margin associated with spread trades or to perceptions about seasonal or cyclical relationships between commodities or different contract months within the same commodity.

The analytical techniques and forecasting methods discussed in the preceding chapters of this book are applicable to spread trades. They can be applied in two ways. First, the individual sides or legs of the spread may be analyzed and forecast as in prior chapters, and the spread based on the forecasts. Second, the historical spread relationship itself may be analyzed and forecast.

In this chapter three spreads out of the great number of possibilities are used for purpose of illustration: Chicago Wheat vs. Chicago Corn; T-bonds vs. Eurodollars; and Gold vs. Silver. No claim is made for these combinations offering the most profitable trading potential. They were chosen simply as representative of agricultural, financial, and metals futures. Many others, such as the Standard & Poor's vs. Value Line Index could have been used, but would not add anything to the exposition. Although the techniques can in principle be applied to intracommodity spreads, that will not be done here.

WHEAT/CORN

Chicago wheat is the soft red winter variety. The crop is planted in the late summer or fall, and the established grass passes the winter months under the snow. Without snow cover the crop suffers in cold weather. In the spring the grass has a head start on growth, and it matures in the summer and early fall, depending on the latitude where it is grown. It is used primarily for cake flour, soda crackers, and similar products (the hard red variety is used for bread products).

Chicago corn is planted in the late spring or early summer since this plant is not frost-hardy. Late spring thaws, too much rain, especially at planting time, not enough rain during the growing season—all can adversely affect the crop.

Most corn is used for animal feed or for processing into high-fructose corn syrup. Little is used directly for human nourishment. Wheat, in contrast, is used mostly for products consumed directly by humans, and only inferior grades are used for animal feed except when the price is so low relative to feed grains like corn that its use for that purpose is cost effective. Both grains figure prominently in export sales to the Soviet republics and other nations. Both can be grown on much the same land in much of the midwestern United States and thus an increase in production of one may lead to a decline of the other.

What makes a wheat/corn spread interesting is that the two grains are similar in many respects yet maintain distinct differences. Thus there is a logic to their relative prices over time. This serves to explain the popularity of this spread among traders. The Chicago Board of Trade features charts of the spread in its regular *CBOT Ag/Metals Update* series.

Figure 13-1 is a chart of daily wheat and corn prices for September 1988-December 1990 as well as the price of wheat less the price of corn. We shall

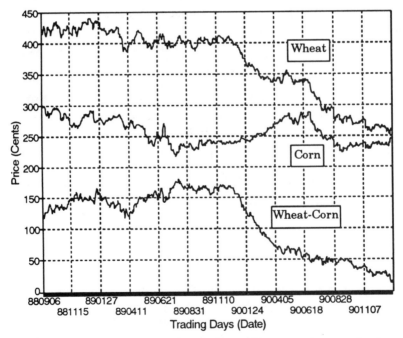

Figure 13-1   Wheat and corn, daily settlement prices and price difference, September 1988–December 1990.

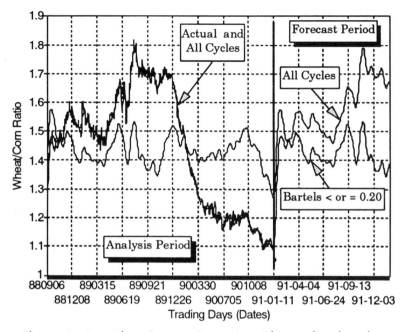

Figure 13-2   Wheat/corn price ratio with two fitted cycles.

analyze the individual price series, and the *ratio* of the price of wheat to that of corn.

Figure 13-2 is a plot of the wheat/corn ratio along with two fitted series.[1] The first of the fitted series contains points synthesized from all cycles extracted from the data. The second contains only those cycles with Bartels' test values of 0.20 or less. In this analysis no backcast holdout sample was reserved. We note immediately there is something suspicious: The fitted series appear to be repeating their exact form in the forecast period. (Remember the Fourier transform for an ascending straight line in Chapter 7.) The problem is not so much in the synthesis of all cycles but rather in that for those significant at a Bartels value of 0.20 or less. A synthesis of significant cycles does not normally repeat itself in the period immediately following the data subjected to analysis.[2] One thing we might do is synthesize only those cycles for which the Bartels test value is 0.10 or less. This can be done, but the synthetic series is little different from that of the significant cycles in Figure 13-2. Next we shall see what happens when we analyze wheat and corn prices

---

[1]Note that the x-axis dates in the form 880906 correspond to year, month, and day in the actual data series, while those in the form 91-01-11 correspond to forecast (future) year, month, and day.

[2]When only integer (whole-number) harmonics are used in the spectral analysis to scan for cycles, the problem is more likely to occur than when fractional harmonics are used. The reason is that when only integer harmonics are used the results are constrained so that the entire pattern of the data under analysis must be fitted by a fixed and finite number of cycles that might not correspond to those actually present in the data.

separately, then combine the separate synthetic series and compare to those in Figure 13-2.

In Figure 13-3 is a plot of the series from Figure 13-2 plus the two synthetic series obtained by calculating ratios of the separate forecast series. The fit is good, so close that one must look carefully to see a distinction. The close agreement in the forecast region between the projection of the synthetic ratio series and the ratio of the synthetic corn and wheat series suggests that perhaps our concern about the repetitiveness of the wave form was possibly greater than it need be. Nevertheless, extra caution should be exercised. In the forecast region we should place emphasis on the series based on cycles gauged to be significant at a Bartels test value of 0.20 or less. Furthermore, before placing any trade orders for the spread, especially since we have some lingering concern about the projection of the synthetic series, we should obtain additional supporting information. This could be either of a fundamental or technical nature, but whatever its form we should seek guidance from outside the price data used in the analysis.

If the projection based on significant cycles is accurate, the wheat/corn ratio will drift sideways to downward until late June or early July of 1991, then head upward until mid-September. Then it will fall for about a month before rallying sharply for a month. At that point it will fall sharply into 1992.

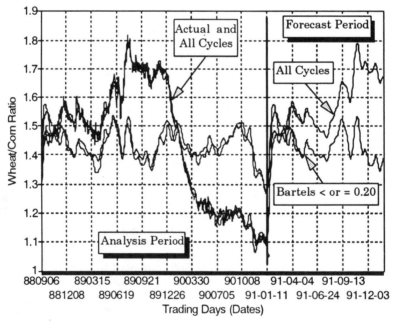

Figure 13-3   Series from Figure 13-2 with ratios of synthetic prices.

GOLD/SILVER

The gold/silver ratio is one of the most persistently popular spreads among traders. For many years the ratio was approximately 20:1, when both gold and silver had fixed values in terms of the U.S. dollar. That ratio no longer has any economic significance, even though some traders for reasons of their own may feel it does. But a case might be made for a ratio of gold to silver that makes sense in terms of relative production, usefulness as stores of value, or industrial applications.

The Chicago Board of Trade suggests that the gold/silver ratio (GSR) has become more popular than the metals themselves among traders because the initial speculative margin for the CBOT spread is only $300, while it is $203 for a 1,000-ounce silver contract and $405 for a kilo gold contract.[3] In trading this spread, or any spread, the ratio of the dollar value of the gold and silver contracts should be approximately equal. Otherwise the spread will be more of a speculation on one or the other metals rather than on the price relationship between them.

Figure 13-4 displays a chart of the settlement prices for gold and silver. Note that the price of silver is in cents per ounce, while that of gold is in dollars per ounce.[4]

There are clear similarities in the two series, but it is apparent that the price of silver fell relatively more steeply than that of gold during the period.

In Figure 13-5 the results of analyzing the logarithm of gold/silver prices for 600 days are displayed. Note that a 200-day backcast holdout sample was retained at the beginning of the data series. Vertical lines indicate the demarcation between holdout and analysis range and between analysis and forecast range. Although we once again need to be suspicious of the synthesis of all cycles because it appears to repeat the price series used in the analysis, the synthesis of cycles significant at a Bartels test value less than 0.10 (one chance in ten that the cycle could have arisen by chance in the data) appears to catch a number of minor turning points in the backcast holdout data. While

---

[3]"Heavy Gold Selling by USSR Has Weighed on Gold Prices." *Night Nuggets* (January 1991).

[4]Since silver trades in 1,000-ounce and 5,000-ounce contracts, and gold in kilogram and 100-ounce contracts, to maintain approximately equal dollar values in each leg of the spread at the outset one needs to solve for the number of contracts of silver, S, in the following equation in terms of gold, G. The futures contract prices are s and g, respectively. If both s and g are expressed in dollars the equation is given in the following equation.

$$S = \frac{100gG}{1,000s} = \frac{1}{10}\left(\frac{g}{s}\right)G$$

But if the price of silver is in cents and gold in dollars we have the simpler

$$S = \left(\frac{g}{s}\right)G$$

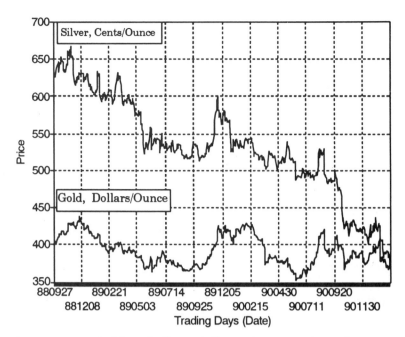

Figure 13-4 Gold and silver, daily settlement prices, September 1988-December 1990.

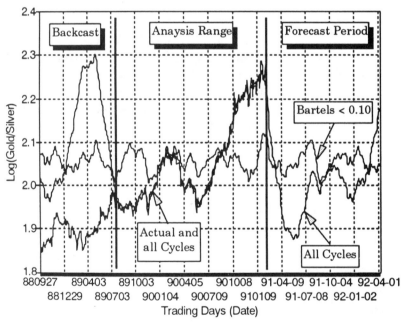

Figure 13-5 Logarithms of gold/silver prices with backcast and forecast.

caution should again prevail, the projection of significant cycles indicates that the gold/silver ratio will fall until mid-April 1991, at which time it will rise until mid-July or early August, when it will fall sharply. Going out further with a forecast based on daily data becomes increasingly tenuous and therefore no interpretation will be attempted for points beyond this.

T-BONDS/EURODOLLARS

This spread is based on the yield curve or term structure of interest rates. When the yield curve is normal, long-term rates are higher than short-term rates. Every so often, however, interest rates go up, and when that happens short-term rates climb at a faster pace than do long-term rates. If the change continues, eventually short-term interest rates become higher than long-term rates. This is termed an *inverted* yield curve. Inverted yield relationships seldom last long, and rates eventually come down. Short term rates fall at a faster pace than long.

Figure 13-6 displays a chart of daily T-bond and Eurodollar price indices and T-bond index less Eurodollar index. A note of caution is in order, however. The T-bond index is based on the price of a $100,000 T-bond with 8 percent coupon and 20 year maturity with semi-annual interest payments. The Eurodollar index, in contrast, is based on $1,000,000 times the result obtained by subtracting the annualized Eurodollar rate from 1.00 for funds

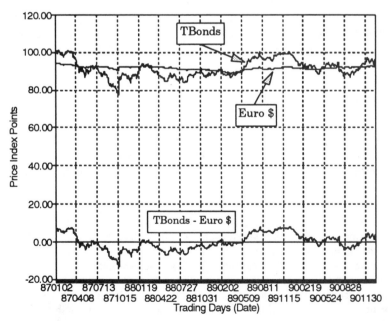

Figure 13-6 T-bonds and Eurodollars, January 1987–December 1990.

maturing in 90 days. Because the Eurodollar contract is ten times larger than that for T-bonds, an interest rate change of the same magnitude will have a larger effect on the value of a Eurodollar futures contract. However, because the value of long-term financial instruments is based on discounted cash flow, the relationship is not linear.

The chart suggests that when the T-bond price is significantly above that for Eurodollars the spread trader should sell T-bond futures and buy Eurodollar futures. And when the T-bond price is significantly below that for Eurodollars the opposite should be done. Clearly the trader would not want to set up the spread too early, because that would lead to losses. Thus the key is to determine approximately where the turning points will occur. Analysis based on cycles can assist in this task.

HEDGING

The term *dynamic hedging* has become part of the standard vocabulary of business and financial firms. It means that risk management (that is, risk reduction) efforts via hedging need not be restricted to fixed hedge ratios, however those may be determined, but that the ratio of futures contracts to cash position may be modified based on assessment of the likely direction of prices.[5]

As a consequence of the flexibility implied by dynamic hedging, the techniques of futures price forecasting illustrated in this book may be applied to hedging. Forecasts of sharply higher price in an item held in inventory by a producer would thus suggest a lower hedge ratio for short positions in futures, or perhaps no short position. Forecast of sharply lower prices would, on the other hand, indicate full hedge coverage to be in order.

SUMMARY

This chapter illustrates how intercommodity spread trades may be analyzed using the same techniques of cycle investigation discussed in previous chapters. Caveats were made regarding cycle projections that seem to replicate too

---

[5]One needs to be careful to avoid letting dynamic hedging become speculation. When does dynamic hedging become clearly speculation? It is often hard to say. One might argue that as long as the futures position is opposite the cash, the hedge ratio may vary from zero to somewhat more than one. But few would argue that a hedger that holds a long cash position and then goes long futures in the same commodity is a hedger. The same applies to a hedger that holds a short cash position and goes short futures. And even if they would argue from such a point of view it is doubtful that they could convince a jury of the validity of their view if stockholders were to challenge their results in court.

exactly the patterns of data in the samples analyzed. Such exact replication is much more likely to occur when only whole-number harmonics are used in the spectral scanning. It was shown that the same cycle projection can be obtained by analyzing the wheat/corn ratio and by analyzing the ratios of the separate projections of wheat and corn.

14

The Foundation for the Study of Cycles

by Richard Mogey[1]

Author's Note

This book demonstrates how commodity prices and other time series can be forecast by applying analysis of cycles to market data. The emphasis is on relatively short-term cycles. But the principles apply also to longer-term events. Understanding longer-term cycles and their timing can help one to see the stage setting in which the shorter-term actors play out their roles. This clearer perception can assist in predicting more precisely how those roles will be played.

For those who would like to learn more about the study and uses of cycles in understanding markets, I asked the executive director of the Foundation for the Study of Cycles to write a chapter on the Foundation, which in 1991 celebrated its fiftieth year. Foundation members from around the world study cycles not in just economic phenomena, but in physical events as well. The data bases available through the Foundation contain data which are in many cases unavailable elsewhere.

–A.F.H.

The origin of the Foundation for the Study of Cycles is the story of the first documented systematic investigation of comparative cycle analysis. Little had been done in this field and, ironically, it took the Great Depression to bring it about.

The Hoover administration asked the young Harvard economist Edward R. Dewey to search for the causes of the Great Depression. The result of

---

[1] Executive Director of the Foundation. The Foundation has several thousand members in 45 countries. Members receive the bimonthly magazine *Cycles*. A not-for-profit organization, the Foundation is located at 2600 Michelson Drive, Suite 1570, Irvine, CA 92715.

his search was disappointing, as he learned that economists did not agree on the cause. However, one economist, Chapin Hoskins, told Dewey he did not know *why* business fluctuated but that by using rhythmic cycles he could calculate *when* changes might occur. After the Hoover administration left office, Dewey began to work with Hoskins; and their consulting service used cycles to forecast the level of business activity and stock market movements on Wall Street.

Dewey became fascinated with cycles and began to read everything he could find on the subject. In 1940, he came across the *Proceedings* of the 1931 Matamek Conference on Biological Cycles organized by Copley Amory. He was amazed to find that some of the cycles he was using in stocks, interest rates, and the economy appeared to correspond to those that scientists had found in data unrelated to economics, such as population dynamics in animals.

The implications of Dewey's conclusion that rhythmic behavior was pervasive and might be synchronous were staggering. He immediately wrote to Copley Amory, a student of biological cycles; and the two men met in October 1940. When Dewey told Amory about the apparent connection between economic and biological cycles, Amory too was amazed. They agreed to form a foundation to study comparative cycles in all disciplines. The permanent committee for the Matamek Conference became the Committee for the new Foundation, with Dewey as the chief researcher.

The purpose of the Foundation was and is to identify and measure as precisely as possible cycles in all disciplines, and to attempt to find the cause or causes of cyclic behavior. Since its inception in 1940, the Foundation has catalogued more than 4,300 cycles in nearly every field of inquiry.

CYCLE SYNCHRONIES

Dewey discovered that cycles in different fields were related—that a six-year cycle, for example, in one field often made crests and troughs at the same time as six-year cycles in other fields. He called this correlation "cycle synchrony." In 1971 Dewey delivered his seminal paper on the subject at a European conference.

Figure 14-1 illustrates the synchrony of the six-year cycle. It shows the average time of crest for six-year cycles found in 19 different series. Although some of these cycles might synchronize by chance, it is unreasonable to think that all could. Consequently, it is difficult to accept this degree of synchrony without searching for some kind of underlying causation. Since 1941 the Foundation has conducted and sponsored research—first to verify the synchronous nature of cycles, and then to find the underlying causes.

Many people have little idea what cycles are. Some connect cycles with something that borders on the arcane, that somehow mysteriously makes things happen. Cycles are not occult phenomena, yet their causes remain, to a certain extent, unknown.

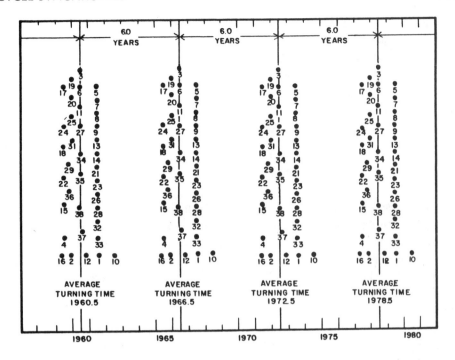

Diagram to Show the Calendar Timing of All Idealized 6-Year Cycles.

The dots are numbered to indicate the phenomena and are repeated time after time across the page at cycle length intervals. The dots represent idealized time of crests. Their vertical positions have no significance.

1. International Battles	14. Goodyear Tire & Rubber Co. Sales	27. Sears, Roebuck & Co. Sales
2. Lake Levels, Michigan and Huron	15. I.F. du Pont de Nemours & Co. Sales	28. Standard Oil Co. of Cal. Income
3. Allis-Chalmers Manufacturing Co. Sales	16. Industrial Stock Prices	29. Stockham Valves & Fittings
4. American Viscose Corp. Shipments	17. Inland Steel Co. Sales	31. Steel Production
5. Armco Steel Corp. Sales	18. J & L Steel Corp. Sales	32. Swift & Co. Sales
6. Armour & Co. Sales	19. Monsanto Chemical Co. Sales	33. U. S. Rubber Co. Sales
7. Bethlehem Steel Corp. Production	20. Montgomery Ward and Co. Sales	34. Wilson & Co. Sales
8. Continental Oil Co. Income	21. National Lead Co. Sales	35. Youngstown Sheet & Tube Co.
9. Cotton Production	22. Pittsburgh Plate Glass Co. Sales	36. Stock Prices
10. Diptheria	23. Proctor and Gamble Co. Sales	37. Hog Value, Per Head, On Farms
11. General Electric, Orders Received	24. Rayon Production	38. Sugar Prices
12. General Electric Co. Sales	25. Republic Steel Corp. Production	
13. B. F. Goodrich Co. Sales	26. Seaboard Air Line Operating Revenue	

Figure 14-1 Ideal crests of alleged six-year cycles.

At one time, Edward R. Dewey called cycles the mysterious forces that trigger events. He believed the causes of cyclic behavior are rational and thus can be discovered through research. Dewey referred to cycles as mysterious because their causes were often unknown, and because they suggest a connection between things which seem otherwise to be unrelated. For example, cycles in weather seem to be related to solar phenomena, growth, economics, and even human emotions.

Cycles are not central to a system of beliefs or prescribed doctrine, nor are they the result of assumptions and theories. Rather, evidence of cycles is the result of observation. Cycles are "history," the record of what took place in the past. For example, a four-year cycle in the stock market refers to highs or lows in the stock market that are made approximately every four years. Sometimes the period is a little shorter than four years, sometimes a little longer, but the average period is about four years. There is nothing mystical about the four-year period—it may be caused by events associated with U.S. presidential elections—but there *is* something statistical.[2] A four-year cycle appears to be present, and it manifests itself persistently over time.

ORIGINS OF CYCLE ANALYSIS

An awareness of cycles has been with us from earliest times. Ancient records show that humans have recognized rhythmic behavior for millennia. For instance, the ancient Egyptians well understood the cycles in the level of the River Nile. From observations of the seasons, the position of the sun and length of the day, from floods and other natural phenomena, people developed a keen sense of repetitive events. Therein lie the origins of the study of cycles.

Yet, as scientific knowledge of the universe grew, the knowledge of cycles generally did not, with the exception of cycles in celestial mechanics, the motions of planets and stars. One of the most important events for modern study of cycles was the discovery of the sunspot cycle in 1843 by Schwabe. In a sense, this event brought the idea of cycles into the mainstream of scientific thinking.

At about the same time, the birth of the Industrial Age began to change how people thought about economics. The theory of economic cycles began during this period. People had been keenly aware of economic and industrial fluctuations throughout the eighteenth century as in both the South Seas and the Mississippi speculative bubbles burst, but early attempts at understanding these fluctuations were not based on cycles. Adam Smith referred to the South Sea Bubble as "knavery and extravagance," while Ricardo refers to "revulsions." Marx relegates the rise and fall of the business cycle to the deficiencies of capitalism. But a new way of thinking about economics was being born.

In 1860, Clement Juglar, originator of the famous Juglar cycle, published his treatise *Des Crises Commerciales et de leur Retour Périodique*. Juglar was one of the pioneers in accurate observation of economic cycles. Several researchers had been interested in cycles prior to Juglar, such as Wade in the 1830s, but Juglar appears to be the first to approach the study of cycles scientifically.

---

[2] A 48-month "Presidential Election Cycle" has also been shown to be statistically significant for the U.S. stock market. See for instance A. F. Herbst and C. Slinkman, "Does the Evidence Support Existence of 'Political Economic' Cycles in the U.S. Stock Market?", *The Financial Analysts Journal*, 40, No. 2 (March/April 1984): pp. 38–44. Reprinted in *Cycles*, 35, No. 6 (August 1984): pp. 151–156.

In 1875, Samuel Benner in Ohio published his famous *Prophesies*. Benner had been personally devastated by the panic[3] of 1873, and thus became obsessed with finding the causes of panics. This research eventually led him to cycles.

The work of Benner, Juglar, and others like them differed from that of earlier commentators on crises and panics. Instead of concentrating on individual events, they focused on the *process* of moving from a panic or depression back to prosperity. In essence, the modern notion of cyclical oscillation was born.

MODERN CYCLE ANALYSIS

At end of the nineteenth century modern cycle analysis was still in a developmental state. The next stage in its advancement would have the greatest impact—the genesis of modern statistics. Statistical inference based on mathematical probability was in its infancy near the end of the nineteenth century, but it was destined to have enormous impact on both economics and cycle analysis.

A major factor in the development of modern statistics was recognition of the importance of precise observation. Reasonably reliable records had been kept since the Dark Ages, but not until the nineteenth century did a concern develop for more precision in the observation of economic data. Today, we have nearly 300 years of reliable data in many commodities and economic series—in some cases (wheat, for example) more than 700 years. Much of the work in compiling these data was done by Rogers, Beveridge, Gay, Warren and Pearson, and Cole, among others.[4]

By the end of the nineteenth century, the important ingredients came together to form modern cycle analysis: observation, reliable data, the concept of cyclic oscillation, and statistical and mathematical methodologies.

COMPARATIVE CYCLE ANALYSIS

In the second half of the nineteenth century, when modern scientific and economic cycle theories were evolving, another important field also arose: that of comparative cycle analysis. This new area of cycle research investigated the underlying relationships between different, seemingly unrelated fields—such as agriculture, animal populations, economic fluctuations, and solar activity. Speculation on such relationships had been made since the beginning of the century, but hard data would not become available until nearly 1900.

---

[3] *Panic* is used to describe the events preceding, as well as conditions in, economic depressions prior to the 20th century. Panics were generally marked by runs on the banks, as depositors withdrew money from accounts, fearing that there would be no cash left if they delayed.

[4] Many of these data series are available only from the Foundation for the Study of Cycles.

Early in the 1800s, astronomer Sir William Herschel suggested a relationship between sunspots and the weather, and hence prices and the economy. This hypothesis, although not strictly cyclic, led W. Stanley Jevons to speculate that economic cycles were caused by the sunspot cycle.[5]

Jevons was not the only one to search for the causes of economic fluctuations. In this century Professor Henry L. Moore proposed a connection with the planet Venus. Sir William Beveridge proposed a connection with meteorology. Professor Ellsworth Huntington postulated that cycles were due to general levels of health. Though none of these theories ever won acceptance, they eventually had great impact on cycle analysis. The proposal that cycles might be interrelated led to the concept of comparative cycle analysis.

Little was done to further these ideas until the 1920s and 1930s, when several conferences on cycles were held. Most notable was the 1931 Matamek Conference organized by Copley Amory, an amateur biologist. Although the conference was organized to discuss biological cycles, relationships between fluctuations in animal life and many aspects of human life began to emerge. Following the conference, a permanent committee was formed to study these issues.

THE FOUNDATION'S METHODS OF ANALYSIS

The Foundation is committed to the use of scientifically admissible methodologies to accomplish its purposes. These include various implementations of Fourier transform-based methods—spectral and harmonic analysis—and newer methods, such as maximum entropy spectral analysis.

With modern computerized tools and methods, the Foundation has been able to identify, catalog, and validate thousands of cycles in a wide array of fields in the ongoing search for cycle synchronies and causes.

CYCLES IN ECONOMICS, BUSINESS, AND WEATHER

Economics is one of the areas that offers promise in the search for synchronies, since so many factors contribute to economic change and data are readily and continuously available. The Foundation has studied a great variety of important economic indicators—equity prices, interest rates, real estate, currencies, and commodities. This research indicates that economic phenomena are clearly cyclic.

---

[5]This hypothesis elicited ridicule and scorn from many persons who did not understand the scientific basis for the connection. Unfortunately, this attitude persists even today in some quarters despite growing body of evidence in support of Jevons' hypothesis.

U.S. Stocks

The Foundation has isolated more than 50 significant cycles in the U.S. stock market. Stocks can be described as having a 30-year pattern, in which two major bull markets culminating in hear markets are followed by a long period of congestion, or generally sideways price patterns (see Figure 14-2).

Two shorter cycles also tend to influence stock prices: a 24.08-month and a 40.68-month cycle.[6] These cycles maintain the same basic relationship every ten years, because five of the 24-month and three of the 40-month cycles occur in each 10-year period. Two periods in which the cycles appear not to be synchronized occur in the "zero" and "five" years (see Figure 14-3). Note that "triangular" wave cycles are a commonly used alternative representation to sine waves.

Based on this description of price patterns, it is my present opinion that long-term cyclic guidelines for stocks can be postulated thus: Two important bull markets occur every 30 years. The first occurs in year two of the pattern (1922, 1952, and 1982) and is the longer. It usually ends in the ninth or "0" year (1929, 1959, 1989), with a major correction in the seventh year (1927, 1957, 1987). The second bull market occurs in the twelfth year of the pattern (1932, 1962, and 1992). It is shorter, and ends in the seventeenth year (1937, 1967, 1997). A consolidation period of approximately 13 years then

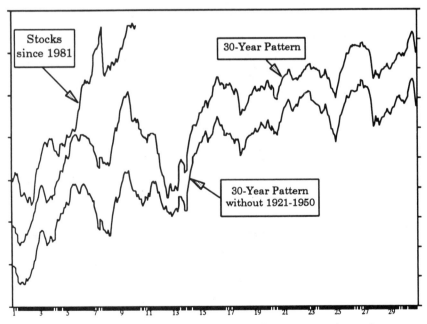

Figure 14-2 Thirty-year pattern in the U.S. stock market.

[6] A four-year cycle was mentioned earlier.

takes place. Since stocks have a persistent, secular uptrend, this consolidation shows an upward bias.

Interest Rates

Interest rates have been studied for centuries. Clement Juglar first postulated the 10- to 12-year, or Juglar cycle, in the nineteenth century. Kondratieff, the Russian economist, postulated his famous long wave, or 54-year[7] cycle, in the early twentieth century. Although Kondratieff's long wave referred to the action of the economy, it was chiefly based on British interest rates.

Both E. R. Dewey and Gertrude Shirk did extensive work on the 54-year cycle, and other cycles, in interest rates for the Foundation. Of more than 20 possibly significant cycles in interest rates, their work suggests that the most important are a 54-year, a 12-year, and a 40.83-month cycle.

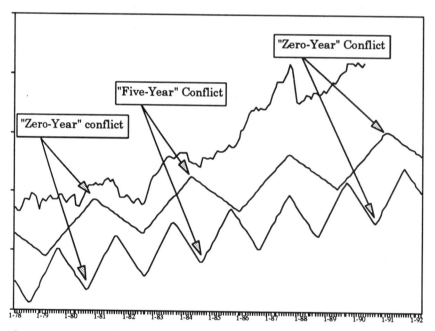

Figure 14-3   Cycle patterns of 40.68 and 24.08 months in U.S. stock market prices.

[7]Kondratieff suggested a long cycle or wave in the range from 50 to 60 years. Dewey found that a 54-year period fits many data series better than any other fixed-length in this range.

The 54-year cycle (Figure 14-4) has made a little less than five repetitions within the available data, hardly enough for any statistical significance. When Kondratieff first postulated the long wave in prices and British Consols, it had made only two repetitions. Since then, the cycle has continued to repeat over another two periods. This is one of the most important aspects of cycle analysis. Once a cycle is discovered, it should continue to perform well.

Some uncertainties remain, however. This long-wave cycle may be related to the prices of commodities, because cycles of nearly the same length occur in both commodity prices and climate. If so, commodity prices may no longer have the same impact on the economy and on the cost of money that they once did. If this is the case, interest rates may no longer follow the long cycle. This cycle will thus have to be closely monitored. The last high was in 1981, and the cycle currently points to lower overall interest rates until about 2008.

The Juglar cycle of about 12 years that dominates interest rates does not seem to be agriculturally dependent, although the Consumer Price Index (CPI) has a cycle of similar length. Figure 14-5 illustrates this cycle, which topped in 1981 and is due to top next in 1993. It last made a bottom in 1987. Despite the downward pressure of the 54-year cycle, the shorter term should bring higher rates within the context of a downtrend, so interest rates probably will not reach the 1981 levels.

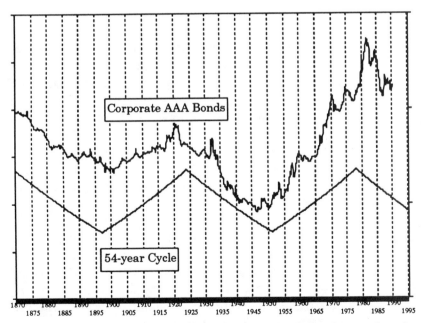

Figure 14-4 Long-wave (54-year) cycles in high-grade U. S. bonds.

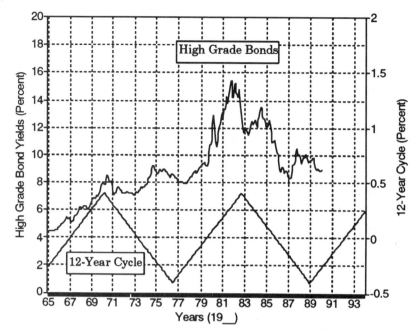

Figure 14-5   A 12-year interest rate cycle.

Metals

Cycles are in a constant state of change. Usually, this change is gradual. But some exhibit abrupt changes, as is the case with precious metals.

At various times over the years, gold and silver were monetized, and so behaved like money, not commodities. Since the Middle Ages, the length of cycles in silver shifted as silver changed from being monetized to being a commodity. Gold followed a similar pattern. These metals also are related to interest rates and the pace of inflation. In periods of lower interest rates gold and silver, as commodities, suffer when prices generally deflate. But, when they are money they normally rise.

The movement of these two metals during the Great Depression provides a classic example. Silver, which was not monetized, collapsed like all commodities. But gold, which was monetized, continued to rise on the black market. Today, both gold and silver are essentially commodities, since they no longer back the major currencies. Therefore, the old patterns found in gold and silver may no longer hold.

One of the cycles in metals is an 18-year cycle, which may be a monetized metals cycle. It is due to top in 1998. If this cycle remains in place when metals are non-monetized commodities, that would argue for more price inflation and higher interest rates. That would call into doubt the 54-year cycle in interest rates. However, the 5-year cycle in metals appears to be related to

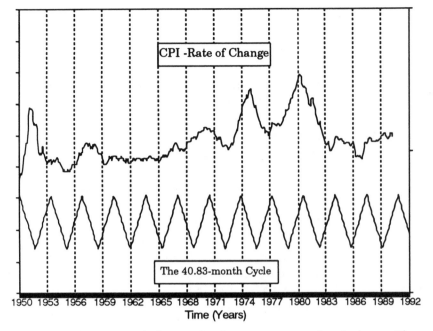

Figure 14-6   Rate of change in the consumer price index, with a 40.83-month interest rate cycle.

metals as commodities. It calls for a top in 1995, followed by lower prices. This would be in step with the cycles in interest rates.

Commodities

Most agricultural commodity cycles are dependent on the weather and, to some extent, changing tastes and production innovations. This tendency led to some of the early work in comparative cycle analysis by researchers such as Jevons.

Scientists working in the fields of climate, astronomy, solar physics, and related fields have long been tantalized by the correspondence between planetary orbits, solar cycles, and climate. But until the advent of satellites, hard data were difficult to come by. Now, serious scientists support many new hypotheses, including recognition that the sun is the engine behind the weather and climate, and that planetary tidal force is a significant expression of solar phenomena.

Since many commodities are weather dependent, it follows that solar activity can be related to commodity prices. This is exactly what the cycles reveal. Most commodities have an approximate 40-month cycle, as does solar activity. There also are major cycles of about 9.5, 18, and 54-60 years in both commodity prices and solar phenomena.

Weather and Climate

Another of the pioneers in the study of cycles was Dr. Raymond Wheeler, a professor of psychology at the University of Kansas. In the 1930s, he made an extensive study of the relationship between climate and human behavior. He concluded that significant changes in climate had a significant effect on human behavior.

Wheeler tracked battles and conflicts and recorded major historical events through more than 2,500 years. His study shows strong correlations between climatological changes and wars, various forms of government, and cultural achievement. He also discovered how climate affected major changes in the business cycle. In an agrarian society, this would be expected. Whether this relationship holds in an industrialized world remains to be seen.

For an alleged cycle to be taken seriously, it should perform well once discovered. This is certainly the case with results from the work of Raymond Wheeler. His forecasts based on climatological and weather cycles have been exceptional, from predicting the shift of industry to the Far East to foretelling the changes in Eastern Europe.

The Economy

The general economy was one of the first areas cycle analysts researched. Cycles have been isolated in unemployment, growth and decline, money supply, industrial production, real estate, and many other important economic indicators.

These cycles generally fall into one of two groups according to length: about 9–12 years and about 18–20 years. The cycles of 9–12 years, like the Juglar cycle mentioned above, seem to relate to interest rates and prices. The cycles of 18–20 years, which particularly affect real estate and building, seem to relate to the rate of growth and population changes in the U.S.

Population does not increase at a constant rate. Every other generation tends to have smaller families, so population grows at a greater rate about every 20 years. This creates greater demand for housing about every 20 years, with the attendant price increases and acceleration in building. As the rate of change decreases, demand falls, building declines, and the cycle continues.

These kinds of trends are of great importance to the economy and have an impact on nearly every aspect of our lives. The growth rate of the U.S. population peaked in the late 1980s and is now declining, which means slower growth in the decade ahead.

CONCLUSION

The goal of cycle analysis is not just to discover significant cycles, but to understand why these cycles work. The first step in this process is to realize that cycles provide a way for understanding change. The concept of cycles is a model for measuring the process of oscillations. The underlying theme behind cycles is that history repeats itself.

This is not an extraordinary idea. Indeed, it is so fundamental it is often overlooked. Nearly every celestial body rotates, as it revolves around some other celestial body. The entire galaxy is in motion—a spiral of star systems, none ever quite returns to the same precise position with respect to the others. (Note that the word "cycle" originates from the Greek word *kyklos,* meaning circle.)

Cycles are historical averages. Each repetition is in some respects unique, yet similar—like the annual recurrence of the seasons. Human beings likewise go through similar patterns of change. Yet each individual meets life in his or her own unique way.

Every time series is a combination of pattern, trend, and randomness, of cycles and individualization. The key to the proper application of cycles to prediction is recognition that the future is a mélange of order, pattern, and randomness. This recognition prepares the cycle analyst for each unique recurrence of a cycle.

Appendix A
Fitting Cycles with a Spreadsheet Program

Sometimes we may want to create an artificial or synthetic time series that contains one or more cycles of specific characteristics. Or we may wish to find the best fit of a cycle of a specific period to some market data in such a way that its amplitude and phase are determined by the data. Both of these tasks are easy to do with almost any spreadsheet program, if we use the right formulas. The two spreadsheet examples that are used in this Appendix may be used as templates to do these things on your own.

The following assumes that you have some knowledge of how to use a spreadsheet program. It is not important which one, since the more popular ones are very similar. The examples were created with Quattro Pro™, but could have just as easily have been done with SuperCalc5™, Lotus 1-2-3™, Framework™, or Excel™.[1]

CREATING A CYCLE

Suppose you want to make a synthetic time series with a cycle or two in it, such as the one in Chapter 7 that is composed of a trend, a seasonal cycle, and a longer cycle. Suppose further that the trend starts with a value of 300 and then will grow at 0.0025 ($\frac{1}{4}$ percent) per period, plus or minus a random amount defined as two times a random number that ranges between -0.005 and 0.005 ($\frac{1}{2}$ percent).

---

[1]This author's preference for Quattro Pro is largely because of its early superior graphics capabilities, flexibility, and the responsiveness of its developer, Borland International, to suggestions for improvements (such as the ability to plot open, high, low, close data).

In Figure A-1, spreadsheet cell B11 contains the formula that gets things started for the trend, and B12, B13, and so on contain the formulas for generating the rest of the trend.

To create a seasonal cycle of exactly 12 periods, an amplitude of 30, and a phase that reaches its first peak in the fifth period, one must perform some additional calculations. Cell E5 contains the amplitude, E6 the phase, and E8 the period. In Cell E7 is the formula that assures that the seasonal cycle first peaks in the fifth period: -2π (Phase/Period) or, in a common spreadsheet terminology, $-(2*@$ PI $* \$E\$6/\$E\$8)$. Then in cell D11 we have the formula that creates the first point in the seasonal, $+\$E5*$ @ COS(2*@ PI*A11/$E$8 + $E$7), which corresponds to the equation Amplitude $\times \cos(2\pi t\omega + \Phi)$, where ω = 1/Period = frequency, t is the time period, and ϕ the phase. This formula cell is then copied down the D column for as many seasonal terms as are desired.

alloutFigure A-2 contains the formulas corresponding to the cell of the worksheet shown in Figure A-1.

In addition to a seasonal, a cycle of period 120, phase of 10, and amplitude 120 is created in the worksheet. It is created exactly as the seasonal is, but in column E. Column F contains the sum or combination of trend, seasonal, and cycle.

Additional cycles may easily be created as desired. However, unless your computer has a lot of memory you will soon reach its limits. And even with a great deal of memory, the time for recalculation will soon become excessive unless you set it to manual—and remember to invoke recalculation when it is required! So, some advice is in order.

	A	B	C	D	E	F	G
1							
2	Trend, Seasonal, and Cyclical						
3							
4							
5		Constant		Ampl=	30	Ampl=	120
6		300		Phase =	5	Phase =	10
7		Growth			-2.61799388		-0.52359878
8		0.0025		Per =	12	Per =	120
9							
10	t	Trend		Seasonal	Cyclical	Combined	
11	0	301.95		-25.9808	103.9230	379.8935	
12	1	301.26		-15.0000	106.9208	393.1848	
13	2	300.73		0.0000	109.6255	410.3595	
14	3	300.31		15.0000	112.0297	427.3437	
15	4	301.68		25.9808	114.1268	441.7863	

Figure A-1 Spreadsheet setup for making synthetic series.

```
A2:  [W4] 'Trend, seasonal, and Cyclical    A11:  [W4] 0
B5:  "Constant                              B11:  (F2) +$B$6+(1+$B$+0.01*(@RAND-0.5))
D5:  "Ampl=                                 D11:  (F4) +$E$5=@COS(2*@PI*A11/$E$8+$E$7)
E5:  30                                     E11:  (F4) +$G$5*@COS(2*@PI*A11/$G$8+$G$7)
F5:  "Ampl=                                 F11:  (F4) +B11+D11+E11
G5:  120                                    A12:  [W4] 1
B6:  300                                    B12:  (F2) +B11*(1+$B$8+0.01*(@RAND-0.5))
D6:  "Phase =                               D12:  (F4) +$E$5*@COS(2*PI*A12/$E$7
E6:  5                                      E12:  (F4) +$G$5*@COS(2*@PI*A12/$G$8+$G$7)
F6:  "Phase =                               F12:  (F4) +B12+D12+E12
G6:  10                                     A13:  [W4] 2
B7:  "Growth                                B13:  (F2) +B12*(1+$B$8+0.01*(@RAND-0.5))
E7:  -(2*@PI*$E$6/$E$8)                      D13:  (F4) +$E$5*@COS(2*@PI*A13/$E$8+$E$7)
G7:  -(2*@PI*$G$6/$G$8)                      E13:  (F4) +$G$5*@COS(2*@PI*A13/$G$8+$G$7)
B8:  0.0025                                 F13:  (F4) +B13+D13+E13
D8:  "Per =                                 A14:  [W4] 3
E8:  12                                     B14:  (F2) +B13*(1+$B$8+0.01*(@RAND-0.5))
F8:  "Per =                                 D14:  (F4) +$E$5*@COS(2*@PI*A14/$E$8+$E$7)
G8:  120                                    E14:  (F4) +$G$5*@COS(2*@PI*A14/$G$8+$G$7
A10: [W4] "t                                F14:  (F4) +B14+D14+E14
B10: "Trend                                 A15:  [W4] 4
D10: "Seasonal                              B15:  (F2) +B14*(+$B$8+0.01*(@RAND-0.5))
E10: "Cyclical                              D15:  (F4) +$E$5*@COS(2*@PI*A15/$E$8+$E$7)
F10: 'Combined                              E15:  (F4) +$G$5*@COS(2*@PI*A15/$G$8+$G$7)
                                            F15:  (F4) +B15+D15+E15
```

Figure A-2   Formulas for fitting a synthetic series in a spreadsheet.

Once you have created a cycle, use your spreadsheet's ability to convert formulas into fixed values, and do that for all but the first cell containing the first item in the cycle's series. That cell formula should be saved in case you later change your mind about the parameters of the cycle you want to fit; if you do this you need only copy the formula down the column again, without reentering it.

FITTING A CYCLE OF GIVEN PERIOD

In learning to work with cycles it is helpful to be able to see the process that is involved and to gain an intuitive feeling for the process by experimentation. The widespread availability of spreadsheet programs makes them ideal for illustrating how a cycle of a given length can be easily fitted to data, and then synthesized and plotted against the original data series. For one or two cycles these spreadsheet programs work well, especially if there are not a great deal of data. However, for working with several cycles, or with more than two hundred or so data points they tend to become slow and to lose accuracy compared

```
        A        B        C        D        E        F        G
 1 FITTING A SINUSOIDAL CYCLE USING QUATTRO PRO(TM)
 2 S&P500 Spot Data -- Fitted period is ==>==>       34.85 <==<==<==<=
 3
 4 (C)   Copyright 1990 by Anthony F. Herbst. All rights reserved.
 5
 6                                    CALCULATIONS FOR
 7                       --------- FITTING CYCLE HERE  -------------
 8                       Omega(w)=    0.1803          N=         500
 9
10                             A =    6.7594 = sine coefficient
11                             B =   11.7414 = cosine coefficient
12
13                             R =   13.54804 = amplitude
14
15                       Phase =     0.52235  in radians
16                                   2.89724  in time units
17
18                  Intermediate phase calculations
19                                   2.89724 for time units
20                                   2.89724
21
22                  Check,G30      327.648 (Alternate Formula)
23
24
25
26        ColAvg                        ColSum     ColSum
27      314.8851                      1689.8409   2935.3496
28
29  t      Data  cos(wt)  sin(wt)  Xt*cos(wt)  Xt*sin(wt)  Synthesis
30  1    272.05   0.984    0.179     267.640      48.783    327.648
31  2    270.51   0.936    0.353     253.114      95.442    328.256
32  3    268.47   0.857    0.515     230.148     138.232    328.431
```

Figure A-3   Fitting a specific sinusoidal cycle.

with compiled programs that use efficient computational procedures and double precision variables.[2]

Now suppose that you want to fit a cycle of a certain period to some market data. Let us assume it is a 34.85 day cycle you want to fit to 500 daily values of the S&P500 index. This is not to say that a 34.85 day cycle is genuine, just that you want to see how well it fits the data.

Figure A-3 contains the worksheet display for fitting a cycle to the data. Figure A-4 contains the key equations used in the worksheet. Note that an

---

[2]Such as the Cycle Analysis Programs (CAP) developed by this author.

```
A1:  PR [W4] 'FITTING A SINUSOIDAL CYCLE USING QUATTRO PRO (tm)
A2:  PR [W4] 'S&P500 Spot Data -- Fitted period is ==>==>
F2:  U [W12] 34.85
G2:  PR [W12] \<==
A4:  PR [W4] '(C)   Copyright 1990 by Anthony F. Herbst. All rights reserved.
E6:  PR [W12] "    CALCULATIONS FOR
D7:  PR
E7:  PR [W12] "   FITTING CYCLE HERE   --
G7:  PR [W12] \-
D8:  PR "Omega(w)=
E8:  (F4) PR [W12] (2*@PI)/PERIOD
F8:  PR [W12] @MAX(A29..A1000)
D10: PR "A =
E10: (F4) PR [W12] 2*F27/N
F10: PR [W12] "= sine coefficient
D11: PR "B =
E11: (F4) PR [W12] 2*G27/N
F11: PR [W12] "= cosine coefficient
D13: PR "R =
E13: (F5) PR [W12] @SQRT(A^2+B^2)
F13: PR [W12] '= amplitude
D15: PR "Phase =
E15: (F5) PR [W12] @ATAN(A/B)
F15: PR [W12] "in radians
E16: (F5) PR [W12] @IF(E19>PERIOD,E19-PERIOD,E19)
F16: PR [W12] ' in time units
D18: PR "Intermediate phase calculatons
E19: (F5) PR [W12] @IF(E02<0,E20+PERIOD, E20)
F19: PR [W12] ^for time units
E20: (F5) PR [W12] +PERIOD*RPHASE/(2*@PI)
D22: PR "Check, G30:
E22: (F3) PR [W12] +MEAN+A+@SIN(A30*W)+B*@COS(A30*W)
F22: (F4) PR [W12] "(Alternate Formula)
G25: PR [W12] "Cycle
B26: PR "ColAvg                    A31: PR [W4] 2
F26: PR [W12] "ColSum               B31: (F2) U +P441
G26: PR [W12] "ColSum               C31: (F3) PR @COS($W*A31)
B27: (F4) PR @AVG(B30..B529)       D31: (F3) PR @SIN($W*A31)
F27: (F4) PR [W12] @SUM(E30..E529) E31: (F3) PR [W12] +B31*C31
G27: (F4) PR [W12] @SUM(F30..F529) F31: (F3) PR [W12] +B31*D31
A29: PR [W4] "t          G31: (F3) PR [W12] +MEAN+$AMPL*@COS($W*A31-$RPHASE)
B29: PR "Data                      A32: PR [W4] 3
C29: PR "cos(wt)                   B32: (F2) U+P442
D29: PR "sin(wt)                   C32: (F3) PR @COS($W*A32)
E29: PR [W12] 'Xt*cos(wt)          D32: (F3) PR @SIN($W*A32)
```

Figure A-4 Formulas for fitting a specific sinusoidal cycle.

```
F29:  PR [W12]  'Et*sin(wt)              E32:  (F3) PR [W12] +B32*C32
G29:  PR [W12]  "Synthesis               F32:  (F3) PR [W12] +B32*D32
A30:  PPR [W4]  1              G32:  (F3) PR [W12] +$MEAN+$AMPL*@COS($W*A32-$RPHASE)
B30:  (F2) U  +P440
C30:  (F3) PR  @COS($W*A30)
D30:  (F3) PR  @SIN($W*A30)
E30:  (F3) PR  [W12] +B30*C30
F30:  (F3) PR  [W12] +B30*D30
G30:  (F3) PR  [W12] +$MEAN+$AMPL*@COS($W*A30-$RPHASE)
```

Figure A-4 (*continued*)

alternative form of the cycle-generating equation is shown in cell E22. This form does not require that the phase be explicitly provided. However, it requires that two sinusoidal values be calculated, and that computation can significantly increase the time required for some computers[3] to do the work required. That is why the alternative form is not used in column G.

It would seem that the built-in regression capability of the spreadsheet program could be used to estimate the A and B coefficients for fitting a cycle. However, data containing a significant cycle do not meet the assumptions used in developing least-squares regression, and the coefficients will not be nearly so correct as those obtained by the method illustrated in this Appendix.

Note that the method illustrated here is *not* the same as performing a spectral analysis on a data series to identify possibly significant cycles, even though the mathematics are similar in some respects. As the preceding chapter reveals, such techniques are more complex and rely on "windowing" or smoothing the parameter estimates to obtain superior estimates.

Also note that by putting all the formulas at the *top* of the spreadsheet it is much easier to add some more data later and extend the work columns downward to match them because there are no formulas at the bottom to get in the way.

---

[3]Especially if the computer does not have a math coprocessor.

Appendix B
The Bartels Test[1]

The Bartels test is based on the idea that if we have a perfect cycle the A and B coefficients obtained in fitting the cycle to each row of the array will all fall upon a single point in the A, B plane. To the extent they do not, the cycle is not a perfect or pure wave. Thus, assuming we will work with an A, B plane in the Cartesian coordinate system, it is possible to measure how close a given cycle comes to the theoretical ideal. With the notion of moving from one point in the plane to another, we can trace through Bartels' development of the test (see footnote 9 of Chapter 8, p. 142).

Bartels in his original development assumed a random walk of n steps, each of length λ (lambda), repeated a large number of times, N. The distance from the starting point, 0, is $L_1(n), L_2(n), \ldots, L_N(n)$. The mean square distance, $M^2(n)$, is defined by

$$M^2(n) = \lim_{N \to \infty} [L_1^2(n) + \cdots + L_N^2(n))/N] = n\lambda^2 \tag{B-1}$$

and

$$M(n) = \lambda \sqrt{n} \tag{B-2}$$

which is the *expectancy* of the random walk.

The probability that after n steps we are a distance between r and $(r + dr)$ from the starting point is given by

---

[1]An alternative exposition may be found in C. E. Armstrong, "Cycle Analysis—A Case Study, Part 25: Testing Cycles for Statistical Significance," *Cycles* (October 1973): pp. 231–235. A reprint of the Foundation for the Study of Cycles Publication No. 12.

$$w(r) = \frac{2}{M^2} r e^{(-r^2/M^2)} \tag{B-3}$$

where e is the base of natural logarithms, and $e^x = \exp(x)$. If we let r be a multiple of the expectancy, M,

$$r = \kappa M \tag{B-4}$$

then

$$w(\kappa) = 2\kappa e^{(-\kappa^2)} \tag{B-5}$$

Integrating Equation B-5 from κ (kappa) to ∞ (infinity) yields

$$W(\kappa) = e^{(-\kappa^2)} \tag{B-6}$$

To apply Bartels' test to a specific *hypothesized* cycle and a given data series, we proceed as follows. Using the finite Fourier transform

$$X_t = \overline{X} + \sum_{i=1}^{m} [A_i \cos(\omega_{it}) + B_i \sin(\omega_{it})] \tag{B-7}$$

where $\omega_i = 2\pi_i/n$ and $m = 1 + n/2$ if n is even, $1 + (n+1)/2$ if n is odd, we fit the hypothesized cycle to each consecutive segment of the data series, each of length corresponding to the cycle. (In an array we fit a cycle for each row.) Next, we fit the cycle to the entire data series. In each case we calculate the coefficients A and B defined by

$$A = \frac{2}{n} \sum_{t=1}^{n} [X_t \sin(\omega_i t)] \tag{B-8}$$

and

$$B = \frac{2}{n} \sum_{t=1}^{n} [X_t \cos(\omega_i t)] \tag{B-9}$$

Next we take the expectancy of the average vector, which is given by $[\sqrt{(A^2 + B^2)}]/N$, and then take the reciprocal of the expression exp [(Average Amplitude/Expectancy)^2].

The example in Chapter 8 should make clear the technique for applying the test.

Appendix C

Forecasting with Exponential Smoothing

A forecasting technique that sometimes performs better than sophisticated (that is, complicated) methods in *short-term* forecasting is *exponential smoothing*.[1] The method works well for very short-term forecasts and is very easy to use. Exponential smoothing is adaptive; that is, it responds to recent actual data in adjusting the forecast for the period ahead. Clearly this is different from forecasts based on fitting a linear or other trend by regression, because the latter do not adapt to the forecast errors inherent in any forecast in calculating the next forecast value.

Exponential smoothing lends itself readily to spreadsheet programs.[2] The key to making exponentially smoothed forecasts is to find the best weighting parameter, W, $0 \leq W \leq 1$. From this value the level smoothing constant lambda is calculated as $\lambda = W(2 - W)$, and the trend smoothing constant tau as $\tau = \lambda^2$. How does one find the best W? Let the computer do it by trial and error. In a spreadsheet program a sensitivity analysis can be performed automatically by setting up a table of values to be entered into a worksheet cell. The results of substituting a column of values, one at a time, into that cell are recorded and the mean square error calculated from the forecast errors (that is, actual forecast value). The mean square error is the variance of the forecast errors plus the square of their mean.

[1]In a contest among forecasting experts, exponential smoothing turned in the best one-period-ahead forecasts, although it did not do so well for longer time horizons. See S. Makridakis, ed., *The Forecasting Accuracy of Major Time Series Methods* (New York: John Wiley & Sons, 1984), p. 5.

[2]For detailed development of a spreadsheet for creating exponential smoothing forecasts see E. S. Gardner, Jr., "Using Exponential Smoothing," *Lotus* (March 1987): pp. 61ff.

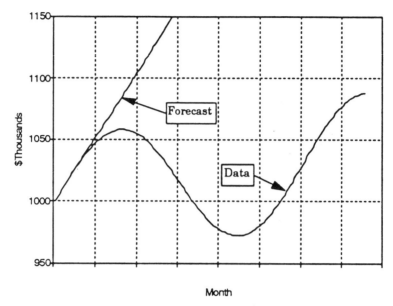

Figure C-1   Exponential smoothing forecast.

How well does exponential smoothing work when a market series contains a cycle with a trend? Look at Figure C-1. The exponential forecast works extremely well for the first leg of the first manifestation of the cycle, which is basically a subtrend. However, if we do not re-estimate the parameters, then as the rate of upward movement diminishes the forecast becomes increasingly inaccurate, and finally impossibly bad. If the exponential smoothing parameters had been periodically re-estimated the forecast would have been much better. But the method is essentially a trend-following procedure, albeit one that adjusts to changes in data series from errors in the previous forecast. A point to remember is that exponential smoothing can only be relied on for forecasting a few points ahead *from data that were used to estimate the parameters*. Successful use requires frequent parameter re-estimation but may be worth the modest effort required.

Appendix D

References and Selected Readings on Market Efficiency

Bidwell, C. M. III. 1979. "A Test of Market Efficiency." *Journal of Portfolio Management* 5 No. 4 (Summer): pp. 53–58.

Black, F. 1973. "Yes, Virginia, There Is Hope: Tests of the Value Line Ranking System." *Financial Analysts Journal* (September-October): pp. 10–14.

Bonin, J. M., and E. A. Moses. 1974. "Seasonal Variations in Prices of Individual Dow Jones Industrial Stocks." *Journal of Financial and Quantitative Analysis* 9 (December): pp. 963–991.

Boothe, P. 1983. "Speculative Profit Opportunities in the Canadian Foreign Exchange Market, 1974–78." *Canadian Journal of Economics* 16, No. 4 (November): pp. 603–611.

Brenner, M., M. G. Subrahmanyam, and J. Uno. 1990. "Arbitrage Opportunities in the Japanese Stock and Futures Markets." *Financial Analysts Journal* 46, No. 2 (March/April): pp. 14–24.

Brinegar, C. 1970. "A Statistical Analysis of Speculative Price Behavior." *Food Research Institute Studies* 11, No. 3 (November).

Cootner, P. H. 1964. "Stock Prices: Random vs. Systematic Changes." Reprinted in P. H. Cootner, ed., *The Random Character of Stock Market Prices*. Cambridge, MA: M.I.T. Press, pp. 231–252.

Fama, E. and M. Blume. 1966. "Filter Rules and Stock Market Trading." *Journal of Business* 39 (Supp.): pp. 226–241.

Flood, R. P., and R. J. Hodrick. 1986. "Asset Price Volatility, Bubbles, and Process Switching." *Journal of Finance* 41, No. 4 (September): pp. 831–842.

Fortune, P. 1991. "Stock Market Efficiency: An Autopsy." *New England Economic Review* (March/April): pp. 17–40.

French, K. 1980. "Stock Returns and the Weekend Effect." *Journal of Financial Economics* 8 (March): pp. 55–70.

Gibbons, M., and P. Hess. 1981. "Day of the Week Effects and Asset Returns." *Journal of Business* 54 (October): pp. 579–596.

Hall, T. W., and J. J. Tsay. 1988. "An Evaluation of the Performance of Portfolios Selected from Value Line Rank One Stocks." *Journal of Financial Research* 11, No. 3 (Fall): pp. 227–240.

Holloway, C. 1981. "A Note on Testing an Aggressive Investment Strategy Using Value Line Ranks." *Journal of Finance* 36 (June): pp. 711–720.

Houthakker, H. S. 1959. "Can Speculators Forecast Prices?" *Review of Economics and Statistics* 39, No. 2 (May): pp. 143–151.

Houthakker, H. S. 1961. "Systematic and Random Elements in Short-Term Price Movements." *American Economic Review* 51: pp. 164–172.

Huberman, G. and S. Kandel. 1990. "Market Efficiency and Value Line's Record." *Journal of Business* 63, No. 2 (April): pp. 187–216.

Jensen, M. 1978. "Some Anomalous Evidence Regarding Market Efficiency." *Journal of Financial Economics* 6 (July-September): pp. 95–102.

Joy, O. M. and C. P. Jones. 1986. "Should We Believe the Tests of Market Efficiency?" *Journal of Portfolio Management* 12, No. 4 (Summer): pp. 49–54.

Labys, W. C. and C. W. J. Granger. 1970. *Speculation, Hedging and Commodity Price Forecasts*. Lexington, MA: Heath.

Larson, A. 1960. "Measurement of a Random Process in Futures Prices." *Food Research Institute Studies* 1, No. 3 (November).

LeBaron, D. 1983. "Reflections on Market Inefficiency." *Financial Analysts Journal* 39, No. 3 (May/June): pp. 16–17, 23.

Lehmann, B. N. 1990. "Fads, Martingales, and Market Efficiency." *Quarterly Journal of Economics* 105, No. 1 (February): pp. 1–28.

Makridakis, S., and S. C. Wheelwright, eds. 1982. *The Handbook of Forecasting: A Manager's Guide*. New York: Wiley.

Neftci, S. N., and A. J. Policano. 1984. "Can Chartists Outperform the Market? Market Efficiency Tests for 'Technical Analysis'". *Journal of Futures Markets* 4, No. 4 (Winter): pp. 465–478.

Ogden, J. P., and A. L. Tucker. 1987. "Empirical Tests of the Efficiency of the Currency Futures Options Market." *Journal of Futures Markets* 7, No. 6 (December): pp. 695–703.

Pearce, D. K. 1987. "Challenges to the Concept of Stock Market Efficiency." *Economic Review* 72, No. 8 (September/October): pp. 16–33.

Reinganum, M. R. 1981. "Misspecification of Capital Asset Pricing: Empirical Anomalies Based on Earnings' Yields and Market Values." *Journal of Financial Economics* 9, No. 1 (March): pp. 19–46.

Reinganum, M. R. 1982. "The Anomalous Stock Market Behavior of Small Firms in January: Empirical Tests Tax-Loss Selling Effects." *Journal of Financial Economics* 12, No. 1 (March): pp. 89–104.

Rendleman, R. J., Jr., C. P. Jones, and H. A. Latane. 1982. "Empirical Anomalies Based on Unexpected Earnings and the Importance of Risk Adjustments." *Journal of Financial Economics* 10, No. 3 (November): pp. 269–287.

Rohrer, J. 1985. "Ferment in Academia." *Institutional Investor* 19, No. 7 (July): 68–78.

Rozeff, M. and W. Kinney. 1976. "Capital Market Seasonality: The Case of Stock Returns." *Journal of Financial Economics* 4 (October): pp. 379–402.

Smidt, S. 1965. "A Test of the Serial Independence of Price Changes in Soybean Futures." *Food Research Institute Studies* 5, No. 2.

Stevenson, R., and R. Bear. 1970. "Commodity Futures: Trends or Random Walks?" *Journal of Finance* 21, No. 1 (March): pp. 65–81.

Strahm, N. D. 1983. "Preference Space Evaluation of Trading System Performance." *The Journal of Futures Markets* 3, No. 3 (Fall): pp. 259–281.

Working, H. 1967. "Tests of a Theory Concerning Floor Trading on Commodity Exchanges." *Food Research Institute Studies* 7 (Supp.): pp. 5–48.

INDEX

Five-Dog Epiphany

Marianne Leone
a memoir

How a Quintet of Badass Bichons Retrieved Our Joy

GRACIE BELLE

Published by Gracie Belle/Akashic Books
©2024 Marianne Leone
All photos courtesy of Marianne Leone other than where indicated.

ISBN: 978-1-63614-192-3
Library of Congress Control Number: 2024935823

Gracie Belle
c/o Akashic Books
Brooklyn, New York
Instagram, Facebook, X: AkashicBooks
info@akashicbooks.com
www.akashicbooks.com

Also Available from Ann Hood's Gracie Belle Imprint

Planet Claire: Suite for Cello and Sad-Eyed Lovers
by Jeff Porter

Now You See the Sky
by Catharine H. Murray

For all the rescuers of creatures large and small

Know that joy is rarer, more difficult, and more beautiful than sadness. Once you make this all-important discovery, you must embrace joy as a moral obligation.
—Andre Gide

PROLOGUE

*I*N NAPLES ON THE VIA CHIAIA, I am captured by a
pack of stray dogs. They look like wolves and there
are four of them. One places his jaws around my
upper arm, lightly, not even menacing. It feels like a bid
for ownership, an invitation to join them. Why not? My
son is dead not a year. Why not join the wolves of Napoli
and try to survive? To understand the why of survival after loss. They are a foreshadow of the pack of rescues we
will join at home, the ones that will help us survive.

CARPE DIEM

I AM NOT CAPABLE OF SEIZING the entire day, so I settle for hours, even minutes. I know that being alive in the moment is the basis of some religions, like Buddhism, but for me it's a hedge against the memory train that can quickly become a funeral cortege. It is my goal to take joy in the bee alighting on a wildflower, in the raspberries turning a dark purple on the vines I plant, in the smell of the ocean that is the divine odor of life, however fleeting. This practice can reap rewards, and then joy returns, untrammeled by grief.

But there's a joy that can be summoned without the conscious effort needed to sustain a practice. That's the feeling that comes when you look into the eyes of another damaged creature and know that your happiness is a mirror and an echo and a prayer, and that the little soul reflecting all that energy is happy too, at last.

~~

BEWARE OF DOGS

~~

I HATE AND FEAR DOGS until adulthood. When I am
a kid, they all seem inexplicably violent and capricious, like my friend Joyce's alcoholic mother,
who snarls and snaps at us with no provocation whatsoever. Dogs and I have a grace period lasting until the age
of five. Before then, my only canine references are television and film dogs, and they are all either glamour girls,
like Lady from *Lady and the Tramp* and the gorgeously
coiffed Lassie, or adventurous sinewy dog heroes like
Rin Tin Tin. There are also lovable rogues like Tramp or
sweetly dumb cuties like Pluto in my make-believe dog
universe. Dorothy's dog Toto seems like a barky cipher,
but I love him because she does.

I am growing up in the Jurassic era of child-rearing
when parent/child negotiations are not the norm. We
kids have actual nondebatable rules, and rule number
one when I am five years old is: don't leave the yard. The
yards on our street are all attached to arts and crafts–
style houses built in the twenties, treasured hard-earned
fiefdoms of the former serfs of San Donato Val di Com-
ino, now ascendant in post–World War II America. Those

in our neighborhood who aren't former *contadini* from the same impoverished village in southern Italy are first-generation Irish whose grandparents came from equally desolate villages in the south of Ireland. There is also a smattering of French Canadians in the neighborhood mix, like the dangerous Poissons, whose name we pronounce "Puss-ons," two mischievous brothers who inspire fear in the kid universe and once tied up my little brother and left him in the local haunted house. (It traumatizes him worse than the first day of school at Our Lady Help of Christians when he points his chubby little finger at the nun and screams "WITCH!" like a Puritan elder.) All the Italians on our street have riotously blooming backyards with a bounty of grapes, tomatoes, and even tenderly nurtured figs—in New England!—the crowded plant life mimicking the closeness and squabbles of the neighbors themselves.

The first time I break my mother's rule and explore the Farinas' tempting overrun garden in their lot abutting our yard, filled with tall tomato plants, even taller weeds, and an actual broken-down chicken coop, I find treasure. It is a discovery beyond the wildest imaginings of a five-year-old girl—a fat, furry, squealing trove of newborn puppies. There they are, nestled on a bed of old rags—squirming, real-life versions of the stuffed creatures that protect me at night from fairy-tale demons and monsters, making adorable snuffling noises and begging to be picked up. I reach out dazedly for one of them, in a Christmas-morning state of bliss.

Snap! A pair of monstrous jaws come out of nowhere. And then there is blood around my eye. Fear roots me to the dusty floor and beats back any pain. My vision clouds.

It is the hungry crocodile from *Peter Pan*. It is a flying monkey sent by the Wicked Witch of the East. It is the Big Bad Wolf. It is an enormous German shepherd, who outweighs me by about fifty pounds, ferociously protecting her young. I have no memory of my five-year-old self staggering back to the house. I know my native Italian and volatile mother sang the last act of *Tosca* at the sight of my bloodied face. I wear a big white bandage for a while over my right eye. The bandage comes off after a few weeks, but the fear of dogs stays with me for a lot longer.

There are, after the bite incident, three Skippys in rapid succession living in the Leone household. Skippy #1 gets hit by a car. Skippy #2 gets hit by a car. Skippy #3 gets hit by a car. My mother and father give up. I can't remember size, color, or breed, though I know all the Skippys were mutts. Except for "police dogs," which is what we call German shepherds, no one has purebreds in our neighborhood. I keep a wide berth around the Skippys and am equally relieved and guilty when each nonentity dog meets his premature demise.

When I am eight or nine, walking to Our Lady Help of Christians elementary school every morning is a gauntlet of terror. After carefully crossing Watertown Street, the busiest street in our neighborhood, I pass Magni's Bakery, stop to inhale the divine odor of fresh bread issuing forth, and walk by my father's bar, Leone's Café. Even without seeing my father, just knowing he is in the back kitchen, stirring the gravy and meatballs for the lunch crowd, I feel his invisible protection, but it only lasts for a few blocks. An unchained police dog is waiting to arrest me at the midway point to school, and he can smell my fear three houses away. What is it with this breed? They look like the wolves my mother speaks of with fearful reverence, a legacy of her girlhood in a village beneath the spiky Appenines. Walking on the other side of the street doesn't work. My personal tormentor bounds happily across the street, unharmed, every single day. If only he could meet the fate of the late, unlamented Skippys, but he is obviously protected by his best buddy, Satan, Lord of the Hounds of Hell. He playfully leaps up on his hind legs, Godzilla-like, and places his paws on my shoulders, owning me. I float above my actual body while the German shepherd and I stand face-to-face, frozen in a place beyond fear. In that moment I understand the concept of limbo, the place the nuns tell us that unbaptized babies go, where there is no time, yet there is an underlying feeling of dread. Finally, his annoyed owner bellows out Godzilla's incomprehensible name, whereupon he bounds back across the street in a magical circle of safety. Where are all the out-of-control cars that conveniently eliminated the three Skippys? This scenario continues the entire school year, proving to me that Godzilla dog is stronger than the power of prayer. I have the wasted hours racked up on novenas and rosaries to prove it.

Every year I spend the summer with my Aunt Ellie and Uncle Benny, who live a more countrified existence on the South Shore of Boston. They have thirteen acres and beachfront. They also have dogs: Ram, the rescued beagle, who lives in a pen because of his tendency to take off after rabbits, and Lillian, the morbidly obese Boston terrier, a silent Buddha-like presence. Ram isn't terrifying, just too wild to establish a relationship with anyone except my Uncle Benny, who found her crippled by buckshot on Martha's Vineyard and patiently nursed her back to health and the use of her four legs. Lillian is a recovering-alcoholic stray rescued by my aunt and uncle. Aunt Ellie discovers that Lillian has an addiction to beer when she catches her stealing Uncle Benny's after-work brew more than once. As soon as she goes on the wagon, Lillian has no personality at all, which my aunt tries to rectify by posing her in hats. Aunt Ellie's sister-in-law, Louise, lives downstairs. Her dog is the irritable and haughty PooPoo the Pekinese, a one-woman creature who literally spits upon anyone other than Louise and does not welcome petting.

I meet the occasional beguiling dog after I become an adult: my friend Gail's cockapoo, Macaroon, who collapses to the floor like a folding mop and flirts with me, batting her chorus-girl eyes; an elegant Afghan hound I see every day in the Fenway, picking her way through the grass like a tipsy debutante on six-inch Louboutins; muscled labs soaring like Nijinsky after plastic Frisbees.

I don't really get it. Dog people seem like cult members to me. What inspires the devotion, the kitsch art, the drippy poetry, the songs of praise, the enshrinement after death? Lassie knows somehow that Timmy is trapped in the well, and alerts people to rescue him. Lady and Tramp save the Darling baby from being bitten by a rat. St. Bernard dogs are in the cartoons I watch as a kid, bringing brandy to frozen-stiff people lost in the snow. This dog thing must be about rescue.

But I never need rescuing.

And then my mother dies. And my aunt who is like a mother. And my uncle who is like a father. And, most grievous of all, my son, my only son, gone in an instant. And then his dog, the link to him.

Now I live with Lucky Dog and French Fry, rescues

from a puppy mill. And I'm hoping that if they can't rescue me in return, they can at least find me huddled in my chair, bring me a brandy, and attempt to resuscitate my frozen heart. They've been freed from puppy prison. I'm clinging to a life raft after Jesse's death. We'll either save each other or drift away. We have found each other. That's the first step.

GOODY, PRINCE OF DOGS

L ONG BEFORE LUCKY DOG and French Fry enter
our newly diminished lives, there is the story of
Goody, Prince of Dogs, who lives with us in the
time of plenty, when it feels like our son Jesse's light is
drawing a never-ending scenario of laughter and good
people to our raised ranch on the tidal river. Memory
is selective, though. I remind myself that the next year
would bring a brutal two-year struggle with the local

school system to get our son his basic civil right to a "free and appropriate public education in the least restrictive environment," as the law states. Nevertheless, the winter arrival of Goody, Prince of Dogs, is always conjured in a wreath of Christmas cheer, the singular kind that involves believing little ones. Santa delivers Goody on Christmas morning, upon the urgent request of our nonverbal quadriplegic son. Our boy, who always leads the way without steps, without words, wants a dog—this is clear to us by the way his face lights up whenever a dog crosses his path, by his six-year-old excitement at reading about one in a story or seeing one on television or at the movies, and finally, and most decisively, by his dredging up and articulating the actual word "dog," foghorn-blatted without fear in the lap of Santa, that most intimidating of jolly old elves.

Jesse is nonverbal and nonambulatory because of a cerebral hemorrhage suffered on the third day after his premature birth, two and a half months before his due date. Only occasionally do we hear a word or phrase spoken when the planets align and whatever neuromotor axons it takes to fall into place allow his sculpted lips the temporary gift of coherent speech, like a beneficence tossed from a capricious god. But despite the spasticity of his limbs, Jesse's renaissance cherub face is mobile and expressive, and we understand him through a series of lip-smacking clicks and head shakes and, later, through his use of a computer. Jesse and I have an intuitive mother/child relationship too, one that often renders bulky electronic communication superfluous. When Jesse sits stiffly on Santa's lap, though, the importance of getting across the dog message is paramount. He says "dog" loudly and clearly, and it is up to us to make a dog appear on Christmas day.

And then we do the worst possible thing: we go to the pet store at the mall and buy Goody. Before I am pilloried on social media, please try to understand what research was like before the Internet made us all goopy about LOL-cats and smiling dogs and "viral" meant some kind of possibly serious illness. This was 1994. Any serious research I did in that year was all about Jesse: cerebral palsy, moving to Massachusetts, and inclusive education for severely disabled but brilliant children whose brilliance is, as yet, unproven by standard, unadapted tests and eye-rolled in disbelief by school authorities. I research bichon frises after I meet a charming one at a yard sale that first summer. I get an actual dead-tree book about bichons. I find out they don't shed: check. They are lapdogs, good for a kid in a wheelchair: check. They adorably resemble Jesse's favorite Muppets: check. Average size: around thirteen pounds. We know it will be a bichon if we ever get Jesse a dog. The horrible truth we don't know at the time: pet stores sell adorable pups like Goody that come from dog mothers who are forced to breed over and over until their early deaths in a puppy mill prison.

Little Goody was purchased at the cutely named pet store at our local mall. That store is out of business now and I can't remember the actual name, but let's say it was an artificially sweetened one like "The Puppy Palace," when it should've been more rightfully called "Dodgy Dumping Place for Dogs Bred in Appalling Circumstances."

Goody appears on Jesse's bed early Christmas morning after lots of frenzied machinations on our part the night before involving our good friends puppy-sitting while we drive thirty-seven miles in the opposite direction to spend Christmas Eve with my family. My husband, Chris, retrieves the puppy from our friends late that night and Jesse finds him on his bed the next morning, a three-pound ball of white fluff, snuffling and snorting into the bedclothes beside him. Jesse looks delighted but not surprised. He had asked, and Santa had delivered. What could be simpler in a six-year-old's purview? He had been good, so good—we tell him every day that he is the best little boy we know and will ever know. Of course Santa has brought him a dog.

Forever after, Goody is Jesse's fur-sibling, named by Jesse that Christmas Day. He begins the name, the long, drawn-out "Gooooh"—and we complete it. "Good?" "Goody?" Jesse clicks, a kiss sound, for "yes," and the name "Goody" elicits his most emphatic, reverberating yes. Being a fur-sibling means that like human sibs, Goody is jealous at times, and shows it by humping Jesse's leg in a bid for dominance, a move that always makes Jesse laugh and makes me want to sweep Goody off the bed and onto the floor like a mother bear swatting away an intruder. Jesse is helpless, lying on his bed, and Goody is in a position of power, transformed into a beast with working canines (*tiny ones*, my rational mind screams, to no effect), his furry cuteness gone in a flash of instinct. At other times Goody licks Jesse's curled fingers with an obsession that is almost admirable in its single-minded focus. Why? He never licks my hand, or my husband's, or anyone else's. Is it a healing attempt on Goody's part? It seems like some section of his dog brain registers Jesse's disability and then follows the instinct to comfort him.

Each weekday, a wheelchair van whisks Jesse up

the long driveway to school; twenty minutes before his return, Goody takes his place at the top of the stairs, a miniature sphinx awaiting the miracle of his idol's daily phoenix-like resurrection. After begging for pieces of Jesse's toast, Goody rides the elevator we had installed off the deck down to the ground floor. When the disability van appears, he goes aboard to inspect the premises, his little shoulders squared with purpose. You can almost picture him with a tiny plastic badge and peaked cap during the discharge of his bus duties. On Fridays, Holly, Jesse's craniosacral therapist, arrives for her weekly session. Goody whines until someone lifts him onto the table she unfolds in the middle of our living room. There he lies on his back, his head resting in the hollow of Jesse's arm, ready to be unkinked or just to receive a spillover of the energy radiating from Holly's medicine-woman palms. At night when Jesse and I rock together in the oversized green chair, Goody clambers aboard, settling into his shared lap domain, sighing with contentment.

In fine weather, Goody accompanies us on walks into the nearby woods, Jesse in his jogging stroller that takes us over rough terrain, Goody off-leash, trotting beside us and sometimes in Jesse's lap when the terrain gets too rough and the brambles too near his low-slung little belly. By summer, Goody is clamoring to join Jesse in the pool. We hadn't been looking for a house with a pool during our search, but having one turned out to be a wonderful resource for Jesse. The pool is the one place where he has freedom from gravity's impossible limitations. He wears a head float and is able to be eye level with his friends, for once, buoyant and gloriously untethered. Goody hovers anxiously at the edge of the pool, afraid to take the leap, whining to be picked up and dunked so he can swim circles around Jesse, like a miniature tugboat, or a tiny planet orbiting his sun.

We all orbit Jesse. The light he throws sustains every one of us, and Goody senses it too. After his swim, we are treated to Goody's "bichie buzz," the racing madly around and around the pool, in a circle dance of delight. Goody always wears a transcendent expression of sheer joy during the bichie buzz, reflected back by Jesse, looking on and laughing at the creature who embodies his own delight.

That morning, the January day I find our son dead in his bed, that is the day Goody doesn't run ahead of me to wake Jesse, like he does every morning. I never notice. I never think about it until days later, after the universe has shattered and my husband and I are postapocalyptic wanderers in a desolate place, a one-dimensional, sunless (sonless) dim land that radiates pain and only pain. Jesse was seventeen. He was our center, our true north, the little soul who shaped our vagabond lives and guided us to a place of unconditional love.

Years later, the image of Goody comes to me, a memory of him on that black day. Goody after the screams, the rough hustle of men and women in uniforms rushing through the house, the sirens blazing as they take Jesse away, my husband and I following in the police car, rigid, silent, stilled by incalculable loss. We follow not Jesse, but the beautiful husk of Jesse, life excised from his huge brown eyes, gone, gone, gone to hospital, to funeral home, to ashes. And Goody, alone in the house that still vibrates with terror, with loss, with death. What did he do then, among the crumpled detritus of the emergency technicians? Did he leap onto Jesse's bed, as he had so many times before? Or did he sense desecration, and stay away? Did he look for him? Did he sit sentinel at the top of the stairs, waiting in vain for our return as an intact family?

I don't know. I don't know because the next few hours, the following days, are still a blurry howl of pain when I try to recall them. When those who tried to give us comfort left, after the service, when the house was silent in a new and ominous way, when the last friend and family member closed the door like the clanging of a jail cell, I know that I picked Goody up and hugged him to me. And I know that his soft fur was the repository of tears unchecked, and I know also that his trembly little body that had brought all of us such joy brought me no comfort because I only wanted then to hold flesh, the smooth and living flesh of my son, my only child.

Goody sees Jesse after he's died, in his room that has become a sepulcher. He runs into Jesse's room, his mockery of a kid's room that still has *Lord of the Rings* posters and the print of the knight and his lady from our son's courtly phase, and his high school awards for honor roll and his baby cuddlies and his boom box and his music, rap and classical and oldies and silly show tunes. Goody runs into Jesse's room and then stops short, his head raised, tail wagging a joyful greeting. He does this more than once. And every time he does, I feel a strange combination of wonder, and envy and rage. Why can Goody see my son? Why can't I? Is he seeing Jesse? I have no proof of this, just my longing, my visceral need to believe that Jesse's energy still vibrates in his room. Maybe, I think, I need to develop dog eyes and strip myself of whatever is blocking my human senses to take me to Jesse. I stand behind Goody, willing myself to see, to feel something, but my clunky humanness breaks the spell every time. Goody turns and races out of the room as if nothing has happened, careless about his amazing power to invoke my son, a magician profaning a miracle.

After Jesse dies, both Goody and I start to die too. We go on long walks together in the nearby conservation land, woods leading to the bay with paths forking off into private places where a name shrieked in a high-pitched sob disturbs only the nesting birds. Jesse died in January. That summer, Goody collapses on one of our walks. Jesse's damaged brain had told his heart to stop. Now Goody's heart is failing too. I know then, when Goody is twelve years old, that puppy mill dogs are often unhealthy, that they are inbred and this can lead to devastating illness. Goody's vet confirms his weakened heart. But it's clear that heart failure is only the scientific diagnosis. In fact, he is giving up, like I am. That's all that makes sense to me, this truth that drums in time to the beat of my heart: I don't want to live in a world without Jesse. And it seems like Goody doesn't, either.

My reptile brain, deformed by sorrow and independent of conscious thought, tries to recreate something that once grew inside me, something beautiful that had become Jesse. But grief has produced instead a monstrous tangle of blood and veins, a tumorous, malignant ball that looks like an alien life form: the not-Jesse. The not-Jesse is slowly draining me of life. I waste away to a hundred pounds, from a previously slender body. My husband, viewing me from his own grief island, finally takes action, and gets me to a doctor.

Goody dies the night before my surgery to remove the not-Jesse.

LUCKY DOG AND FRENCH FRY

AFTER THE OPERATION to remove the not-Jesse, I receive good news. All the cancer is gone. I will live. I am not celebrating. I am numb. Now I am "recovering" after the surgery, spending hours on my daybed like some neurasthenic Victorian lady on a fainting couch. There is an angry red scar vertically bisecting my torso. The physical pain is at least keeping my mind off the soul pain. Getting from lying prone to propped up on one elbow is an ordeal that requires sequential thought to avoid the kind of gut stab that makes me gasp. I remain flat on my back, seeing the world through a haze of pharmaceuticals and pain. But I lack the ability to have sequential thought, as evidenced by my newfound ability to watch reality TV. I stare, uncomprehendingly, at television shows about spoiled rich women bitching at each other over byzantine slights, the origins of which escape me no matter how hard I try to concentrate. I lie there, only semi-returned to the world of the living. I can't read. Listening to music is too shattering. The reality shows are turning my hamster brain to kibble. It is February in New England. The daybed affords a view of the river at low tide, its muddy banks covered with rime. There is a tidiness to the frozen universe, a symmetry to the wintry landscape: the icy bleakness outside matches perfectly the grayed-out condition within my soul.

I really hadn't thought that losing Goody would cause the sorrow that it does, the lingering ache eclipsed just behind the huge one for my son. I am not callous, I tell myself; Goody's death has followed a long litany of human ones. Jesse's is the one that will never heal. Ever. My mother, my aunt who was like my mother, and my uncle who was like a father—they each evoke a separate step on the via dolorosa, but my mother, my aunt, my uncle each lived into their eighties. Jesse—that loss is the one that makes me catch my breath, gentling the pain before it roars into the inevitable conflagration, raging, out of control. In a month, the first crocuses will be raising their dauntless heads, peeking through the splinters of ice. And now here is Goody, his impish little spirit poking like a shard of glass through the remains of my already splintered heart. I miss him. I think of how he made me laugh when he reacted to the word "shit!" That's how I respond to the irritation of the doorbell when I'm trying to work. Therefore, Goody associated that word with *Someone's at the door! Must run to greet them!* It got to be his party piece, the trick we showed visitors. All one of us needed to do was whisper "shhhhh" and Goody would go into a wild and highly amusing frenzy. Everyone would laugh, Jesse's high chortle triggering us all. I barely remember smiling now. It seems to belong to a bygone era, one that will never come again.

The physical pain ebbs in the coming months. I become functional, at least on the outside. In April, I sit at my computer looking at Petfinder, the website for people who want to adopt a dog or cat. I berate myself for visiting the site, as though I am cheating on Goody. Some finger-pointing, fierce inner voice keeps insisting there will never be another dog like Goody. Goody was a part of Jesse. Getting another dog would be like saying I could replace Jesse. I can't replace Jesse. There will never be another fur-sibling. There will never be another Goody.

I click on *breed* and click again for *bichon frise*.

I keep going back to the same page that has not one, but two homeless bichon frises. Lucky Dog and French Fry stare straight ahead at me, their silly names a cruel joke. The hopelessness in their eyes says that they are unfamiliar with laughter or play or any sort of kindness. French Fry is half poodle, half bichon, the site informs me. But I think he is a dead ringer for Giuseppe Garibaldi,

Italy's national hero. Frenchy looks like Garibaldi's American dog son: both have scraggly white beards and big brown eyes filled with sorrow. Lucky Dog is full bichon and looks just like Goody, except that his eyes are different, battle-scarred but defiant. He stares out boldly and I get the feeling that he is French Fry's protector, even though he looks smaller in the picture. He comes across as the scrappy one, the George to Frenchy's Lenny. The site tells me that they may be adopted only as a pair; there is no getting one without the other.

But we're not *adopting a dog*, I tell myself. And we are certainly not adopting *two* dogs named Lucky Dog and French Fry.

SEDUCING MY HUSBAND
FOR DOGS

I SHOW THE PETFINDER PICTURE of Lucky and Frenchy to my husband. I have already dropped their almost–mockingly cute last names.

"Look at these two orphans of the storm," I say, keeping my voice even.

His blue-gray eyes soften, and the curve of his lips rises in an almost-grin, the same lips that were voluptuous on Jesse, the marker of his half-Italian heritage. Chris gentles animals and humans. They sense the kindness that is at his heart's core. I remember him putting a little frog into Jesse's hand with a meticulous care that was respectful of both Jesse and the frog. I think of the snapshot of sleepy Chris in bed, Goody posed on his hind legs, saluting him, Chris smiling, his eyes crinkling with amusement and, yes, love. Could he, could *we*, love these two damaged creatures? Or are we too damaged ourselves. Chris needs time, time to process, his inner self still staggering backward, reeling from a blow.

But even before the time-space continuum was shattered, when we became different versions of ourselves, even as far back as acting class when I was enjoined to work on stillness for six long months, Chris was already there, at the stillness point. He could go deep. I am sure he could probe that place of love, of giving again for this ragtag pair of dogs from a puppy mill.

When we were first married, my husband's favorite gift from me, the one he still speaks of with awe, was an hour in an isolation tank in lower Manhattan. When I saw him afterward, he was exactly like someone who'd had a religious experience, shaky to be out in the world, marveling at the jangly streets of the city, senses enhanced, reinvigorated, a man reborn. Isolation tanks were a thing in the early eighties, popularized by the film *Altered States*, where William Hurt immures himself in a soundproof, lightless tank, floating in body-temperature salt water. Chris tried to articulate what it felt like to regain the lost silence of the womb, to still the clamorous mind.

I can only reaffirm that he is my complete opposite, the yin to my yang, and that my experience of being enclosed in a dank, dark, body-sized space would leave bloody scratches on the capsule cover and echoing screams as I begged to be let out.

Newly married at the time, I experienced a brief pang, fearing that his introduction to my raucous world, including my boisterous Italian family, had driven my new spouse to finding relief in a simulated coffin. I don't remember our wedding poem; it was a second choice because my ex-boyfriend used the one I wanted: Shakespeare's "Sonnet 116." We were careless about the whole event, snarky, treating it without reverence, leaving out our families, making the whole thing spur-of-the-moment (we lied about imminent acting commitments and the need to leave town). I wasn't romantic or religious, but even I balked at the atmosphere at the New York City office where we got our marriage license. The clerk bellowing: "COOPER! NEXT!" before we said our vows was too much even for me. We found a Unitarian church in Manhattan. We posed ironically in the anteroom, mimicking a nineteenth-century couple, my husband standing with his hand on my shoulder, I sitting demurely, wearing a crown of flowers. My ring was from a pawnshop on Canal Street, my antique dress from a jumped-up secondhand store, Chris's suit a sixty-dollar special from 14th Street. Five close friends attended, all of us feeling absurd, as if we were impersonating adults. I giggled during the ceremony: the minister switched voices when she began the ritual, intoning the words in a fake-majestic tone. My new husband, though, had tears in his eyes; for him, the solemnity of the moment resonated.

Despite his misty-eyed turn during our wedding ceremony, many years later, my gentle, generous partner can still make me laugh like I'm five years old. That's his best gift to me, besides being the father of our son, for as long as we had him. The ups and downs of the acting profession, the absences it has demanded, rewards it has bestowed, the cataclysmic blow of losing our only child—these events and others have deepened and changed our perspectives and have left us in an altered state. But I've taken possession of that poem my ex-boyfriend used, *Love is not love which alters when it alteration finds*, because it belongs, really, to us. Our life has altered, we've altered, but the love has never changed.

* * *

Chris hovers nearby during my recovery from surgery, supplying tea and sympathy, but I keep going back and staring at Lucky and Frenchy, the orphans of the storm. I leave the site with their tragic faces on his iPad where he can't miss them. They are still available, still bedraggled, still bereft, looking even more hopeless somehow.

No one is adopting them.

Then, almost without our conscious consent, *we* are adopting them. But first, my husband and I must acquire three recommendations, including one from a vet, and have an in-home visit from a representative of the rescue organization. A very nice middle-aged lady arrives at our house one spring morning. Chris stays long enough to meet her, then bails on urgent and faux "errands." I smile at her and send him telepathic death threats, hoping they don't show on my face. I offer coffee to the interview lady. She shows me pictures of her nine Pomeranians. (*Nine?* Yes, reader, I judged her. Seven years later, I found myself thinking that it wasn't totally an insane idea that *we* could actually accommodate nine or ten bichons.) The lady and I sit stiffly in our yard sale–themed living room that I hope screams shabby chic but fear looks merely shabby. I ramble nervously on about Goody, Prince of Dogs, and try to reassure her that we are normal people who would never add more harm to already injured animals. I promise daily walks, healthy food, reassuring routines. She asks about the portrait of our son. I tell her about Jesse in my dispassionate-for-strangers voice, the one that insures my not getting emotional. She cries anyway, when I tell her that Jesse had been disabled and that he had died. I brace myself.

"Then you'll know how to nurture these dogs, because you had a special-needs son."

She is compassionate. She is kind. She is absolutely right. We have patience because of Jesse. We have tolerance for differences. Am I offended by this warm-hearted lady's comparison of rescue dogs to my disabled son? Absolutely. But then again, nothing she can say will be harmless. Nothing. If I riff through the catalog of horrendous things uncomfortable people have said to me regarding the death of my son, I could dredge up some real gaspers. This is low on the scale. People offering sympathy to bereaved parents are at a huge disadvantage. I feel a certain sympathy for *them* because anything they say is terrible and wrong. The situation is the definition of awkward and no-win. This is the all-time chart-topper: "I can't imagine," they say. *No, you fucking can't*, you think. *Be glad you can't, but don't say that to me. Shut up.* That's the go-to for most people: "I can't imagine." I want to say, *Then it's lucky you're not an actor, isn't it? Or a writer. It's lucky you have no imagination. How great for you.* This dog-adoption woman does have some imagination. She can picture how we once made the leap to loving a damaged child and might now be able to love damaged dogs. This is better than the people who say, who actually verbalize the words, "Oh, he was disabled? Then it's for the best," to us, as if they are the directors of eugenics at Hitler's Operation T4, and their job is now a little easier with the removal of one more "useless eater." On the terrible day of Jesse's death, my elderly ninety-something neighbor across the street was the first one on the scene that frosty January morning, after the fire trucks and paramedics arrived. As Chris and I scrambled to the police car, she stood at the top of our driveway, an angel of death swaddled in mufti.

"Jesse's dead," I said, stunned at saying it aloud.

"Then it's for the best," she said, the progenitor of many Grim Reapers, all echoing the same unbelievable sentence.

I hope none of these fevered inner rants show on my face to the Pomeranian Lady, only the strained smile I am projecting along with assenting head bobbles.

It works, somehow. We are deemed worthy, even after Chris ditches the initial interview and returns in time for the wrap-up, which consists of him smiling shyly and silently at the lady who is the gatekeeper to Lucky and Frenchy. The Pomeranian Lady gets his gentle aura, and thankfully doesn't confuse him with the more unsavory characters from some of his films. (Believe it or not, this has happened a few times, most notably with the famous Boston quit-smoking guy. During our session, he confused us with the couple he had just seen in *Great Expectations*. In that film, the wife—not played by me!—is cheating on my husband's character, and at our session, the quit-smoking guy accused me of cheating on Chris, to our utter confusion. The quit-smoking guru left the room hurriedly and never came back. A young woman assistant came in and told us our session was free. We left, still confused until the *Great Expectations* mix-up finally dawned on us. Once outside, we lit up.)

The Pomeranian Lady gives us official papers to sign, and sets a date to pick up the orphans of the storm in Connecticut from the kind people fostering them.

Lucky and Frenchy arrive at our house four months after I had major surgery, sixteen months after our son Jesse died, and four months after the death of Goody, Prince of Dogs.

WELCOME TO YOUR FOREVER HOME

*T*HE CAR IS VIBRATING LIKE A CARNIVAL ride as-
sembled by a drunken roustabout. Two little bodies are at the epicenter of the shaking:
Lucky and Frenchy, on their way to what the rescue or-
ganizations call their "forever home." I sit in the backseat, holding them in my lap, trying unsuccessfully to
calm the outsized terror that is filling the car like a toxic
cloud. It is my first real inkling that human touch means

the opposite of reassurance to puppy mill survivors.

My husband and I have driven to Connecticut from the South Shore of Massachusetts to pick up our rescues from Deb, their warm-hearted foster mother. Lucky and Frenchy are housed with about ten other small breeds awaiting families. The other dogs are lively, yapping happily when we come to the door, swarming us with glad-dog greetings. Lucky and Frenchy are off by themselves, sequestered, bathed in an aura of doom. They allow Chris and me to hold them, but they seem indifferent, resigned. They remain passive as we sit on the floor cuddling them.

We arrive home in time for dinner, but Lucky and Frenchy aren't interested in eating. Even cooked chicken can't lure them to their food bowls. They cower on the ratty orphanage dog bed they came with, their eyes following our every move. We are humans, and that means hurters. They remain on hyper-alert when we go to bed. I hope they will finally relax after the lights go out, but I doubt that will happen. I picture them scanning the horizon like sentries, Lucky relieving Frenchy and vice versa as the long night wears on.

The next morning, I stagger into the kitchen for coffee. Our floor plan is wide open, living/dining room melding into a kitchen area; we chose our house for its wheelchair-accessible open space—and its rock-bottom price. When I look around, eyes newly opened via jet fuel–level coffee, I see what can only be described as the aftermath of a shitstorm. The living room is a poop mine-field. Lucky and Frenchy remain on their orphanage bed, trembling, their eyes apprehensive and following my every move.

My reaction is crazy, but not so crazy for those of us

who inhabit the planet of the bereaved. Our world is up-ended; nothing makes sense. So, when I survey the devastation before me, I smirk at the sight, and think: *Grief made manifest.* I can't help it; a quote from C.S. Lewis arises: *No one ever told me that grief felt so like fear.*

"Don't worry, I've been there," I tell Lucky and Frenchy to no comprehension whatsoever. "I have PTSD too. I mean, I haven't literally shit myself yet, but . . ."

"Who are you talking to?" My husband walks in and sees the transformation of our living room from shabby to shitty chic. "Shit!" he yells.

I smile. "Right."

It's such an extreme version of "shit happens," it is almost cosmic. Well, comic anyway. Not that anyone's laughing.

Chris and I watched hours of Cesar Millan's *Dog Whisperer* show in preparation for the arrival of our two rescues. We never, however, saw an episode devoted to the rehabilitation of such fearful creatures. Most of the dogs featured on Cesar's show express fear as aggression. Lucky and Frenchy seem numb, shell-shocked, remote, but never aggressive. More pressing is the immediate situation. Our rescues have never been house-trained, have never walked on leashes or even walked on anything other than wire cages for the first years of their lives. If I assume the "alpha" stance and lead them outside, will they follow me? Will they run away? We do not live on a busy street—in fact, there are no sidewalks in our part of town—but cars occasionally zoom by. I picture the Pomeranian Lady unleashing the entire Shih Tzus & Furbabies rescue organization on us after Lucky and Frenchy meet their premature demise under a rogue school bus.

I summon up a movie-villain voice, and the dogs respond to my Darth Vader "Come!" I only have to say it once. They scramble down the stairs and through the open front door. I feel a rush of confidence at the same time that I feel absurd about my pasted-on leadership skills. I plan to have them follow me to the fenced-in area where they can run around on the grass bordering the pool. I hope to have them follow me, to be more accurate.

It is a glorious spring day. I look at the grass studded with buttercups, and I hear Jesse's little-boy giggle. Just for a moment the vista before me shimmers and Jesse's face appears, laughing, as I hold a yellow flower under his chin. A fairy-tale troll lurks just behind the appreciation of the fragile new blossoms and whispers, "Butterbutterbutter," jabbing me with a memory of loss. Bitterbitterbitter. I have one for each season—my new normal. Spring is the worst—all that new life, hope, and promise. Ask me again in October, though, and I will tell you that autumn is the worst, with Jesse's looming birthday and memories of the new school year. Or maybe it's the holidays: Thanksgiving, with its missing place at the table, or Christmas, the all-enveloping matrix with the surround sound carols that always seem to be playing *"Through the years we all will be together"* in an inescapable jeering infinity loop. All of them. It's all the seasons. Each one has a grief sniper lying in wait behind spring flowers, birthdays, school buses, Christmas trees, with my heart in the crosshairs.

I glance back at Lucky and Frenchy, my fearful charges. They follow me onto the asphalt of the driveway like little windup toys, their stick legs stiff and robotic, a hateful legacy of their former lives confined in a wire cage. I wonder if they will ever run or play. I lead them to the pool area and Lucky begins to respond to the grass under his feet. He prances in a sudden balletic pirouette of springtime almost-joy, and my eyes fill with tears at his resilience. Frenchy follows gingerly, testing the ground for hidden pitfalls, like a little old man navigating an icy sidewalk.

I sit in a lawn chair, tilt my face to the sun, close my eyes, and drift, content, listening to the happy sounds of Lucky and Frenchy becoming bolder by the minute, chasing each other, truer to their doggy selves with every grassy leap. I am congratulating myself and reliving my power moment as pack leader when I hear the splash. My eyes fly open. Lucky has fallen into the pool and is now swimming in panicked circles at the deep end. There are no steps into the pool, and he is too small to leap out of the water or use his paws to leverage himself up and out. The water washes over his face and I scream and jump into the pool. I guide Lucky's flailing little body to the edge of the pool and heave him onto the side. He shakes himself and runs off without a backward glance, indifferent to my lifesaving heroics and on to the next adventure. I haul myself out with much more difficulty, weighed down by water-bloated sweats. Up on the deck overlooking the pool I hear Chris's laughter, and even in my soaked and shivering condition, it's contagious. I join him. He comes down and brings me a towel. We look at each other and I know we are both thinking the same thing: *How long has it been since we have laughed like this?* I look over at Lucky. Even if our bold little rescue doesn't care that I have saved his life, I am grateful to him for returning laughter to ours.

NATURAL BORN KILLERS

*I*ARRIVE HOME FROM ERRANDS one late-spring
morning to find Chris standing inside the pool
enclosure with a strange expression on his face.
When he speaks, his voice climbs a couple of octaves.
"Baby, I thought it was a squeaky toy!" he babbles at me.
His hands are gripping the fence like a prisoner of war.
He has just witnessed what could be called an atrocity,
unless you're the pragmatic sort who is blasé about the
food chain and the circle of life in the wild kingdom.
Lucky and Frenchy have killed and eaten a baby rabbit
and mauled another one, now in its death throes nearby.
Frenchy Garibaldi, in a psychotic break from his little

white ballerina dog appearance, has blood on his ruff and a feral look on his face. Lucky, prancing happily nearby in the middle of the murder scene, seems quite at home surrounded by blood, guts, and dismembered limbs.

I think of Goody, Prince of Dogs, and how he would have dealt with a baby rabbit in his territory. A vision rises of Jesse's dog, immaculate in a monocle and top hat, intoning in a plummy accent to the offending little creature: "What on earth are *you* doing in my exclusive pool area? Begone, rodent!" That's if he had noticed the rabbit at all. He would most likely have had eyes only for Jesse and anyone who could lift him into the pool to be near his adopted sibling and ward.

As for these two white, fluffy ex-prisoners, I am certain that each little dog has only one thought at the sight of the newborn kits: *Food source.* Followed by: *Meat. Protein. Kill now. Eat.*

Chris jokes about how maybe it's a good thing that Lucky and Frenchy have so far declined to share our bed, preferring to sleep on their spiffy new dog digs by the fireplace in our living room. My husband says it will be awhile before the disturbing image of blood on Frenchy's ruff goes away. I agree with Chris but don't tell him that I feel a secret thrill at the dogs' ability to use their tag-team ferocity and resurrect their survival instincts. They want to live, despite all the pain and abuse they have experienced. They don't ponder the existential crisis of whether life after puppy prison is worth living.

I want to be fierce too. I was a warrior mother for seventeen years, fighting for our son's personhood, for his right to be regarded as whole even though his body was broken. I need a little of the rescues' spirit to pierce the gray gloom that drops randomly from the sky, immobilizing and shrouding me in loss. And though the wildlife in our yard is safe from my savagery, I vow to take note of Lucky's and Frenchy's will to survive their shattered beginnings and learn a thing or two about ferocity and life as we now know it.

~~

SUMMER SCHOOL

~~

B Y SUMMER IT IS CLEAR: we must teach Lucky and Frenchy to swim to the newly installed stairs at the shallow end of the pool. They love their time outdoors around the pool and the area is fenced, so we don't have to worry about them running off and turning feral, living on rabbits in the nearby woods. However, ever since Lucky fell into the pool during one of his mad, zigzagging chases with Frenchy as "it," I have been afraid to leave them alone. If he isn't trained to swim to the stairs, he might just swim hopelessly in circles until he drowns like the chipmunks we occasionally fish out of the pool filter, a thought so horrifying it spurs my husband and me into a frenzy of swimming instruction.

Lucky runs away when we walk toward him with intent, no matter how reassuring Chris and I try to be, crooning his name or singing it out brightly. Lucky sees right through our false heartiness and glowers at us from under a lawn chair. Frenchy is more passive, almost depressingly so. If you approach Frenchy with intent, he just shrinks into the ground and stares up at you, hopelessly awaiting his certain death, his Eeyore eyes glistening and resigned. Frenchy is the first, therefore, to brave the waters of the pool. He begins furiously dog-paddling the air the moment Chris picks him up. It's both hilarious and heartbreaking, that cartoonlike desperation. Lucky is riveted by the spectacle. But the minute Frenchy hits the water, Lucky leaps up, and, barking frantically, follows Frenchy's progress, sometimes nipping the top of his head, egging him onward toward the stairs like an Olympic coach in sight of the gold. Frenchy reaches the stairs and scrambles inelegantly out of the water and over the side. We cheer his triumph. He shakes himself, emitting palpable blame-rays toward us. *You have used me horribly,* he beams. *But I forgive you. Don't do that again, please.* He slinks under a wrought-iron table. He stares at us with disappointment at our betrayal.

We turn to Lucky, who reads our minds and flees. A chase ensues; Chris and I split up and finally employ a successful pincer move. I pick Lucky up and he flails and kicks, but when he is lowered into the water he swims like a pro even without the reciprocal encouragement of Frenchy, who remains safely under the table. When Lucky emerges, triumphant, to our cheers, he shakes himself, then takes several victory laps around the pool. He ends his gleeful run on his back, wiggling in ecstasy against the scratchy cement.

Lucky knows how to take in joy. I wish I could be like him, instead of feeling more like Frenchy's soul sister. My operating system, like his, seems like it's set to default mode for resignation and suffering. If my friends and acquaintances read this, they will be flummoxed. I don't appear to be a mater dolorosa on the outside. But my inside thoughts are dark, dark, dark. I applaud Lucky, more for his jubilation than the swim, and a little of his delight spills over to me.

For the rest of the summer, the Lucky-and-Frenchy-coach-and-swim act is in high demand for both kids and adults, and laughter is heard again around the pool. This laughter, more than anything, evokes Jesse, lying on his little blue raft by the water's edge, ready to lose the chains of gravity and scream for joy, the same joy I know Lucky feels and has channeled somehow to us. A distant and alien radio wave of hope reaches us on the planet of Grief, one we're not sure is real or a cosmic joke on us.

~

LOVE

~

"**I** THINK YOU'RE STARTING TO LOVE ME," I taunt Lucky after he lets me fondle him without flinching for the second day in a row. He so doesn't want to love me. It interferes with his tough-guy self-image. Summer is over and it's the grim season of canvas skies and early dark. I attempt to invade Lucky and Frenchy's favorite new space on the big green chair. My husband is working in another state, and I have been living in my head all day, communing with ghosts. I need contact with a beating heart.

Frenchy Garibaldi is a pushover. He lets me stare directly into his eyes, big and brown and dolorous, like his dogfather, Giuseppe Garibaldi, the storied unifier of Italy. Frenchy lets me see his suffering. He has a noble yet vacant face, the scars of abuse making him see the world through an invisible barrier. He has officially succumbed to my siren charms.

Frenchy and Lucky climb onto the biggest and most comfortable chair in our living room. They sleep there every night. They allow me to sidle onto the chair and pet them. I make this as much as a routine as the morning

run outside to sprinkle the shrubbery, followed by breakfast bones. But recently Frenchy has decided that this
petting thing is a drug to which he will become addicted.
The first night, I climb onto the chair, and he is on the dog
bed. He immediately sits up and raises his paws onto the
hassock, but he doesn't dare jump up. I encourage him,
though he stays immobile, unable to take the leap. I help
him up and pet him. He is so overcome with pleasure he
begins panting heavily. The next night he jumps up without any prompting. This is exactly like seducing a boyfriend. A boyfriend named Frenchy Garibaldi from my
old working-class neighborhood outside of Boston. That
doesn't seem like a stretch.

Lucky, the full bichon, is bolder than Frenchy, and his
bluster at the approach of strangers is over-the-top theat-
rical, especially in light of the fact that he weighs thirteen
pounds soaking wet. I, too, am included in the stranger
category if I do something suspicious, like go downstairs,
then come back up, my face and scent transformed into
sinister intruder by disappearing for two minutes. First
Lucky barks madly, then he howls, finally subsiding into
huffy snorts and low growls, his huge black eyes never
leaving the intruder. But for all his *haka* dancing, the
mini-Maori warrior is terrified of touch. Even adjacent
touching is threatening; he jumps off the big green chair
every time I snuggle with Frenchy. It makes sense: Lucky
is smarter than Frenchy, and he has a better memory of
what touch means. It means bad things. It means being
kicked and hit and picked up by the scruff of the neck and
flung to the ground. My memory of touch is silky golden
skin covering a slender, spastic body that responds to a
massage with a grateful clicking sound for "yes." My

memory of touch is also colored by sudden loss and the ephemeral solace of dreams. The rescue dogs and I have formed a pack, all of us wary of the way life can without any warning grab you by the scruff of the neck or kick you aside. But at least I remember love.

It's time to move this along. I sidle gently toward the chair and Lucky stands nervously, ready to bolt. I put my hand out and he flinches, but he doesn't leap away. He settles down and lets me stroke him, a first. I try to calm the excitement I feel at this major step. Lucky averts his face as I rub his head. He allows only a few strokes before he jumps off the chair.

A few days later, I creep into the chair again. This time they both stay put. I roll their necks and try to rub out the memory of fear. I pull the fleece blanket over all of us. Lucky puts his head on my chest, over my heart. I am thrilled and afraid to move. He still won't look at me, the fearsome combination of petting and direct love too overwhelming for his crumpled little soul.

The next morning, he runs away just because I happen to make eye contact. I can't help it—I'm insulted. Suddenly this little fluffball is like every bad boyfriend who never called after a hot date like they said they would. An absurd image of Lucky superimposed over a surly boy in a torn T-shirt and low-slung jeans comes roiling back from my tormented teenage past. He watches me from a safe distance through half-lidded eyes. His lip curls into a sneer. He's bad, he wants me to know. He doesn't need me, or anyone. I half expect him to jam a cigarette into his mouth and grab my lighter, staring at me as it dangles from his smirking lips.

Sometimes the sheer work of getting these dogs to be

dogs just infuriates me. They're bichons—they're supposed to crave laps, affection, doting. That's why they're tucked smugly under the arms of all those eighteenth-century royals in paintings, coddled to a fare-thee-well. But when I'm overtaken by impatience, the dogs' core-level fear looks to me like spite. I forget temporarily that they are ex–puppy mill prisoners. At the moment, I don't care. They are stubborn. Ungrateful. I boil marrow bones and bestow them every morning, sometimes even before I pour my own crucial start-up coffee. I am their Bone Goddess. Can't they just love me?

Back on the chair the next night for another try, I channel the Temptations and serenade Lucky in my cracked-from-years-of-smoking falsetto:

I'm gonna shower you with love and affection
Look out it's comin' in your direction . . .

A flip of the tail and he's gone. Lucky thinks I'm a crazed stalker. Or worse, he's embarrassed by my ironic torch-singer pose. He peers at me from his safety zone, under the oak table across the room—as far away from me as he can get and still inhabit the same space.

He comes sniffing around when I'm on the floor doing yoga the following morning, but I ignore him. Two can play at this game, buddy. He leaps onto the hassock and his eyes never leave my outstretched legs as I move them left to right, right to left, his head windshield-wiping like he's in the stands at Wimbledon. I move into the cobra position. When I lift my head, Lucky backs away as if I am a real viper.

You know what? This is good, I tell myself as I scrub

out the oil-slicked pan in which I boiled another batch of marrow bones. Lucky and Frenchy are damaged. These dogs are too damaged to need me, except for food, water, and shelter, and I'm too damaged to nurture them. They're the perfect dogs for right now, for this walled-in-by-grief time of life. They're zombiefied by pain. So am I. They stare dazedly at things and totter stiffly around. So do I. They are afraid of everything. So am I.

We're made for each other.

Jesse was damaged too, but that was just on the outside. He was quadriplegic and nonverbal and brilliant. He wrote poetry using his computer and made the honor roll every semester. But he wasn't damaged inside, like these dogs. He could take love in and reflect it back like the world's biggest magnifying glass. Love in, love out—that's how it worked with Jesse.

It's time to walk them. Frenchy is stunned and compliant and easy to get on the leash. Lucky slinks round and round the oak table, slithering under chairs, always just out of my reach. I almost give up; this feels too much like some kind of sneaky Zen koan or a horrible life metaphor, drearily going around in circles, chasing after something I don't even want. I bark out his name like a drill sergeant, like all the books say I'm supposed to do, and Lucky flattens to the ground. I hate it. I hate the pack-leader thing, and I hate seeing Lucky abject and cowering and—what? Thinking I might just morph into one of his former jailers? The sky, too, looks threatening, adding to the gloom of an already dark day.

On our stop-and-start walk, I look down at these two rescues. Frenchy skitters along with his back hunched, ready to duck and cover at a moment's notice, his ears lifted by the wind, which only adds to his fear factor, amplifying sounds and ramping up the nameless terror of crackling leaves. I stop to pet him reassuringly, but he hunches even further, bending like a comma at the approach of my hand. Finally, he accepts the caress; his liquid eyes telegraph a mute apology for flinching.

Lucky surges ahead, a dog on a mission, turning his head back occasionally to bite the leash. Then, a doggy revelation. He turns to look at me after a particularly satisfying sniff at a clump of weeds, a gap-toothed smile of pure joy stretching from ear to furry ear. I'm so shocked I smile back. A minute later he's back to biting the leash and I'm wondering if I imagined the smile.

But when I unleash Lucky at our door, the metamorphosis continues. He cavorts wildly at my feet in a paroxysm of delight, his eyes never leaving my face. He swirls like a Sufi mystic in the throes of religious ecstasy. He prances like a man dancing for his beloved. He invites me to play, but by his rules. I take him up on his invitation eagerly, immediately forgetting my former dark and brooding thoughts.

I learn the rules by trial and error. They are: *1) Clap your hands. 2) Freeze in position. 3) Now chase me, and I'll run away—but I'll always come back.* It's a tiny, skewed version of "love in, love out." He's still damaged, and so am I, but maybe this outside game can lead us in, and there we will begin.

Inside/Outside
by Jesse Cooper

On the inside, I walk
On the outside, I give
On the outside, I am mute
On the outside, I give
On the inside, I speak
On the inside, I walk

DREAM

I N THE EARLY MORNING GLOOM, I make coffee by rote because I'm still thinking of my dream where I had a baby that was Jesse but not Jesse and I wanted to change his little shirt. I asked Chris to get me one of Jesse's T-shirts. Chris said, as if to chide me, "He'll always be in Jesse's shadow." I realized then that the child in the dream was not my child, and the fleeting hope that I could have it all again, the surrounding joy, was gone. Chris was right. He wouldn't be Jesse. It would never work.

The sense of futility is loss squared.

Jesse would have turned twenty-one years old in nine days. I start to cry in the kitchen, remembering the silky feel of the baby's skin in the dream. I grind the coffee beans, place the paper filter in the coffee maker, fill the kettle, sobbing.

Frenchy is suddenly alert. He stands erect and freezes, looking like a ceramic dog knickknack my mother would have given pride of place in our kitschy living room. He emits shrill yips at regular intervals, like a smoke alarm, his eyes never leaving my face. Frenchy is the Emotion Police, the Cerberus guarding my own private Hades.

I immediately stop crying, arrested by the Emotion Police Dog.

STRANGER DANGER

I N THESE FIRST FEW YEARS WITH US, Lucky and Frenchy are put to the test regularly when we have visitors. And we have a lot of visitors, especially in summer. We live on a tidal river, close to a marina and a bay. Family and friends arrive in hordes when the weather is good. At the first sound of the car doors slamming, Lucky and Frenchy are on high alert. Even after the wild barking from Lucky and supportive yips from Frenchy have subsided to low growls and grumpy sounds of exasperation, the visitors are eyed by the dogs like prospective shoplifters for the duration of their time at our house. Old friends who remember Goody just can't grasp the fact that Lucky, who looks exactly like Goody, is a dog traumatized by abuse. Unlike Goody, he won't jump on a seated stranger and claim his breedright as a lapdog. Lucky sneers at an outstretched hand as if it's an obscene gesture. He backs away, glowering from a distance. It makes me feel like a failure as a host, as if I'm subjecting our company to broken toilets or bad food.

When our overnight guests open the door of the guest room on the same floor where the dogs sleep, the barking that greeted them upon arrival begins all over again. The dogs no longer cower in a corner shaking, so that's progress, I tell myself. Now they raise their heads like meerkats from the plush green double-sized chair. Their eyes follow the intruders with suspicion. When visitors emerge from the bathroom, Lucky and Frenchy bark them back into the guest room, only subsiding when the door closes. *And stay there!* they seem to be saying, as they settle back into a wary sleep. I don't like to think about what a door opening in the night might have meant to them in puppy prison.

For casual drop-ins, like the FedEx guys, I find myself explaining the dogs' sad history, so they will forgive Lucky and Frenchy's rudeness and not think of me as a neurotic dog owner. "They were prison dogs," I tell them. That line just makes the delivery guys look at me strangely, so I amend my excuse to, "They spent their entire lives in wire cages," in a blatant bid for sympathy. "They don't bite," I say, even as Lucky is employing his rushing maneuver, the one where he runs at their legs, exactly like a dog about to take a vicious bite out of a tender ankle. I fly out the door after Lucky, yelling, "He has no teeth!" in an effort to be reassuring, but the delivery guy usually looks less than reassured. Lucky's bark betrays his anxiety, it seems to me. It's querulous, more like a howl, and he paradoxically wags his tail during the whole display that's meant to be menacing. Way to win friends, Lucky. But he doesn't care about human friends. And he does just fine with dogs.

On one of my walks to the nearby marina with Lucky and Frenchy, we meet two well-raised little bichons. Their names are Mary and Molly, and their owners are two shy gray-haired ladies who are roommates. Mary is the alpha dog, and she immediately goes into play position with Lucky. It's delightful to see Lucky reciprocate like any normal dog. Molly cowers away from the fray and Frenchy hides behind me, his nose occasionally nudging the back of my knee, like a shy toddler entering a new preschool. I notice when I pick up Mary that she seems to weigh nothing, though she looks to be the same size as Lucky. I remember that this is what Goody felt like in my arms, and realize that Lucky holds himself with the kind of tension that turns his body into steel, much like what the cerebral palsy did to Jesse's muscle tone. But the cerebral palsy was a result of his intraventricular hemorrhage on the third day of his life that left scarring on the brain. Lucky and Frenchy are rigid with fear, an emotion I hope Jesse never, or very rarely, experienced in his lifetime. If you turn Frenchy onto his back, his four little legs will stick straight up like a mini four-poster bed or a cartoon drawing of a dead dog. When does the scarring effect of fear leave the body?

On our walks, the dogs stiffen and stand like statues when people approach—joggers, parents walking with strollers, or people riding bikes, as if freezing in place renders them invisible to others. People often stop to comment on how adorable Lucky and Frenchy are, referring to them as "puppies" because of their diminutive size. Inevitably, their heads will be down while they are being showered with praise. When they look up, they will have giant brown smears all around their mouths. This is because they have been eating dirt, their favorite pastime, whenever the walk is interrupted.

"I don't know why they do that. They get chicken at

home," I explain irrelevantly, as the dogs' former admirers recoil from the dirt-eaters.

We resume our out-of-sync walk. Lucky plows ahead and Frenchy lags behind. I walk with my arms stretched out like a Balinese shadow dancer. I want to give these former prisoners the illusion of freedom, so that someday they can actually be free. I think about Goody, and how he never needed a leash when he accompanied Jesse and me on our walks. I wonder if the day will ever come when the dogs will trust us enough to not need tethering. In these first years together, the only way they will stay close is to be leash-bonded. My impatient heart wants the bond to be love, only love.

~

HOWL

~

IT'S JANUARY, THE MONTH I HATE, the month of loss, of Jesse leaving for good. The marsh surrounding the tidal river looks like a frozen moonscape where nothing can live. But the coyotes are alive and howling in the icy black night. The chorus saves me the trouble of opening my mouth. I'm tired. I lie with the dogs on the green chair and close my eyes, listening. The wind rises, adding an eerie dissonance, plinking neural notes on a devil's harp. The dogs are still, alert. The screaming of my surrogates goes on until it's inside my head and we are all screaming together, even though I am silent.

Then the sound is closer and outside my mind. I open my eyes. Frenchy has his head tilted back and it is Frenchy Garibaldi, little white fluffball, who is emitting a wail that is a whisper. It takes a minute to comprehend the absurdity. Then I laugh at the sight of this amuse-bouche for coyotes joining the fray. "No, no," I tell Frenchy, "not your tribe." And now it's as if his timid keening has summoned Jesse's laugh because I hear it bubbling and can picture— no, can *feel*—us together laughing at Frenchy, the hors d'oeuvre who thinks he's part of the pack. We're outside the pack too; we don't belong to the regular world, Jesse and I. And now we're howling together because it was a sound that Jesse could make. We are howling together and our howls tumble downward into laughter. And I am grateful to Frenchy for taking us there, to a place we never were in this life.

∿
LIE DOWN WITH DOGS . . .
∿

Paul Fox

*L*UCKY IS SO BOLD, DARING TO COME all the way downstairs into the unexplored outer reaches of our new master bedroom. We have renovated the downstairs part of our house that used to be Jesse's playroom and my office, and now the dogs have the upstairs to themselves when we don't have guests. Lucky can hear the shift in breathing that precludes waking, even from upstairs. But the object for Lucky is breakfast bones, and so every morning I begin the slow ascent to consciousness with the help of a new kind of alarm: the *tickticktick* of Lucky's paws on the hardwood floor. He peers around the corner and stares at me. Sometimes I pretend to be asleep.

I'm careful to regulate my breathing and not move. But Lucky always knows. How do dogs automatically know when you're conscious?

When I don't acknowledge him immediately, Lucky goes into his dance. He lies on our new rug, legs splayed, and rocks to and fro, luxuriating into the deep pile with a yoga-like fluidity I can only envy. Then he stands and shakes himself out of his trance and trains his black eyes on me. *Get up*, he transmits. *Get up, human. Get up now, before you force me to rake my claws across your closet door. You wouldn't want that, would you? Get up, before I pee on your new hardwood floor.*

I really want Lucky and Frenchy to start sleeping with us. Goody used to split his time between our bed and Jesse's. I try to make the rescues sleep on the bed this frigid night, without success. Chris is away and the dogs have become self-appointed but terrified protectors, the Barney Fifes of watchdogs. The swirling leaves blowing by the door are the massed enemy. The rescues stand as if they are carved-stone griffins at the top of the stairs, arfing in sync. They bark at the leaf intruders, putting the full force of their combined thirty pounds between themselves and the evil winter wind.

I think maybe they would feel calmer if we were all together in a pack, sleeping curled around each other, safe and content on our soft flannel sheets. I know I would. I retire downstairs without them and try to sleep. Listening to them bound across the floor every time the wind rises makes me feel like the stock counterintuitive character in a horror movie. The phantom audience in my head is frustrated and screaming, *There's someone outside! Don't you get it? Lock the doors! Get help! You're gonna die!* When the audience becomes deafening, defeating any possibility of sleep, I get up, resentful of my fifteen-pound protectors, and I carefully check the lock and even open the front door to peer into the blackness, half expecting to be yanked into the marsh, a lizard-skinned hand over my mouth.

I carry Frenchy downstairs and Lucky follows anxiously, as I knew he would. I put Frenchy beside me on the bed and he meekly lays his head on my chest and allows me to pet him. But Lucky paces at the foot of the bed, and then jumps down and runs away. *Ticktickticktick*. After about ten seconds, Frenchy gets restless. He can hear Lucky running around upstairs. He can't relax without his partner. I plod up to corral Lucky and bring him back to bed, after whispering a fruitless "Stay" to Frenchy. But Frenchy jumps off the bed and runs upstairs right behind me. I give up. As much as I don't want to be the lead in a generic slasher film, I have no desire to be Margaret Dumont, comic foil in a Marx Brothers movie, either.

When Chris returns home, the dogs relax their vigilance—but only by degrees. They still bark every time Chris comes upstairs from the bedroom, their wary brains on a Groundhog Day loop of fear and anticipation. Chris and I watch a movie and the rescues settle behind my head in the big green chair. Their favorite new spot is to lie behind the pillows, wedged so that their fluffy bodies overlap. Frenchy sleeps with his head an inch from mine. He's not watching the movie tonight. Usually, Frenchy is intrigued by television. He reacts to dogs on the screen and sometimes appears comically absorbed in a story even when his fellow canines aren't featured. He becomes aroused and barks at the television if the large head of another animal looms. Lucky gets it right away and, after being initially interested, seems to realize that television isn't real. But Frenchy remains skeptical. Maybe that lion could come through the screen, open wide its jaws, and devour him. You never know.

There are layers to Frenchy. Or not. But I am revising my initial opinion that he's not too bright. I think he has PTSD. He has bad dreams every night. Lucky is often the victim of Frenchy's night terrors. It all happens in a flash. We hear muffled growls and a yip, and the next morning Lucky may have a streak of blood on his face. This is worrisome but we don't know how it happens or what to do about it. If we separated them, they would be upset. And drugging Frenchy into a stupor is not something we want for him.

On the night we are snuggled on the green chair watching television, it finally happens: Frenchy has a nightmare and bites my head. There is a muffled growling, a subterranean roar from the depths of his unconscious, then silence. He doesn't break the skin on my head but it's alarming, to say the least. Chris, observing from a few feet away, says that Frenchy never woke up from his dream during the entire ten-second incident. This horrifies and saddens me.

I wonder what is in Frenchy's recurrent nightmare, and if it bears any resemblance to mine. Mine is picking my way along swaying catwalks high above a cityscape. Frenchy's is probably about balancing on the wire rungs of his too-small puppy mill cage and being threatened by nameless men in hats or bullied by bigger dogs, snarling and slashing at him. Or worse things I don't want to imagine.

We are PTSD mirrors, Frenchy and I. I think of finding my son dead and my breathing becomes quick and shallow and my heart pounds, and I want to leave my body. Frenchy bites people's heads. I bite people's heads off. Figuratively. But we have different takes on the world. I'm not afraid of the world, since it's already done the worst to me it can do. Frenchy doesn't know that yet, and still fears giant animal heads that can come through the television. It's my job now to instill in Frenchy the fact that the worst the world can do to him has already happened, that he is in a safe and loving place, and that every day he can expect good things. And while I'm teaching him that, I can learn it myself, over and over, to expect good things and to be grateful for the small things now, to count them like jewels in a treasure hoard against depression and fear. I don't expect big things anymore: Jesse writing another poem, getting into college, falling in love. But I still dream of the impossible. I'm expecting Lucky and Frenchy to sleep with us someday.

SEX ED

G OODY WAS A SEX FIEND. He had an adorable white teddy bear, filched from Jesse, that was the object of his lust. "Lucy," no longer white and fluffy, was humped regularly and with gusto no matter the weather, no matter the company, no matter the place. Chris and I perfected euphemisms for Jesse's young cousins about Goody's "playtime" with Lucy. We got it, though. We knew it was really about dominance and that Goody was taking out his frustrations about being low man on the family totem pole. It was normal dog behavior, we thought. Not that we knew anything.

But it's hard to figure out what is going on between Lucky and Frenchy in the context of normal dog behavior, much less disguise it. Lucky is always the lucky recipient of Frenchy's devoted and amazingly noisy attentions, the sounds of which filter through dinner parties and family gatherings. All heads turn to Lucky and Frenchy, and Lucky stares at us with insouciance, a thought bubble of *What are you looking at, ogler?* nearly visible above his head. It never goes the other way. Lucky is always the giftee and Frenchy always delivers the "gift." They are graphic. Once, when Lucky was upright, leaning against the back of the green chair, pushing Frenchy's head with his paw, our gay friend watched them, agape. "It's the baths, 1968," he proclaimed. That was my cue. I delivered my best Bette Midler version of "Friends." Lucky just stared at us both, his eyes glazed over with pleasure.

Pleasure. An unknown quality in the first three years of Lucky and Frenchy's grim lives as puppy mill prisoners. I feel the familiar drive to make pleasure something our little rescues expect as a birthright, the gift of being on this beautiful planet. I had often felt this way about our son, for whom the pain of constricted limbs and frustration were a daily reality. I wanted nothing more than for my son to experience bodily pleasure, a release from his tight and twisted limbs. I felt keenly his happiness when I massaged the tight muscles in his back and legs and heard his long, drawn-out kiss sound, the one that meant "yessss." And we too, as parents, had dealt with the reality of sex and disability with regard to our son when he came of age. That event, the day I addressed the mechanics of how my helpless son could give himself pleasure in full privacy and on his own is one of my fondest memories. I know that sounds strange and makes some people uncomfortable. Many still may think of people with disabilities as sexless, neutered. Those people are wrong. My son, a fully cognizant human, was a sexual being. When he entered middle school, he was as hormonal as all of his other classmates.

There was a tiny shadow on Jesse's upper lip. Overnight, a scattering of pimples migrated across his forehead. His high-pitched giggles descended into a seal-honk laugh. And even though his skinny limbs, elongated now, remained tight and flailing, there was one muscle that worked very well and surprisingly often. He was twelve years old and in middle school. He should have been masturbating like a zoo monkey every five minutes like all of his peers. But Jesse had severe cerebral palsy and not one of his muscles worked the way they should have. His brain functioned very well in every other way, earning him straight A's in Latin at our local high school and honor roll status every year. I was sure his already rich imagination had ratcheted up exponentially since his hormones went wild.

I wanted to talk to him about pleasure, specifically self-pleasure. Very little about Jesse's body could give him pleasure. It was often a vessel of frustration, his arm not following his brain's intention to pull his computer switch, his head lolling just as he tried to focus on something. He had immense pleasure from food, but the spoonful of ice cream or morsel of turkey was delivered to his mouth by other hands.

I wanted to talk to him about privacy. Other hands had always washed him, lifted him to his commode, dressed him, stretched his tight limbs. It was what always had been, and there was no place for shame or prudery in his world. He didn't know it, because it hadn't been taught to him and it never would, not in our house. What could Jesse do independently? He could communicate and he could use his left hand to rake at his computer switch, which opened the door to his imagination. But masturbation using his hands wasn't an option.

That's how I came to spend all my time thinking about how my son could masturbate without using his hands, with a body that was betraying him in yet another way, once again denying him pleasure. I brainstormed with my husband, feeling like we were on some bizarro-world X-rated episode of *Leave It to Beaver*. Chris's usual engineering genius failed him in this case. He claimed to be "thinking about it," but for whatever reason—shyness? squeamishness? transference of my Catholic guilt?—there was no action. It dawned on me that Chris dreaded formality. And talking. As in, Having An Important Talk. Or maybe when he thought of jerry-rigging his son's penis, his brain froze.

I was getting Jesse ready for bed. I pulled the pajama top over his honey-gold chest, still hairless. I felt the pang I always felt when I saw the circular scar where a chest tube had been inserted during the first fraught days of his life. I winced inwardly thinking about the medical staff pushing the tube and what agony he must have felt in that newborn world of blinding lights and giants' roaring voices and pain without end. Jesse was lying on his back on his soft blue flannel sheet. Neil Young was singing "Hey Hey, My My" on his stereo. And Jesse was erect. This part of his body worked gloriously. I admired this functioning part of him. Then I turned down the stereo.

"Okay, Jesse, here's the thing. You know the whole reproduction story from health class and that book we read. But I'm sure they didn't go into detail about orgasm at school. Orgasm is great. Fantastic. Better than all the rides at Universal rolled into one. It's something that happens during sex with other people. And sex with yourself. In fact, I bet you've already had one, in your sleep?"

No comment, but I had Jesse's full attention.

"Well, you can make it happen. Yourself. When you're by yourself. And you can just tell us when you want to be alone."

I walked over to Jesse's bookcase and took out a CD.

"If I roll you over on your stomach, you can move back and forth. And you can have an orgasm. You can make it happen yourself. And I'm leaving now."

Before I left, I clicked on the CD. I closed the door. The muted sounds of the "1812 Overture" pealed triumphantly. I smiled, listening to the cannons exploding. And thinking of Jesse's pleasure.

Now, in the life I'm living with huge swaths of it intentionally blurred, the tiny redeemed joys of two small victims are the lights that gleam in the foggy night. I snatch them like a kid greedy for fireflies, and I hold onto the light for as long as I can.

INTRODUCTION TO PARADISE

WITHIN WALKING DISTANCE from our house on the tidal river is the sort of place I pined for when I lived in the city. Even though the insistent buzz of Manhattan powered my twenties self, and I gloried in the everyday drama of my life there (a tall man roller-skating in a dress! A bald man with black painted-on hair playing on the pavement with drumsticks! Oh my God, that was Baryshnikov who just walked by!), my child-self remembered the peace and beauty of the bay and I went through fierce pangs of wanting it now! right now! with the same broken-hearted rage and sobbing of a toddler melting down over absolutely nothing at all.

Now there are eighty public acres of woods, meadow, and bay at my disposal less than five minutes away. When we first moved to the South Shore of Boston from Hoboken, New Jersey, we bought a bright red jogging stroller for Jesse that required very little adapting for his disability. We were free to walk the conservation area in every season, little Goody off-leash trotting beside us or riding in Jesse's lap. We sang Christmas songs and gathered pine boughs and pepper berry branches for decoration in the glinting winter light. In summer we walked the trails to the bay, arriving at a stone outcropping with a giant boulder overlooking the water and a view of the coast that went all the way to neighboring Plymouth. The ancient boulder had a stone "lane" that went down to a sandy beach dappled with marsh grass.

Jesse's ashes are buried there, at the crest of the seascape that never fails to evoke deep sighs and groans of pleasure in the visitors we bring. It is a site you could imagine as holy to the native people who lived in that place years and years ago. The surroundings bespeak reverence and calm and agelessness. Finding beer bottles and graffiti there is like the imposition of a crass loudmouth stumbling into a sacred rite. My friends and I swim from the rock overlooking the bay. When the tide is high you can slide into water over your head, swim out a little way, and enjoy the panoramic view from yet another perspective, the best one, we all agree.

We can't wait to introduce Lucky and Frenchy to this earthly version of doggy heaven that awaits them in the conservation land. Chris and I decide to take them in the car so we can park by the road and start out the long way around. Big mistake. The minute they are corralled into the car, they both begin shaking, Frenchy so wildly that his ears rise, and he looks like he might lift off like a furry helicopter. The dogs side-eye each other warily. It seems like Lucky is berating Frenchy: *You were the one who peed on the floor near the guest room. It's* your *fault they're getting rid of us.* They quiver for the rest of the mercifully short ride.

Everything changes a few minutes later, when we arrive at our destination. Out of the car and back on terra firma, Lucky's pioneer spirit resurfaces. He prances and sniffs in the parking area, intoxicated by the smells of so many dogs in one place. For Frenchy, it is as if we have asked him to participate in the Iditarod, when all he wanted was the comfort of caresses while tucked into the green chair, safe at home. Lucky, by now mad with delight, sniffs and sniffs, as if he could inhale all eighty acres of the conservation land and the cumulative dog scents within.

Once on the well-worn path toward the bay, Frenchy is beset from every direction by dogs of all sizes and shapes. They race inside the high grass and burst through, startling our rescues. Lucky greets the giant drooling labs and rotties with friendly, dog-approved social responses: the serious introductory business of butt-sniffing and getting into play position. If the dog is larger than a toy breed and relatively young, Frenchy hides behind me. If the dog then gets too curious and too close, Frenchy bares his teeth in a pathetic show of faux ferocity. He isn't brave enough to actually growl, so he just barely lifts his lips like he's showing a dentist the state of his gingivitis. The big dogs just stare stupidly at Frenchy and then move on. The ones who insist on socializing make Frenchy clack his jaws and snap at the air. I pull him away, afraid his bad dog manners will escalate into an all-out dogfight.

Unlike my childhood self, I love all dogs, but I can't help regarding these big bruisers who leap randomly out of the tall grasses as scary intruders. I feel as protective of Frenchy as I did of Jesse when he reached middle school and the boys around him were hormone-pumped and prone to fights that arose out of nowhere, like young antler-butting stags. I was always afraid they would knock into Jesse's wheelchair and tip him over.

I retro-fear the big dogs: there are two aggressive ones in our neighborhood, sleek and muscled, and they bark ferociously like weightlifters with 'roid rage whenever they catch even a glimpse of Lucky and Frenchy. They jump in place near a barrier fence that looks too low, closer and closer to the top with every frenzied leap, their dog voices shrill and menacing. Once they got loose and ran right for the rescues, like out-of-control semis on a wet highway. Lucky and Frenchy reacted each according to temperament: Frenchy flopped over on his side offering his neck, as if to say, *Kill me now and let me shuffle off this mortal coil.* Lucky stood his ground with a *Bring it, bitch* pose.

Back in the conservation land, Lucky runs ahead and tugs on the leash. He looks back at us and dog-smiles. Chris and I catch some of his glow. But really it is the memory of Jesse's radiance that shimmers between us like something tangible, something shared without words. This place. Our son. Hours and hours of joy, the little red jogging stroller pulling the natural world closer to Jesse, thrilling his senses, freeing him in those moments from the confines of his body. All this passes between us in what is no time at all. Freedom. I long to let go of the leash and watch Lucky's flying-squirrel running mode that always brings a smile to onlookers watching our short runs down the driveway, the reward ending to our walks around the neighborhood. I have to remind myself to be patient, and to temper the goal of future freedoms with a foundation of trust and security. One day soon, Lucky will run free. The loyalty in his smile is a guarantee.

INSOMNIA

IT STARTS WITH A QUATRAIN that seesaws in and out of your consciousness like the blade of a mezzaluna knife. This time it is the echo from Hozier-Byrne's "Take Me to Church": *I'll tell you my sins and you can sharpen your knife / Offer me that deathless death / Good God, let me give you my life.* You understand that you will not sleep that night and you try to suppress that thought, but it rises anyway, and surrounds you, a miasmic canopy over your fancy sleigh bed. In the next stage of sleeplessness, you revolve on your bed like a suckling pig on a spit, but no position brings sleep. You try to read a book. It doesn't work. Instead of your eyes growing heavy, the quatrain gets louder, more insistent, drowning out the words on the page. *Good God, let me give you my life.* You turn out the light and lie still, pretending to be asleep, trying not to disturb your husband who has joined you in bed. Now your thoughts multiply, along with phantom, lost limb pains that leap around in a mad game of body tag. The lost limb is your son. You are "it."

Every once in a while, a memory separates itself from the pushy horde of disparate voices crowding your brain and you are sliced open a little more: your hand rakes through the impossibly fine hairs on the side of your son's head and you bleed that for a while. You see his chest with the puncture mark where they pressed in the breathing tube. You unfurl his long fingers. Blood is filling the bed. Your husband, lying beside you, breathes deeply and evenly. You begin to recite your gratitudes like the catechism you learned in parochial school, the lists of sacraments, deadly sins, holy days of obligation. Your lists are long. You begin: You have fresh water when you turn on the tap. You have never gone hungry. You live in a beautiful place. You have good friends. You love your husband, and he loves you. You keep going, telling your gratitudes like beads on a rosary. You run out of grace. The nuns taught you that the eighth deadly sin, the unforgivable one, is despair. You despair. You give up and leave the bed. You prowl around upstairs, your rescue dogs eyeing you warily from their protective perch behind the pillows on the oversized chair. You are an intruder from the world of not-sleeping. You don't belong upstairs. You lie on the daybed and look up "insomnia" on your iPad. It says that you could be depressed. You almost laugh out loud at that one. It also says not to read from electronic devices, because that will impede sleep. You close your iPad and lie down again. The full moon glares down at you, silvering your world. You glimpse the room that was once your son's, but you don't go in. It is empty, a taunt. You let yourself cry, gingerly, afraid of an onrushing tide of tears that will never stop, and you remember that the nuns told you St. Peter cried so hard after his denial of Christ, he wore grooves in his face. You wonder when that will happen to you. But the only effect of your puny tears is a stuffy nose and a heated face.

You think of the handsome young man who came that day with his parents, old friends on a visit. The young man remembered your son and how he tried to communicate with him when they were both children, your son in his wheelchair with his computer and his clicks, the language of the nonverbal cerebral palsy tribe. You were so grateful for this mention of your boy, for his cameo appearance in the world of the living, you almost wept right there, with both of you waist deep in the pool, the pool your boy loved so much, the pool where he could defy gravity with his neck brace and be eye to eye with his friends. You secretly called it the Pool of Tears and thought often of Alice trying not to drown in hers, swimming wildly in circles. You knew that you were Alice, growing and shrinking and unable to return to yourself and swimming wildly in circles.

Later, up on the deck, you and your old friends had lunch surrounded by flowers and the smell of the sea. You all heard the scree and looked up to see the hawk that signified your son circling low, and you thought it was a sign he was joining you for lunch.

Now, tossing on the daybed, you think of how that solace doesn't work when you are denied sleep. The hawk isn't your son; the hawk is a coincidence. The hawk is synchronicity, drawn by the power of your need to find meaning in a meaningless existence. The clock says four a.m. *Offer me that deathless death.*

Finally, around five a.m., you fall asleep. You dream you have found an infant who nobody wants. Everyone seems to think the infant can survive without your care, by itself. They tell you to leave it. You wonder why anyone would abandon such a beautiful baby. But when you look back the baby isn't a baby, it's a grown thing, hideous and deformed. You wake up in the same bed where you found your son dead on a January morning. The first thing you hear is the dull sound of the quatrain, fainter now, drained by your fitful sleep and the disappearance of the moon.

~

TEETH

~

*T*HE VET DELIVERS THE DIRE NEWS at Lucky and Frenchy's annual home checkup: Lucky needs to have nine teeth pulled. It turns out to be a huge drama—for Frenchy. And for me. The part that worries me is putting Lucky into a kennel at the vet's office where the surgery will take place. I wonder if being caged will send Lucky hurtling back into the fearful and depressed little dog we rescued from what would surely have been a short and unhappy life. Lucky was the first of the pair to recover little broken mirrored shards of joy. Now at the end of every walk we have a new ritual to celebrate and enlarge upon that joy. At the top of our long driveway, I remove both dogs' leashes. Then I adopt a runner's crouch and announce: "On your mark, get set—GO!" I race down the drive, Lucky running before me. Sometimes he circles back like a fighter in a victory dance, coming perilously close to sending me into a spiraling fall as I maneuver around his taunting little figure. He always wins and I always acknowledge his win with a high-pitched calling of his name over and over, alternating with simulated crowd cheers. Lucky prances at my feet grinning, long pink tongue lolling, claiming his bichie birthright as a creature of light. Midway down the drive comes Frenchy, loping at his own diffident pace.

But now Lucky will be shut up in a cage. Again.

And then there is the anesthesia he will have during surgery. Anesthesia. The word hurls me back to a corridor at St. Vincent's Hospital in Greenwich Village, 1989. Our son, Jesse, is not yet two years old and is having surgery to remove his adenoids, since he has been breathing through what sounds like wet cement. His tiny form is barely a bump on the gurney as he is wheeled into surgery. I follow as far as I can, but just before I have to let him go, at the moment when I am smoothing my son's curls to stem the rising panic, the anesthesiologist tells me that it's highly possible Jesse could have another, even fatal brain bleed during the surgery. This is the first I'm hearing about that. My husband and I agreed to the surgery on the recommendation of our trusted pediatrician. There is no Internet in 1989 for me to do extensive research. I just want my son breathing without effort. The anesthesiologist's timing is a cruel joke and it's everything I can do to resist snatching my baby's inert body and fleeing the hospital. I am alone during this surgery because Chris is working in another state. I sit in the hospital cafeteria and smoke, lighting one cigarette to the end of another, a carcinogenic rosary to an unknown god of mercy that I fear is not there.

Jesse survives the adenoid operation without another brain bleed, and he never breathes through wet cement again. Today, as we deliver Lucky to the vet's, I force myself to believe that he will be okay. Chris is with me for this ordeal, and I stay in the room, holding Lucky until he is unconscious. When we return to pick him up, the vet warns us that Lucky will be wobbly because of the drugs and to place him gently on the dog bed when we get home. The vet doesn't know Lucky. I carry him inside, handling him like a Fabergé egg, and lower him onto the dog bed on the floor. Frenchy watches us anxiously from the big green chaise that has replaced the oversized green chair. The moment Lucky is settled onto the dog bed, he leaps up onto the chaise. He settles into his usual comfy place between the pillow and the back of the chaise. He ignores us and closes his eyes.

I tell Frenchy it's time for his walk, put on his leash, and leave Lucky to sleep it off. Frenchy only makes it half-way up the driveway before collapsing onto a snowbank. He lies there quivering, looking back at the house. The thought bubble over his head screams, *Luckeeeeeee!* The yearning is worthy of a gothic novel. I give up and lead Frenchy back to the house. When I open the door, Lucky leaps off the chaise and runs down the stairs to meet us.

"Really?" I say. He looks up at me. Really. I put the leash on Lucky, and he swaggers up the drive, Frenchy walking in sync. Lucky looks back at me. His thought bubble reads: *Anesthesia? I laugh! Hahahahaha!* He makes a balletic leap over a pile of snow to make his point.

~~~

SNOW DAY

~~~

S NOW BLOWING SIDEWAYS, the dogs burrowed into the velvet throw, and split pea soup bubbling on the stove, a witches' cauldron of delight. My friends from California think they are taunting me with announcements of temperature and degrees, but I think of the brown air, the selfish palm trees that don't offer shade, the dystopian celebrity culture, and I embrace the quilted silence of my New England like a lover. I sit at my father's old poker table, oak scarred with the names we carved when I was thirteen, and think of snow days past, neighborhood kids crowded beside Jesse on the oversized chair, a roaring fire, BLTs, brownies, a movie, every single element a facet of a crowning joy.

DROP THE LEASH

*F*OR THE SECOND DAY IN A ROW, Frenchy collapses in the street like a femme fatale getting a bad-news telegram in an old-timey movie. We are on our daily slogging walk through another brutal winter. Today the sun is so bright it's blinding, but the cold isn't knife-sharp, and breathing in and out is possible without pain. We walk to the marina, and I watch the sluggish tide move under the patchy ice and snow that covers the water but cannot contain its relentless ebb and flow. There are no cars, so I drop Lucky's and Frenchy's leashes. Lucky prances a bit, but the marina parking lot and streets have been salted in the night and Frenchy begins lifting one paw, then another. We are about halfway home when Frenchy drops. I pick him up and carry him like a war buddy. He weighs about twenty pounds at this time, and carrying his muscle-clenched little body in my arms after a little while is like some kind of medieval penance. Then Lucky begins to falter. By now Frenchy's weight has grown to eighty pounds—or that's what it feels like—and we are still about a quarter mile from home. Walking off-road where there is no salt is impossible, since the drifts are so deep. I pick up Lucky and feel like we are all in some cartoon version of a World War II movie about the siege of Stalingrad.

It is the last time Lucky and Frenchy walk the streets of our neighborhood on-leash through that salty trail of tears.

The next day I dragoon Chris into the new adventure of dropping the leash at Bay Farm. If this works, it will be the go-to place for our daily walks and Lucky and Frenchy will run free. It's bright today, windless and cold, and I'm hoping the snow is tamped down from bigger dogs and that there will be a path. Lucky and Frenchy are wearing their fake-sheepskin coats, a gift from Bernadette, Jesse's Irish nanny and angel made flesh. I like to turn up their collars, so they look like young juvenile delinquents from a fifties B movie. But right now, they just look terrified, cowering in the backseat, Frenchy shaking so hard it feels like he alone is powering us through the snowy streets. Bay Farm Conservation is only five minutes away, so we arrive at the parking lot before Frenchy levitates from his own anxiety. We park, and I can see a path. There are cars, but no other dogs in sight. I lift them out, and Lucky immediately begins sniffing. Frenchy huddles behind me, trying to disappear, so I won't surrender him to his newer, crueler owners, or whatever horror scenario is storming his brain. He obviously has no memory of the trial run here last summer.

Once the dogs have done their business and we are safely away from the parking lot, we follow the trail toward the bay. Lucky begins to scamper and strain the leash. Frenchy stays close to Chris's side. I drop the leash, and Lucky runs ahead, free. He looks back at us for a moment, his face a wonderment, then he runs ahead, the leash trailing on the snowy path. But then he stops, turns, checks to see that we are following. Chris drops Frenchy's leash. He doesn't run to catch up with Lucky, but he moves ahead, cautiously at first. As Frenchy gains confidence, he trots behind Lucky, but can't keep up, because Lucky has joy spurts that propel him to run far ahead—but always looking back to see if we are still there.

And we are always there.

~~

VOICES

~~

T HIS IS HOW GRIEF RENDERS MEMORY: picture a minefield where even a flower can detonate, and though you continue your walk through the woods, you no longer see what is before you, only the face of your beloved inhaling a sprig of jasmine, its delicate white tendrils caressing his face. And though you are shattered, you pull the pain toward you like a cloak and wrap it tightly, and you call it to you aloud, more afraid of losing the memory of touch, of sight, of sound, than feeling the shrapnel that pierces your senses.

The voices of the dead all fight for space and crowd my memory, each one yelling over the other to be heard. Entire ancient conversations float above random song lyrics and bleatings from the unrelenting ads on television. Some jingles are so deadly and infectious that I race across the room to mute the sound before their noxious rhymes embed themselves within my brain forever, corrupting the memories of love I hoard and resurrect like invocations to a god I know isn't there. My son's laughter rises above it all, like the pure tone that sets the universe in motion.

WHERE'S THE BEEF?

IT'S SPRING, THE SEASON OF GALAS and fundraisers. We get invited to a lot of them, so my husband can lend some kind of celebrity glow to the occasion, even though we are usually shy and stiff at these things and never know what to say. We want to help, so we smile for the photographers and go inside to a hotel banquet room glittering with strategic lighting and tinkly with the sound of ice clinking against glasses raised in toasts to whatever cause we are celebrating. The people sitting with us are mostly strangers. More than once I have slipped off to the ladies' room and returned to find a huge hunk of beef sitting on my plate, usually filet mignon. I don't eat beef anymore in my wimpy attempt to help the planet along and save bovine lives (bacon is still a challenge, though; sorry, my porcine friends). But I never miss an opportunity to steal napkins and stuff the hunk of beef in my fancy evening purse, oversized for just such an occasion as this. Sometimes my neighbor, perhaps a Nobel Prize–winning scientist or a captain of industry, will side-eye me for slipping meat into my purse, but just as often my seatmate will volunteer his or her beef too. I accept donated bloody meat whenever it's offered, even notched with other people's teeth marks. It's for a good cause, as they say on the invitation.

Lucky jumps down from his fifteen-hundred-dollar dog bed the moment the key turns in the lock. He and Frenchy have adopted the green down-filled chaise as their bed, spurning the spiffy one actually meant for dogs on the floor by the fireplace. I am allowed on the chaise at night but they never snuggle with me. When I sidle onto it, they peer down at me with a faint disdain, annoyed at my disarranging the pillows where they like to lie.

On high alert, Lucky stands at the top of the stairs and backs away as we climb them, never taking his eyes off me. Frenchy remains nestled into the downy green pillow, not even bothering to lift his head. I remove the bloody meat from my evening bag with a flourish and pass it under Lucky's nose, alarming him by coming too close. But his interest is definitely aroused. He trots over to his dish and waits while I slice the tender meat into pieces. Frenchy finally gets up and jumps down. They stand before their plates staring at me while I ponder the absurdity of these two little orphan Annies eating filet mignon and sleeping on downy pillows. It makes me so happy; I feel momentarily celestial, a bestower of karmic balance, a righter of wrongs. Of course, I realize that unless I get the chance to capture whatever cold-blooded trolls tortured Lucky and Frenchy and put them into a too-small wire cage for three years, there will be no karmic justice. They will remain unavenged. And the scars will be there forever, like mine, whether or not they are avenged. But for tonight, there is filet mignon.

* * *

They finish their beef dinner and jump back onto their oversized dog bed, their movements synchronized like Olympic swimmers.

It's enough.

HATE CAROUSEL
(JUST AFTER THE
ELECTION, 2016)

*T*HE UNIVERSE HAS SHIFTED and speeded up and now my days are a blur that have no center, just a progression of hours punctuated by outrage after outrage and a sense of spinning into the void of outer space. Not even the recovered joy of my abused dogs can comfort me. Not when I picture what has become a meme, the leader of our country mocking a person with a disability who held his hands the exact same way Jesse did. And the crowd that watches him do it laughs. Eyeing the beefy men parking their pickup trucks at the Stop & Shop, I wonder which ones burn with rage about women and Black people and immigrants, and I don't want to understand them at all. I just want a remnant of kindness as a reminder we were once human, but the carousel we're on is going too fast and we're all on that ride, whirling out of control and giddy with hate, thrilling to the demons we've unleashed.

MY ITALIAN AFFAIR

IN THE SUMMER OF 2017, I travel to Italy and cheat on Lucky and Frenchy with two irresistible Bergamasco shepherds, Brina and Alina, a mother-and-daughter pair with matching dreadlocks and shamanic souls. These haunting creatures belong to my friend Davide Ferrario, who lives in Turin on a magical rise so close to the city center it seems illusory, as if his house could disappear at any moment. My dog love affair happens at the end of the trip. The dogs seem like an award to someone on a vision quest who finally gets enlightened after a journey that leads her through a series of tasks and trials.

Italy has always been a place where all of my senses are heightened. It's as if there's a giant tuning fork over the land and my brain adjusts immediately to another level, one that's always been there, thrumming in the place my mind goes right before sleep, that sweet spot where whole, perfect novels are born.

I have been preparing for this trip for months. Nutrimenti, an Italian publishing house that brought out books by Andre Dubus III and Barack Obama, published my first book, *Jesse*; it is through Andre's generosity that my book comes to their attention at all. Nutrimenti submitted *Jesse* to the prestigious Festivaletturatura, an international festival of writers that is held every year in the walled city of Mantova. This year will feature my noir passion, Maurizio de Giovanni, with Chimamanda Ngozi Adichie and Elizabeth Strout, among many other literary bright lights. I am thrilled when Ada Carpi, Nutrimenti's publisher, tells me that I have been invited to present, and that she and her partner, Andrea Palombi, will take me on a mini book tour after the festival. One of the places I will read is my mother's hometown, Sulmona, surrounded by the Appenines, Italy's tallest mountain range that runs like a spine along the middle of the country. It is the birthplace of Ovid, famous for confetti, the candied almonds given as favors at weddings, renowned also for an Easter procession called the Running Madonna.

On Easter morning, a huge crowd gathers at the main square, Piazza Garibaldi, to see this pageant of redemption. Six men carry the Madonna Addolorata, draped in black. They use a slow, swaying step. Suddenly, across the piazza, the doors to the church open and the risen Christ appears. The grieving mother, seeing her son again, "runs" across the piazza toward him. Her black mourning clothes fly away. Under them, she wears green, signifying hope. The mother meets again the son she thought she had lost forever. Doves are released. The crowd gasps. Old ladies weep. Handel's "Messiah" blares. I had seen this procession two years after losing Jesse. Still wrapped in the unreal, gauzy throes of grief, a small part of me understood why my mother had spoken of this ritual with awe.

I am determined, in tribute to my mother and all my peasant forebears, to read my book about my son aloud in Italian.

For weeks I have been struggling with the mysteries of the Italian language, a language with which I have always had a complicated relationship. The Italian of my youth was never the soft and sexy *lingua dell'amore* that made others wax rhapsodic. The dialect I heard from my mother and the old people in my neighborhood was harsh and guttural, brutish throat-clearing sounds that were to me the dreary stuff of daily life, no different than gargling or hawking up phlegm. There was no trill and flow, no operatic flourish to the dark phrases my mother hurled like maledictions, nothing but shame in the sound of my grandfather's comical attempts at English, mangled by his Chico Marx pronunciations.

I was alert to every cultural stereotype around Italians, smelling slurs like the foul cigars my grandfather smoked: my chubby brother assigned to play Tony Spumoni the ice-cream man in a school play, the buffoonery of Italians portrayed on television and in the movies as fussy waiters or big-nosed cartoons, all of them hilariously trying and failing to *speaka da Engaleesh*, the way people talked down to my mother. Child snob that I was, insecure all-American wannabe, I shrank from anything to do with the embarrassing sounds of those alien words. I learned French in high school, proudly and unwittingly flaunting the Quebecois accent bestowed upon me by Sister Cor Marie and earning, years later, looks of incomprehension and disdain from the Parisians I was so earnestly trying to impress.

But now I want to read from my book about Jesse in Italian. For months I have been dedicating an hour a day to learning Italian online. The stigma I once felt about the language is fading away as my present-day American culture newly embraces all things Italian with an *amore pazzo,* a mad love that admittedly seems focused on Tuscany, but nevertheless encompasses even the lowly southerners, my antecedents. Tuscany is Italy's magic kingdom. The fairy-tale version of Tuscany haunts the collective unconscious of America like Jesus sightings on a *panino.* There's a little restaurant in our small town south of Boston called Tuscany Tavern, though the owners are actually from Salerno, near the toe of Italy's boot. I can get "Tuscan" bread at my local supermarket, where I can also pick up a couple of cans of "Tuscan beef stew" dog food for Lucky and Frenchy. I can wash my hair with a pricey bottle of Tuscan Soul shampoo and, presumably, get in touch with my spiritual side while I lather up. And when I go for a doctor's visit, I can even avail myself of Tuscan lemon antibacterial soap for a germ-free Tuscan medical experience.

The word *Tuscan* evokes golden hills, heart-stopping

vistas studded with endless rows of orderly vineyards, heavenly food, and a land filled with people who know the secret of *la dolce vita*. Tuscans lead simple, earthy, tranquil lives only a stone's throw from some of the greatest art treasures in the world. Tuscans speak a beautiful, standard Italian complete with trilled *r*'s and lovely round vowels soft as the sexy leather goods you can buy near the Ponte Vecchio.

But I don't care if my Italian is standard or Tuscan—my aim is to not humiliate myself in front of a crowd in Mantova. So I am diligent about my language app, Duolingo, suffering the setbacks of the beginner as I probe the mysteries of Italian grammar. I know my Italian will ring true, if slightly southern, my *s*'s pronounced with the telltale slushy *sh* sound that bespeaks the *meridionale*. I heard all the adults in my family use Italian as a secret language when they wanted to discuss something we kids weren't supposed to hear. I was a master lurker, avid for news from the top, and a mimic who could expertly and nastily recreate my mother's Italian accent as my weapon of choice in our adolescent battles. I feel like my Italian is there somewhere, submerged in a deep well from my childhood, waiting to be tapped. If only I can locate that place, I will sound like a native. A southern native.

When I last visited Italy in 2014, I decided I would speak Italian with no shame about bad word usage or mangled tenses. When I am in Italy, I live in the present. I don't know how to phrase the future, so *domani* (tomorrow) or *la prossima settimana* (next week) has to suffice. As for the past, that's *molti anni fa* (many years ago) or *ieri* (yesterday). I like the fact that my poor Italian vocabulary means I must find some strange synonyms when I can't pull up the exact word. It's poetic, in a skewed way. And the southern Italians are forgiving: "*Tu parl' bene, signora,*" they say, invariably, even after I know I have grammatically slaughtered their *bella lingua.*

I know exactly the paragraph I want to read: it is about the Italian culture and the acceptance of death as a part of life, something that barely exists in my eternally jejune American environment. The last sentence in the paragraph reads, "I keep going back to Italy because that is where I found him." In Italian: *Torno di continuo in Italia perche è li che l'ho trovato.*

But I cannot say those words without tears clogging my voice. Why am I weeping every time I speak the language aloud?

When I did readings of my first book about my son in English, I never choked up, or became too emotional to continue. My eyes were dry. I avoided the chapters I knew would be triggers and distanced myself by becoming a character reading from her first book. But every time I practice reading aloud from that same book in Italian, my voice becomes unsteady. The tears drop like an iron curtain, shuttering my words, sealing my voice.

"*Torno di continuo in Italia perche è li che l'ho trovato.*"

Those words were always about connecting with my son in Italy before and after he was with me in the flesh. I don't know why he is more present there. Maybe it's because I'm in a place where the repetition of everyday chores is suspended and replaced by a re-perception of the world around me. But in a flash of insight, I realize that what connects me is absorbing everywhere the first language that I ever heard beyond my mother's heartbeat. It was never English. Of course it wasn't. The language she crooned to me when I was still inside her, the language she whispered when she held me close, triumphant at finally producing a child after seven long years of trying, was her mother tongue: Italian.

I don't get through my first Italian reading in Mantova.

The presentation is at the deconsecrated fifteenth-century church of Santa Paola. Even denuded of its statues, votive candles, and linens, the space still feels holy, awash in a strange, green-tinted light, as if we were underwater. The church is almost full, with a secular congregation of at least three hundred and fifty people to hear Jesse's story. I am introduced to the interpreter who will sit beside me and murmur English into my ear. I sit in the middle, facing the crowd, beside my old friend Davide, a writer and film director. He is an important link because he knew Jesse, and has written a moving, funny preface to the Italian version of the book, one that honors my son, his singularity, his puckish humor, the wordless boy who had a way with words, the poet admired by award-winning poets.

We begin with Davide interviewing me about the book, but before my mind has registered the Italian susurrating into my left ear and the English quacking into my right, a weeping father appears before us like a living Pietà. He is carrying a young, spastic girl who looks to be around six years old. He says, through sobs, in heavily accented English, "I want you to meet my daughter, Maddalena."

Maybe he isn't speaking English. Maybe my memory doesn't serve me, blurred by emotion. Maybe it is Italian he speaks, or an international parent-to-parent lingua franca that is beyond words. It doesn't matter. I know what this father is saying, because it was what I had said in my head so many times when introducing my son to people he didn't know: *I want you to* see *my son*. See beyond the disability, the spastic limbs, the wheelchair. See his essence, his soul. See my child first, not his physical differences. I see Maddalena, her shining self, her father's love. A beautiful daughter of love. I kiss her. The man goes back to his seat. The audience and I remember to breathe, waking together. I begin to read the paragraph I have chosen, in Italian. I speak about invoking my son "like an amulet, like a scapular, like a precious stone against the world and all its woes." But I falter before the end, and Davide seamlessly picks up the reading where I left off: *"Torno di continuo in Italia perche è li che l'ho trovato . . ."*

In Sulmona, I leave Jesse's holy card at the shrine to St. Anthony in a thousand-year-old church. The holy card is a laminated photograph of a portrait we commissioned from talented artist Adrienne Crombie when Jesse was four. He is depicted as a punk angel, his cowlicky hair standing on end, his spastic arms foreshortened by cerebral palsy. Floating under the sun, his white angel wings keeping him aloft, Jesse looks directly at you, his medieval saint eyes a little narrowed, his full lips lilting toward a smile. He looks somehow knowing, as if the sun directly above him is conferring insight along with its golden rays. On the back of Jesse's holy card is his "Inside/Outside" poem and the dates of his birth and death. I like to leave the card at shrines, both secular and holy. In Rome, I left his card at the statue of Giordano Bruno, the monk burned as a heretic in the Campo dei Fiori for believing in reincarnation and life on other worlds. Jesse had been there with us that July thirteen years earlier, shouting with delight as we laid flowers at the base of Giordano's cowled and mysterious statue in the center of the piazza.

At the Santa Maria della Tomba in Sulmona, I look for the inevitable shrine to St. Anthony. The tonsured saint was my mother's favorite. He's almost always shown holding the Christ child and is the patron saint of lost things. I want to leave a memento of her grandson in a church my mother must have visited as a young girl, before immigrating to America, before she lost her mother and the life she had known, before she lost her land, her language.

I walk through the arched stone doorway into the clear light of the September afternoon, and stand for a moment, trying to adjust to the lightheadedness the altitude always brings. A white feather seesaws in front of me, floating to the ground.

Ada and Andrea have booked us into Sei Stelle, a bed and breakfast overlooking the Piazza Garibaldi, where the Running Madonna ritual happens every Easter Sunday. In the breakfast room, Chris, whose passion is architecture, listens intently to our host, Filippo Fraterolli, as he explains how they have incorporated an ancient aqueduct into the wall of the breakfast room after a renovation. The engineering is clever; on the wall where the aqueduct ends, the stone pylon embedded in the wall looks like it has always been there.

But I am looking at the tic-tac-toe set on the sideboard

in front of the wall. Oversized *X*'s and chunky circles in red and black on a blond-wood tray. Jesse's set, which I have never seen anywhere else and which still sits on the bookcase in his room, the giant pieces easier for his spastic fingers to pick up. Jesse, at our kitchen table, crowing in delight after beating his father at the game. An incongruous child's toy displayed in front of this ancient aqueduct arch now blended into the wall of an elegant Italian breakfast room, like a madwoman's dreamscape. I feel giddy and charged and overcome. I am the madwoman in this place, legs suddenly weak, mind untethered.

That evening we cross the Piazza Garibaldi and I read from my book at the Sala della Comunità Montana. My cousins are there, children and grandchildren of my mother's half sister, and I feel both warmed by their presence and dismayed by the fact that the place where I am reading about Jesse would have been inaccessible to him and others who use wheelchairs. I tell this to the crowd in my halting Italian and take questions after my reading. I can't stop thinking of how impossible it would have been for Jesse to negotiate the stairs to participate in a discussion about a book that describes his life, its challenges and triumphs. The otherworldly feeling of that afternoon begins to dissipate, replaced by a familiar sadness and the residue of anger from past battles for my son's inclusion. After the reading I ask my cousin about my aunt and say that I want to see her. He bursts into tears and tells me that she would not know me any longer. Her memory began to fail after the loss of her husband a few years ago. I only met her seven years earlier, a treasured link to my mother's early life. Another loss.

My husband and I clatter through the now empty Piazza Garibaldi, our footsteps the only sound in the night. It is the end of the summer season. The night is moonless and clear and empty of people. The silence is suddenly broken by a sublime voice singing in Italian.

"Where is that music coming from?" I ask my husband.

"Your purse," he says.

I pull out my phone, which is playing an aria from Rigoletto, *"Bella figlia dell'amore,"* sung by Luciano Pavarotti.

Beautiful daughter of love.

An electronic gift from somewhere. One of the singers in the quartet is named Maddalena. The little girl in the underwater church in Mantua. My mother. And finally, Jesse. Jesse, who told me once in a dream that was not a dream, "I'm always with you."

The tuning fork that exists over my ancestral home has aligned all the missing voices I long to hear again, their hum in the perfect pitch of love. Yet another message knocking at the chambers of my skeptic's heart. Despite all the insistent beeping and dinging from the universe, I never pick up. But I am a receiver, whether I leave the phone on or off.

I dream of Jesse that night, in my bed that overlooks the piazza where the grieving mother looks for her son. It is just his face in close-up. He is still a boy, not the man he would be now if time were real in his world. He makes his kiss sound for "yes." Or maybe it means "Get it?"

The last of the readings is in Torino, with Davide. We stay at his renovated farmhouse, a wonder of Italian design, thanks to his partner Francesca, who works as a production designer in the film industry. The tomato garden feels more sacred than any of the churches I have visited, and the view from the veranda is enough to make me wish I had been more diligent about applying for dual citizenship.

I take delight in Davide and Francesca's menagerie: felines Lilla and Bandiera; magical donkeys Maia, Parigi, and Maria; and lastly, Brina and Alina, the mother/daughter pair of shaggy dog healers. Brina and Alina know how to nuzzle and soul-snuffle like a pair of mountain *streghe* dispensing love charms. They feel like a preparation to returning home, where the connection to Jesse will surely be clouded by the return to daily life. I take a last look at the sacred tomato plants, the donkeys grazing, Brina's soft, matted curls under my arm. I whisper what has become a prayer: *"Torno di continuo in Italia perche è li che l'ho trovato."*

I stand in my kitchen, where I had last seen the hawk. It sat in the dogwood tree outside my window like an avatar on Jesse's twenty-first birthday. The hawk perched calmly on a scarred limb of the tree. He turned slowly to show me his profile, like a handsome young man aware of his youth and power and beauty, but keeping his distance, to also display his independence and his ability to fly away on a whim, should he so choose. I am home now, and the connection is strong. I have forgotten that I am a receiver. I turn to Lucky and Frenchy, who stand by their empty food bowls, watching me warily, probably wondering why breakfast is delayed. They don't know the connection is humming, the line engaged.

~~

ANOTHER WAY DOGS
AREN'T LIKE CHILDREN

~~

*T*HEY GET OLD AS FAST AS YOU DO. In fact, they outpace you. As you begin to lose your balance, they do too. As your teeth start to rot and fall out, theirs do too. As your aches and pains multiply, you can see that theirs do too. They begin every day with stretching, like you do, to stave off calcification. All of us have only mixed results, no matter how deeply we achieve the down dog pose. We all groan when we have to move up or down from the comfortable chair. We're getting old together, but they're getting older faster. Still, how can Lucky kick up his heels like a newborn foal or streak down the driveway like a furry meteor? He is ancient in dog years, yet he's discovered some secret bliss that powers him to run. I stare at him, trying to absorb his magical effluvium, wishing in vain for the bliss spillover.

~~

MELANCHOLIA

~~

*T*HE TURKEY WITH THE WEIRD-COLORED head is at the window again this morning. It's early. Very early. He stands there, mesmerized, staring into my snazzy walk-in closet on the lower level of the raised ranch, and I feel like he's making eye contact with me, telegraphing his need. I hurry into my daily writing fundamentalist compound dress so I can go outside and feed him. He begins banging his head on the glass and I realize what he's seeing is his blue-headed reflection. And it pisses him off. I empathize. My reflection pisses me off too, especially now that I seem to grow a new wrinkle every day and my mouth is becoming a string purse and my neck is growing wattles that make me a human version of the bird in the window. My hair is not yet blue, at least. But I've learned not to stare too long at myself in the glass, something my blue-headed friend has yet to figure out.

"Melancholia." I say it aloud and it slithers out my lips, startling me like the black racer snakes I see sometimes around the cranberry bogs. The word serves as a prayerful entry to the cathedral of high pines I walk under every day with Lucky and Frenchy. The sandy East Street bogs are the nonmuddy alternative to Bay Farm, which leaves you in ankle-deep muck from late autumn to late spring. Lucky and Frenchy, already low to the ground, become living mud balls once the thaw sets in, so we don't return to their Bay Farm paradise until the summer solstice. At the East Street bogs, the pines tower over us, no longer threatening now that it's spring. Last winter they suffered the ravages of climate change, cracking violently in two, groaning thereafter like wounded soldiers in a Red Cross tent. After the storms, they dangle their damaged limbs, threatening retribution to the humans below who brought on their devastation. Evidence lies strewn about everywhere and the dogs are like marine recruits leaping over felled tree trunks and sharp branches. Lucky and Frenchy follow me now along this path, panting their crooked dog-smiles, content, oblivious, enjoying the adventure. I scan the sky, looking for wooden swords of Damocles teetering above.

This walk around the Duxbury bogs includes a side path alongside a lily pad–covered water called the Golden Reservoir. The water is tranquil and bucolic, a dreamlike setting, until the roaring sound of traffic reminds me that a two-lane highway, Route 3, runs parallel to the pond, masked by vegetation. There are dead trees standing upright at the other end that evoke an ultra-modern war monument. Every time I see them, I hear my grandfather's Italian-accented old-man voice. Whenever we would drive by, on our way to the town where I now live, he would cackle: "Heh, the dead soldiers," like he was greeting old friends, and I wondered why he saw the dead trees as dead men. Now, of course, I understand that morbidity is genetic, and that I have inherited a darkness of spirit along with darkness of feature from both sides of my family. I walk under damaged pines and picture instant death by tree limb. The other dog walkers I see don't seem to be awaiting the revenge of the pines. They're talking on their cell phones, jogging virtuously, or warning their labs to stay out of the water. They aren't looking up, thinking of death.

This spring at the pond there is a swan couple and a pair of cygnets that sail along in their wake as their elegant parents dive for bugs and fish. The swans appear to be devoted to one another, but that love doesn't apply to nonswans, so I steer clear when they are near the shore. I've heard these birds can be aggressive and picture refereeing a battle between the swan parents and intrepid, curious Lucky while Frenchy paces fretfully behind my feet, tripping me and sending me headlong into the fray.

The cranberry bogs are working bogs and they are flooded after harvest. In early spring the cranes and herons return, soaring above like prehistoric reptiles or standing on one leg, utterly still, as if posing for a Japanese watercolor. Leftover cranberries pool and bob at the edges, vivid as blood against the stubborn remains of the snow. There's a magical, lonely quality to these bogs.

One day I take the long route with Lucky and Frenchy, around Old Bog, bisected by the remains of a dilapidated pump house and a smaller bog left to the wild. I see a group of very young children throwing rocks into the ditch around the cultivated section. They appear after I round a curve, and I am startled, not just by how young they are, but also by the fact that there are no overseeing adults around. In my own childhood, I would have been just as free-range as this band of children, but in these days of helicopter and snowplow parenting, it's surprising no one has called and reported the parents to some disapproving official entity. The oldest kid, a boy, is maybe seven, and he boldly asks me where Frenchy's tail is (it's bobbed). A little girl who looks around five pauses from hefting rocks and informs me cheerily, "We're breaking up the ice!" "Good for you!" I say fakely, moving on, my smile wavering as the morbidity gene kicks in and I concoct a fantasy of the children turning feral, braining me from behind with a fusillade of rocks.

The magical quality of the bogs can at times be sensory. There is one particular place on my everyday walk that during just one week of spring holds such a concentrated aroma of pine that I am compelled to stop and look for the source whenever I pass through this invisible cloud of the pure distilled essence of Christmas past. Every day for a week I stop and scan the vegetation on both sides of the sandy path when enveloped by the smell. I think there must be a downed tree nearby—immediately, of course, linking the scent's origin to death. Finally, one day I realize the point of getting a piney gift like that is to stop and smell the memories. It is just in time, because the scent disappears a few days later. I will have to wait until next spring to know if it's a yearly occurrence or just a particularly active figment of my imagination. I hope it's an annual event, like the solstice. I mention the peculiarity of the area pine cloud to one of the dog walkers but her response is to look puzzled and politely humor me.

"Yes, they're rescues," I say over and over to people who meet Lucky and Frenchy at the bogs, trying to explain away my dogs' standoffishness. Worse, sometimes Lucky will act interested in the extended hand, the cooing voice, then back off and scamper away, the dog equivalent of the withdrawn handshake—*Haha, gotcha, sucker*. There is often a weird feeling of mutual embarrassment after Lucky's snobbery. "They're damaged," I say. "They'll always be damaged." Then I walk on and, without irony, look for heart-shaped stones on the sandy ground, hoping for a sign from Jesse when I don't even believe in signs.

Maybe melancholia is just end-stage grief, now that Jesse has been gone so long, a terminal condition that metes out only the occasional knife thrust, the random stifled scream of remembered pain. But this end stage spreads and colors everything, tie-dyeing it all into one blotchy funny/sad Chekhov play, a carnival of empathy, a shared *weltzchmerz*. Now when I hear the wild turkey call for a mate in the reeds behind our house, I pity his loneliness and wonder if his head is too blue to lure a partner. It's crazy to share a sense of loss with a creature whose head holds a brain the size of an indica gummie.

Old Blue Head has finally found a mate. One morning, a skinny, underfed female shows up in our front yard after I throw out the critter crunch for Blue and his underlings, the squirrels, and one bold whaddayoulookinat rabbit. I can't help but smile, watching them. I think of that bumper sticker, the one that says, *Coexist*. All that disparate life, sharing dried corn and sunflower seeds, even the bold little Badass Bunny darting in and out around Old Blue Head, who fans out his feathers, but then goes back to munching his corn. They're coexisting. It's a good way to be in the world for those of us who are damaged, this coexistence with melancholia and communal celebrations of food.

HER OWN PRIVATE FATIMA

I AM A TOWERING SHRINE OF OPPORTUNITY, a magic wellspring of goodness, the goddess of secret deliciousness, distributor of manna that comes not from heaven, but from the pocket of my gray all-weather parka. Like one of those gods who inhabit multiple incarnations, these are the guises in which I appear to Zoey. Zoey is an eight-year-old yellow lab I meet from time to time at the bogs. My left pocket is the sacred source, the origin story in Zoey's religion, and I am the beneficent but mysterious deity who sometimes manifests as a human being.

Zoey goes into transports of joy at my appearance because I once reached into the left pocket of my winter puffy coat and gave her a treat. The memory of that snack has converted Zoey into my most devoted follower. When I approach, she dances and whirls with more intent than an ancient tribal elder begging for rain. Her trance state makes her impervious to the demands of her companions, a nice older couple imploring her to rein it in, to no avail. The fact remains: there was once a treat in my left pocket, and it could appear again at any time, like an apparition of the Blessed Mother. Zoey is a true believer, optimistic in her belief of an eventual blessing from my left pocket.

Lucky and Frenchy stand at a distance watching Zoey's fervor with a disdain that is palpable as they shift their paws and direct glares toward her over-the-top display. Their impatience reminds me of New Yorkers pushing past open-mouthed tourists in Times Square. They want to move on, so we do, but I miss being a true believer, in anything, and remind myself to refill that pocket and, next time I see her, deliver unto Zoey her earthly reward.

~~

THANKSGIVING NOW

~~

*T*HANKSGIVING IS ONE OF THE HOLIDAYS we now try to ignore. We spend it in the arts and crafts house where I grew up, peopled with the ghosts of our parents and grandparents and aunts and uncles, all laughing and smoking and telling stories and passing the homemade ravioli and finally the walnuts and figs. The same dramatic or funny stories, told and retold every year, are the stuff of our family legends. We kids supply the questions and laugh or gasp on cue. It is a passion play we enact every year. For my husband and me, of course, the missing person at the table is our son, fierce lover of both turkey and ravioli, enthusiastic listener to family stories, loudest laugher and first person at the table to get the joke. The holiday is the second speed bump in the memory minefield that begins with Jesse's birthday on October 15, and barrels along like an armored truck on the perilous holiday highway until January 3, the day I found him dead in his bed. In those past seasons of celebration, we had enormous feasts at our house on the tidal river with family, neighbors, and friends around our scarred oak table. *The Silver Palate Cookbook* provided the blueprint for my throw-dietary-caution-to-the-winds Thanksgiving feast. I made the full American meal using more butter than my mother had in her entire life, and, in the necessary nod to my Italian forebears, a giant pan of lasagna and stuffed-mushroom appetizers. It was Jesse's favorite holiday, and he wrote a poem about it when he was eight. The opening line was, "My family is fancy," and it ended with, "On Thanksgiving, I thank, I give." But Jesse always gave us more than we ever gave him.

Thanksgiving now means driving forty miles to the childhood home where my sister lives. We travel with two elderly dogs in the backseat, shaking enough to power our journey on anxiety alone. Lucky, always a braveheart, seems to adjust once we get on the highway, as if he at last realizes that the long trip promises new adventures, new sniffing grounds, new dog meetups. For Frenchy, the long drive seems only to stoke his fear. Usually I sit in back with them, trying to pet away the terror. It feels surreally like the times I sat with Jesse in the backseat on long car trips, keeping him entertained.

When we arrive at my sister's, we park nearby in the huge, deserted parking lot. What was once a factory across the street from our house is now an office park. I leash the dogs and take them to do their business on the grass before going inside. My nieces arrive like industrious elves and form a line, ferrying the lasagna, lemon squares, and other goodies into the house. I wave from across the street, smiling at the single-file caravan of food, a secular procession of which my mother would have approved.

I look down to see Frenchy on his back in the throes of a massive, silent seizure. The outside world goes quiet and I'm in a limbo-like time zone that is eerily familiar, the one I used to inhabit when Jesse had a seizure. In that godless place, I became an automaton that snapped at once into motion and did whatever I could to protect my child. But I couldn't actually protect him, beyond giving him medication while my own heart remained beatless, frozen in place, and my breath short-circuited in my chest.

My niece briskly takes Lucky, telling me she has texted me the address of the nearest animal hospital. She has three kids under four and I briefly marvel at her supermom competence. Frenchy's seizure is mercifully short, though he is now limp. He is breathing normally, as if the seizure blew away his accumulated anxiety. I take him into my arms and my husband drives us all to the nearby hospital.

We give the person at the desk all the vital information and Frenchy is whisked away. We are told to wait, and for the next three hours we sit in molded plastic chairs watching the sad parade of sick and maimed animals brought in by their distraught owners. All the while, *"It's the most wonderful time of the year"* seems to be playing on a nonironic, mocking loop. I'm painfully familiar with the jeering taunts of holiday music, all that *"through the years we all will be together"* stuff that makes me want to run across a field of snowmen, knocking their heads off like little Margaret O'Brien in the holiday movie *Meet Me in St. Louis*, the originator of the saddest song lyric in yuletide history. My husband and I smirk knowingly at each other when the dreaded line comes up on the inescapable music playing in the waiting room, but the limping and sick animals are getting to us. We're worried about Frenchy and wondering what's taking so long.

Finally, we are summoned to a treatment room. Frenchy is sedated and subdued. A young and enthusiastic veterinarian informs us that Frenchy "could have brain cancer," in which case, she tells us, "he will have to have chemo," and that they will have to keep him overnight and give him an MRI in the morning. I burst her bubble immediately by telling her I wouldn't have chemo if *I* had brain cancer, and that we are taking Frenchy home and calling our own vet in the morning. The thought of what an overnight in a kennel would do to Frenchy spurs me on: all of the work both Chris and I have put into the last ten years, of reassuring Frenchy and Lucky that they will never be caged again, that there will be a calm order to the day, routines that always end in cuddles and treats— we have not done all this to leave him forty miles away in a cage, shaking and suffering in a place where time is measured in a steady drumbeat of escalating fear mirrored by the panicked barking of other dogs.

I feel briefly sorry for the young and enthusiastic vet, who only means well for our elderly rescue. She has been the undeserving recipient of the Jesse backstory in my cold and swift reaction, a leftover backlash from all those doctors who wanted to fix him, all those years ago with unnecessary operations and painful probings and drugs that never helped. The neonatologist who wanted to put a shunt in his head because "his clinical course might be better." The callow, clueless interns who stood outside the emergency room as my son writhed from dystonia, whispering about drilling a hole in his head. The orthopedist who wanted to fix him by cutting his hamstrings. The neurologist who wanted to give him drugs that would distort his beautiful features and cloud his mind. I held him close and fended them off, waving the torch of my rage like fire to flesh-eating zombies.

Once Jesse was all ours, and the otherworldly over-bright lights of the neonatal intensive care unit began to lower in memory, we were fearless, invincible. When my husband called from his unimaginably swanky suite in Miami, we were on a plane, courtesy of *Miami Vice*. I felt like I could fly the plane myself if I had to. We were fleeing the winter, racing toward new freedoms. My four-month-old was the size of a newborn, but he was in my arms on a terrace in the natural light of the sun, expelled from his plastic sarcophagus. And the hospital could never have him again.

We take Frenchy away with us, along with a prescription for a drug that's supposed to prevent future seizures. No drug ever prevented seizures for Jesse.

We wolf down our belated turkey dinner, barely tasting it. The Lucky and Frenchy reunion occurs at my sister's house, and the dogs take their places on a pillow behind a chair in the living room, snuggled together. When we finally get home, Frenchy prances in delight and gobbles down a meal, revived by familiar comforts and smells. The next morning, I speak to our fantastic, calm vet, who tells us to keep an eye on him and not to panic. I give Frenchy half the seizure-med dose for a few days, then stop.

Frenchy never has another seizure. Nor does he ever have another long car ride. His travels beyond our town are over, but that's a small price to pay. I'd rather watch him prance, never to see the inside of a cage again.

THE BOYS

WE ARE WITH THE BOYS who are the boys that Jesse would never have been. But they are the same age as he was the year he died and there is something that brings to mind our son, so different in body, so alike in the yearning, the curiosity, the talent, the vulnerability these boys wear like an upturned collar on a favorite shirt.

Chris and I are judging these boys. Our friends, the parents of one of the boys, have asked us to watch the scenes and monologues they have chosen to perform for a national competition.

We sit in our friends' comfortable living room and are introduced to the boys, who are all polite and wary, and to their teacher, a Catholic brother. The boys' wariness is catching: Chris side-eyes me and wonders if I'll launch into a tirade about my years as a parochial school student suffering the tender mercies of the sisters of St. Joseph, a favorite rant at dinner parties and in print. The boys, in turn, side-eye my husband, probably thinking about his Academy Award and wondering what he'll say about them.

But I am remembering Jesse, who arrived two and a

half months early on a chaotic day filled with confusion and fear. He was born in a Catholic hospital, St. Vincent's in Greenwich Village. Gone now, that old building the size of a city block, as if it had never been there at all. Statues of saints lined the halls, their impassive faces offering a cold sort of mute succor, but I knew even in the dire aftermath of his birth, when Jesse's life was connected to a serpent's nest of tubes, that he would never be baptized in the Catholic Church. His pure light shone through the opaque plastic of his enchanted prince Isolette. I wanted to spit at the thought of some priest removing the church's arcane notion of an original sin from my son's pure, incandescent being. I don't think of the first fraught birthday, the icy fear, the grim pronouncements.

Now I remember the later birthdays, sunny still-warm October days on our deck, my son encircled by cousins and friends, laughter and cake, the surrounding marsh in hues of gold. I want to find the multiverse where this day exists and reside there forever. When the need for palliative spiritual care overwhelms me, I study quantum physics, the secular religion for the grieving unbeliever, and try to understand. I no longer pray to a father god or make the sign of the cross. A religion that eradicates the mother won't give me back my son. But I bypass these anticlerical thoughts. I'm not here for religious debate with the Catholic brother, who seems very sweet; tonight, we're both an audience and mentors to the boys.

Jesse wrote poetry on his computer, each word a hardwon victory over his wavering, disobedient hands and flyaway arms. "I am sometimes invisible" was placed dead center in one of his poems, at his insistence.

I am sometimes invisible.

He was aware of the struggle to make his mark on his world. And he never stopped trying to use his voice, not the teenage croak of his last years, but the one that appeared in pixels on the page.

And here now, these vibrant, eager boys, so present in the world Jesse has left behind forever. If he were sitting in this cozy room, in his chair, how would they relate to him? Jesse's friends were into theater and writing. I picture him writing a scene for one of these kids. I see him, his spiky hair, his long, furled fingers grasping the pull switch as he chooses or rejects words. He would watch as the boy spoke the words he wrote but could not speak except through a computer.

The first scene is a two-hander about a pair of brothers, one of them autistic. I brace myself for either a treacly or ableist presentation, but the boys perform a sensitive and believable dramatic scene, imaginatively blocked and well-acted. The rest of the boys follow, some in pairs, some performing monologues. We give feedback and ask questions about intent and preparation.

They stand in the living room, thanking us. I swallow my own thanks, knowing they wouldn't understand how grateful I am for the gift they have given, how their shaky, truth-seeking light has, for a brief moment, re-illuminated my son's luster here on earth.

DOGS AS METAPHORS—
OR NOT

THE BOGS IN WINTER ARE ENCIRCLED by icy water. That moat is studded with veins of cranberries left over from the harvest, like an abstract painting that's both beautiful and macabre, nature's broken artery. Lucky loves to get close to the edge when lifting his leg, tempting fate, or at least a sudden, unwanted dip in freezing waters. He skirts the border so often that I lose my initial fear for him and return to my phone, spitting out yet another recording of a proposed opinion piece that will be incoherent with rage and thus unprintable. I know that Frenchy will be right at my heels and that Lucky will eventually race back to both of us in an always-stunning blast of geriatric energy. Frenchy is crafty: aside from a first marking when we arrive at the bogs, he doesn't pee once during our hour-long walk.

When we get home, he immediately asks to go out on the deck, remembering the early training days when a visit to the deck meant a treat as his reward. My exasper-ated "You just came back from a two-mile walk!" doesn't register. He bounds back into the kitchen and stands there, panting, waiting for his reward. Playing dumb or mad ninja skills? Whatever, it works. He gets his treat. Every single time.

Lucky pushes it, finally succumbs to gravity and old age, and falls into the moat surrounding the bog. There isn't even a splash. True to his name, he is lucky. I am not at that moment ranting into my phone and look up just in time to see that he's disappeared over the edge of the bog. He keeps his head above the icy water, his paws pump-ing furiously in full survival mode, and I haul him out. Unabashed, deposited on terra firma, he prances wildly, a triumphant grin on his face like he's just completed the Iron Dog triathlon. Then the exhilaration wears off and the frigid air hits him. He begins shivering and I snatch him up and put him inside my coat and begin the quarter-mile jog back to the car. I know that faithful Frenchy Garib-aldi will be following just behind me, a perplexed look on his face as he plods along. Is Lucky the reason we're cut-ting the walk short? Well, okay then! Dinner that much sooner!

In the car I remove my gray puffy coat and Lucky huddles underneath it, disappearing totally, not even the wisp of a tail showing. I crank up the heat and worry he'll have a coronary after the shock of the bog water. I keep checking the rearview mirror to see if the tiny bulge in the parka is moving. When we get home, I carry him in, still wrapped in my coat, and deposit him on the wooden floor. He revives instantly and runs to his favorite place in front of the fireplace, where he flips over, wiggling his spine on the braided rug. Lucky dog Lucky begins a sort of ecstasy prayer, a one-dog revival meeting celebrating his own resurrection from near death.

Frenchy (always the acolyte) catches his religious fervor and dances over to greet the born-again Lucky.

I have never been so thrilled as Lucky at my deliverance from near-death experiences, but I can relate to the teetering-on-the-edge-and-tempting-fate part of his foolhardy, risk-taking temperament. The seventeen-year-old me who wore a little Betsey Johnson minidress and hitchhiked with a friend from Boston to New York City never once paused to give thanks that the four older guys who picked us up and dropped us off in the Bronx didn't take us instead to some deserted rest area and murder us. Ditto for the ride home to Boston, in the cab of a giant tractor trailer with two guys who gave us whiskey and donuts that weren't laced with barbiturates.

But Lucky . . . is he really just foolhardy? What is that thing that makes him push limits? Fearlessness? Fecklessness? He has both, but there's something else, a noble edge to what he does.

Lucky is the Marvel superhero whose secret power is defiance.

Lucky is the old lady who hits Nazis with her handbag.

Lucky is Icarus, flying too close to the sun.

Lucky is the worst boy in my fifth-grade class who used to pretend to sneeze and yell "Fuck you!" and the bully nun always blessed him, to our suppressed hilarity.

Lucky is Jesse, the bravest boy I ever knew.

(I have actually called Lucky "Jesse" a few times by mistake.)

Lucky is none of these things: deliverer, superhero, righter of wrongs. He is a little dog with an oversized presence in the world.

Jesse was a little boy whose presence in our world was so big it blotted out the sun.

(But Frenchy is undoubtedly Eeyore, if Eeyore could bargain for treats in a souk.)

~~

CHILD'S POSE

~~

I WRENCH MY BACK. IT'S A FIRST in my life, and shocking that it took so long, since an MRI view of my spine ten years ago showed something resembling a corkscrew or an amusement park roller coaster. My doctor says I should be three inches taller. I lifted my son Jesse for seventeen years without a problem, even with what I now know is severe scoliosis. How this back tragedy happened: I got into one of those manias that can occur when shoveling snow. You're congratulating yourself for the cardio you're pumping, you're deep-breathing the crisp air, a dance number throbs in your head, you're killing it. Unfortunately, you're shoveling late-winter snow with the consistency of wet cement and it's killing *you*. In the latter throes of what escalated into a soul-consuming frenzy, I found myself lifting the shovel over the deck rail again and again just to hear the satisfactory *thwack!* when the snow hit the ground ten feet below.

Now, a month later, I feel like I'm living with a sadistic ghost who can appear from anywhere and stab me in the sacroiliac at will. These are the wages of body dysmorphia, i.e., thinking I still have the resilient muscle tone of a thirty-five-year-old. The only cure for the random stabbing attacks is to drop to the ground and assume the child's pose I learned in yoga, a position that resembles someone making obeisance to an interplanetary overlord. I found a kind chiropractor who prescribed continuing the child's pose, and other exercises, including lying on the floor with my legs elevated.

Lucky's and Frenchy's reactions to child's pose vary wildly, consistent with their temperaments, though both are intrigued by the sight of me groaning and gasping and prostrate on the floor. Frenchy is the first to approach. He looks concerned, then begins sniffing and licking my hand. Before long, he is nudging me to pet him, any worry about my unusual prone position forgotten. Lucky follows Frenchy, but keeps his distance, hovering behind him. When I reach out for Lucky, he backs away. I change positions and lie on a blanket with my legs resting against the sofa. When the spasm passes and I struggle to my feet and walk away, Lucky takes his place on the blanket and licks the pillow where my head was resting.

I am absurdly touched by this gesture.

AT LAST, PUPPYHOOD

*T*HE SECOND CHILDHOOD that you hear about is real, at least for one of our rescues. At the age of a hundred and five in human years, or fifteen in dog ones, Frenchy Garibaldi has recovered at last his lost puppyhood, a redo of the original one that was destroyed by abuse for two years.

Now when visitors arrive, Frenchy prances over to them, and eagerly sniffs, then licks their outstretched hands. When it's time to come in for dinner, he capers like a baby goat, in ecstasy at the thought of the food in the bowl before him. His formerly Eeyore face lights up in a surprised-looking grin as he lopes along on his daily walk through the meadow. He follows me faithfully into the bay, no longer frightened when the ground gives way to water. Some old cautionary habits remain, though—he still snaps at overly friendly giant labs, and when there's a scrum of happily carousing big dogs nearby, he paces nervously, looking around for me so he can hide behind my knees and make himself invisible. But the anticipatory delight before every routine of the day? That joy is now a permanent feature.

The satisfaction I feel when I look back at Frenchy's lopsided smile framed by a canyon of wildflowers has a distant parental echo. I remember this, the reflected happiness and the knowledge that I helped to make it happen. Those other smiles, Jesse's smiles, belong to another time and place in a collection of digital images that can be accessed if you know the password. But that password is just a spectral code, and not the real opening that now remains deeply buried in the inner core under the strata of years. To access those memories beyond the digital is to frack the heart, and I am afraid to do that, to expose myself to the earthquake of grief that might follow. But there are places, songs, and sensations that remind me of Jesse even now, even without my conscious intent.

Sometimes I am standing on the edge of a grief vortex and don't know it. I think I am a free agent, just someone shopping for groceries or driving my car. Then a song creeps up and pushes me from behind and I topple into white sleepless nights. The song itself is meaningless until it means everything. The song repeats until I understand something, but what am I supposed to understand? The song blots out the world.

It is Jesse's physical presence that I miss with a yearning that makes me gasp. Holding my two-year-old great-niece in the pool this summer opens a portal to a time when my son's golden summer skin felt firm yet soft in my hands. I lift my great-niece in and out of the water, and her high-pitched baby giggles add to the sense memory of that time, here in this place on the tidal river. The water conducts memories. I lift baby Mia up and down, her downy head inches from my face as my mind returns to Jesse.

When Jesse was born, I thought his hair would be black,

with highlights of blue, the recessive gene made dominant by my mother and his paternal grandfather. Instead, it was an ordinary brown, but edged incongruously in platinum like a halo or a crown, and fine as silk, littered with unruly cowlicks that stood up straight, even if he could not. It was my delight to run my fingers over and over through the sides of his hair, lowering his eyelids like a magic spell, delivering a bliss that became a chord humming between us.

I clutch at memory like a drowning person snatching at flotsam after her boat is torpedoed. I am desperate to retain the sound of my son's voice in all its incarnations: his baby giggles, the deepening belly laughs after his voice changed, the uncontained laughter that was punctuated by a satisfied yell, like the end of an aria. I curse the fact that we have very little of him recorded on video or audio— because the lesson Jesse taught was to live in the moment, we never thought to capture it for the unthinkable time when he might not be here.

Time is the factor. In two years, we will have spent as long on this earth without Jesse as the time we had with him.

My scars and Frenchy's, covered over with new layers of experience, remain. But—here is what I know: despite the lasting scars of Frenchy's early abuse, he smiles now when he walks in the Bay Farm, he loves his daily routines, and he prances his happiness every day.

And I know, too, that holding little Mia in the pool, the smile on my face in the picture snapped by her mother, is a replica of the smile on my face holding Jesse in the pool all those years ago.

A PRAYER TO THUNDERPAWS

*H*E IS ANCIENT IN HUMAN YEARS. How does he bound over the boggy trail like that? Tiny thunderpaws drumming the ground, rapturous with the joy of almost-flight, a goofy smile you can see twenty feet away, punctuated by the cartoonishly long tongue that streams beside him like a banner.

O Lucky dog, let me in on your secret. Let me access that joy.

Have you forgotten the cage, Lucky? I see how you sometimes stand, disoriented, on our walks, how you don't see me, can't hear me. And then you wander off, in whatever direction you choose. You have forgotten, at last, the cage. The door opening to bad things. The man in the hat. The fear. The pain. How wonderful that the thing you most remember now is joy.

A new litany: Let me in on your secret. Let me access that joy.

~~~

AVATAR

~~~

THE LAWN AND TREE SERVICE ARRIVES like they do every year for the fall cleanup. We have a couple of acres of land that is mostly marsh. Our house is situated well away from the road with lots of cedars in front. Workers fan out over the yard and the infernal sound of leaf blowers fills the air. I contemplate another year of inactivity with the lawn: a failure on my part. I hate the lawn and want our yard to be a meadow. I belong to a Facebook group that I check too infrequently about becoming a pollinator haven for bees. The sight of pristine patches of unnaturally green, chemical-laden, obsessively maintained lawns disgusts me. I'm a bee saver who lifts them out of the pool when they fall in and is often rewarded with stings for my acts of mercy; I made an escape plank for them when I found their tiny little corpses in the birdbath. They deserve the pollinator-friendly lawn I keep delaying, though the grapevines and lavender bushes sustain them for now.

When the yard workers are here, I run around trying to protect my wild raspberry bushes from the mowers and the center garden that has overgrown oregano and mint from my husband, who wants that mown too. There are tree limbs down from last winter, and the tree planted in my mother's memory has succumbed to the ravages of moths last year (the same year my memoir about her was published; I try unsuccessfully to not attach any meaning to that event). The roar of heavy machinery fills the air as teetering branches from last winter crash to the ground.

Ross, the arborist, calls us over to the dogwood that I look at every morning from my kitchen window. The tree is ailing, has been for some years now. It only flowers spottily in the spring, and one half of the tree doesn't flower at all. There is a gentle split in the middle of it, and the non-flowering part has scarred bark and a curving branch that the birds love to light upon. I even saw a turkey roosting there once. I hang suet in a cage on that split and appreciate the sight of woodpeckers industriously hammering away, their crimson heads bent on getting something to eat before a murder of crows arrives, Hells Angels on a mission to wipe out every last scrap of food. Ross wants to take down the tree, a suggestion met with horrified, high-pitched noises on my part. He then suggests just cutting off the dead branch, the curving one where the birds like to sit. No, no, a thousand times no.

I don't explain my vehemence to Ross, but I wonder if my husband remembers that the hawk has visited us a number of times, lighting on that branch. And that I, in the insanity that follows losing your only child, have made the hawk Jesse's avatar. For that reason, the branch cannot be removed, or I'll never see the symbolic representation of my son again. I know this is not sane. Still, I need to protect the dead branch so I can get visits from the hawk who represents my son.

The dogwood is spared, complete with the dead branch, a renewed invitation to the hawk avatar.

I have not accounted for my son's mischievous spirit.

A week later, I sit at our scarred oak table working at my computer. The table faces a wall of windows, and my view is of the backyard, the marsh, the tidal river and the deck, complete with a rainbow flag with the word *Pace*, Italian for *peace*. Wikipedia says the Italian peace flag became popular in 2002 with the *Pace da tutti I balconi* campaign to fly it from every balcony in Italy, demanding peace. Jesse could see that flag rippling from our deck every morning at breakfast. During a break, I look up and notice something I have never seen before. And I laugh. Then I grab my phone. And I again hear that voice I have heard only in dreams: *I'm always with you.*

Not only is it a hawk, it's a Cooper's hawk. Good one, Jesse. Thank you. I'll still try to save the dogwood, but I get the message. *Pace, tesoro.*

NINE GRATITUDES 2019 (THINGS THAT HAVE DELIGHTED ME IN SPITE OF THE HOLIDAYS)

*T*HE DECEMBER WIND GRABS and shakes our haunted house like a human entity, an enraged toddler Ghost of Christmas Past, shrieking for attention, unconsoled—like us. We tune into an old movie, hoping for a Preston Sturges antidote to the reality of our Christmas Eve. Barbara Stanwyck and Fred MacMurray offer us up a dream Christmas that only makes things worse. I am bone-weary, a hundred years old. I fold my stiff body into bed and lie there listening to the swirling howls that mimic my ugly, pointy thoughts.

"We don't do Christmas," I tell people now. "We ignore it." You have to eat, though. And even if you avoid the Great Satan—the mall—the tinsel and music of the season envelops you at the supermarket and the drugstore. You still run into people who ask how many years it is now since Jesse's gone. You retreat further and further into yourself until you are a dying Tinkerbell, clad in black, your light growing dimmer as the Christmas lights around you suck it away like a greedy, insatiable beast.

Trying not to annoy others with your sadness during this season makes you feel like an actor in an endless, very bad play. You are the Ghost of Christmas Present. Trying not to remember Jesse in his dark-green thermal pajamas, waking with a smile when you whispered, "It's Christmas!" in his ear. Trying not to remember the blueberry pancakes for breakfast, or Jesse in his father's lap laughing and trying out his new electronic piano. Or his mounting excitement with each new knock on the door as the house filled with friends and neighbors. Trying not to remember when he didn't wake at all, eight days after the last time you did Christmas.

Since Jesse's death, the rollout to the holidays has been a looming obstacle course that happens earlier every year. Even now, approaching year fifteen, I'm still walking swiftly out of rooms where a Christmas song plays, to avoid the sadistic phrase *"through the years we all will be together, if the fates allow."*

I'm doing the gratitudes this year. I have no alternative. Because thanks to the planet ending, there are no snowmen anymore for me to run around and behead with shovels, like little Margaret O'Brien did so satisfyingly in the same film that gave us that endlessly recurring holiday song.

Gratitude #1 involves my great-niece Mia, who is almost two. For months my sister, who is Mia's grandmother, and I have been calling her the poster girl for the current political era, since she basically repeats one phrase—"I don't like it"—then turns her head away. Sometimes she just closes her eyes, as if hoping when she opens them you'll be far, far away. My sister texted me a picture of Mia with her head on the tray of her high chair. Underneath my sister had written: *I just said good morning*. But a few weeks later, at the Christmas Eve daytime gathering, she has turned a corner. I find her happily sitting at the kids' table, a naked doll in each fist. I pick up a nearby blond doll and walk her over to Mia's Barbies. Then I speak to the dolls. Mia's baby Madonna face becomes aglow with an expression of wonder for which Christmas commercial directors would kill. Mia looks at me, incandescent, mouth agape, as if to say: *You speak Doll! You're old, but you can speak Doll! You must be magic!* It's so fulfilling when two-year-olds think you're magic.

Gratitude #2: Maybe it's the current national mood, the upside of living in turbulent times, but the Christmas music in the supermarket (place of no escape) seems more subdued this year, even nonexistent in some supermarkets. Very much appreciated. Number of shopping carts left deserted in the coffee aisle this season: none.

Gratitude #3: A sighting of the extremely out-of-place Cooper's hawk that whooshes just feet above my head outside Trader Joe's in a mall parking lot.

Gratitude #4: Riding home from the family Christmas party, my husband confesses to me that when he first met me, my double-jointed thumbs gave him the uneasy feeling I might be a witch. This revelation irrationally thrills me.

Gratitude #5: A Christmas-week visit from a red fox that smiles obligingly when I snap his picture. He stands right outside my window, by the dying dogwood tree. I leave bones for him under the rhododendrons.

Gratitude #6: I am the scourge of the neighborhood for feeding an ever-growing flock of wild turkeys. When I emerge from the house in my medieval-looking black sweatshirt bathrobe with the hood up, the birds run toward me like we're lovers in a bodice-ripper and all twenty-three of them think I'm lost at sea. At least that's what it feels like. I know that instead we look like characters in a dystopian sci-fi novel. This also delights me.

Gratitude #7: Today was my unbirthday, January 2. I no longer celebrate my birthday, since it was sometime in the night between the second and third that Jesse left us. I decide to go to tai chi, like any other Thursday morning. At the end of my street, sitting calmly on the stop sign, sits the Cooper's hawk. I burst out laughing, wondering what Jesse is trying to tell me. *Stop?* Stop what? Tai chi? Driving? Watching too much CNN? I fumble for my phone to snap a picture, then as I make the turn, the hawk takes wing directly over the car. *Stop.*

Gratitude #8: Lucky's squeaks. As Lucky ages into a practically weightless bundle of fur, he is dropping his badass swagger and alerting me that his ancient bones ache and he would like it if I would pick him up and pet him, please. He does this by emitting the tiniest of squeaks. You would think such a sound would be easily overlooked, but somehow the exhaled noise is penetrating enough that I always hear it. I love this new communication. Lucky asking for help and sitting serenely in my lap for caresses is a gift that tells me it is possible to be healed and, more importantly, to *ask* for healing/help.

Final gratitude: This past year, forty thousand more people learned about Jesse and his life. Our friend Dan Habib, a documentary filmmaker, has a son who is quadriplegic and nonverbal, like Jesse was. He made an important documentary called *Including Samuel*, about his son's inclusion in New Hampshire public schools. Chris narrated his newest documentary, *Intelligent Lives,* which chronicles the ways that testing marginalizes people with disabilities and immigrants. Jesse's story bookends this documentary about three young adults with disabilities. Chris and I agreed to be executive producers and have helped Dan promote the film.

In Jesse's case, we fought a two-year battle to get his basic civil right to a free and appropriate public education. The school assigned a neuropsychologist to test Jesse when he was six years old. The test went on for hours without a break, and when Jesse's tutor and aide came out, she was rattled. She told us that the test had no adaptations whatsoever for Jesse's disabilities. Every time the psychologist would ask Jesse to point to something on a page he was holding, the man would flip the page before Jesse could get his wandering arm to cooperate enough to point. The test went on and on, more absurd by the minute, with no way for Jesse to complete it. In the end, even the school had to admit it had been a waste of time. When Jesse was finally tested correctly, with a computer and adaptations for his disabilities, like a switch he could click with his one volitional movement, he scored in the ninety-ninth percentile. But many young people with disabilities are not so lucky and, due to inaccurate testing, are consigned to institutions or segregated classrooms.

We first saw the entire film last April at its premiere in Ashland, Oregon. We sat in the packed theater; by the end of it, we were overwhelmed. We hadn't realized how much of Jesse would be in the film. It starts and ends with photos of him, and Chris's narration tells the story of how testing had almost derailed his inclusion in his local school. The film concludes with a video of Jesse and me in Tuscany, floating in a pool overlooking fig trees, and rosemary and lavender bushes.

We were sodden heaps when the lights came on. We floated to the stage, the applause for Dan's work in the background, to talk about Jesse, his struggles and triumphs during his seventeen years on earth, filled with gratitude for our son's ability to touch people, and to change lives so many years after his time on earth.

~~~

UNLUCKY 2020

~~~

L UCKY DOG DIES IN JANUARY. Like Jesse, he was seventeen. Like Jesse.

He fails in a matter of days, fluttering down like an autumn leaf from his aged, spry self to a ghostly whisper, stumbling, blind. I carry him for his last walk. He can no longer stand. We call our calm and trustworthy vet, Dr. Pat Hess, who comes for home visits. We ask her if we should let nature take its course. She counsels that it might not be good for Lucky. Or for us. We agree to the option that would cause him the least pain. Ours is just beginning.

We watch Frenchy to see how he comprehends. Chris, braver than I, cradles Lucky. Our vet explains the process, the drugs she is injecting, and then, dazed with sorrow, we watch Lucky close his eyes and drain away, his fierce little anima finally stilled. We ask about what is best for Frenchy right now. Dr. Hess explains that she will go out to the car and wait, because her presence is elevating his anxiety, and that we should lay Lucky down in the bed on the floor that he shared with Frenchy, now that they are both too elderly to jump onto the chaise.

She further instructs that we should let Frenchy sniff Lucky's body. Then she comes back in and takes away Lucky's body. We leave the towel that had wrapped Lucky on the bed. Frenchy inspects the dog bed and that night sleeps there, in Lucky's towel. And the sight of Frenchy, curled into the memory of his soulmate, is the end of this sad day.

Dr. Hess returns three days later with an intricately carved wooden box containing Lucky's ashes and Mary Oliver's book of poems, *Dog Songs*. Healer. She is so kind that I am nearly undone.

Then I am. Undone.

Cry. Cry. Cry. Look too many times at too many videos of Lucky running, airborne, possessed by a joy so palpable it makes you feel like you are flying too, just looking at him. Remember joy. *My best dream is to fly*—from Jesse's last poem. Remember joy.

Then, heart-struck, think about what it would be like if you had cell phone videos of Jesse, if cell phones had video then, when he was growing up in the nineties. Hundreds of cell phone videos, his sounds, his laugh, oh—his laugh. To have all that. You don't. You have only memory that is tricky and blurry and crisscrossed with scars.

Cry. Cry. Cry. It's January.

It's the year of the pandemic, and that will soon change everything.

AFTERMATH AND BEGINNING

*A*FTER LUCKY DIES AT THE END of January, Frenchy and I still walk every day, even though Frenchy was never as avid as Lucky for the chance to run free. We return to the bogs, where one after another, dog walkers who knew Lucky approach, begin to ask, "Where's . . ." and then stop, abashed. "Oh." I stand, smiling, awkward, heartsore, unable to speak. But the confused people who knew Lucky as the cute tongue-hanging member of the rescue duo that was once Lucky and Frenchy and is now missing? Those kindly people and their inquiries are not the worst part of our daily bog slogs.

The part of our walk that occasions the most wounding heart stabs happens when Frenchy stops and looks behind him, perplexed, waiting for Lucky. At first, Frenchy stands, confused, his head turned, peering all around for his furbuddy. I encourage him on, my voice falsely cheerful, rising in pitch as my sorrow deepens and Frenchy continues to search for his former cellmate. Our walks are becoming Beckettian playlets, mini expressions of hopelessness and despair, both of us waiting for someone who will never come back.

Or maybe, I tell myself, Frenchy is seeing Lucky, or some version of Lucky only dogs can see, and Frenchy's simply waiting for him to catch up. Maybe what transfixes him is the sight of Lucky flying above the ground, in one of his grands jetés, his eyes mad with the joy of liberation. Maybe Lucky comes to him in a dream when he misses him the most, when the pain level is high, like Jesse has done for me. Maybe Lucky tells Frenchy in dog-speak: *I'm always with you.*

I hope so.

NEW YORK, I LOVED YOU

*O*N FEBRUARY 20 OF THIS PANDEMIC YEAR, before we know there will be a pandemic, Chris and I sit in the packed house at the Broadway Theatre for the premiere of the long-awaited revival of *West Side Story*. We are blissfully unaware that in a month we will be quarantined in Massachusetts watching death tolls mount on CNN and hoarding toilet paper. All we know is that we are ready for a respite from mourning Lucky and eager to see a groundbreaking cast of diverse young people recreate the musical I have loved since I was twelve. We decide to make a quick trip down to New York City and back by train. Our friend Andrea, known and loved by Frenchy, will dogsit while we are away.

I lived in the city for seventeen years, met and married my husband there, gave birth to my son at St. Vincent's Hospital, acted my recurring role in *The Sopranos* there, and was brokenhearted and thrilled and overexcited every single day I ever spent there. It is always exhilarating to be back in the hustle and flow of Manhattan.

The last time I had been to an opening was in 2017,

for the premiere of a new play by Lucas Hnath, *A Doll's House, Part 2*. My husband was one of the four people in the play, which received eight Tony nominations, including one for him as Best Actor.

The last musical we had seen on Broadway was *The Lion King*, with Jesse, years ago. Before that, we had taken him to the Broadway revival of *Oklahoma*. It was his first big musical, and we had listened to the score for weeks to prepare. Jesse knew every song. He sat with his beloved caregiver, Brandy, behind us in the space reserved for wheelchairs. When the curtain rose, I was the only person in the audience facing backward, watching my son's face open like a flower to the sun. Years later, at the service celebrating his life, we sang "Oh, What a Beautiful Morning." Outside the Unitarian church, the rain fell in sheets, blotting out the world.

New York, teeming with memories . . .

There is a cocktail party before the *West Side Story* premiere in the lounge of the Broadway Theatre, crowded with spiffily dressed people nose to nose talking excitedly, air-kissing one another, waiters shimmying through impossibly small openings to proffer drinks and hors d'oeuvres.

The show is stunning; we marvel at the talented young cast, join the standing ovation at curtain, blow off the after-party to meet a friend for drinks at our hotel, and are back on the train to Boston by noon the next day.

We score seats at a table for four on the Acela thanks to a kindly porter who points to the place where the line will soon form for the train, usually a guessing game leading to frantic last-minute dashes. Chris and I sit together. I am by the window, facing a middle-aged guy. At the last minute, an Asian man boards and sits beside the middle-aged guy. On February 21, the pandemic has not yet roared into the worldwide conflagration it will become. We are news junkies, but all we have heard are unsubstantiated reports from Wuhan, China. It doesn't seem real to us.

On the train, the new Asian seatmate begins coughing juicily into his elbow. The guy opposite me and beside him begins scrunching farther and farther away, until he is cartoonishly plastered against the window. This goes on for some time, until the window guy gets up and disappears forever. The Asian man scoots over to the window seat and never coughs again. I smile at him. He smiles back. None of us realize that train rides and trips to New York City (or to Italy) will not be in our future anytime soon.

A week or so later, my friend Soo Sheung and I sit talking on our deck. I tell her about the guy coughing on the train. She says that she only has to clear her throat on the red line into Boston to have the train empty. We laugh—but that was before our then-president started calling the virus sweeping the northeast by an Asian slur, and the repercussions began affecting Asian Americans, and Soo Sheung had the additional worry about possible violence against her adult children.

The next time I see Soo Sheung, we are both masked and meeting gingerly outside on our deck, six feet apart.

I don't know when I will next be in New York City or sit in a theater audience. I mourn for my former city, and for all of us.

~~

SORROW, REFLECTED

~~

Pandemic, two months in

I CRY EVERY DAY NOW. Nothing has changed from the year 2005 except that the rest of the world has caught up with me. I listen to "Va, Pensiero," a virtual choral piece from Verdi's *Nabucco*. It is my morning and evening devotion and I weep at precisely the same line every time: *"Oh mia patria, si bella e perduta"* (*Oh, my country, so beautiful and so lost*). My son was pure love. And remained so throughout his life. He left abruptly. My country lingers, drowning in a rising tide of cruelty and apathy, leaderless. So lost. So beautiful, once.

This longing for touch, this feeling of loss, of diminishment—this is all familiar. This is the echo of the cataclysmic, permanent, and life-changing loss of our only child. I wanted no other's touch, not our downy-furred rescue, not my family's hugs, not even my husband's embrace. I wanted only my son. Now I look around and see others who long to touch their dying loved ones and I know their anguish, I know it too intimately.

It is surreal, this reflection of my own sorrow on such a worldwide scale.

What is also familiar is the remoteness of everything. The social distancing mirrors my own, just after we lost our son. Then, I would've welcomed a mask. I didn't want anyone to recognize me in the supermarket and offer their condolences. Or to look into their eyes, alive with pity and fear, the fear that the losses of others could be contagious, like a virus.

After Jesse's death, everything in the world felt strange and unfamiliar, but eerily the same. It was as if I had been dropped onto a stage set of my life with the same people I knew, house I lived in, work I was obligated to produce, but now it was an inescapable, artificial construct, and I was trapped in an endless troubling dream powered by the undercurrent of a rumbling panic attack.

That elderly neighbor who told me it was "for the best" that my son died on that January morning? She was a nurse during World War II, working in the European theater. It is clear that she would've denied Jesse a ventilator should he have needed one during this pandemic. And that is happening right now in ICUs across our country, and it haunts me every single day, that this pandemic is yet another occasion to deny the humanity of people with disabilities. After all, the person who sits in the highest office in the land denied medical coverage to his nephew's child, who also had cerebral palsy.

People like Jesse are disappearing daily, becoming permanently invisible, dying in group homes and institutions at a rate that would warm the eugenicist hearts of our "leadership," if those hearts weren't also invisible. And Jesse was first introduced to life on this planet in a neonatal intensive care unit, where he was on a ventilator for weeks, until he could breathe on his own. That ventilator would be denied to him today in a hot zone, should he have been unlucky enough to be a victim of this raging pandemic, as a harried emergency worker judged his quality of life and future contributions to society and found them wanting on the basis of his spastic limbs.

Jesse died suddenly at seventeen, from sudden un-explained death in epilepsy (SUDEP). His life was worth something not just to us, his parents. He brought joy. Re-member joy? And the party in power, the "prolife" party, the one that gets apoplectic over a clump of cells, has re-mained silent on what this pandemic is doing to people with disabilities, actual full-grown people with lives and loves and purpose. So has the media, for the most part.

The worldwide grief as the daily death toll mounts surrounds me the same way my own grief did in those early days of loss.

Jesse was an honor student, defying the people who would deny his worth in the world. The reminder of how fragile that victory was, of how easily his life could be de-valued, is what I don't want to remember. But I am seeing it every day now in this, the country of his birth.

Oh mia patria, si bella e perduta.

Oh, my country, so beautiful and so lost.

Oh membranza, si cara e fatal.

Oh, memories, so dear and yet so deadly.

~~~

DIMINISHMENT:
QUARANTINE SPRING
IN LIMBO

~~~

HERE THEY ARE, MY DAYS of diminishment: word puzzles, grain to the wild turkeys, suet for the quarrelsome starlings, death counts, racism, fascism, planetary rage, climate rage, and loss loss loss loss loss . . .

Always, loss.

Screens for pay. Screens for play. Screens every day. Screens all day.

Rain every single day. Overwatered cannabis and mute reproach from Frenchy, who blames me for his arthritis and the rain, and who doesn't understand that though I am the goddess who dispenses all that is delicious in the world, I cannot control the rain or his arthritis. I'm working on the arthritis, though. Nightly massages and CBD oil. Rewarded with a few seconds of prancing when we go outside and come back in for dinner.

* * *

Tonight, I experience the old-age, stay-at-home version of being pepper-sprayed in the face without even going to a protest march. Frenchy, equally elderly (he is a centenarian in dog years, and I feel like a centenarian, so we're twins), is limping again from arthritis so I pull out this evil-looking thing I find in the medicine cabinet, a twisted little tube of something that contained capsaicin, the stuff you find in hot peppers. I hate really hot food, and have never by choice eaten a hot pepper, so I am unfamiliar with the main ingredient, but I know that it produces heat and that will probably be good for Frenchy's aching haunches. I rub it on the affected areas, and then forgot I did, and rub my eyes, and it feels like someone has pepper-sprayed me point-blank in the face.

It's a demented scenario of what I actually used to do, which is protest illegal wars and other evils in person and risk getting pepper-sprayed in the face. Now I just do it on my sofa to myself by accident while trying to help my ancient dog. Age appropriate.

Woke up thinking again about diminishment, how now when I swim my obligatory twenty laps a day, if the rain lets up, Frenchy paces. He comes with me to the pool area where he used to hang with Lucky and ferociously bark at any and all intruders who dared approach. Now he paces dangerously close to the edge of the pool, going around and around in circles. He looks confused, like he remembers the pool area but not why he is there, and even more poignantly, he knows somewhere in his addled brain that someone or something vital is missing. He reminds me of nothing so much as the evening I spent with my elderly Aunt Sara after a surgery, when she walked in endless circles around her little four-room cape, wringing her hands and muttering, sensing the beginning of the end. Frenchy is doing the dog version of that and it has diminished my last joy.

But—when the rain finally abates, there is one remaining glimmer of joy, and as always, it is aquatic. When I pick him up and lower him to the pool, Frenchy remembers his old life with Lucky and begins moving his front legs in a paddling motion, as if he were already in the water, and about to be coached by the ghost of his furry soulmate. Frenchy swims two laps a day, even now, possibly with Lucky's invisible support powering him.

And I can't outrace him. I have tried.

THE CUSTODY DOG AND
THE TURKEY TROT

*I*N EXTREME OLD AGE, Frenchy Garibaldi Cooper finally gets his shot at movie stardom. And my husband and I get to act together for the first time in years.

In the middle of May 2020, Chris, and I receive an interesting offer: a British producer, Celine Rattray, asks if I would be willing to write a ten-minute scene on the subject of quarantine, as part of a compilation film about the pandemic. Ten families or groups will be involved, and we will be the actors, directors, camera operators, sound people, script supervisors, costumers, and all the other millions of jobs on an active movie set. The production company will ship the equipment to us. We will shoot the film ourselves, a terrifying but exhilarating thought. Chris feels this is an insane idea. I point out that it is the only work that will be forthcoming for months. I also point out that we haven't acted together since before we were married—and he finally agrees. It will be fun, I say, having no idea of if it will be fun or a marriage-ending nightmare.

We receive, shortly thereafter, two giant metal suitcases full of equipment. We find a note from Julianne Nicholson, who had done *August: Osage County* with Chris; the letter advises us to "breathe." Looking at all the equipment spread over the guest bed, I realize that I have indeed been holding my breath. We have two days to shoot this thing, and one day for reshoots. To add to the pending chaos, I have written the wild turkeys into several scenes.

What mad folly born of quarantine dreams have I dragged us into?

The ten-page scene I write is about an estranged couple, Claire and Brian, who share Frenchy the Custody Dog. They are now reasonably amicable when they make the weekly dog exchange. As he walks off, Brian sneezes and we get our first clue that Claire has misophonia, an extreme reaction to the sounds of people chewing, sneezing, etc., that might have led to their separation. Brian returns with Frenchy within minutes, claiming that he was howling in the car. He offers to stay the night, just to make sure Frenchy's all right. Claire agrees and Brian follows her up the stairs, smiling. The next few days under quarantine will determine whether Frenchy the Custody Dog has effected a reconciliation, or if misophonia wins.

Fun fact: I kind of have misophonia. I once moved my seat on a train because someone sitting two rows behind me, kitty-corner, was chewing gum too loudly.

We are nervous that first morning, but excited.

One unsettling factor remains. The portrait of Jesse that we commissioned from painter Adrienne Crombie has been mounted on an easel in our open living area since we moved here from Hoboken. It was a focal point when Jesse was with us in body and remains so now. We hope people don't think we are morbid, though we also don't actually care if they do. Jesse belongs there, his presence still informing every beat of our lives.

But our scene is about a couple who don't have children. So I have to cover the painting, lest it draw attention away from this estranged couple. I find a beautiful tapestry cloth my mother gave me to cover the painting, but it feels, somehow, like I am excising our son from our lives, putting him under a shroud, hiding him from the world, something we never did when he was alive. And yet, even though Jesse himself had acted with us in a film directed by John Sayles (*City of Hope*), playing the adorable baby with a disability belonging to a single mother, our acting jobs had remained separate from our daily lives with Jesse. He had reaped the benefits of worldwide travel, exotic locales, even lunch with his little-boy idol, Jim Carrey, but our performances were apart from our life with our son.

Except—he is always there, underneath, powering our choices as actors. I have played mothers, and Chris has played fathers, even abusive fathers, but that doesn't mean we used the emotions we called up as parents in those scenes from the feelings aroused by our actual son. Jesse made us both better actors. Our son inspired the emotions needed for rage, from the battles fought with the clueless in the medical world or those in education who would deny him his full personhood. On the opposite spectrum, we could call up joy from our daily life with our boy, and from myriad events, pride in his hard-won accomplishments, hilarity from his mischievous wit, the contagious sound of his unbridled laughter. And later, a battery of emotions could be rekindled from the deep, howling abyss of loss, enough to make me faint during the filming of a scene in *The Sopranos* in front of my television son's coffin, enough to make Chris's last scene in *Breach* evoke shudders in me to this day.

It is months later, still in quarantine, that I think about the first time Chris and I acted together, so many years ago in a little classroom above a carriage house on 56th Street in Manhattan, just across from the backside of Carnegie Hall. Our performance of the incestuous brother and sister scene from *Mourning Becomes Electra* was the culmination of many days and nights of rehearsal and feverish talks over coffee at La Parisienne coffee shop on Seventh Avenue. Those delirious rehearsals were enhanced by an undeniable attraction, at least on my part. As far as that attraction being reciprocal, Chris was a lot harder to read. The same cowboy-like shyness and taciturnity that mesmerized me also made him a mystery boy. The fevered coffee shop talking was mostly on my part. But his focus during rehearsals was something to behold. When he turned his gaze on me, I felt illuminated, seen in way that was new. When he touched my cheek in character, I felt undone in real life.

We finally performed the scene in class. Our revered teacher, Wynn Handman, seemed pleased. He told another class that we "blew the roof off" the space, but never told us. Still, he was happy when the scene ended, and we were too. So much so that we continued to see each other even when we weren't in class.

Our next chance to act together was in our friend Nancy Savoca's senior thesis film at New York University, *Bad Timing,* which won the Haig Manoogian Award, the first given to a woman director. We played a married couple, which foreshadowed our own wedding the following year, in 1983. Chris played a failed actor who worked in a garage, and I was his heavily pregnant wife. I recently rewatched the film and marveled at how young we were and how our lives had turned out: Chris was never a failed actor, and I never reached that far in my pregnancy with Jesse, delivering him at thirty weeks.

And now we're playing a separated couple who still have affection for one another, and who share an ancient, overweight dog and a history together. But the thing I can never, ever picture is separating from Chris. In real life, Chris and I are preparing to be together 24/7 into the indefinite future as we shelter in our home during this pandemic. Over the course of our long marriage, one of us has often been away (Chris more frequently than I) while the other holds down the fort at home. Jesse and I had often visited Chris's sets, especially when they were in delicious locations like Tuscany (*My House in Umbria*) or Prague (*The Bourne Identity*) or Montana (*The Horse*

Whisperer). When neither of us has acting jobs, we are together all the time, and we are fine with that.

In our prepandemic life, even when we were together all day, every day, there was still the option of going out to see friends, alone or together, or to dinner parties, book readings, theater. In quarantine, we are putting to the test my initial fears at the beginning of our relationship about things that might drive us demented about each other. Now we are in constant contact, and will be into the foreseeable future, with no chance of separation and no social encounters outside of the virtual realm.

What might actually drive me demented now? Well . . . Chris is a cleaning freak, which I can't complain about. Believe me, I have tried, but have always been drowned out by friends saying things like, "He vacuums? Does laundry? Cleans the bathroom? Shut. Up. Forever. Do. Not. Dare." Okay, but the smell of Windex permeating your breakfast omelet? The sound of the vacuum cleaner invading your every creative attempt at coherent thought when you already have pandemic brain and besieged by the dissonant sound of the republic imploding? The decision to deep-clean the sink fixtures while you are about to drain the pasta?

These can definitely be irritants. But I don't lose sight of the big picture, even in quarantine. Living with the man my mother called "Mistuh Clean-a" is a gift, even when he shrinks three favorite sweaters in a row to Barbie size. And he is thoughtful enough to try to restrict the vacuuming to when I am out on errands. Despite the notable laundry failures, I also know that the meticulousness he brings to his bouts of cleaning mania will be transferred to the filming of our scene.

* * *

Shooting in sequence, day into night, is a saving grace for the two days we have to complete our ten-page scene. We manage to stay on schedule right through to dinnertime. Chris improvises a line in one of our early exchanges that is funnier than anything I wrote in the original script. This nags at me more than it should. Frenchy never barks or squirms during the takes where we pick him up endlessly and put him down again. I enjoy the persona Chris has chosen for his character; I wrote something close to his own laid-back style, and he embraces it. In playback, my own character seems bitchy, but I was the one who wrote it, and maybe in doing so I have tapped into my own truest self.

At the end of the first evening (and by *end*, I mean long after midnight), I contact the producer and upload what we've shot. At two a.m., we stagger into bed, our only failure that day the lack of wild turkey footage. We will get it tomorrow, we sleepily reassure each other, oblivious to what will soon become a looming turkey obsession.

It is late in the second day of our shoot and not one turkey has appeared. I have scattered critter crunch around at various intervals in the filming. Nada. That evening, we are officially finished filming the scene. We are also still turkeyless. So there will be a reshoot day, we've been told, after our takes are reviewed by the producers.

Following this long day of false sightings, nervous lookouts, and increasing despair, a band of six intrepid turkeys materializes as if summoned by some snarky god. Where have they been lurking? "Hurry!" Chris hisses at me. I race inside and change into what I was wearing in the original turkey scene. Chris wields the camera from a discreet distance, and the turkeys are finally captured on film.

Our at-home film experiment is complete. We have a ten-minute scene, haven't murdered each other, and have actually been able to work together during a jangly, scary, once-in-a-hundred-years worldwide pandemic. And the finished film, *With/In*, is still streaming on STARZ and other channels.

The very first thing I do is unveil the tapestry covering Jesse's portrait. Uncovered, or under a tapestry, he was never really gone.

GRASS ROOTS

ON ONE OF MY YEARLY DOCTOR VISITS, I am asked to list any "meds" I am taking. I tell the nurse assistant that I do not take any meds. Then I mention that I use cannabis. Her face changes and she warns me, in the kind of stern voice you use to remind a four-year-old to stop kicking the back of your seat while you're driving, that "we don't know the long-term effects of cannabis." I reply, "You're looking at fifty years of cannabis. Which may be why I'm not on 'meds.'"

I always try to keep the exasperation that covers the actual bitterness I feel out of my voice when I talk to medical personnel about cannabis. I always fail.

Jesse's seizure disorder had loomed over all of us like an evil spirit that hungered to possess him, to steal his consciousness, to paralyze his limbs, to own his very soul. He hated the tonic-clonic seizures that would catch him unawares just as he was trying to complete a poem or play a video game, distorting his pre-Raphaelite features, tightening his muscles into painful, jerky, puppetlike appendages. He told me so when I asked him one day, replying with his most emphatic click of the tongue.

Every time it happened, I went into suspended animation alongside my son, pressing him to me, willing him to come back to me, forking the evil presence away with every anti-*malocchio* power I possessed. The seizures always returned, lurking outside our every moment of joy. Until at last, they took him away from us forever.

"His brain told his heart to stop," Jesse's pediatric neurologist told me, trying to explain the incomprehensible reason for his death that cold January night. The medical term, sudden unexplained death in epilepsy, is a condition we, his parents, had never heard from any of the neurologists who treated him. The official medical title of what killed my son still enrages me. It sounds like a flippant toss-off of that shattering, tectonic event, like an afterthought label by professionals who can't be bothered to invent something Latinate and medically obtuse, and who finally decide to tell the truth: *We don't know how the brain works. Not really. We will prescribe drugs that make your child sleepy, coarsen his beautiful features, muddle his thoughts, but none of them will work to stop the seizures. We don't know why this happens. It's Sudden and Unexplained, so just accept that. You look upset. Here, take these meds. That should mute the pain of losing your only child into a hazy side effect, along with bloating and kidney failure or any other of the maladies listed at warp speed at the end of a televised drug ad by a demonic auctioneer, insidious and deceitfully soothing at the same time.*

I wanted to give our son cannabis, but we were terrified that if anything happened to him at school and for some reason he was hospitalized and they found cannabis in his bloodstream, he would be taken away from us by some child protection agency. We would have no recourse then; we would be responsible for our son having ingested an illegal substance and we would be liable and lose him into the maze of child "services" that would then place him in an institution.

That horror scenario kept me from ever attempting cannabis as a remedy for the seizures he had every day of his life on earth, the seizures that no drug ever controlled. Not the phenobarbital that colored his supplement formula a sickly pink, not the Dilantin that hardened his gums and made teething a rite of particular torture, not the highly addictive Klonopin (called the honeymoon drug because it loses its effect after a short period), not magnets taped to headbands, not acupuncture, not herbs, not prayer, not Reiki, not holy water from Ireland, not the ketogenic diet that twisted his insides into pulsing implements of torture and required giving up nursing my son, my most joyful nurturing of him after two months of pumping while he was in the neonatal intensive care unit. Nothing. Worked.

But all along I had a feeling that cannabis might work.

Now, eighteen years after Jesse's death, his pediatric neurologist tells me that she has been using cannabidiol on her patients for the last nine years. On the Epilepsy Foundation website, under the heading *Does Cannabis Help Seizures?*:

> *Early evidence from laboratory studies, anecdotal reports, and small clinical studies over a number of years suggest that cannabidiol (CBD) could potentially help control seizures. Research on CBD has been hard to do and taken time due to federal regulations and limited access to cannabidiol. There are*

also many financial and time constraints. In recent years, a number of studies have shown the benefit of specific plant-based CBD product in treating specific groups of people with epilepsy who have not responded to traditional therapies.

I am happy for the children with seizure disorders who are experiencing relief from the use of cannabidiol. I will never get over being sorry about not using it to relieve my son's agony, and perhaps saving his life.

Leafly, a cannabis information site with over forty million views, posts that Americans spent nearly eighteen billion dollars on cannabis in 2020, 65 percent more than in 2019. But the reason I now grow a forest of cannabis every summer is so that I can actually sleep at night. Without a pinky-sized piece of brownie before bed, I will inevitably wake up, gasping, at the same time every night: 3:25 a.m. Is this when our son left us, while I slept, unaware? Is this when "his brain told his heart to stop"? Is this my body remembering, belatedly, to wake up, to do something, anything, to save him? The panic attacks are always suffused with the same feeling of dread, overlaid with a bottomless pit of loss. My cannabis crop allays the panic, at least for the night.

I nurture my seedlings like I once nurtured my son, counseled by the wisdom of the ancestors. They learned how to coax life from a starved earth, all that they had in the old country. Unlike them, I am not growing for sustenance; I am growing to stay sane.

~~

COMPLICATED GRIEF

~~

S O, THIS POEM I FOUND is as true now as it was whenever I wrote it. And when was that? I am an archaeologist uncovering layers of grief. This wasn't written during the first years, when I was actively dying, the grief forming into a cancerous tumor, a living, brutal elegy, an alien-looking mass that made you draw back, as you would from maggots swarming a dead thing, the dead thing being my insides, roiling, creating an ugly, living manifestation of loss. No, this was the Mesozoic era, after the period when I knew I would live but not sure yet how, how, how, how.

Complicated Grief

On the eleven-year anniversary of your death
The world is even more atilt
There are primroses blooming in January
And the rest of the world is awash in blood
We hurry toward a mass extinction
To join you
Wherever you are

And the drug companies and their lackies
Call what I am feeling "complicated grief"
So I can be soothed by thinking it's medical
And I can swallow a pill
And be another satisfied customer
And amble the world with the rest of the walking dead
Remembering nothing
The pain buried under an eiderdown opiate quilt
But I want to remember you
I want to touch the fading contours of your teenage face
that were changing every day Like the tidal river ebbing
and flowing outside my window
Even if it means covering my ears and contorting my
face like a scary crazy lady
When a song ice-picks my head in a public place
And stabs me with a wheelchair dance
Even if it means weeping unnoticed at after-parties and
crouching in restrooms
To get away from everyone who isn't you
Even if the random sniper pain makes me drive off the
road sometimes
Or spend the day in bed without speaking
Because I want the memories more than the people
around me
If I can't have you I want the memories, I whisper in my
head to the uncaring universe That has scattered you
everywhere
But the memories flutter and die all around me
Like the masses of moths that cling to our door
And I grasp at them
And hope for dreams that never come
I saw a picture once of an eiderdown baby duck with all

its feathers plucked
It was bleeding but still stunned and alive
And looking at us, the people who did this
There is no such thing as burying pain
And there is blood on the eiderdown quilt
It's complicated, grief

ELLIE'S BEACH

July 10 of the pandemic summer

Dear Jesse,

After a hesitant, wary dip in the sea, on the lookout everywhere for translucent bobbling creatures that sting, the jellyfish have finally moved on and the sea has invited us in. Bliss. A watchful bliss for now.

The ocean offers a gift today on its rocky shore, after a choppy-waved swim. It is a gift of magic at the place of magic: an undersized robin's egg with a perfect, wheelchair-sized escape hatch. Blue was your favorite color, and this is such a perfect blue that just gazing upon it could heal an entire day of sadness with enough spill-over to glide into an untroubled sleep. Fragile as a wisp of hair. The lock I took from you in that other blue room: not enough. That was a bad blue, in that room that held your husk. Your hair. Your lips. You. Your navy-blue shirt that said, *Anime fiammagenti*. Souls on fire. But you were cold.

This egg today has a different message, about shedding something that holds you back.

Thank you.

All the love, forever and ever,
Mumma

PANDEMIC SEPTEMBER:
MORE LOSS

*S*O, ALL THE DEATHS THIS WEEK, the daily and growing counts on cable news, then my cousin's husband Andy's death, his wake and the strange new world of masked condolences six feet apart and a closed casket at the end of the room.

And now—Frenchy. An agonizing lifetime-long five days of him staggering, splaying, shedding weight, disappearing before our eyes, hours spent holding him, feeling the high ridge of his backbone emerge like the fox skeleton we saw revealed over days at the bogs one winter as the snows gave way to spring. I sit with him on our sofa and try giving him squirts of water from a dropper, an array of food spread regally before us like a tasting menu, all rejected by Frenchy, who averts his head, not to be distracted from actively dying. He is tenacious to the end, holding on to life, leaving at his own pace. When he was in his prime and healthy, he was ruled by fear, but dying seems to now free him and make him strong in his conviction to do this thing right: to refuse food. To attempt to drink on his own by staggering over to his water bowl, a journey almost as hard as it is to die. He isn't in pain. Our vet told us the signs when Lucky was dying. I am glad he didn't suffer.

Again, the visit from our gentle vet, the shot to end what is inevitable, the last look into Frenchy's always sad Giuseppe Garibaldi eyes before his light dims forever.

Chris and I are weary and sad. Even all the rainbow-bridge tropes about Frenchy romping with his soulmate Lucky in another, happier place bring no relief. We are trying to appreciate all the good things we have—with our exalted privilege in this hideous world, we don't even feel worthy of sadness. I am bereft for the whole damn world.

A dogless household is bleak.

ANHEDONIA AND THE
ANCIENT ROCK CURE

IT KEEPS RAINING IN THE MORNING and the paint crew hasn't come again and it's another day behind the plastic they taped over the windows and the door to the deck. I am trapped. I am immured.

I'm encased in plastic and the toilet is screaming again and I can't write and I feel anhedonic in our dogless household. The screaming toilet sounds like a woman howling in an agonized contralto, a woman who has abandoned all hope of ever being released from captivity. The screaming toilet is the ghostly echo of my own writer voice searching for release. It is the concentrated sorrow of the whole world. I am, like our toilet, a living metaphor for this pandemic.

Anhedonic even walking on Duxbury Beach. Even putting my feet in the water in October. Even walking barefoot on sand. Even after Chris found a magic rock that looked like a black chunk of magma, one that emerged from the Pleistocene era of volcanoes and was somehow carried to Duxbury Beach with the image of ancient green ferns seared into it.

The roar of the surf. The seagull posed in a warrior stance before the waves, not even flinching at the crash of the surf, daring it to come for him. The sandpipers, chipmunks of the sea, as Chris pointed out, darting everywhere. The clattering of the rocks resettling after a wave carries them to shore, then changes its mind and hustles them all back into the ocean. Chris using the word *clattering*.

A memory of Jesse on that beach, red jogging stroller skimming the sand, Goody beside him, prancing along and pausing to sniff the tempting, rotting sea wrack. Jesse's echoed shriek of laughter as Chris pushes his stroller faster and faster, darting close to the waves, breaks the spell.

I am grateful for this particular memory and for Chris finding the ancient rock and naming the sandpipers and curing my anhedonia. At least for today.

The next day, I can hear voices and sense movement behind the suffocating plastic on my deck. The faraway murmuring and the soft laughter is what brings me to consciousness.

The plastic is ripped away in majestic, sweeping gestures and the outside of the house is being scurried over by young, shy, adorable painters who pop up in random windows like monkeys out of a toy box. Writing, already a slog, seems impossible with an audience of haphazard jacks-in-a-box. I feel stalked even putting on clothes when I lift the curtain in the downstairs closet and stare directly at the denim-clad knees of one of the shyboy painters. (Usually, it's a giant male turkey from the flock I feed, looking disdainfully at me).

I push muffins and coffee on the painters, but they don't want it. They want their own Dunkin's, both coffee and donuts. They act uncomfortable around me, like I'm a bomb about to go off. Is it the black clothes? The crone-like, hooded thing I wear every day that is so soft I can't quit it during this quarantine? It's black too, witchy. I don't want to scare young painter boys, but I will never give up my witchy hooded cloak.

It's far better now that I can see out my window to the marsh, better than when the toilet was inexplicably shrieking like a woman being tortured or when I caught sight of the sign across the street telling me that the best is yet to come.

Small mercies, but I wish that Lucky and Frenchy were here, overseeing the work of the shy painters. Maybe they wouldn't be so afraid of me if we were not a dogless household.

GRANDIOSE PLANS AND QUARANTINE DREAMS

I HAVE PLANS FOR THE QUARANTINE. Many plans. In the summer, we can still see family and friends outside. But the sonorous, forbidding teaser for *Game of Thrones* keeps up its mocking repetition in my already-swimming head: Winter is Coming.

First up: Marie Kondo my closet and then the entire house. My closet looks like it belongs to a postulant in a cloistered convent from 1943: three quarters of everything is black. So—arranging according to color, as Marie suggests, is out. Most of my clothes are thrift shop, and then some expensive outfits needed for preplague glamour events due to the business we're in. All I care about now is wearing something that feels soft against my skin. I discovered these sweatshirt material dresses at my local thrift shop and they are my pandemic everyday outfits when I venture out without underwear, because they put a barrier between skin and the softness of the fleecy stuff. No one may ever wear a bra again after this. At home I wear either a hooded sweatshirt dress or one without a hood. Black. And a black fleece cloaky thing with a hood. I like how witchy it looks to the neighbors when I feed the turkey hordes. I don't care. A small, mean part of me hopes it's unsettling.

We are rewatching *My Brilliant Friend* and tonight I see a glittering beach scene and a walk-on by a crone around my age wearing black clothes and a kerchief and I realize that my daily wear is a direct line to my peasant ancestors: my black fleecy hooded cape, my long black jumper, my black clogs. Only the hood replaces the kerchief.

End result of the wardrobe cull: I pick off a few non-fleecy dresses and fancy duds I have no longer any need for, and then move on to household items. I can't lose any books because that's my hoarder default. But I do manage to get rid of kitchen doubles (I will never make a Bundt cake, I have faced that and moved on, nor do I need four loaf pans) and some doubles of chotchkes, like my three boxes of nun bowling pins (I keep two).

What I haven't faced yet? Old technology, like the millions of CDs and DVDs and the iPod player. I await the mockery karma from my nieces for laughing at my Aunt Ellie and Uncle Benny's eight-tracks.

What I settle for: I will get rid of one thing a day. Even if it's a small thing. If I remember. If I'm not too distracted by the sounds of power tools. If I can stop scrolling and looking at screens. (What am I looking for?)

Next: Literary pretensions revived (rereading Ulysses*)*
Books are off the radar for my Marie Kondo clean-out, but while gazing at my cluttery hallway, I rediscover my ancient copy of James Joyce's *Ulysses* shoved under a clunky

table (one that definitely doesn't spark joy). The book has appropriately bright-green tape holding its spine together, but most of the crispy pages are loose. The cover is black and forbidding. Inside are my earnest late-teen liner notes, in Palmer Method cursive, that writing now so retro it reads like some fourteenth-century monk's annotations in an illuminated manuscript.

I open the book and see *"Liliata rutilantium"* and my margin note, "Mass for the Dead." How did I know that particular Latin phrase was from the Mass for the Dead? There was no Google then, in the Priorscreen era. Did I actually go to the library and look this up? It doesn't matter. Reading the first pages brings me right back to all the Irish boys, so many Irish boys, all the ones my mother warned me against, thus transforming them into gotta-have lust objects. Which is how I read *Ulysses* the first time. Because of my then-current Irish boyfriend and the course I was taking on Irish literature. The Irish literature had then a dual purpose: it worked as a syllabus for deciphering the Irish boys.

Irish boys blush so easily. It's wonderful to be able to read their signals when you are a bookworm teenager and boys are an alien map with unfathomable routes, all leading to the boys ending the conversation that you begin with, "Have you read . . ." by looking at you and saying, "You're weird," and walking away. Italian boys are all swagger and bravado, never revealing themselves. The blushing of the Irish boys is revelatory, a way to finally interpret that strange other gender. Watching their faces suffuse with blood, I feel cognizant of the real meaning of communion, of understanding another person's discomfort, one that mirrors my own, this form of communion realer and more useful to my life than the papery wafer you receive at Sunday Mass and spend the rest of the rite trying to dislodge from your upper palate.

But I digress. I re-dive into the world of "fearsome Jesuit" Stephen Dedalus. Weirdly, one of my boyfriends had Dedalus as his middle name and Steven as his first. But that was later. I was in my second year at UMass Boston, enrolled in a course that was all Joyce taught by goddess professor Mary Curran. Middle-aged, plump, and carrying her tiny dog, she informed us at our first class that today would be the last time we would meet in the classroom and that all future meetings would be at night, once a week, not twice, at her apartment on Beacon Hill. She warned us not to show up without a bottle of wine. My joy was complete and may have colored my first reading of *Ulysses*. I was as enthusiastic about reading that giant tome as I was about having sex four times a day with the current Irish boyfriend who thought sex was dirty and whose subsequent gusto was something wondrous to behold, his guilt somehow hurtling us into the orgasmic multiverse.

Half a century later, quarantined with the man I've been married to for thirty-seven years (and whom I adore more than any blushing Irish boy), following death counts and watching too much television, *Ulysses* is somehow more of a challenge, even with Google now available as an option for deciphering arcane words and Latin phrases.

Maybe it's the political atmosphere of perennially barking men on talk shows, maybe the brain-piercing sound of incessant power tools in the neighborhood, but rereading this book is starting to feel more and more like I'm listening to men bloviate endlessly in bars. I have read and reread Molly Bloom's monologue a number of times since originally reading *Ulysses,* but now it feels like too long a slog through men talking in pubs to get to Molly's brilliant stream of consciousness. And while I appreciate the lovely prose, Stephen Dedalus is getting on my nerves. Without the rosy glow of Irish-boyfriend infatuation, Dedalus seems like a boring prig who never shuts the hell up.

Reader, I abandoned *Ulysses* (like most of my Irish boyfriends abandoned me). I do not suffer *agenbite of inwit,* either, like Dedalus. (Look it up. Google is your friend.)

Next: Record my Christina short stories for possible future podcasts

Before the pandemic, I was reading my coming-of-age stories at local venues to enthusiastic response. Now I have convinced my husband to read the male parts of the stories and we plan to set up a microphone in the closet and record two stories.

We haven't done this.

We're blaming the power tools.

But it's more likely it's because we are glazedly sitting in front of the TV nervously watching the real-time disaster movie that is 2020.

Lastly: Remedy the problem of the dogless household

The ad with the suffering caged dogs shaking with cold keeps popping up on cable news. I scream every time it flashes on-screen and run for the remote to erase the sight of those poor creatures. Those ads haunt me. I find myself again on the Petfinder site, two months after losing Frenchy. I don't tell my husband, but I think about the coming winter, how we are going nowhere, not even to see my family only an hour away. About how we could shelter and begin reintroducing a suffering dog to their innate dog joy in the coming winter months.

I broach the subject with Chris. He says he's still mourning Frenchy. I tell him I understand. I sneak back onto Petfinder.

And then I find them. The next rescues.

~~~

TITI AND SUGAR

~~~

E XOTIC DANCERS TITI AND SUGAR flounce into the dimly lit topless bar, shrieking with fake laughter, their eyes scanning the horizon for fresh marks, guys who are shit-faced drunk, flush with payday loot, and looking for love.

No, that's not the beginning of this story. This is really a story about two rescued and abused bichons named Titi and Sugar, Louisiana natives, who only sound like they should be exotic dancers.

Titi is listed on Petfinder as "special needs." She is six years old and has spent her entire life in a backyard cage, giving up multiple litters. When she is finally rescued by the Cenla Alliance of Animals, they find her harness growing into her flesh. She is a fear-biter as a result of her years of abuse. (May her oppressors suffer my *strega* curse on them and never know another happy moment.) In spite of the years of suffering, her photo on Petfinder shows Titi smiling hopefully. She looks broken but loving and I am jittery and shaky all night after staring at her picture. I keep thinking about how she gave up so many litters and feel a connection to her because we have both lost offspring, and then laugh at myself for being so maudlin and absurd. I ask the universe for a sign. Should we adopt this severely wounded girl?

Everything is loud now, even in lockdown, the mad would-be king, the Nazis rising, the militias, the sign across the street that says, *The Best Is Yet to Come*, the assessing and somehow sinister look from the sign owner when I park at the top of our driveway to get our mail, the whine of power tools, the rage of broken, frightened men.

I can't hear if I'm supposed to have Titi.

Just give me a sign, Universe, I keep asking, then demanding. *Give me a fucking sign!*

No sign comes: no hawks, dragonflies, not even the visitor fox, smiling or unsmiling.

It doesn't matter. I don't need a sign. I *know* we should adopt Titi. That smile, the resilience of it tells me we need to have Titi in our lives.

I present my case to Chris, who again says he is still mourning the loss of Frenchy.

My rebuttal: No one will be adopting Titi, who is six years old and "special needs"—never walked on a leash, never walked anywhere, caged for her entire tragic life, unsocialized, a fear-biter. A fear-biter! That will be a challenge, an inner gulp that I hide from Chris. But we will know how to bring her back to dog joy. We have done it before.

We are heading into a dark, cold, lonely quarantine winter, where our only socializing, outside of masked grocery store visits, will be virtual. Film production is at a near standstill because of the pandemic. So are book events. We will have the time to devote to this little six-year-old who has lived her entire life in a cage and has produced endless litters of puppies that were taken from her too soon. We can be her liberators.

What I don't say: We need, in this time of mass trauma and grief that mirrors our own from losing our own source of light, to relive the giving part of ourselves, the distant echo of the selflessness that comes with parenting, in hopes of the joy that can bring.

Chris finally says yes. I think it is Titi's hopeful smile.

I immediately push for a second dog. And Chris agrees. After all, Lucky and Frenchy had been good companions to one another and to us.

I text Sarah Kelly, the Louisiana rescue contact, and ask her to find a companion for Titi. Lucky and Frenchy were a bonded pair, and had to be adopted together. We found that having two dogs was great and lessened our guilt when we had to go out. When we had only Goody, he would hurl accusatory vibes at us that made us feel like we were unwilling participants in a knife-throwing routine.

After Sarah proposes a few possibles that won't work for various reasons, she shows us a picture of eight-year-old Sugar, never caged, not abused, just given up when her elderly owners had to go into senior housing in a place where they don't take dogs. Sugar is a bichon/Maltese mix and a matted mess who smiles impishly at us from her photograph. Sarah shows us a video of Titi and Sugar together, and from what we can see, they get along.

I ask Sarah how to go about adopting Sugar so she can travel north with Titi.

"You know she's already yours," she says.

And just like that, we have a pickup date for two rescues one week before the quarantine Thanksgiving we plan to spend alone together.

COMING HOME

WE ARE DRIVING ON THE BACK ROADS from our house on the South Shore to Westport, Massachusetts, to pick up Titi and Sugar. We have treats and, ominously, a towel and gloves to deal with Titi's fear-biting. The rescuers told us that we should wear gloves while handling her and throw a towel over her to pick her up. We are scared, but resolute. After all, she isn't the snarling German shepherd who terrorized me in my youth, just a twelve-pound, six-year-old bichon who has spent her life in a cage. How bad could it be? But I have been warned that she drew blood from one of the workers at the rescue place in Alexandria, where Titi and Sugar are sheltering before their trip north.

The rescue center housing Titi and Sugar is on the main drag and we find it easily. The young women tending to them are friendly and, after we verify who we are, bring them out to us in the car. We head home, Titi trembling in my lap and Sugar, excited, smiling, hopping up to look out the window. I marvel at that. None of my dogs have ever expressed interest in the outside world while in the car. Sugar has obviously never suffered abuse and has been on many car rides.

We take the highway home and Titi relaxes, gentled at last by petting. I think of her life, the pain that made her snap, the cage, the rough handling, the harness growing into her flesh, a horrific vision that makes me wince every time. Rosemary Clooney comes up on the playlist, singing, *"Come-onna my house, I'm gonna give-a you candy,"* and I laugh and think of my mother and sing to Titi, only a bar before my voice strangles, choked by tears. Sugar unceremoniously tramples us both as she investigates the view from the other side of the car. I follow her gaze to the avatar of my son, the hawk soaring over the woods at the side of the road. Finally, a sign.

Of course, Jesse always, always approved wholeheartedly of dogs. And told us so in whatever way he could. I hungered for every one of my son's words, the jeweled few that fell from his perfectly shaped lips. How he blurted "dog" when sitting on Santa's lap. The effort that took. How he slurred "I love you" when we snuggled in the big green chair before bed. How we laughed when, as a six-year-old, he stared at my well-endowed Swedish friend sitting beside him at the pool, and then crooned a drawn-out "booooooobs" as if it were an incantation to a Norse goddess. His kiss sound after I massaged his spastic limbs. The words of his poems, each one the fruit of a Herculean labor as his wavering hand struggled to pull the switch connected to his computer, each one a priceless gift.

I have my sign at last and we have our work ahead. What will it be like to lift Titi out of the car when we get home? I put that thought aside for the moment and sing along with Rosemary Clooney. Titi stops trembling.

Finally, we arrive home. Deep breaths as Chris takes hold of Sugar. We have been warned that she is a bolter. I throw the towel over Titi and she struggles, breaking my heart a little. We carry them inside and introduce them to their forever home, the scarred oak floor now cleared of carpets and dotted with puppy pee pads.

Titi and Sugar look around as I get their dinner ready, and they bypass the dog bed, the same way Lucky and Frenchy had done, as if they have left them a note (*Hold out for the chaise if you're addicted to burrowing. We were. Don't worry about them. They're pushovers. Enjoy, Lucky & Frenchy*). They find their way to the chaise in front of the picture window and Titi snuggles down into the pillows until only her head is visible, creating her own thunder shirt. She periscopes from her comfort submarine, rotating her furry little head to follow me as I move about the kitchen. Her eyes are so intense they're borderline disturbing. The white fur under her eyes is stained a blond color, adding to her look of world-weary exhaustion. She watches my every move as I put together chicken and rice for their dinner. Sugar is alert and concentrates on the chicken. I hope they will gobble their dinner and then sleep deep and hard after what must have been a noisy and terrifying ride in the big semi picking up dogs in kill shelters all over the South and delivering them north. I try to telegraph my wish for them: *Sleep in quiet and wake up to freedom and peace, ladies.*

"Come-onna my house, I'm gonna give-a you everything. Everything. Everything," I sing.

FIFTEENTH CHRISTMAS
WITHOUT

*T*HE FORCED CONFINEMENT OF THIS quarantine Christmas makes this holiday finally feel right for us. We are alone together with our rescues. We haven't decorated (again). We only have thrift shop gifts for each other, and books. Rain lashes at the windows outside. On the news, there is deadly contagion and a rising death count and the world is grieving, not celebrating. We haven't celebrated this holiday for fifteen years, and the relief of not pretending to be joyous in a world of surround-sound carols and holiday specials, a world without Jesse, is finally—dare I say it? It's . . . comforting.

At the end of my neighbor's dock is a Christmas tree with multicolored lights that illuminate the cloaking dark with a brave, foolhardy act of hope.

BLOOD AND KISSES

ON HER FIRST FULL DAY WITH US, Titi bites Chris on the hand and draws blood.

I think about taking Titi and Sugar for a walk, but my husband points out that neither dog has any clue of how to walk on a leash and that we and they will be better off if we bring them out to the fenced-in pool area and let them run around. The day is sunny and fine, and we look forward to watching the dogs finally run free.

I put on gloves and throw a towel over Titi and then pick her up. She struggles against the towel and then goes still, her body tense. I feel like a kidnapper or one of Titi's abusers, and I wonder how long it will take before she trusts us enough to let us lead her on a leash. Sugar is perpetually excited, jumping into our laps, licking our faces. She was most likely never abused, but we have been warned that she likes to take off running, so we both feel like we're on some kind of mission from one of Chris's action movies just getting the two straining, struggling-against-the-leash rescues out to the pool area. Once we get the gate open, Titi flies out of my arms and runs around in a mad circle. Sugar races around as well, and their joy is ours too.

Watching Titi's low-slung little body run, her wide, open-mouthed smile as she races along, her interior voice screaming, *FREEEE*, is the solace I haven't realized that I need. It is such a relief to let go of the festering resentment that has been roiling in me since the rise of the incessant neighborhood power tools and the ever-more-frightening news stories that split my brain and cause sleepless nights and irritable days. Nothing like what Titi has endured. Nothing like what many people we've been hearing about are enduring in this pandemic. Gratitude and patience. It's my practice now.

But these last four years have almost taken me down. Not to mention the simmering disgust from staring at my neighbor across the street with the *The Best Is Yet to Come* sign placed prominently on his unnaturally green lawn. The sign assaults my eyes every day when I sit down at my writing desk. Titi's freedom hurls me back to Jesse's right to a "free and appropriate public school education," one that we had to struggle for every single day.

During the education wars, we played Bruce Springsteen's "Born to Run" over and over, blasting it back at the assholes in this town who were keeping Jesse out of school, a defiant anthem. *"It's a suicide rap, it's a death trap, we gotta get out while we're young, because TRAMPS LIKE US, JESSE, WE WERE BORN TO RUN!"* Screaming, twirling his wheelchair, we sang our equal parts rage and exhilaration, me using words, Jesse screaming, *"BRUUUU . . ."* catching the high, secure in the knowledge that I would sweep away anyone who couldn't see his light, propelled by that power, lifting us to a place that was almost divine.

After an hour outside we begin to get chilled, even in

the sun. Elaborate plans are put in motion to get Sugar's leash firmly in hand and to somehow pick up Titi. We give that up after a few minutes of running in circles, and I take Sugar back to the house, terrified she'll wriggle out of her harness as she strains against the leash, quivering, aflame with the twin desires to chase squirrels and explore the neighborhood.

I get her indoors and race back to the fenced-in area. We try a pincer move to trap Titi. That doesn't work and, out of breath, we upend the metal lounge chairs and create a barrier. Then Chris makes the mistake of looming. And wearing a hat. And being a man (Titi has obviously been abused by a man). And yanking her leash. I throw the towel over her, and her head begins whirling and snapping frantically. Chris picks her up and the towel falls back, and that's when she bites him, drawing blood.

He blames himself.

But Titi never blames him. Just the opposite.

Everything changes a few nights later, in the guest room. How did we end up in the guest room?

Our bedroom in our raised ranch is downstairs. We assume that Titi and Sugar will sleep upstairs on the chaise that they have claimed as their daytime hangout for naps, just as Lucky and Frenchy had done. Lucky and Frenchy slept entwined throughout the night and never wanted to sleep with us downstairs. But Titi and Sugar are only recent acquaintances. They get along, though Sugar tries to dominate Titi in the beginning. During the first week, we are awakened by Sugar barking after we go to bed. We finally figure out that she slept with her previous people. We take her onto our bed, and she sleeps there happily until we get up the next morning.

But then Titi starts barking in the middle of the night, probably wondering where the hell everyone's gone. I drag myself upstairs and Titi jumps down from the chaise. A fruitless chase ensues, around and around the sofa, reminiscent of my no-win chases with Lucky. I give up and collapse onto the couch, where I spend the night.

Chris and I confer the next day. This can't go on. We decide to move up to the guest room. I am secretly thrilled to be sleeping in our old bedroom with its view of the marsh. We are now on Jesse's bed. His memory quilt, created from his old T-shirts by our beloved family member Claire, adds a layer of literal and soulful warmth to our new sleeping arrangement.

Now that we are sleeping upstairs, Titi and I are inventing rituals for touching and for trust. I capture her by throwing my fleece over her after she comes to me and clearly indicates she wants to come to bed. She struggles, then submits and lets me carry her to bed. She paws the quilt and approaches where I am lying. She rolls in my red fleece, imbibing my scent. She settles near me and bites the corner of the book lying by my hip. I put out my hand, palm down. She pushes against the covers with determination, bunching them. I call her to me, my hands patting the bed. She continues to push and bunch the covers, eyeing me the whole time. She gets closer and closer, and her nose brushes my hand. I don't move.

This interaction is on her terms. She is brave and I tell her so. I tell her how good she is, how brave, over and over. What a beautiful energy she has, and how is it that a force so great can emanate from her tiny body and its low-pitched, almost manly bark? Titi isn't wimpy. Her burning onyx eyes flash a warning—she is so wary. So watchful.

Chris tells me the next morning that when he came to bed, much later, Titi inched up and licked his hand, under the protective cover of darkness. He makes a joke about her biting him in daylight, then being totally different in the bedroom. We both crack up. Oh, these dogs, how they save us.

I laugh with Chris, but also feel the teeniest bit of envy. Titi hasn't licked my hand yet.

My own reward comes the night before the fifteenth anniversary of losing Jesse. The date I dread every year.

I watch Titi on Jesse's bed. This breeder bitch emerging from years in a cage. She lets me pick her up if I am slow, if I talk to her tenderly, if I respect her fear. Now she wriggles on her back in a canine ecstasy, grunting her pleasure. Her back is against Jesse's memory quilt, on the bed where I found him that January morning. And I think about the power of healing from a powerful soul, even one whose spirit has been gone so long.

Chris has Titi's tender approach under cover of darkness, and I have the sight of her ecstasy on Jesse's quilt. And both of us are grateful, so grateful.

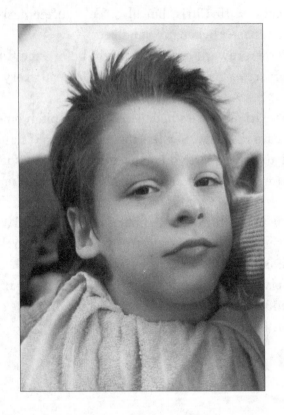

O N THIS DAY, THE DAY I HATE MOST every year, I
can relive every moment in every cell of my body.
I can microparse time down to the zeptosecond

and replay those minutes, that loss, but I won't. Instead, I do what I need to do: walk Sugar in the early morning; it is then, on our brisk and march, that I receive an unexpected gift.

A herd of deer appears on River Street and then disappears into the woods, as if I were in a waking dream. They cross the deserted street, unhurried and unafraid, aware of their own magic, gracing it like a ball gown. I thank Jesse aloud. Sugar wants to chase them, but as I told her, she won't ever find them if she looks so hard. They are gone now, like a glimpse of the perfect happiness you know is somewhere, yet no longer here once the vision is gone.

~~

BOLTER

~~

M Y HEART WANTS TO ESCAPE my breast, still clanging like a sledgehammer in a forge. I am racing in a desperate frenzy after Sugar, the escape artist. She bolted when I opened our front door after retrieving feed for the wild turkeys from the trunk of my car. I am chasing her in my nightgown and robe, running down the street like a crazed crone looking for her coven, shouting, "SUGAR! STAY!" Possessed by her evil-flirt persona, she stops, sits in the exact middle of the street, cocks her head, and smiles, as if to say, *Isn't this fun? Now chase me, bitch!* She takes off again, and I head after her, legs buckling, coughing, breathing heavily, cursing my many years of smoking cigarettes and feeling like I am in some dystopian writers'-room pitch for a *Jackass* film possibly titled: *Grandma Runs a Marathon: Hilarity and Heartbreak Ensue.*

(It is decided in the writers' room that "ensue" is too fancy a word for the *Jackass* franchise.)

Grandma Gets Run Over By a Semi is the final choice.

~~

BITCHEZ BITCH

~~

I'M GETTING SUGAR A LITTLE PLEATHER domina-
trix outfit. She has revealed her true nature to me.
Every morning she compels me to do a mile-long
march in the snow. She does this by threatening to bark and
wake up Chris, who loves to sleep in. Since getting these
two girls was my idea, I feel guilty waking him so early,
even though he has said he is very happy that we have Titi
and Sugar now. (As he should be, since he is the recipient
of their unadulterated adoration every minute of the day.)

I want to note that this morning drama all happens
before coffee. As soon as I stir, Sugar's on high alert. Her
gopher head pops up from the bedclothes and she watches
my every move as I stumble to the bathroom right next to
the guest room. She jumps down from the bed and waits,
vibrating. Titi remains on the bed, but gives me a long,
stern look, as if warning me to obey Sugar, or else she
will add her basso bark to the mix. Sometimes Titi stares
at me with those intense black eyes and begins to growl
low. She says without speaking, *You better not leave me
here again. I will do bad things.* I try to quell the unsettling
image that immediately comes to mind from yesterday

when I had clicked to *Silence of the Lambs* on television and looked over to see an entranced Titi smiling weirdly while Anthony Hopkins chewed off a prison guard's face. That image propels me to immediately cave and take her for the walk, even though it's terrifying to do the leash dance with two unhinged bichons who have no idea what to do with freedom yet (except bolt, in Sugar's case). I'm like an amateur doing a Scottish sword dance as the dogs bumble into each other and the leashes entwine and I hop fruitlessly around, hoping to never drop the leash because if I do, Sugar will bolt and a car will come and she will die before I've even had a cup of coffee and it will be my fault.

Today, though, it's just Sugar who wants to go on the forced march before coffee. I close the bathroom door. When I emerge, it begins, the low pulsating bark ready to escape Sugar's lips. She never takes her eyes off me as I hurry into the layers of clothes required to walk in the single-digit cold. By the time I get to my stockings, the bark has risen higher in her throat. When I reach for my witchy hooded fleece, a sharp, truncated sound escapes. I hiss at her to be quiet. She bounds down the stairs and stares up at me, the smothered barks still safely in her throat, but the warning hum rising in volume.

Outside, adding to the cacophony, a turkey flock has arrived. I struggle into my parka and grab Sugar's leash with one hand while trying to fill a cup with critter crunch with the other. Sugar pulls at the leash with the strength of a ninety-five-pound rottweiler. She is a dog on a mission. She must scatter the turkeys! She must at last capture the red squirrel who has been eluding her every morning. She must greet the neighborhood dogs! Her arfs have reached a crescendo.

I wrench open the door with a death grip on Sugar, whose mighty struggling causes me to spill dried corn and sunflower seeds all around the hall. I manage to scatter some critter crunch to the young turkey flock, as Sugar drags me past them to the foot of a giant cedar where the red squirrel has ascended to a high branch, a rodenty smile of triumph on his face. Sugar is foiled and momentarily crestfallen. I admit I feel a small satisfaction observing this. The turkey flock sometimes follows us to the street, and I feel complete then, a total *strega* who draws giant small-brained birds to be part of my tribe.

I have never had female dogs. I wonder if this extreme possessiveness is something that happens with the canine female. At this stage of their rescue saga, boy dogs Lucky and Frenchy mostly observed me from the safe space of the chaise. My friend Dot tells me that her female pugs bark wildly in tandem if she dares to leave her chair in the living room to walk into, say, the kitchen. Sugar and Titi are also bullying me in this same way, and there is a growing list of Things That Are Not Allowed or We Shall Bark.

Things that are not allowed: closing the bathroom door, going downstairs to get something, raising my voice for any reason, sudden movement, dancing and, to a lesser extent, singing. Singing mostly seems to be puzzling to them. Of course, I looked up solutions on the Internet. Most said: *Pay no attention and it will stop.* But when, exactly? After they've awakened Chris too, every morning?

At first I think they have confused me with a lesser deity, since I am feeding them breakfasts and dinners they never had in their old lives, but now await reverentially.

They receive daily pork jerky treats (ultimate manna) and bones (rapt attention for at least an hour). I also control access to Outside, the gates to their heaven, which they crave endlessly. I think maybe the barking is an invocation not to leave them, a petition of sorts.

But then I see how they are with Chris, especially Titi. Pure love. Delight. The absence of fear.

Chris has only to look her way, and Titi becomes Marilyn Monroe in *The Seven Year Itch*, shimmying her entire body and wagging her tail so quickly it becomes a blur. I picture Chris and Titi sharing a spaghetti dinner like that iconic scene from *Lady and the Tramp*, a noodle joining them mouth to mouth across a table as they are attended by a grossly stereotyped Italian waiter. I suppose I should also picture my head Photoshopped onto the Italian waiter, since I'm the one who fixes and serves them their dinners.

Sugar uses her cuteness to enhance her tyranny. I have seen her charm people on our forced marches. She is adorable and knows it. She greets people with infectious enthusiasm and bright-eyed looks. Titi, on the other hand, is moody and suspicious. They each reflect their earliest years, Sugar probably cosseted and loved, but also ignored and untrained, and Titi brutalized daily.

Titi and Sugar, the bullying bitches from Louisiana. Each one works on me. Even knowing I'm being manipulated, I can easily succumb to the charms of once again having dogs that look into my eyes, leap into my lap and lick my face, evoking distant memories of Goody and Jesse and the halcyon past. Titi, whose dark eyes hold the memory of abuse and whose body bears the scars, has earned forbearance from her years in a cage. When she creeps into my lap in the backseat of the car on the way to the bogs for our long walks, I feel tender toward her and grateful that despite her scars, she can show affection and look for caresses.

In the morning, I find her snuggled between my husband and myself. I think of the long, lonely nights in the cage outside. We stare into each other's eyes, and she says, *I could tell you stories.* I respond, "I know. You're a survivor."

I throw back the covers and move to get up. She growls.

BOGTROTTERS

IN JANUARY WE INTRODUCE Titi and Sugar to the East Street bogs. We run into many of our old dog-walking friends, including Andrea, Lucky and Frenchy's former dogsitter, who snaps a picture of us at the end of our walk. But traversing these trails is a lot different than the last time we have done so, with Lucky and Frenchy off-leash, little totterers barely skirting the steep edges of the bog, nearly blind, nearly lame, but still game for adventure.

The picture Andrea snaps is a perfect portrait of things as they now stand. Sugar looks right at the camera with a big, open-mouthed smile, because she knows she's the prettiest being in the photo. Titi crawls up the side of Chris's leg like the cast-off stepchild in a Victorian melodrama. She looks at the camera plaintively as if to say: *You see my situation. The mean pretty girl is in Daddy's arms and I, short, stocky Titi, am left to hang onto his leg, where I can barely reach his knees.*

I look unengaged, though I am hanging onto Titi's leash for dear life because Chris and I both fear dropping the leash and the rescues getting away, a gnawing ever-present anxiety when we consider that Titi barely knows her name and would never come to us if we frantically called, and Sugar would just bolt. Off to greener pastures? Surely she knows by now that we are the source of organic hamburger and endless pork jerky snacks?

Sugar is unable to contain herself on the way to the bogs. Paws on the glass, she looks out the window and inadvertently keeps pushing the power button to open it, letting in the arctic air and making me lurch to shut it before she somehow manages to fly out the window. When we arrive at the bogs, her excitement peaks; finally, we are at the primal source of dogs, people, and intoxicating smells and sights.

Chris walks Sugar and I walk Titi, who barely stops to sniff anything for fear of losing proximity to my husband. I am convinced she thinks he is a magical unicorn, since he is kind and speaks softly to her, and caresses her—unlike, I am sure, any other male person she has ever encountered. Sugar is in awe of the mallards that suddenly honk and arise from the water in a V-shaped flock. I'm curious and a little apprehensive about the coming spring when she will encounter the six-foot black racer snakes that never fail to alarm me, sunning themselves on the main walkways. Lucky and Frenchy ignored them, but somehow I don't think that will be true of Sugar. I love her curiosity, her willingness to engage. Just not so sure about close encounters with snakes. Or snapping turtles.

On the ride home, Titi creeps into my lap, a move that touches and puzzles me. She runs from me if I address her, even though I am careful to use a wheedling, nonthreatening voice when I am at the scarred oak table working on my computer or if I stand suddenly. I take advantage of the time in the car to pet her, my hands working through her dense fur, all along her backbone, wondering where the scars are under those sweet, deceptive curls. I think I can feel them, a ridge apart.

I remember the scar on Jesse's chest, which looked like a bullet wound, a flesh flower. Maybe that's what I am feeling, a sense memory of Jesse's battle scar, the very first one, his warrior choice to stay despite the pain, when life won. We all have them, mine a wavy line bisecting my torso. Testaments written in blood and tissue, odes to endurance, pledges to carry on.

Sugar is finally drained of her almost manic enthusiasm after our two-and-a-half-mile trek, one in which she got to meet and intimidate goofy labs three times her size, and an array of cute doodles and one dangerous doxy. And the people walking the bogs who we knew from the years before, who smiled when they saw us: "Oh," they began delicately, "you got new . . ."

We presented Titi and Sugar, the exotic dancers from Louisiana, and gave the people their origin stories.

Chris steers the car past the shuttered farm stand on the way to our street. It will be two months before the surrounding fields soften and yield color back to us in the riotous flowers and vegetables of early spring. Now, in the dead of winter, we are driving through a living Breughel painting, a landscape of browns and whites dotted with touches of gold.

Sugar perks up, renewed, when we make the turn onto our street, and I marvel at how she can already recognize where she is after only a few months: home.

Titi raises her head, affirms what Sugar knows.

We're all home.

WHY I (MOSTLY) DON'T
WRITE FICTION

W E ARE WALKING THE BOGS on the first nice morning in March, after too many days that made us want to rethink this New England life. I am speaking of the cruel teasers in mid-March, when we're taunted by one or two sunny afternoons heralding spring, weather approaching sixty degrees, the temporary banishment of face-biting winds, the wary return of the blue herons, posing midbog like ancient Roman statuary. Today is one of those days, the sun warming our faces, steadily obliterating the last traces of ice on the sandy pathways of the East Street bogs.

Chris walks Sugar, and Titi and I follow, Titi reassured that she is only inches away from the heels of her god in human form. Now, four months into walking our rescues, Sugar still pulls at the leash like an out-of-control freight train, especially if there are other dogs to meet up with. Titi never strains the leash anymore, which is why I don't notice she has slipped out of her harness until she prances in front of me, an apparition from one of my nightmares.

I experience a mini version of this nightmare every

morning, shortly after waking, ever since I decided to start taking Titi and Sugar to the Bay Farm instead of walking the neighborhood. Titi and Sugar are great about jumping into the backseat of the Camry for the short drive to Bay Farm, but once we stop in the gravelly parking area, Sugar's accelerated frenzy makes getting her out of the car without having her somehow slip by me and bolt into the street like the ticking doomsday minutes in an action movie right before a bomb is dismantled. Or isn't.

But what to do now, here at the East Street bogs, with Titi prancing free and no way to capture her? Chris and I sit down abruptly at the side of the path, him holding Sugar's taut leash. If we approach Titi, she will back away. If we try to trap her by throwing a coat over her and miss, she might take off. Does she know her name? We think she does. But does that mean she will come to us if we call? Apparently not. We try, to no avail.

A dog-walking lady stops, concerned, and we explain the situation. Her little unleashed doodle playfully joins the party, socializing with Sugar. Titi, fearful of dogs she doesn't know, stays about five feet away. Another lady stops and we discuss encircling Titi. We dismiss that idea—what if she feels threatened and dashes away?

Titi stays close but at one point starts to run down the path, away from us. We stand and call her, my voice betraying my nerves. Chris warns me not to sound panicked and spook Titi. But the anxious solo morning forays into the Bay Farm have left their mark. I keep picturing myself alone there, Titi running loose and absolutely no way to get her back into a harness. I see myself blubbering hopelessly on the ground, too distraught to even dig out my phone to ring Chris. I holler out to Titi again and realize that my husband is right—every time I call her, she edges farther away, alarmed by the agitation she and everyone else can hear in my voice. I shut up, take a deep breath. I offer to take Sugar, who is squirming in Chris's lap, crazed to continue the walk.

I hold onto Sugar and we sit quietly with the two ladies. Even the doodle relaxes. With calm restored, or at least the appearance of calm restored, Titi ambles ever so slowly over to us, drawn by Chris's steady blasts of cool and unflappable energy, like a Xanax mist. And he is, after all, Titi's shrine, her deity, the human love of her canine life. We all fall silent, even squirming Sugar.

We watch, in real time, as Titi surrenders her fear and love wins. Chris takes her into his arms. We all breathe big sighs of relief. Chris looks up, silently points skyward. This message, this coda, is for just the two of us. Circling above is the hawk, Jesse's avatar.

And that's why I write mostly nonfiction. Because it really happened that the hawk that is the avatar (to us) of our son appeared just at the moment that Titi, brave, resilient Titi, conquered her fear and surrendered to love. And if this were fiction, you would be right to call this bogus, a too-neatly wrapped end to a sweet little story.

But it really happened, and it happened just this way, and even if spring was coming and the hawk was simply looking for the voles that emerge after winter, I don't care. Because the truth is this: the hawk that is the avatar (to us) of our son appeared at just the right moment to let us know that love wins.

~~~

MISPLACED MOTHERING
AND THE TIME CONTINUUM

~~~

*T*HE TURKEYS GURGLE AND COO outside my kitchen window. I rush to feed them at the side of our house, the one area that's hidden from the neighbors. The turkeys know the sound of the dried corn hitting the ground and pinging off the propane gas tank. They race toward the critter crunch, ungainly as a gabbling bunch of portly matrons from some old black-and-white comedy. I love watching them jab at the earth, serenely oblivious to the zigzagging chipmunks grabbing seeds, filling their cheeks, and darting away.

The squirrels arrive next. They look up at me and lift their hands prayerfully for the walnuts I bestow like airborne communion, then race off with them to their nests. A rabbit quietly munches clover studded with feed, unruffled by the frenzy surrounding it. I stand high above them on our deck, barefoot; I catch a glimpse of myself in the picture window, a crone in a tattered nightdress, long white hair streaming messily, scarily, down my back.

I look more like myself now than at any other time in my life.

* * *

The rescue dogs stare at me beside their empty food bowls. In two short years, Titi and Sugar have perfected their Dickensian orphan looks, belied by their bordering-on-pudgy little bodies. But I don't need that prompt. I fill their bowls before making my own start-up coffee. The tech guy comes to check the generator. I race outside with concord grape muffins and make him take one. Is it my imagination or does he look a little frightened? He takes the muffin and walks quickly away.

I am Artemis, reincarnation of the many-breasted goddess I saw at the National Archaeological Museum in Naples that first terrible, joyless Christmas.

I am Artemis, feeding a world that no longer has my son in it.

This year is the eighteenth we have lived without Jesse. He was here on earth for seventeen years. But time, for the griever, is meaningless, so why obsess about it? I read articles greedily, looking for news about the nature of time, how to exist in time, how to live in another time while still alive in this one. But time remains elusive, and access to memory is jangly and uncertain.

Since the worldwide devastation of COVID, time has become both malleable and stretchy, and concurrently regimented and speeding like a commuter train during the Manhattan morning scrambles of my lifetime there. Hours back up on each other, predictable dominoes clacking into familiar places. And even in a beautiful arboreal place, where nature can pretend it's not mortally wounded, even as we find encouraging words painted on rocks in the woods, chatter in supermarket lines and act overly friendly with strangers, we are all internally staggering around like zombies, limbs drooping and falling after each new daily atrocity. The grieving parents' lonely trek through time is matched now by a worldwide army of those who have suffered loss. All of us have a new, distorted relationship with time.

What comes with the passage of time? Regrets.

Here are two of mine. There are many more.

We never took Jesse to swim with dolphins. I wonder if their strange language would have spoken to him, to the sounds he was able to emit despite the words locked in his mind, expressed in poetry. I picture him conversing with a dolphin, two sentient creatures laughing together, that sound as deep and ancient as the ocean, as the amniotic fluid that didn't hold him long enough, a temporary and joyous return to the womb of our water planet, courtesy of a magical creature.

Gnawing regret:

Now that I am old and various parts of my body cramp and bring me to my knees like lightning bolts from a vengeful god, I have found relief, instant relief, in oil of magnesium sprayed directly on my twisted limbs. Why didn't I know about this when Jesse was writhing in this same agony I now understand in every fiber of my being? Why doesn't modern medicine know about this, why had not one doctor suggested it to ease my baby's suffering when he writhed with spasticity? Because it costs less than ten dollars and there's no kickback or trips to the Virgin Islands to incite peddling it? I can't go there.

The two young interns outside the room at Children's Hospital who were casually discussing drilling a hole in my son's head during one bout of dystonia come to mind. Can't go there. I don't want to revisit my former home in the medical-rage vortex. After we finally won inclusion for Jesse, I took down the punching bag. And anyway, if I go there, it will probably just cause cramps in my hands.

What else comes as the years mark time without the beloved? The ever-constant desire for contact remains, a nagging, useless longing, a hunger unfulfilled, relieved only by strange and synchronistic events that would have gone unnoticed before the absence of our child made us cling to these events, clutching a life raft on a torrent heading for Crazytown.

I have a file called the Crazy List. It numbers all the signs and wonders that have happened since Jesse left us, the signs I interpret as messages, communications that are done with intent from . . . somewhere in time or space.

Does one year past mean the deadline for signs has passed?

That there will be no more hawk avatar sightings?

No more songs in the car that arrive precisely in response to my beseeching tears and strangled screams?

No more dragonflies alighting on my hand?

No more dream messages?

No more tiny, ephemeral moments of remembrance for what was once here on earth, embodied?

Or should I interpret, in my desperation to find connection and meaning somewhere, anywhere, that my surprising old-age friendships with young men who would have been Jesse's age might be the final sign, the legacy, the coda to his time here? These young men, my friends, have varied backgrounds, but most are writers. One is a neighbor I watched grow up here in the AhDeNah, where we live; one is someone I met walking the rescues; three are the sons of dear friends; one was Jesse's best friend.

We text, we email, we visit, we exchange recipes, we joke and banter in the way I think I would've done with my nonverbal son using his ever-evolving computer skills. The eye-gaze computer, once a prototype, is now a real device used in schools, and thought-to-screen will be here soon, we are told. Jesse was a poet, and I dream of what his poems would have been if he had become a grown man, what the passage of time would have done to his always startling perceptions. These young men are conduits, portals to a time that never was.

And in another time, not even that long ago, I thought people who treated dogs like babies were just . . . sad. But now, with this passage of time away from the cage, Titi stands on her hind legs and smiles, asking us to pick her up and hold her close. And like a baby, she puts a paw on either side of my husband's shoulders and lays her head there. She has conquered her fear. She remembers the pain of the harness biting into her flesh, but the pain is dimmer now. He holds her like a baby every night. And so do I. She is a dog, not a baby, but for us who hold her, it feels like the polar opposite of sad. It feels like the whisper of a joyful deliverance. So it's easier now, when time makes a gesture that is a repetition of the one that had fortified my soul for any struggle in the world, when time allows me that memory of holding my son close.

Time heals all wounds is a bullshit platitude, and that tired old saw makes me want to retrieve my punching bag from its place in the back of the shed. But while holding Titi, I time-travel to the remembrance of joy. For Titi the embrace is a triumph of resilience over fear, for us a gift. The Sufi poet Rūmī wrote, "Don't grieve. Anything you lose comes round in another form." I will grieve as long as I am in this body, Rūmī, sorry. But I recognize Titi, that she embodies Jesse's love in another tiny form, and I welcome the embrace.

It has been eighteen years since Jesse left us. What was his body is ashes. His essence is everywhere. His avatar visits me often (not often enough). His name is on the charity that fights for inclusion here in Massachusetts. And on the scholarship awarded at his high school, to those who want to give back to society. There is a book telling his story, bearing his name. In his memory, the little rescues teach us the life lessons he taught every day. Love. Unconditional love. Always and forever.

THE KILLDEER

I KNOW THIS BOOK IS ABOUT DOGS, primarily rescue dogs, but I would be remiss if I didn't tell you
about the birds, all the birds that have been in my
life these past eighteen years, all who have been drafted
somehow, into acting as go-betweens for the multiverse
where a spark of consciousness still flares. All the information crackling on those humming wires from the cast
of hawks, murder of crows, murmuration of contentious
starlings—and now this singular, totemic one, this mystery bird guarding our son's tree.

I arrive at Jesse's high school to deliver a check for the

recipient of the Jesse Cooper Give Back to Society scholarship, a small stipend given every year in his memory to
a student with a disability. I pass along the route my son's
short bus took every morning; back roads studded with
cranberry bogs that have not yet come aglow to create
autumn's glorious crimson panorama. Girding myself, I
park the car and walk toward the weeping cherry tree at
the entrance to the school, nervously checking to see if it
is still healthy. Losing your child makes you hyper-aware
of the anvil falling out of the sky, of inexplicable things
the universe might be trying to tell you, of wild ideas you
must entertain to preserve what's left of your sanity.

Eighteen years ago, Jesse's best friend, tall, reedy, brilliant Kyle, planted this tree in a ceremony where he read
my son's last poem. He had commissioned a plaque that
quoted from it: *The world is my book, I hear all its voices.*
My nonverbal son could not answer the world's voices except through his computer, but his best friend would go
on to get his doctorate in linguistics, fascinated by every
aspect of language, and the ways of acquiring it. Today is
a clear, sunny day, cold for late May, but in New England
the weather is not immune to the latter days of climate
madness, and Jesse's tree is still standing and looks to be
healthy. I am so relieved. A part of me unclenches.

Then the bird emerges like a three-dimensional
painting created to trick the eye into seeing something
else. This trompe l'oeil bird sits under the tree, a study in
stillness, its brown and white feathers blending so perfectly into the mulch that its sudden emergence seems
otherworldly.

The bird's gaze is steady, and it never looks away even

after I made a cartoony sound of surprise when its camou-flage somehow dissolved, and I could clearly see it sitting beside the trunk of Jesse's tree. I finally detach from the bird's compelling stare, and raise my phone, certain that it will startle at the movement and fly away. It doesn't. It just sits calmly, and continues to look at me, strange white-circled eyes unwavering, piercing me, somehow opening a portal to loss like a laser seeking a cure.

I force myself to turn away, and walk over to the door of the school, standing dazedly at the entrance even after being buzzed inside. Going through these doors reminds me of the two-year battle we fought to get our son his basic human right to a free and public education in the least restrictive environment, and the special ed director whose words were the inspiration for the scholarship we now bestow every year.

The special education director's deathless quote, as relayed to me by another parent, was: "Why should we spend money on these kids? They don't give anything back to society." During the education wars, I bought my punching bag, lost fifteen pounds, and began a campaign with other parents of kids with disabilities. There were six lawsuits that year. The result of those legal actions, including ours, was the full inclusion of our son and the Jesse Cooper Give Back to Society scholarship. The first one was given by Jesse and Chris on awards night. The special ed director was in the audience, though he no lon-ger had a job. (Never, ever mess with an Italian mother.)

I remember the way to the guidance office, just down the hall from the entrance to the school. I drop off the check, and the kind secretary, Judy, gives me a gift in re-turn: her enthusiastic remembrance of my son when he was alive in the world. We hug, and she walks me to the door. I immediately step over to the tree. The bird is gone. Another line from Jesse's last poem: "My best dream is to fly."

I can only emit strangled cries on the ride home, as if I am part of an extinct species of a flightless bird.

I would stop at the supermarket if we were all still wearing masks, but now the public can easily see my face spasming. I discovered the added utility of masks during quarantine, when Nellie Furtado came over the Stop & Shop loudspeaker sniper-singing, *I'm like a bird, I'll only fly away,* from a song Jesse and I listened to over and over, floating in the pool. The mask hid my crazy-lady contorting face. My wet eyes could be explained by allergies. It was the season. But Jesse. Me. Hours floating, hearing that song. And then he did. Fly away. As if the song was offering instructions.

The rescue dogs provide a full-throated welcome at my return, which they think means their walk at the bogs is coming soon. But I must find out what kind of bird this is, the bird I met at Jesse's tree. Titi begins her hilariously low basso bark to remind me to get a move on, and I ignore her, but as I begin to hunt down the mystery bird, I think about the strange swallow last week at the bogs that played a game of tag with Titi. I have never seen anything like it before. Titi, with a huge grin on her face, looking up at the little bird, then racing back and forth. I am not the only one having interspecies interactions, it seems.

The bird under Jesse's tree, I learn, is a killdeer, also

called a plover, a shore bird even though it doesn't inhabit the shore; it hangs around railroad tracks, like the ones on the other side of the tidal river behind our house. I am curious about this bird that was so insistent to catch my eye and then hold onto it, like it had an urgent message for me, as if it were a courier pigeon instead of a killdeer.

This is the kind of magical thinking that is the purview of the eternally bereaved parent. I'm all for anything that can assuage pain. But what is the message? I missed the one on the day of the night Jesse left us. On that day, the last birthday I have ever celebrated, a bird slammed into the slider opening onto our main room while my son and his best friend worked on their project for school, a piece from *To Kill a Mockingbird*. I remember a brief shudder at that message, recalling the Irish superstition about birds crashing into windows bringing bad luck. And then there's the synchronicity of the title of the book Jesse and Kyle's project was based on.

I hate the name of this bird. *Killdeer* seems like a terrible word, calling up memories all the way back to the shattering "Bambi, your mother is dead" that Disney served up to my four-year-old self, and visions of my father's return from his annual hunting trip with a dead deer on top of his station wagon. *Killdeer* is supposed to be the sound this bird makes as it flies off. I listen to the birdsong on the Internet and it sounds nothing like "killdeer" to me. It sounds like the highest pitch of Jesse's giggles before his voice changed.

The strangest aspect of this non-deer-killing bird possessing such calm, such discomfiting stillness, is that the killdeer is an actor. Like my husband and me. The bird is famous in ornithology for pretending to have a broken wing to divert prey from its nest, which is made on the ground, often indistinguishable from the pebbles surrounding it. The bird hobbles along, dragging its wing, luring a possible predator away from the nest, then flies away, emitting its famous, though (to my mind) wrongly named cry, described as "jeering" on one site.

Is this the message? It sounds like something I would do if someone tried to harm my son—lure them away, then jeer at their inability to hurt him. It's an urge I recognize (the special ed director in the audience on awards night, for one—I expressed a silent internal jeer that night, but it didn't sound like "killdeer"; instead, it was a much more common epithet, recognized by anyone on or off social media).

But maybe this plover sighting today is just a hello from Jesse, who could be, if not an actor, most definitely a trickster, who delighted in teasing his tutors and friends and myself, fake-outs his specialty, like pretending to get every answer wrong on a history test his tutor gave, then pulling his switch correctly for every answer when I exasperatedly took over.

It's the eerie stillness that bird possessed that haunts me. This bird and I, staring at one another, in a stop-time minute. My acting teacher, the late Wynn Handman, after watching one of my frenetic monologues in his class, had me work on stillness for months. And when I did my first scene on *The Sopranos*, after a ten-year absence from any acting (besides embodying a rage-crazed warrior mother in real life), the director suggested that I "take it down about 90 percent." Then there was Chris in our first acting rehearsal for a weighty O'Neill play, touching my face and drawing it to him, whispering, focusing my attention.

Maybe the universe is telling me to be still, so I can hear something.

At Jesse's service, his girlfriend Jamie's parents performed the Beatles song "Blackbird."

Take these broken wings and learn to fly
All your life
You were only waiting for this moment to arrive . . .

Jesse's best dream was to fly.

Acknowledgments

I was so thrilled to work with Ann Hood as my editor. Ann, more than any other writer I know, understands the key to what this book is about. I have, as long as I have known her, admired her ability to access joy after the worst loss any parent can experience. Ann midwifed this book and made sure it had a safe delivery with her honest, incisive, and always perfect-pitch notes. My gratitude to her is enormous. And she also had a bichon frise named Zuzu, who hung out with Lucky and Frenchy!

Immense thanks to Johnny Temple and Johanna Ingalls at Akashic Books, who streamlined my sometimes spilling-over-the-top prose due to COVID brain. Gratitude also for your patience and encouragement. A huge thank you to Topher Cox, who provided the photograph for the cover of this book.

My agent, Colleen Mohyde, has been a supporter of my writing since my first published book, and I owe her a lot for her undying loyalty.

Finally, Chris Cooper, my husband and partner of these past forty-one (!) years, has always—always—been there for me, whatever my endeavor. For this book, he was both inspiration and ballast, as always.

The Jesse Cooper Foundation

The Jesse Cooper Foundation supports inclusion in public schools through the Federation for Children with Special Needs, adapted sports for disabled kids through AccesSportAmerica, and the disabled orphans of Romania through Romanian Children's Relief.

For more information, write:

Jesse Cooper Foundation
PO Box 390
Kingston, MA 02364